GOA AND PORTUGAL

Xavier Centre of Historical Research (XCHR) Studies Series

No.1 : João de Barros: Portuguese Humanist and Historian of Asia/ *C.R. Boxer*
No. 2 : Coastal Western India: Studies from the Portuguese Records/ *M.N. Pearson*
No. 3 : The Black Legend of Portuguese India: Diogo do Couto, His Contemporaries and the Soldado Prático-A Contribution to the Study of Political Corruption in the Empires of Early Modren Europe/ *George Davison Winius*
No. 4 : Health and Hygience in Colonial Goa (1510-1961)/ *Fátima da Silvà Gracias*
No. 5 : Trade and Finance in Portuguese India: A Study of the Portuguese Country-Trade, 1770-1840/ *Celsa Pinto*
No. 6 : Goa and the Revolt of 1787/ *Charles J. Borges* (Ed.)
No. 7 : Goa and Portugal: Their Cultural Links/ *Charles J. Borges* and *Helmut Feldmann* (Eds.)
No. 8 : Goa-Kanara Portuguese Relations 1498-1763/ *B.S. Shastry* and *Charles J. Borges* (Eds.)
No. 9 : Goa's Foremost Nationalist: José Inácio Candido de Loyola: The Man and His Writings/ *Charles J. Borges* (Ed.)
No. 10 : Goa and Portugal: History and Development/ *Charles J. Borges, Óscar G. Pereira* and *Hannes Stubbe* (Eds.)
No. 11 : Conversions and Citizenry: Goa under Portugal 1510-1610/ *Délio de Mendonca*

About the Editors

Charles J. Borges. S.J. is Director, Xavier Centre of Historical Research, Alto Porvorim, Goa. He has been a Jesuit since 1967 and after his training in philosophy and theology, did his M.A. and Ph.D. in history from the Bombay University. He is author of *The Economics of the Goa Jesuits 1542-1759* and had edited or co-edited a number of books including *Goa and the Revolt of 1787, Goa and Portugal: Their cultural links,* and *Jesuits in India: In historical perspective.* He has many published articles to his credit and has also lectured in India and abroad.

Dr. Óscar Guilherme Pereira, a Goan now permanently resident in Germany, has a doctorate in law from the Univ. of Cologne and teaches at the same Univ. He is director, Centro Português de Colónia (Cologne) and was part of the organising team for the 1st Goa-Portugal Conference in 1996, in Germany. He frequently travels for conference and seminars abroad.

Hannes Stubbe has studied ethnology and psychology at the Universities of Freiburg (Germany) and Rio de Janeiro (Brazil) and obtained a doctorate in 1975 for his work on the Indian tribes of Brazil. Since then he has lectured in Germany and has been visiting professor in Brazil, Mozambique and China. He has over 100 publications to his credit.

XCHR Studies Series No. 10

GOA AND PORTUGAL
History and Development

Edited by

Charles J. Borges
Director, Xavier Centre of Historical Research
Óscar G. Pereira
Director, Centro Português de Colónia, Univ. of Cologne
Hannes Stubbe
Professor, Psychologisches Institute, Univ. of Cologne

CONCEPT PUBLISHING COMPANY PVT. LTD.
NEW DELHI-110059

ISBN: 978-81-7022-867-7

Edition 2026

Published and Printed by

Concept
Since 1974

Concept Publishing Company Pvt. Ltd.
A/15-16, Commercial Block, Mohan Garden,
New Delhi-110059 (India)
T : 91-11-41101460
E : publishing@conceptpub.com, *W*: www.conceptpub.com

PREFACE

The 2nd International Conference in the series "Goa and Portugal" was held in Goa (September 6-9, 1999) and had as its focus "History and Development." Organised by a group of Goan historians under the direction of Dr. Charles J. Borges, director, Xavier Centre of Historical Research, it attracted over 30 scholars from India, Portugal, Canada, Germany, Japan and Italy. The 1st conference was held under the direction of Dr. Helmut Feldmann, director, Instituto Luso-Brasileiro (Univ. of Cologne, Germany) and was conducted at the same University in May 1996. The papers presented then were edited jointly by Charles J. Borges and Helmut Feldmann as *Goa and Portugal: their cultural links* (New Delhi: Concept Publishing Co., 1997).

The present conference on "Goa and Portugal: History and Development" was inaugurated by Lt. Gen. J.F.R. Jacob, PVSM (Retd.), the then Governor of Goa at the XCHR, and Prof. B.S. Sonde, Vice-Chancellor, Goa University, delivered the keynote address. He touched, among other issues, on the topic of plant diversity and exchange believing that the Portuguese studied the manner in which Goans used certain plants, and that set off an exchange of plants between the continents in the 16th and 17th centuries. The significance of those exchanges, he reminded all, on the world was so much that today we cannot imagine how the present day world would be without the availability of this plant diversity.

The topics deliberated on during the four-day meet were the role of religion, art, trade, science, inter-cultural exchanges, industrialization, village communities, administration, and literature. Financial support for the conference came from the University of Cologne, Comissão Nacional para comemorações dos descobrimentos portugueses (Portugal), Instituto Camões (Portugal/New Delhi) and Fundação Oriente (Portugal/Goa).

I would like to thank Prof. Dr. Hannes Stubbe and Dr. Óscar Pereira for their help towards making this present volume possible; Centro do

Mundo Lusofono (Univ. of Cologne) for sponsoring this present publication; Ms. Ernesta Bhobe for her competent computer work, and Concept Publishing Company for publishing twenty books so far of the XCHR.

Dr. Charles J. Borges
Director, XCHR

April 20, 2000

CONTENTS

Part IV: LITERATURE

LIST OF CONTRIBUTORS

Teresa Albuquerque is fellow, Heras Institute of Indian History and Culture, Mumbai.

Philomena Sequeira Antony is head, Dept. of History, S.P. Chowgule College, Margao.

N. Shyam Bhat is reader, Dept. of History, Goa University, Bambolim.

Charles Julius Borges is director, Xavier Centre of Historical Research, Alto Porvorim.

Ana Isabel Buescu is associate professor, Centro de História de Alem-Mar, Faculdade de Ciências Sociais e Humanas, Lisbon, Portugal.

Maria Carmen Augusta d'Assa Castel-Branco is lecturer, Dept. of Philosophy, Ensino Secundário, Lisbon.

Victor Anand Coelho is professor, Dept. of Music, University of Calgary, Calgary, Alberta, Canada.

Maria Luisa Cusati is professor, Facolta di Lettere e Filosofia-Portoghese, Instituto Universitário Orientale, Napoli, Italy.

Carmo D'Souza is lecturer, V.M. Salgaocar Law College, Miramar, Panaji.

Livia Baptista de Souza Ferrão is lecturer, Centro de Pré-História e Arqueologia, Instituto de Investigação Científica Tropical, Lisbon.

Ana Maria Pereira Ferreira is professor, Dept. of History, Universidade Nova, Lisbon.

Fátima da Silva Gracias is director, Research Institute for Women, Panaji.

Sebastião Iken is lecturer, Dept. of Philosophy, Univ. of Cologne, Germany.

Engelbert Jorissen is associate professor, Faculty of Integrated Human Studies, Kyoto University, Japan.

Archana Kakodkar was till recently documentation officer, Centre for Latin American Studies, Goa University.

Pratima Kamat is reader & head, Dept. of History, Goa University.

Maria de Jesus dos Mártires Lopes is lecturer, Instituto de Investigação Científica Tropical, Lisbon.

Xavier M. Martins is lecturer, Pednem College, Pednem.

Artur Teodoro de Matos is professor, Universidade Nova, Lisbon & director, Centro de Estudos Damião de Góis, Instituto dos Archivos Nacionais, Lisbon.

Percival Noronha is founder-member, Indian Heritage Society (Goa), Panaji.

Óscar Guilherme Pereira is director, Centro Português de Colónia, University of Cologne, Germany.

Celsa Pinto is deputy director, Directorate of Education, Panaji.

Fenelon Rebello is managing director, Italab (Goa) Pvt. Ltd., Margao.

Rowena Robinson is lecturer, Dept. of Humanities and Social Sciences, Indian Institute of Technology, Powai, Mumbai.

Augusto Félix Francisco Rodrigues is researcher, Instituto Nacional de Investigação Agraria, Oeiras, Portugal.

Maria Pia de Menezes Rodrigues is curator, Central Library, Panaji.

Chirly dos Santos-Stubbe is lecturer, Technical University of Darmstadt, Germany.

Carmo da Silva is historian, Villa Silva, Cansaulim, Goa.

Hannes Stubbe is professor, Dept. of Psychology, Univ. of Cologne, Germany.

Rui de Azevedo Teixeira is professor, Departmento de Lingua e Cultura Portuguesa, Universidade Aberta, Lisbon.

Joseph Velinkar is research scholar, St. Xavier's College, Mumbai.

INTRODUCTION

The 31 papers presented at the Conference on "Goa and Portugal: History and Development" covered a large span and areas of interest in Portuguese contacts with Goa from 1510 to 1961. They have been broadly grouped in four sections dealing with trade and industries, village communities and Goan life, religious issues, and literature.

PART I: In "Liberty goods and private trade: Some reflections on the liberty and subtlety in the 18th century Indo-Portuguese trade", Philomena Sequeira Antony reviews the prevalence of the officially sanctioned practices like liberty goods (*liberdades*) and private trade in the 18th century Indo-Portuguese maritime trade showing the increasing dependence of Portuguese trade on the local agents in procuring quality products. Celsa Pinto in "Spurt in industrialisation: *Fábrica Real de Cumbarjua*", sketches the establishment and working of Goa's official textile-producing factory, *Fábrica Real de Cumbarjua.* Though short-lived, its study shows that the expansion of the Portuguese Indian textile trade in the late 18th and early 19th centuries did stimulate textile production not only in Surat, Daman and Diu but even in Goa.

Fenelon Rebello in "Portuguese Legislation on reopening the mint of Goa in 1845 and issues of overstruck native coinage in Daman", comments on the mint of Goa. In 1845, the worn-out and crudely-struck pieces were replaced, the copper coinage was reformed and mechanical means used to regulate the shape and weight of the new pattern adopted. N. Shyam Bhat while looking at the historiography of the economic history of Goa in "Trade in Goa during the 19th century with special reference to colonial Kanara", examines the emergence of modern economy of Goa which was marked by the development of mines and export of ores from the middle of the 20th century and comments on the nature, significance and various dimensions of trade in Goa during the latter half of the 19th century.

Fátima da Silva Gracias in "The iron ore rush and the quality of life in Goa", traces the development of the mining industry in Goa (the last two decades of Portuguese rule in Goa seeing a rapid expansion of mining activities) and analyses its impact on the quality of life of Goans, particularly in the areas of living, health and environment. Xavier M. Martins in "The organisation of Water Navigation in Portuguese Goa (1935-1961)", studies the office of *Navegação Fluvial* which was the largest Portuguese establishment in Goa and highlights its general setup, syllabus and examination patterns as provided in the order dated 1935 and which remained in operation in Goa even after 1961. Óscar G. Pereira tells us that from the mid 1960s, the government of Goa made tourism one of its main sources of income. In "The tourist industry in Goa: risks and opportunities," he analyses the implications of tourism in the socio-cultural, moral, environmental and economic fields, and shows the alternatives to tourism based on the proposals of non-government organisations which work to prevent a major inflow of tourists into Goa.

PART II: Carmo D'Souza in "The Village Communities - A historical and legal perspective", outlines the legal development of village communities from the 16th century citing the *Foral* (Charter) of 1526, the Regulations of 1735, 1836, 1871, 1886, Decree of 1880, and important 20th century legislation. He goes on to analyse the present legal problems and issues about this institution. Joseph Velinkar in "Village Communities and their Evolution", tells us that the village communities of Goa are an assemblage of various racial and professional groups, originally from across the Ghats or from the northern and southern coast. They formed units of villages (Tisvadi, Sashti and Bardez) and each village was administered by a group of persons (gaonkar, councillor) and the entire group of gaonkars was called the village council. The Portuguese communicated with the people through these.

Pratima Kamat in "Peasantry and the colonial state in Goa, 1946-1961" investigates the land tenurial patterns in Goa, especially the systems of bhatkar-mundkar and comunidades, while studying the colonial transformation of Goa's land system, the impact of the two World Wars, the international economic crisis of the early 1930s, the nature of agrarian stratification, status and power, and the inequitable nature of contemporary agrarian structure. Livia Baptista de Souza Ferrão sums up some of the more relevant aspects of agrarian structures in Daman in "Land Tenure and people in Daman: past and present" and also refers to basic problems concerning landholdings and land use while taking into account the social changes and economic development. She refers to the systems of agricultural production, the importance of agriculture in the socio-economic development of this community and the agricultural development programmes.

Augusto Félix Francisco Rodrigues in "Kenaf, an annual plant for paper industry: Its viability and potential interest for the economy of Goa", informs us that kenaf is an annual herbaceous, sub-ligacous plant and textiles and paper pulp can be obtained from its stem. The prospects of kenaf as a new raw material for the paper pulp industry constitute an opportunity and a challenge to regions with edafo-climatic conditions, like Goa. Percival Noronha shows the technical evolution and stylistic development of Indo-Portuguese furniture in "Indo-Portuguese Furniture and its evolution". Most pieces of this type of furniture disclose, he tells us, a national identity bound within the great framework of Indian art, culture and tradition and are closely integrated with Indian life. The study mentions the attitudes of many Goans towards furniture either by indulging in restoration of old pieces or replicating classical models.

Pia de Menezes Rodrigues in "Emergence of the Goan intellectual elite (1820-1926)", refers to the Marquis of Pombal who introduced in Portugal and Goa liberal ideas and far reaching reforms. The liberal regime was ushered in 1820. Liberal ideas were further strengthened with the establishment of the Republic of Portugal which lasted till May 1926. She studies whether the developments during this period led to the emergence of a Goan intellectual elite. In "Liberation and the Goan Ethos", Teresa Albuquerque believes that most Goans have been concerned with economic liberation more on a personal level, and involvement in political freedom was restricted to just a few individuals like Francisco Luis Gomes, Menezes Braganza, Tristão da Cunha, Ram Manohar Lohia, and Aloysius Soares. She refers to the Goan contribution for uhuru in Kenya and asks why a group so minuscule turned vociferous and effective in Goa and Kenya.

PART III: Artur Teodoro de Matos in "A Glimpse of the Hospitallers of Diu in the late 18th century", informs us that the Hospitallers came to Goa in 1681 and four years later moved also to Bassein and Diu. At Diu their hospital and convent received annual financial help from the Crown. They had their Constitutions updated in 1787 and their Commissary General in 1788 drew the attention of his men to their poor administration of their properties. Maria de Jesus dos Mártires Lopes in "The Sisters of Santa Monica in the 18th century: Details of their daily life", while informing us that the only religious congregation for women in Goa started in 1606 was made up of the wives and daughters of absentee or deceased soldiers, paints a picture of the daily life of these women and of their literary and musical activities and links with the outside world. Maria Carmen Augusta d'Assa Castel-Branco focuses on the poetical output of the sisters of the convent of Santa Monica in "The presence of Portuguese Baroque in the poetic works of the Sisters of Santa Monica in Goa." It reflected the Baroque then current in Portugal, yet merged it with the colours of the local Goan culture, forming a synthesis of western and eastern features. The other activities of the sisters included floriculture, manual arts, and pastry making.

Charles J. Borges in "Contrasting Images: Religious Orders in Goa before their suppressions and after their reinstatement in the 19th-20th centuries", speaks of contrasting images and about how the needs of the hour forced Religious Orders operating in Goa to take on a different stance of work after their reinstatements in the 19th and 20th centuries. If the earlier style was a combination of enthusiasm, understanding for local problems with a strange aggressiveness, their later style was more evaluative and benign. Carmo da Silva in "Goan Oratorians," refers to the Oratory of the Holy Cross of Miracles of Goa, the first religious congregation of clerics of local origin which flourished for about a hundred and fifty years till its extinction by the Portuguese government. Its showpiece is the flourishing Church in Sri Lanka and the origin of the group is linked to the greatest missionary that Goa and India, has ever produced, Blessed Joseph Vaz.

Archana Kakodkar in "Religious rituals and their positive and negative impact on Hindu society" speaks of Goa (described as Konkan Kashi or Kashi of the South) and describes some Hindu religious rituals practised in Goa during the late 19th and early 20th centuries and their positive and negative impact on Hindu society. She refers to the status of women who were involved in religious rituals and praises the Portuguese for banning certain undesireable rituals. Rowena Robinson in "The Construction of Goan interculturality..." focuses on the theme of Hindu-Christian interaction in the area of popular religion and culture and believes that the lives of present day Catholics show a wide variety of syncretic interculturalism. While the symbols and rituals of Hinduism and Christianity clearly differ in religious content, at operational and compositional levels there are parallels between them.

PART IV: Victor Anand Coelho in "*Saudades* and the Goan poetic temper: Globalizing Goan cultural history", commenting on the work by his late father, writes on how he saw Goan poetry as positioned at the crossroads of European and Indian cultures, of village customs and urban modernism, of Latin and Sanskrit, and of a mythical past and an uncertain future built on this myth. He discusses the theme of *saudades* in Goan poetry along with his own work on Goan musical historiography.

Hannes Stubbe in "Abade Faria (1756-1819), the School of Nancy and Sigmund Freud: An unknown Goan source for psychoanalysis" studies the influence of Faria in Europe and looks at the scientific discoveries in the course of his hypnotic experiments which made him appear as the forerunner of the psychoanalysis of Sigmund Freud, born 100 years later. Chirly dos Santos-Stubbe presents Faria in "Abade Faria (1756-1819) in scientific and fine arts literature" within the literary perspective of his time as well as within the scope of the echo which it provoked in the scientific and fine arts European literature.

Sebastião Iken in "Morphosyntactic realignment in Dravido-Portuguese creoles under a diachronic perspective", speaks of the contacts between the Portuguese language and the languages of Asia and how out of this linguistic contact there resulted variants of Portuguese language and languages with a Portuguese base. From this base, he has worked out a realignment of syntax in the variants of Portuguese and languages with a Portuguese base according to the pattern of syntax of Indian languages.

Maria Luisa Cusati in "Angelo De Gubernatis and Goa", analyses the correspondence between Angelo De Gubernatis (an Italian scholar who studied Indian culture and Gerson da Cunha (Indo-Portuguese scholar in Goa). Fifty five of the letters sent by da Cunha (mostly in Portuguese) are housed at the Library of Florence. In "Goa as a literary motif and as a historical subject in Captain Marryat's *The Phantom Ship* and other texts ...", Engelbert Jorissen speaks of this novel as a historical adventure novel, staged in the beginning of the 17th century, in which the hypocritical Catholic-Christian society becomes a major target of the critique of the author/narrator. He refers to Marryat's anti-Catholicism, to the nunneries and the Inquisition in Goa. Rui de Azevedo Teixeira in "*O Signo da Ira* (The Sign of Anger): Ethno-literature and neo-realism in a case of literary excellence", highlights the importance of the novel in the panorama of contemporary Portuguese prose and underlines at the same time the ethnic literary aspects which the novelist employs and his philosophic presuppositions and neo-realist aesthetics, all of which reinforce the intrinsic, global and modernly literary nature of the novel.

Ana Isabel Buescu in "Reports about Goa for the Royal Academy of History (1726)", tells us the Royal Academy of Portuguese History had as its main task the study and writing of ecclesiastical history and also the history of the empire. Those in charge of archives and registry offices in the colonies were asked to send copies of documents preserved with them. The *Memoirs for the ecclesiastical history of the archbishopric of Goa and its suffragans* contains news and information sent to the Academy. In "The Foreigners in India in the time of Afonso de Albuquerque: the Anonymous", Ana Maria Pereira Ferreira relying on the letters of Afonso de Albuquerque gives us details of the origin of the firemen and soldiers who served between 1509-14 in India. The numbers indicate a strong predominance of north Europeans over French and Spanish presence.

PART I

TRADE AND INDUSTRIES

1

Liberty Goods and Private Trade

Some Reflections on the liberty and subtlety in the 18th century Indo-Portuguese trade

P. SEQUEIRA ANTONY

Speaking of the European corporate enterprises in India around 1600-1800, Om Prakash highlights the overall emphasis of corporate groups on the long-distance intercontinental trade while the private traders operated within Asia.[1] He adds that the Dutch E.I.C., however, differed from the rest by participating in both the Euro-Asian and the intra-Asian trade. This paper seeks to look into the role of the private traders in the intercontinental long-distance trade within the Portuguese colonial empire.

Recent trends in historiography reveal that the old eurocentric approach claiming that the Europeans incorporated the Indian Ocean economy into a world economy is giving way to the view that European arrival and domination effected no essential change in the Indian Ocean economic order and that they merely kept the system going.[2] The story of the Portuguese domination over the *Estado da India* indicates continuity and change: continuity of the traditional trading pattern which they integrated into, and change to the extent of initiating a structural pattern that could legitimize and impose their power and orient their commerce in a specific direction.

Control Mechanisms

The control mechanisms of the Portuguese empire, no doubt, underwent profound changes between the 16th and 18th centuries to the extent that by the end of the 18th century the Crown's role in the Goa-based trade transposed *vis-a-vis* the Crown subjects after a cavalcade of policies. The introduction of naval power as a backstay for trade, whatever its strength was, and manifested in the title "Lord of all Conquest, Navigation and Commerce of Ethiopia, Arabia and India" conferred by the Pope on the King of Portugal, was a novel trend, irrespective of the extent of the security it provided the empire.[3]

The Portuguese colonial expansion was flanked by a two-pronged strategy: spiritual and material. The difficulties and uncertainties of the cumbersome voyages to the East were overshadowed by the urge to search for souls and spices. The commercial motive was predominant when the *Estado da India* proved to be a prized possession. Though the process was not precisely reversed after about a century of colonialism in the East, yet, Crown participation in the maritime trade abated. By the end of the 18th century, the Goa-based long-distance trade comprised largely of liberty goods and merchandise of private traders, while the goods on the account of the Crown diminished considerably.

Crown monopoly over trade was another structural feature of the Portuguese colonial empire. Colonial matters were primarily a royal prerogative. The late medieval European society acknowledged the king and his advisers as the ultimate authority that shaped colonial policies. Europe was convinced that it had an inherent right to demand goods from the rest of the world. Wealth from distant lands was therefore funneled home through monopoly control over trade. The spice and drug trade was brought within the exclusive control of the Crown. Later, the English East India Company enjoyed such rights over the Indian trade as part of the charter granted by the Queen. Such a monopoly ensured that the enormous profits of the spice trade amounting to as much as 300 % flowed into the royal coffers.

Goa acquired a new role in the Portuguese empire. Besides being the centre of administrative, religious and other activities, it was catapulted into being an important centre of international trade in the 16th century.[4] Pepper grown in Malabar and Kanara and to a lesser extent from Malacca was brought to Goa for export to Lisbon.[5] When pepper was no longer a cardinal item of trade in the European market in the 17th century and textiles replaced that commodity in the Portuguese trade, Goa continued to play the same role. The Portuguese procured their merchandise largely through the merchant class, rather than by contact with the cultivators. This class of merchants continued to play a key role and actively participated in the long-distance trade even when the Crown had turned away from the Indian Ocean to the Atlantic. The merchants owned ships and secured licenses to trade to Lisbon. More on this later.

Shifting focus and policies

The Portuguese Asian empire suffered from certain inherent structural weaknesses: the maritime empire had little territorial support; the possessions were scattered far and wide, hence vulnerable to attack. The metropolis was a re-exporting agent rather than a producer of goods - factors such as these posed an imminent danger in times of crises. Constant incursions by rivals led to the decline of the Portuguese power in the East by the mid-17th century.

The manipulative role of the Crown resulted in a similar situation. Pressured by the burden of managing three continents, which could not be borne indefinitely, the Crown shifted focus from the Indian Ocean to the Atlantic. Spice trade was no longer lucrative as it had been in the previous century. The Crown even toyed with the idea of building up a new spice empire in Brazil. Meanwhile private trading in pepper and other spices which was Crown monopoly earlier, was sanctioned. The crunch in human and financial resources weighed down the premier colonial empire in the Orient while its European counterparts, particularly the English, were surging ahead. The fragmented first empire took the back seat and the more resourceful American empire was at the core of the Portuguese focus. It is against this background that the significance of the vicissitudes in metropolitan policies are considered in this paper.

Portugal was also the victim of the global struggle for control of the Asiatic trade. When the Dutch and the English overpowered the Portuguese in the spice region, Portugal sought to focus on Brazil, whose sugar, gold and tobacco in turn saved the empire.

Going back to the *Estado da India* and the maritime trade, corollary to the official trade, legitimate private trade was recognised by a *Regimento* of 1515, permitting officers and crew to carry spices or textiles duty free on their return voyage, the volume and value of such goods depending upon the rank of the concerned men.[6] The liberty chests were of a stipulated size and were offered as a maintenance payment. The deck and cabin space above the hold offered to officers for availing a similar facility was called *agasalhados*. It is significant that by an *alvara* of February 13, 1672, goods brought in the liberty chests or cabin space after being registered at Goa, were permitted to be sold in Brazil or elsewhere. It is this provision that led to a burgeoning intra-colonial legitimate and contraband trading operation notwithstanding the fact that such operations were clandestinely prevailing long before.[7]

Lisbon's mindset in recognising these privileges is clear: it was a tactical move to contain the payments made to its servants. Even the English East India Company supplemented the poor pay to its servants by allowing private trade until it was abolished in 1773. Secondly, it was perceived as a means of defending the ships on the high seas more effectively by making the officials partners in that trade. Sailors could also be enticed into the service of the *Carreira* which was otherwise notorious for its lacklustre hardships and risks.[8]

Partly or fully duty free liberty chests were baits meant to offset the resentments of sailors who showed an understandable reluctance to serve the *Carreira da India* and preference for the *Carreira do Brasil.*

The perceptions of the Crown were far from being realistic. On the other hand, the liberty to sell liberty goods at Brazilian ports was sanctioned in the wake of a series of orders disallowing *escala* or stopover of returning Indiamen at those ports. The royal letters of March 18, 1665, June 17, 1667, March 29, 1670 and December 18, 1670 - all these had either disallowed *escala* at Bahia for Indiamen or prohibited the sale of goods on board such ships when they were forced by circumstances to call at Brazil.[9] The purchase of such goods was punishable by the order of March 4, 1671.[10] In the backdrop of such restrictions, the new facility granted on March 2, 1672 authorising returning Indiamen to call at Bahia in case of dire need, and the sale of liberty goods reflected how the Crown had yielded to the persistent pressure of those who advocated *escala.* The sanction granted to larger Indiamen in 1692 to put in at Bahia then justified the stand of the supporters of the move that the ships of the *Carreira da India* were half-empty on their return voyage as they carried the expensive, but less voluminous cotton textile and silks, hence could take on sugar, hides, Brazil wood and other merchandise for the onward voyage to Lisbon.[11] In reality, this sanction was a formal recognition, however reluctant, of a practice in vogue for long. It set in motion a trend that the Crown could hardly check in the years to come. It turned the benefits which the Crown had sought to derive out of the liberty chest facility into opportunities advantageous to individuals. For an empire that was essentially maritime and commercial, this policy indicated the lack of a vision, a strategy. The discovery of gold in Brazil in 1695 acted as a catalyst to the Indiamen putting in at Bahia. The lure for gold by legal or illegal means turned the freedom of selling liberty goods into scandalously abusive practices. Liberty goods were dispatched through friends and even acquaintances, often without registration.

Contrary to expected behaviour, the crew protected personal liberty chests at times of crises, or stored up liberty goods at safe places on board even before consignments of the Crown were taken in. It was reported that the Indiaman, *N. S. da Esperança* on the home run in 1715, carried more merchandise in the captain's chamber, in the *curves,* in liberty chests and in prohibited places, than the rest of the cargo.[12] Overloading the ship to the extent of risking its safety was not uncommon. Influential people did remind the Crown that these privileges would recoil. Yet they were maintained because sailors depended on them for their subsistence. In 1759 *S. António e Justiça* carried 125 sacks, 80 bales and 14 barrels of pepper, 11 bales, 9 bundles of textiles and 2 *pipas* of wine, in contrast to 1858 sacks, 45 bales, 110 barrels of pepper, 1668 different volumes of textiles, 17 pieces of silk, 366 bales, 51 boxes and 29 *amorradas* of cinnamon and some porcelain articles, incense and coffee, besides 21 slaves on the account of officers and individuals. The Viceroy's consignment also consisted of 39 sacks of pepper and 19 different volumes of textiles.[13]

Goa-based trade in diamonds and other precious stones also cushioned the clandestine trade. Their small size, easy concealability and huge profits helped illicit trade distend. In 1706, diamonds taken to Lisbon by two ships, *N. S. dos Prazeres e S. António* and *Salvador do Mundo* on private accounts were reportedly embezzled.[14] Diamonds and precious stones were conveniently concealed in bales and bundles containing other goods and surreptitiously sold at Bahia. Such actions confounded even the most alert officials and reduced any computation of the magnitude of the invisible trade to a near impossibility.

The diamonds exported from Goa were generally not registered, hence the problem of quantifying such exports. The *N. S. da Vitória* which sank near Bahia in 1748 carried diamonds that were not recorded.[15] The alarming proportion of illegal trading at Bahia was partly an escape from the excessive duties levied on goods at Goa and Lisbon. The complex maze of disorderly streets of Bahia were premises of hectic trading in contraband goods. Officials of the India House complained in 1725 that textiles disembarked at Lisbon were those which did not find markets at Bahia.[16] The claim was not totally devoid of truth.

Embezzlement and manipulations involving illegal sale of goods at Bahia was common and convenient when ships dropping anchor at nightfall used the cover of darkness to sell off the goods before inspection of the ship the following morning.[17] At times ships remained far into the sea and sent goods for sale on the mainland by country boats or sometimes deliberately aborted voyage.[18] Men who purchased their offices found the postings at the Customs House where goods were moved in and out of the ship, into the warehouse and back, easy means of enriching themselves by colluding in the back door transactions.[19] For example, guards on duty aboard an Indiaman were dismissed for failure to protect goods from being embezzled in 1711.[20] Repeated complaints at Lisbon pointed to the straying of goods at Bahia and the chaotic maintenance of registers at the Goa port.[21] Crown attempts to contain the trouble was manifested in a decree of November 19, 1737 permitting registered consignments of liberty goods alone to be sold at Bahia.[22] Yet, instances of embezzlement were continuously reported, for instance, aboard the *N. S. das Brotas* in 1766, and *Rainha de Portugal* in 1781.[23] In 1785 the captain of *N. S. da Conceição* was found involved in illicit trading at Bahia.[24] It was individual interest that still prevailed over sincere service to the Crown.

Returning Indiamen also found it convenient to divert some of the textile consignments to Angola from where they were smuggled into Brazil by smaller craft. Coarse cotton piece goods used by Brazilian merchants for the purchase of slaves in Africa had great demand in Angola. Despite decrees prohibiting the sale of textiles and other goods by Indiamen that called at Angola for refreshing and revictualling, the practice continued. The trading network was subtly used for illegal transactions.

Invisible trade of this type jeopardized royal interests by way of evasion of freight and duties at embarkation and disembarkation. By displacing goods which would have earned the Crown sizeable profits, shipping was rendered costlier. The increasing, but futile endeavours of the metropolis to restrict, if not eradicate the invisible trade reflects the weakening of its hold over colonies.

In the 17th century a variety of articles ranging from pepper, chinaware, diamonds, spices and ivory were carried as liberty goods in small quantities, though they were eclipsed by textiles in the following century as the latter were popular in Brazil and West Africa and were prominent in the re-exporting network of Lisbon.[25] In 1764 the *N. S. da Conceição e S. Vicente Ferreira* was loaded with liberty goods of various officers including the *dispenseiro* and the carpenter. They consisted of 155 bundles, 8 boxes, 9 bales, 3 cases, one chest and 23 other volumes of textiles, 9 boxes, 18 *frasqueiras* and 180 cases of porcelain and 11 slaves. Of the 1135 volumes of liberty goods, 97 were for sale in Bahia, in addition to 2 slaves.[26] The chaplain of the frigate, Fr. Eusebio de Jesus Maria José opted to sell at Bahia five of the nine bundles of textiles he had on his *liberdades* account.[27] In 1763 textiles worth 4054=0=00 *xerafins* registered in Viceroy Conde de Ega's *liberdades* account were put up for sale at Bahia.[28] In 1764, the same Viceroy's liberty goods on board the *N. S. da Conceição e S. Vicente Ferreira* containing 725 pieces of textiles were being sold.[29] Even where legitimate trade was involved, goods on the account of the Crown were minimal in the 18th century. Though the quantum of exports was less than of the 16th century, it kept the Goa-Lisbon trade going.

This gains significance in the light of what P. J. Marshal states in a recent work, where he observes that "European purposes in Asia remained essentially commercial."[30] The loss of hegemony in the East had compelled Portugal to shift the focus from the Indian Ocean to the Atlantic. (The British East India Company was turning from the Atlantic to the Indian Ocean by the 18th century, as Prof. Marshall points out) where the current of trade was centered, making Brazil the key zone of Portugal's wealth and what was left of its power. But the market in Brazil strengthened the Goa-based commerce through the unofficial channel thus providing some justification for the commercial presence of the Portuguese in the *Estado da India*.

Private Trade

As stated earlier, considering the high costs and higher risks, together with the waning fortunes of the Crown in the East, involvement of private merchants in the Asiatic seaborne trade was given serious consideration. By the decree of March 9, 1672, made effective from March 1673, freedom of trade was conceded in all types of textiles, pepper, clove, cinnamon, other drugs and slaves to all Portuguese living in the kingdom, Brazil, or any other colony.[31] This measure formally ended the Crown's monopoly of trade and commerce and facilitated the entry of private traders into that arena. However Lisbon-centredness still prevailing, goods had to be carried to the metropolis for payment of duties after which they were re-exported - this factor was a deterrent to the merchants whose interests were focussed on the Brazilian markets rather than of Lisbon.

To strengthen the commercial basis of the Asian trade, the strategy already adopted by the Dutch and English was attempted. In 1691 the plan of establishing the India Company was mooted with a view to invite private capital into the official trade. The cold response of Portuguese-Goa merchants is explicable in terms of the traders' perception of treating the said company as a threat to their own trading network.[32] Wealthy Bahians doled out a meagre sum of 9,950 #000 *réis,* alleging that they faced a financial crunch. The general slump in Brazil notwithstanding Brazilians were not enthused by the scheme.

The gold strike in Minas Gerais in 1695 and royal sanction to the stopover facility at Bahia to returning Indiamen almost simultaneously triggered off flourishing contraband trading at the American capital. About 73 ships on the Goa-Lisbon voyage called at Bahia during the first half of the 18th century, while the number declined to about 53 in the second half[33] when the mining economy attenuated. Realising the adverse consequences of such practices on the revenues of India, the Crown ordered on March 17, 1734 that returning Indiamen could sell goods at Bahia by paying 10 % duty (*dizima*) and a security guaranteeing the payment of other duties at the India House in Lisbon.[34] The unsold cargo could be dispatched to Lisbon for sale, as stated in the order of April 17, 1738.[35] Then on, Bahia came to be glutted with Indian goods. Varieties of Indian piece goods, Chinese porcelain, tea and even slaves found a receptive market in Brazil.[36] Private trade received a further boost by the subsequent orders of 1744 and 1750 permitting officials of homebound Indiamen to take hides from Brazil in their cabin space. Anxiety of private traders to embark goods on their account before those of the Crown were taken in, was a logical sequel. In short, the results were similar to those emerging from the *liberdades* facility.

Private traders were the chief beneficiaries of these measures. With the option to sell their goods at Bahia and Lisbon open, they were never under pressure to dispose off the merchandise. There developed a nexus between merchants and their agents at Goa, Bahia and Lisbon. Cargo accounts of Indiamen that called at Bahia indicate the increasing proportion of private merchants' goods as against those of the Crown. Accounts of the following ships - *S. António e Justiça (1759), S. Francisco Xavier e Todo o Bem* (1756),[37] *N. S. do Paraizo* (1773),[38] *Neptuno* (1778)[39] and *N. S. da Conceição e S. António* (1780)[40] are some of the numerous examples. Official cargo was restricted to limited quantities of textiles, pepper, cowries and saltpetre procured on snuff account in India. In 1795 the goods on the official account of the ship *Princeza do Brazil* were valued at 38918=0=1 *xerafins*, while those of private merchants were worth 68816=2=20 *xerafins*.[41] Lack of flowing capital was perennially a stumbling block in the path of the official trading network in India because of which the Crown kept making short term adjustments like shifting the choice of fabrics from cheaper to finer ones or pepper and saltpetre being preferred to textiles.[42]

The facility to sell goods at Bahia had an added advantage to the private merchants who could take on fresh consignments of timber, sugar, hides and assorted cargo for the onward voyage. In December 1734, gold, bullion, diamonds and other precious stones were permitted to be dispatched to Lisbon.[43] In 1757, *N. S. das Neves e Santa Ana* took 63,000 *cruzados* to Lisbon on the account of private merchants[44] which reflects the extent of trading facility that Bahia provided to private merchants involved in the Goa-Lisbon network.

Private trade did not spare the human merchandise either. Slave trading did occur, though not regularly, along the Goa-Africa-Bahia route of the *Carreira da India*. References date back to 1698, when slaves on board the *N. S. do Cabo* were sold, followed by others. In 1740 the *N. S. da Conceição* offloaded 136 slaves in Bahia; in 1741, 143 slaves were disembarked.[45] In 1794, 17 slaves on board the *N. S. de Belém* were sold at Bahia for 2890#910 *réis*, earning a profit of 838#030 *réis* on the deal.[46]

Heavy imposts charged for the Goa-Lisbon *Carreira* voyages were a major impediment in the progress of trade. Portugal justified the high levies on grounds of the security to goods against heavy risks, but merchants had resorted to the invisible trade, particularly availing the *escala* facility at Bahia. *Escala* was ended in 1765 and a spate of decrees passed to reduce the various duties. *Laissez - faire* advocated by the Physiocrats, the free trade concept of Adam Smith, the fiscal reforms of Pitt the Younger (1759-1806) and the political expansion and consolidation of the English East India Company in India might have pressured the straggling Portuguese empire. Lisbon reoriented the structure of duties as part of a wider strategy.

The royal decrees of January 8, 1783, May 27, 1789, April 27, 1797 and November 25, 1800 unleashed the earlier colonial grip over trade, particularly over the Goa-based textile trade. The results were almost instantaneous: Between March 2, 1784 and March 8, 1785, 14 Portuguese merchant ships and 2 *curvetas* entered Aguada, Goa. During the same period, 6 ships arrived at Calcutta. Between 1784 and 1788, 75 ships from Asia entered Lisbon and 56 ships left Lisbon for Goa, an annual average of 15 and 11 ships respectively.[47] The Goa-Bahia nexus blossomed into a bourgeoning trade between 1792 and 1808. A large number of private merchants' ships were licensed to trade along the Asia-Lisbon route. The *Carreira da India* came to be rechristened as the *Carreira da Ásia*. A few of these ships are listed here :

Year	Route	Name of the ship
1795	Bengal-Lisbon	*N. S. do Carmo, Sta. Thereza, Triumfo*
1795	Bengal-Lisbon	*Princeza do Portugal*
1806	Malabar-Bahia-Lisbon	*S. Thiago Maior*
1811	Bengal-Rio-Lisbon	*Santa Cruz*
1811	Bengal-Rio-Lisbon	*Marquez de Angeja*
1811	Bengal-Rio-Lisbon	*Camões*
1814	Madras-Pernambuco-Lisbon	*N. S. da Paz, Rozalia*
1814	Madras-Pernambuco-Lisbon	*Commerciante*
1814	Bengal-Brazil-Lisbon	*D. José Primeiro*
1815	Bengal-Pernambuco-Lisbon	*Camões*
1815	Bengal-Rio-Lisbon	*Cianno*
1815	Bengal-Rio-Lisbon	*Marquez de Angeja*
1816	Goa-Pernambuco-Lisbon	*Vigilancia*
1816	Calcutta-Tellicherry-Bahia-Lisbon	*Gram careta*
1816	Bengal-Madras-Pernambuco-Lisbon	*Príncipe do Brasil*

(Compiled from *AHU*: *India* and *Baia* Mss).

During the years 1792 to 1806, a large number of piece goods were exported to Bahia, the highest figure being 330,067 pieces in 1799; the lowest - 133,146 pieces in 1797. Trade was spread to other centres like Rio, Pernambuco, Maranhao and Pará, besides Bahia. Asian exports to Rio and Pernambuco reached the peak in 1801. Textile exports to Lisbon also improved considerably during the said period.[48] The prospects of taking on additional cargo was an added incentive to the private ships. In 1806, *S. Tiago Maior,* in 1811, *St. Cruz* (it had 141,345 pieces of textiles on its Bengal-Rio-Lisbon voyage) and *Marquez de Angeja* took large volumes of cotton, coffee, cocoa, rice, sugar and hides to supplement the cargo for the onward voyage.[49]

The Role of Native Merchants

The increasingly important role played by private merchants in the seaborne trade needs to be related to the local agents and brokers in Goa on whom the Portuguese were dependent for timely supplies of goods by force of circumstances. The Goan Hindu businessmen of Panjim and the surrounding areas worked either on partnership basis or as individuals, but did not have a common organization. Though the general Portuguese sense of dislike for the gentiles was well known, for lack of alternatives, they continued to rely largely on the indigenous agents. Driven by considerations of profit, the local merchants played a key role in the procurement of goods through country trade, while confining themselves to a marginal role in the direct Goa-Bahia-Lisbon network. The local merchants used their bargaining power to their own advantage, resulting in loss to the Portuguese in some deals. Complaints about the poor quality and high price of consignments which were echoed in Bahia and Lisbon were but reflections of the nature of deals offered by the native merchants. Murmurs among the Portuguese merchants that they had lost control over trade which was entirely managed by locals, had some truth. Hence, it was proposed to entrust supply work to Portuguese merchants and Catholics.[50] The loss incurred by the sale of textiles shipped on official account by the vessel *S. António e Justiça* (1759) is a case in point.[51] Such complaints and problems did not occur in the private trade sector which amply shows that the local merchants and brokers knew where their interests lay.

Reference needs to be made to two specific instances of Goan traders' participation in the Goa-Bahia trade. One is Rogerio de Faria, a Goan Catholic from St. Inez, settled in Bombay, whose ship *Grão Cruz de Aviz* sailed to Rio with Balaghat textiles and other cargo. This initiative earned him knighthood at the royal court. Soon after, Faria shifted his focus away from Brazil to the more lucrative opium trade.[52]

The second case is of the Mhamai Kamat brothers of Panjim, who, through their agency house not only procured goods from Surat, Malabar, Balaghat and elsewhere, but also undertook export of textiles, saltpetre, coir, incense and other articles directly to Brazil or Lisbon where they had their trading associates. Their business correspondence housed at the Xavier Centre of Historical Research (Porvorim) throws light on the participation of private merchants in the Portuguese trading network at a time when the seat of power was shifted from Lisbon to Rio.[53]

Among the lesser local merchants may be listed Gopala Kamat of Panelim, Babu Naik, Gopala Naik, Rama Sinai Molio, Anta Naik, Narayan Naik and Paraga Naik - all of Cumbarjua, Soirea Parab Lawande of Ribandar and Srinivas Naik of Panjim.[54] As Goa was dependent on the hinterland for the supply of the export cargo, the local merchants exported arecanuts, coconuts, cashew and coconut fenny, cashew nuts, mangoes, tamarind, etc. and procured goods, mainly textiles for the trans-oceanic trade.[55] Small quantities of textiles and other commodities were exported directly to Bahia or Lisbon by these merchants. It was in supplying the procurements to the private traders and officials for the long-distance trade that they earned their profits. The role of the lesser merchants had gained importance in the wake of the opening of the markets of the *Estado da India* directly to Bahian tobacco in 1776, providing room for intra-colonial interaction.

In conclusion it may be said that Portuguese fortunes in the Goa-based seaborne trade in the 18th century can be divided into two unequal periods. The first phase spanned over nearly three quarters of the century when the sale of liberty goods and the Bahia-centred invisible and visible private trade eclipsed the official trade, confining the role of the Crown to limited shipments on the snuff account and largely to the maintenance of the *Carreira* by collection of freight, entry-exit and other levies. The second phase began with the opening of direct tobacco trade between Goa and Bahia in 1776, followed by the liberalization measures in the last two decades of the century which opened the flood gates of American trade to private operators. In the first phase, periodical Crown orders took the officials and private traders from strength to strength and enhanced their participation in the intercontinental trade enormously. Even before Indiamen were allowed to pay 10 % duty at the Bahia customs house as a precondition to the sale of goods there, merchants had found their own means and ways to indulge in such sales without registering their goods at Goa. In 1731 it was reported that on this account alone the India House suffered a loss to the tune of one third of its net proceeds. This phase reflects the inability of the Crown to chart a clear road map to orient its commerce in the mercantalist direction. By cobbling up short-term adjustments to deal with situations, the Crown altered the control mechanisms on which the empire was based. For instance, termination of the Crown monopoly over pepper and other drugs and opening up of Bahia as a stopover for returning Indiamen were moves that benefited the private merchants immensely. The consequences were unintended and worse still, not perceived. Though the Crown tried to retain the Lisbon-centredness of the trading network, the growing invisible trade compelled the authorities to slacken that control eventually, leading to intra-colonial relations.

In the second phase, the manoeuvers were better result-oriented. Though the earlier *escala* facility was ended, Indiamen on the outward voyage put in at Bahia for tobacco consignments to Goa. Moreover, the liberal decrees lowering duties facilitated better trade relations with Brazil - thus marking the culmination of the growing private trade around the years 1796-1807.[56] Expansion of trade occurred in terms of volume and variety of goods, particularly textiles. In short, it was mainly the Brazil-linked private trade that sustained the first Portuguese empire during the exigency as much as it sustained itself through its subtleties.

NOTES AND REFERENCES

1. Om Prakash, "European Corporate Enterprises and the Politics of Trade in India, 1600-1800", in R. Mukherjee and L. Subramanian (eds.), *Politics and Trade in the Indian Ocean World*, New Delhi, 1998, pp. 165-182.
2. Georgio Borsa, "Recent Trends in Indian Ocean Historiography 1500-1800", in G. Borsa (ed.), *Trade and Politics in the Indian Ocean*, New Delhi, 1990, pp. 7-8; Om Prakash, *op. cit.* p. 185.
3. Borsa, *op. cit.*, p. 8.
4. K. S. Mathew, "Trade in the Indian Ocean during the 16th century and the Portuguese", in K. S. Mathew (ed.), *Studies in Maritime History*, Pondicherry, 1990, pp. 22-23.

5. Om Prakash, *op. cit.*, p. 166; Afzal Ahmed, *Indo-Portuguese Trade in 17th century 1600-1663*, New Delhi, 1991, pp. 69-71.
6. C. R. Boxer, *The Portuguese Seaborne Empire; Historical Archives of Goa (HAG): Monções do Reino*, 49, fl. 185.
7. C. R. Boxer, "The Principal Ports of call in the *Carreira da India* (16th-18th centuries)", in Boxer, *From Lisbon to Goa 1500-1750*, p. 63.
8. C. R. Boxer, *op. cit. passim.*
9. *Ibid.*, p. 50, n. 39.
10. Virginia Rau, *Os Manuscritos do Arquivo da Casa de Cadaval respeitantes ao Brasil*, vol. I, Lisbon, 1955, pp. 202-203.
11. José Roberto do Amaral Lapa, *A Bahia e a Carreira da India*, pp. 331-341.
12. *Documentação Ultramarina Portuguesa* (*DUP*), IV, p. 46.
13. *Arquivo Histórico Ultramarino* (*AHU*): *Baia*, nos. 4143-46, 4586-93, 4722-23 c.a.
14. *HAG*: *MR*, 69-70, fl. 378; 76, fl. 151; *AHU*: *Baia*, no. 19737 c.a.
15. *AHU: Baia*, *caixa* 102, doc. 13, dt. 8/7/1748; *DUP*, IV, p. 206.
16. *DUP*, IV, p. 57; C. R. Boxer, *op. cit.*, II, p. 54.
17. *AHU: Baia*, no. 10331 c.a.
18. *AHU*: *Baia*, nos. 8457, 22644 c.a.
19. *AHU*: *Baia*, no. 20695-20697 c.a. The practice of sale of offices was common all over Europe. For details of sale of offices in 1761 in Portugal *vide AHU*: *Baia* nos. 6173 - 6202 c.a. That year, Luis Coelho Ferreira purchased the post of *Guarda-Mor* of Bahia Customs House for 16,000 *cruzados*.
20. *AHU*: *Baia*, *caixa* 7, doc. 21; *DUP*, IV, p. 37; Amaral Lapa, *op. cit.*, p. 233 for royal orders of the 17th century in this regard.
21. *AHU*: *Baia*, *caixa* 64, doc. 49, dt. 17/3/1738; *caixa* 91, doc. 21, dt. 7/1/1746; *caixa* 94, doc. 34, dt. 29/10/1746; *caixa* 99, doc. 24; nos. 7596, 7597, 11711, 19736 c.a; *Biblioteca Ajuda de Lisboa* (*BAL*), 51-VIII-20, no. 72, fl. 84; *HAG*: *MR*, 49, fl. 185; *MR*, 2376; *DUP*, IV, pp. 52, 80-81, 86-87, 102, 175. Amaral Lapa also discusses this issue in his *A Bahia e a Carreira da India*.
22. *AHU: Baia*, *caixa* 62, doc. 21.
23. *HAG*: *MR*, 58, fls. 49, 322-322v; *AHU: Baia*, nos. 7597, 11065-11066 c a.
24. *AHU: Baia*, nos. 11769, 11776 c.a.
25. *Vide* Appendix 1 for the prices of Indian piece goods at Bahia in 1727.
26. *AHU*: *Baia*, no. 6616 dt. 11/7/1764.
27. *AHU*: *Baia*, no. 6656-57 c.a. dt. 11/7/1764.
28. *AHU*: *Baia*, *caixa* 43, docs. 7479-7527 dt. 8/10/1766.
29. *Vide* Appendix 2. The following ships carried unspecified quantities of assorted goods on *liberdades* account between 1693 and 1704 on their Goa-Lisbon voyage:

Departure from Goa	Name of the ship	Liberty goods taken
January 1693	*S. António de Tana*	pepper
December 1693	*N. S. da Salvação*	pepper, amber, textiles, diamonds
December 1694	*N. S. de Nazaré*	pepper, diamonds
December 1695	*N. S. das Necessidades*	textiles, tea
December 1696	*N. S. da Vizitação*	textiles
January 1698	*N. S. do Cabo*	textiles
January 1702	*N. S. da Piedade e Chagas*	textiles
January 1703	*S. Pedro Gonsalves*	pepper, cinnamon
January 1704	*Salvador do Mundo*	pepper, textiles, chinaware
January 1704	*São Boaventura*	pepper, chinaware
December 1704	*Princeza do Céu*	cloves, ivory, chinaware
1704	*N. S. dos Prazeres*	pepper, cloves, chinaware

(Source : *HAG*: *MR*, 69 & 70, fl. 54-59v)

30. P. J. Marshall, "The British in Asia : Trade to Dominion, 1700-1765, in P. J. Marshal (ed.), *The Oxford History of the British Empire: The Eighteenth Century*, Oxford, 1998, p. 486.
31. *HAG*: *MR*, 6A, fl. 114; 37, fl. 194.
32. A. R. Disney, *The Twilight of the Pepper Empire*, pp. 74-81.
33. Amaral Lapa, *op. cit.* pp. 331-341.
34. *HAG*: *MR*, 103A, fl. 130; *AHU*: *Baia*, nos. 19736, 19739 c.a.; Amaral Lapa, *op. cit.*, pp. 257-258.
35. *AHU: Baia*, nos. 1779-1781 c.a.
36. For a glimpse of the *dizima* collected at Bahia on Indian goods, *vide* P. Sequeira Antony, "The Goa-Bahia Intracolonial Relations 17th-19th Centuries", unpublished Ph.D. thesis, Pune: TMV, 1998, Table 5.1, p. 221.
37. *AHU*: *Baia*, nos. 2133-2134, 2010-2211 c.a.; Amaral Lapa, *op. cit.*, pp. 284-285.
38. *AHU*: *India*, *maço* 95, no. 94.
39. *AHU* : *India*, no. 306.
40. *AHU* : *India*, no. 296.

41. *AHU*: *Baia, caixa* 197, doc. 16, dt. 14/4/1795.
42. *HAG*: *MR*, 1508, fls. 110, 208.
43. *AHU*: *Baia*, nos. 87-88, 1079-1080 c.a.
44. *AHU*: *Baia*, nos. 2108-2109 c.a. An account of Bahian contribution to the cargo of *N. S. do Paraizo*, 1773, is available in *AHU*: *India, maço* 95, no. 94.
45. For further details, *vide* P. Sequeira Antony, *op. cit.*, pp. 261-262.
46. *Arquivo Nacional de Torre do Tombe* (*ANTT*): *Casa da India*, no 1500, fls. 47-48; *AHU*: *Baia, caixa* 201, doc. 35, dt. 23/7/1796.
47. P. Sequeira Antony, *op. cit.*, pp. 240-241.
48. *Ibid.*, pp. 243-246.
49. *AHU*: *India*, nos. 303 and 305.
50. *HAG*: *MR*, 63, fl. 458. For complaints about poor quality of diamonds and other goods, *vide*, *HAG: MR*, 1501, fl. 52; *DUP*, V.
51. *Vide* Appendix 3
52. T. R. de Souza, "Rogerio de Faria; An Indo-Portuguese Trader with China links" *ISIPH*, IV, Macau, October 1991, *passim.*
53. P. Sequeira Antony, *op. cit*, pp. 223-225; C. Pinto, *Goa: Images and Perceptions*, pp. 49-60.
54. *AHU*: *India*, cod. 1715; *ANTT: Junta do Tabaco, maço* 105; *HAG*: *Registos Gerais*, 2278, fls. 266, 345, 357, 379, 396, 418, 546.
55. *HAG*: *MR*, 177A, fls. 323-329 for details of the trade link between Goa on the one hand and Portugal, Bombay, Daman, Diu, Balaghat, Cochin etc. on the other.
56. For details, *vide* José Jobson Arruda de Andrade, *O Brasil no Comércio Colonial*, São Paulo, 1980.

Appendix 1

Price of Indian piece goods at Bahia Customs House-1727

Type	Price in *réis*
Dotins de Bengala (a corja)	20 # 000
Alcatifas da Índia	---
Camas pintadas (a pessa)	15 # 000
Colxas da Índia	---
Cangas (a pessa)	# 800
Chaudeos de Bengala (a corja)	18 # 000
Damascos da Índia (a pessa)	14 # 000
Damasquelhos de cores (a pessa)	9 # 000
Escomilhas largas da Índia (a pessa)	4 # 000
Esperregois da Índia e China (a pessa)	8 # 000
Folinho da Índia (a corja)	9 # 600
Gorgorao da Índia (a pessa)	8 # 000
Lenços de ceda da Índia (a corja)	4 # 800
Lenços de China (a corja)	16 # 000
Madrapazes panos de Bengala (a corja)	30 # 000
Sanas de Bengala finas (a corja)	30 # 000
Sanas de Bengala ordinarias (a corja)	15 # 000
Veludos da Índia (a pessa)	16 # 000

Source : *AHU*: *Baia, caixa* 26, no. 8, dt. 3/4/1727

Appendix 2

Sale of textiles from Viceroy Conde de Ega's liberty goods at Bahia - 1764

Quantity		Type	Price per piece in *réis*	Total in *réis*
10	peças	*Demesco*	14 # 000	140 # 000
3	peças	52 covados satim	700	36 # 400
8	peças	cabaias pintados	12 # 000	96 # 000
20	peças	gagara enterfinos	3 # 000	60 # 000
154	peças	chitas ordinarios	1 # 500	231 # 000
20	peças	cobertas ordinarios	3 # 000	60 # 000
32	peças	cobertas perquenos	2 # 000	64 # 000
27	peças	lenços	# 75	20 # 250
7 meyas	peças	cassas entrefinos	2 # 500	17 # 500
300	peças	linhas patavar	2 # 000	600 # 000
26	peças	lenços	# 75	17 # 850
47	peças	lenços (damaged)	# 20	12 # 380
8	peças	cangas bordadas	# 280	10 # 240
4	peças	demitins (damaged)	2 # 400	9 # 600
2	peças	demitins (partly damaged)	1 # 200	2 # 400
20	peças	linhas patavar (partly damaged)	1 # 000	20 # 000

Total =1509 # 070

Duties: Dizima = 150 # 907
Others = 38 # 881

Total Duties = 189 # 788

Source: AHU: Baia, no. 7499 c.a. dt. 25/9/1765

Appendix 3

Textiles shipped to Bahia on snuff account by the vessel *Santo António e Justiça* in 1759

Qty in Corja	Type of textiles	Rate per Corja in Goa (*réis*)	Price offered at Bahia per Corja (*réis*)	Price in Goa (*réis*)	Expected sale price at 30% premium (*réis*)	Actually sold in Portugal (*réis*)
1	Cassas rachadas de falaz	201#000		201#000	261#300	156#000
½	Cassas de flora mormote	225#000		112#500	146#250	88#500
½	Cassa mil flores	261#000	18#000	130#500	169#650	122#600
1	Doriaz of 40 mãos	165#000		165#000	214#500	172#000
1	Doriaz of superior quality	180#000		180#000	234#000	248#000
½	Cassas tapados de flores	365#000		232#500	302#250	246#000
1 &15	Amamos	1032#500		196#000	257#400	213#750
10	Cassas brunas	802#500		802#500	1042#600	
16	Senas	532#500		852#000	1107#600	
52	Folinhas	145#500		756#600	977#600	955#850
17	Borralhos	55#500		88#800	115#400	96#000

Appendix 3 (Contd)..

Textiles shipped to Bahia on snuff account by the vessel *Santo António e Justiça* in 1759

Qty in Corja	Type of textiles	Rate per Corja in Goa (*réis*)	Price offered at Bahia per Corja (*réis*)	Price in Goa (*réis*)	Expected sale price at 30% premium (*réis*)	Actually sold in Portugal (*réis*)
22	Corbandeis	304#500	68#500	289#200	375#960	247#475
3 ½	Cadeas de riscas verdes	562#500		1237#500	1608#750	1320#000
9 ½	Paricaes copoz	490#500		981#000	1275#000	1100#000
20	Cadeas of 19 covados	68#400		58#000	196#900	258#500
1 &15	Cadeas of 24 covados	65#400		70#000	114#300	159#200
7 ½	Chita de Balaghat	142#500	16#000	106#800	138#850	120#000
4	Sarassas	13#200	12#800	52#800	68#640	47#200
14	Panos de cafres	88#500	12#800	123#900	161#600	
12	Zozuartes	772#500	8#000	927#000	1005#100	929#000
30	Linhas Patavar	43#200		1296#000	1684#800	1326#339

Loss incurred at the sale in Portugal : 36 %

Source : *HAG*: *MR*, 1506, fl. 103; *AHU*: *Baia nos. 4117-4122 c.a.*

2

Spurt in Industrialisation
Fábrica Real de Cumbarjua

CELSA PINTO

The lack of industrialisation in 18th century Goa has been too easily overemphasised. This is clearly mirrored in traditional and current historiography on Indo-Portuguese history. In fact the nature of the Goan economy in the said period has hardly received scholarly attention. This lack of scholarship stems from a misplaced belief that this theme is undeserving of appraisal. This paper seeks to disprove this assumption with a focus of attention on the emergence of the textile industry in Goa as an obvious outcome of the revival and expansion of the Portuguese Indian textile commerce in Indian Ocean waters towards the end of the 18th and the beginning of the 19th centuries.

It is instructive to note that Daman and Diu, the once flourishing centres of textile production, made a remarkable comeback in the 18th century. Daman produced *tiadas, canequins, zuartes, beatilhas,* etc., while Diu manufactured *panos de joris, panos de begaris, panos de durgogins, chellas, anagoas, bartingis, chondris,* etc. that formed quite a sizeable portion of the textile cargoes that were shipped officially and unofficially from India to Portugal, Brazil, Angola, Mozambique, South East Asia and Macau in the late 18th and early 19th centuries.[1]

Down south, Goa the capital of the *Estado da India* was not to remain unaffected for long. Textile production was soon to find expression. Not that this economic activity was a novelty to Goa. It must be stated that silk-producing factories had been set up at Betim and Porpangim by Conde de Ega. But this experiment in private enterprise had a limited amount of success and ended in bankruptcy.[2]

This paper is an attempt to dwell upon an interesting dimension to the economic history of Goa, to showcase one instance -- Goa's government-run textile-producing factory, *Fábrica Real de Cumbarjua* that functioned from around 1784 to 1797. A few questions crop up in this connection. What were the circumstances leading to the establishment of the *Fábrica*? What was its significance in terms of profits and losses? What were the odds it faced? How far was it successful in facing them? What implications did its existence have for the Goan economy? In the course of the subsequent discussion efforts will be made to try to answer them to the extent possible, given the limitations of source materials.

In focussing on the above theme the study has been influenced by specific considerations. It is hoped that it will correct misleading impressions, will make a relevant dent into *terra incognita* and above all stimulate interest and research in an area hitherto treated with contempt.

Efforts were afoot in the 1770s to find a replacement for the extinct textile unit at Betim. We have evidence that points out to deliberation and discussion as to whether to take recourse to a fresh project at Cumbarjua that would be under royal protection and run on the account of the *Fazenda Real.* It was estimated that initially its annual expenditure would amount to 3045-3-00 *xerafins.*[3]

There is no denying the fact that such an enterprise was bound to prove advantageous. Textile production would cater not just to domestic demand -- locals, the Royal Hospital and the Arsenal -- but also to the emerging textile commerce of Goa. It would provide labour opportunities to a number of locals including women.

It would also be reasonable to argue that the development of textile production in Goa was bound to attract highly professional weavers from the North and provide them with avenues for employment in a region relatively free of turmoil. This in turn was to work to Goa's advantage for skilled weavers in Goa were admittedly few and far between. This explains why a batch of young men was sent to Diu to acquire sufficient and efficient knowledge of textile production.[4]

Records tell us that there was a strong recommendation that Simão Rodrigues Morreira be commissioned to initiate the venture of setting up the said textile factory on the island of Cumbarjua.[5] This naturally revolved round the necessity of assigning the task to an individual well-known for his expertise and enterprising spirit. It needs to be stressed that Rodrigues Morreira held vital positions as *Ajudante de Intendencia da Agricultura, Escrivão da Junta de Mesa Agricultura, Intendente e Inspector de Reaes Fábricas de Estado.* He also controlled the *Coardaria de Arsenal Real* and the *Establecimento de Cairo.*[6] His approach was known to be positive and held the edge of being better than others. This did not go unrecognised as may be seen from the faith the Goa government reposed in him.

Simão Rodrigues Morreira while keeping in mind the potentials of textile production in Goa, put forth a plan of action that would assist the establishment and functioning of the new industrial outfit *Fábrica de Cumbarjua.* It contained elements of a forward strategy. Some of his recommendations revolved round the nature of fabrics to be produced specially those which in no way would offer competition to the textile industry at Daman and Diu; the necessity to create new posts and appoint special officers to oversee the governance of the *Fábrica*, to monitor the procurement and distribution of raw materials, etc. The appointment of an Inspector, who would be expected to pay monthly visits to the *Fábrica*, was expected to stimulate industriousness of work, ascertain perfection in manufacture and foster textile industrialisation.[7]

The plan indicated above coupled with concerted promotional efforts was bound to produce the desired results. The *Fábrica Real de Cumbarjua* became a reality around 1784. Simão Rodrigues Morreira was appointed its Administrator from November 1784. It produced textiles such as *lonas, meyas lonas, beatilhas, zuzuartes, ardians, tucorins, botians, panos de cafre, chitas, cadeas* and *coromandeis*, many of which were in imitation of textiles produced at Surat and Balaghat. Most of these manufactures were oriented towards Portugal and Mozambique.[8] For instance, we have a reference that textiles produced at Cumbarjua reached Lisbon in 1789 via the ship *São Luiz e Santa Maria Magdalena.* The cargo included 41 pieces having a value of 63$ 620 *réis.* Those who dispatched the fabrics were Pedro Joze de Silva, Manoel Gonsalves Chaves, Manoel Joze Machado and Manoel Ferreria de...[9] From a price list we gather that *lonas, meyas lonas* and *chitas* produced at the *Fábrica Real de Cumbarjua* were acclaimed as fabrics of very good quality that fetched a price of 2700 to 1600 and about 2500 to 3600 *xerafins* per piece, respectively.[10] For sometime even there arose a strong demand to create a commercial network with Portugal specially in *lonas.*[11]

The 1780s marked the high point of the *Fábrica de Cumbarjua*'s existence for it brought tangible benefits to Goa. In 1787 its profit amounted to 3553-0-4 ¾ *xerafins* and in 1789, 2414-0-38 ½ *xerafins.* From fabrics sold at Mozambique in 1791 it brought a gain of 1081-3-01 ¾ *xerafins* for the *Fazenda Real.*

Not only were fabrics produced by the *Fábrica* sold on government account but also on the account of private persons who dispatched them to Mozambique and Lisbon.[12]

The volume of the textiles produced at the *Fábrica* was small, involving a few weavers. After defraying operational costs the *Fábrica* was able to show profits that were not large. But all in all this added to a relatively significant economic enterprise.

It should be pointed out that by *Carta* of March 8, 1786 textile maunfactures of Goa including those produced at the *Fábrica* enjoyed exemption from all customs duties at Lisbon and in the Portuguese empire. Moreover the cultivation of *linho canhamo* and cotton was conducted on a large scale in Goa to meet the shortfall in raw materials essential for the textile industry.[13] All this leads us to infer that the said *Fábrica* enjoyed royal patronage and protection which went a long way in countering any prevailing sense of insecurity.

In the early 1790s the *Fábrica Real de Cumbarjua* fell upon hard times. In encountered increasing difficulties. The crisis was triggered off by a serious and persistent constraint -- the shortage of raw materials. Thread and other expensive materials had to be imported.[14] It can be explained that this high price syndrome not only made textile production in Goa much more expensive when compared to that in Balaghat, Gujarat and other parts of India but also brought the *Fábrica* to facing a life-and-death struggle for existence.

From this development stemmed a debate. Many bemoaned the loss of business and expressed grave concern. It was perceived that appropriate steps and mobilisaion of efforts were the crying need of the hour to provide an effective answer to the malaise. It was felt that the cultivation of raw materials in Goa should be accelerated. This would drastically reduce the expense incurred on imported materials. Such measures as exemption from duties on raw materials were also recommended.[15]

It was also argued that a thorough revamping and streamlining of operational procedures at the *Fábrica de Cumbarjua* -- simplification of and economy in administration, perfection in manufacture etc., were a must.[16]

To give a boost to the textile industry it was believed that payment to weavers should be by the piece as was the practice in other parts of India. This should replace payment by salary.[17]

It is obvious that precisely the exemption enjoyed by the *Fábrica de Cumbarjua* from duties in Portugal and in its colonies together with the measures suggested above, if persued vigorously, would remedy the situation, would reduce expenditure to a reasonable level, bring about perfection in manufacture and would inject new life into the *Fábrica* and help it to prosper and gain profits.[18]

But unfortunately the efforts made to cope with the problems of the *Fábrica de Cumbarjua* were not favourably rewarded. Despite a whole gamut of measures, it did not seem to make any headway.

The deepening crisis was made more serious by the slackness of demand for *lonas*. From Goa moved a bundle of 5 pieces of *lonas* having a value of 122-2-09 *xerafins* on board the vessel *Princeza do Brazil* in December 1791.[19] On its receipt, a report was despatched to Goa that clearly reflected that the market demand in Portugal was essentially for textiles in imitation of those of Surat and Balaghat.

It may be conjectured that the problems of the *Fábrica de Cumbarjua* were compounded by the emergence of the industrial arena in the form of privately-run factories at Taleigão, Mandur, Divar, Talaulim and Mapusa. They gave the *Fábrica* at Cumbarjua serious competition that brought it to the verge of collapse. There was evidence of clandestine (or otherwise) transfer of materials and the weaning away of workers and officials from the *Fábrica de Cumbarjua* to the *Fábrica de Taleigão* specially after the death of Simão Rodrigues Morreira. The state had no clearly formulated policy to combat this menace though orders were issued for their return.[20]

The records provide a few odds and ends on the *Fábrica de Taleigão*. It produced fabrics that were well-received in Portugal and Mozambique. There is a clear reference to 36 *panos retalhos* being despatched in 1791 on board the *Princeza do Brazil* which when auctioned at the Casa da India brought 28$409 *réis*. It produced *panos de cafre* of the kind available in Balaghat, *zuzuartes* in imitation of that produced in Surat and *cadeas* better than those produced in Surat.[21] In short the *Fábrica de Taleigão* appeared to be schooled in the intricacies of production and in the increasing demand of the international market.

Bad administration, sheer ignorance and carelessness had also brought about the progressive deterioration of the *Fábrica de Cumbarjua* and made it a liability.[22] It caused the *Fazenda Real* unproductive expenditure on a daily basis. Needless to say it existed only in name. Despite protective measures by the government to bolster its existence, it showed no signs of recovery.

A dismal picture of economic ruin, the end of the *Fábrica Real de Cumbarjua* eventually came about. It faced closure in 1797.[23]

By order dated March 6, 1798 (?) the *Fábrica de Cumbarjua* was revived. It came to be administered by and on the account of Luis Joze de Souza Machado de Morais who was then administrator of the textile factory at Taleigão. In fact he bought 25 looms together with other equipment and materials of the factory.[24] Thus it seems that the *Fábrica de Cumbarjua* received a new lease of life. But it came to be privately operated. This was essentially in response to the need to find a viable alternative. There were no options left but to accept this fate and continue to function under a system alien to bureaucratisation.

A report submitted in 1800 by Luis Joze de Souza Machado de Morais indicates that the *Fábrica* had 36 weavers and 32 other officials. It produced 118 *lonas* and 573 *atualhados* and *lenços*, 403 *doutins*, 2920 *cadeas*, *chitas* and *coromandeis*.[25] The transition from bureaucratic to private enterprise proved fruitful.

But this seems to have been a temporary phenomenon. After the death of Luis Joze, the *Tecelagem de Cumbarjua* as it now came to be called ran into trouble once again. There arose a tussle for its control between Florencio Joze de Moraes Sacramento, nephew of Luis Joze and the well-known Goan trader António Pereira.[26] There were also tentative moves to amalgamate the *Tecelagem de Cumbarjua* with the *Fábrica de Corduaria* of the Arsenal.[27] Since we have no further evidence of its existence it may be presumed that this merger was its eventual fate. This also seems plausible in view of the fact that a serious effort was made around 1811 by Joze Rodrigues Morreira to install a textile factory at Cumbarjua. His representation was backed by Conde de Galves(?).[28] However it did not receive favourable attention. Why this is so is unclear. Perhaps it would not be unreasonable to suppose that since the island of Cumbarjua was bestowed as a *mercê* to Candido Joze Maurão Garcez Palha in 1810 it was not possible to do so. Rodrigues Morreria was instead permitted to take charge of the factory established at Ribandar by *Officio* June 8, 1811 which had to furnish supplies annually to the troops, the Hospital and the Arsenal.[29]

To conclude, the foregoing study though not comprehensive mirrors quite clearly that the *Fábrica Real de Cumbarjua* despite its shortcomings and though shortlived is a case in hand which supports the line of argument that there was a spurt in industrialisation in Goa that owed its initiative to the winds of change blowing globally in the 18th century ushered in by the Industrial Revolution.

It may be safely assumed that the textile industry of Goa was a direct result of the expansion of the Portuguese Indian textile industry of the late 18th-early 19th centuries and in turn it stimulated and had a profound impact on it. It is important to recall that textiles formed the single most important item of the Indo-Portuguese trade of the period under discussion.

Given the present state of our knowledge, it would not be erroneous to assume that textile industrialisation in Goa contributed in a number of not unimportant ways to the development of the Goan economy at a time when overall development was staging a recovery. Without the growth of the textile industry, Goa's commercial advance might have been slower. If its stimulus to economic advance is viewed in combination with that exerted by other economic branches with expansive tendencies, then evidently its impact was notable.

NOTES AND REFERENCES

1. Celsa Pinto, *Trade and Finance in Portuguese India*, New Delhi, 1994, pp. 189-190.
2. Historical Archives of Goa (HAG): *Monções do Reino* (*MR*) 191B, fls. 1396, 1403.
3. HAG: MR 191B, fl. 1400v.
4. HAG: *MR* 191B, fl. 1404v.
5. HAG: *MR* 191B, fl. 1416.
6. HAG: *MR* 191B, fL 1475v.
7. HAG: *MR* 191B, fls. 1408v-1410.
8. Pinto, *op. cit.*, p. 192.
9. HAG: *MR* 175B, fls. 96-99.
10. HAG: *MR* 191B, fls. 1435v-1438.
11. HAG: *MR* 171B, fl. 402.
12. HAG: *MR* 169B, fl. 687;191B, fls.1391v,1430-1432v.
13. Pinto, *op. cit.*, p.192.
14. HAG: *MR* 172B, fl. 580v; 174B, fl. 591.
15. HAG: *MR* 171B, fl. 402; 173, fl. 245; 174B, fl. 595v.
16. HAG: *MR* 174B, fl. 595.
17. HAG: *MR* 171B, fl. 403;172B, fl. 580.
18. HAG: *MR* 171B, fl. 595.
19. HAG: *MR* 191B, fls.1434-1435.
20. HAG: *MR* 191B, fls.1391-1392, 1440-1440v.
21. HAG: *MR* 174B, fl. 617;175, fl.100v.
22. HAG: *MR* 179A, fls. 322-323; 191B, fls.1365, 1443.
23. HAG: *MR* 177B, fl. 551v; 191B, fl.1392.
24. HAG: *MR* 179A, fl. 325; 191B, fls.1380-1381.
25. HAG: *MR* 179A, fl. 325.
26. HAG: *MR* 182, fl. 318.
27. HAG: *MR* 182, fl. 318v.
28. HAG: *MR* 191B, fls.1360, 1446-1446v.
29. HAG: *MR* 202D, fl.518.
    Fábrica de Tecelagem de Ribandar under Adminstrator Joze Rodrigues Morreira acquired loans for the period 1812–1820 to the tune of 46203–2–44 *xerafins* from the Treasury and provided the Arsenal textiles worth 33057–1-21 *xerafins* for the period 1814–1818. By December 1827 it returned 7091–3-20 *xerafins* and still owed a balance of 6054-3-03 *xerafins*.

HAG: *MR* 202D, fl. 518v; 204B, fls. 696-697.

Appendix 1

Statement of Profits and Losses of the *Fábrica de Cumbarjua*, 1787-94

Year	Value (in xerafins)	Profit (in xerafins)	Loss (in xerafins)
1787	12487-3-14	3553-0-04¾	
1789	11823-4-07½	2414-0-38½	
1792	3715-2-23		2287-1-00
1793-94	10766-3-44		21435-0-48½

Source:- HAG: *MR* 169B, fl. 687;174B, fl. 600; 176A, fl. 274; 191B, fls. 1391v, 1430-1432v.

3

Portuguese Legislation on Reopening the Mint of Goa in 1845 and Issues of Overstruck Native Coinage in Daman

FENELON REBELLO

Available records had given a broad outline of the coinage issued by the Portuguese mainly in Goa, and to a limited extent on the instructions issued to other mints in India, by Governors and their Revenue Councils. However it was the occasional appearance of specimens over the years, that subsequently revealed some unknown aspects of the activities of mints, such as denominations, and patterns of the coinage issued.[1] As a result, some of the assumptions and opinions earlier formulated, had to be then, revised.

Recently, our attention was drawn to the contents of a small hoard of rusty coins. Amidst the lot that consisted mostly of native Indian copper pieces, we could discern Portuguese crowned arms and dates on some of them. There were over two dozen pieces similar to the issues of Goa, but only two denominations, each of one date, 4½ *réis* of 1845 and 7½ *réis* of 1848, and all of them thick and unshapely. We could make out that they had been overstruck on native Indian coins, but there were other notable differences mainly in the crowned arms and weight. They appeared to be a crude job hurriedly executed.

Being unable to obtain any references to them from available sources, it became necessary to find out the reason for the existence of such pieces, possibly through inference from other known facts and it seems that history comes to one's rescue. We shall, therefore, briefly consider, first, some of the circumstances prevailing, both in political as well as monetary systems.

The general administrative situation in Portuguese India, during the reign of D. Maria II (1834-1853) was conducive to a sorry state of affairs. Riddled by political struggles and factionary turmoils, which even led to crime and insubordination, hardly a real stability was achieved, even though a dozen governments took over successively up to 1842.

As for the coinage, the issues of the mint of Goa had begun to show a gradual deterioration mainly in the types of copper coins issued from the end of the 18th century, as evident from the unevenly struck and deformed pieces which even failed to maintain legally adopted weight standards. Subsequently, matters got worse by hurriedly restriking worn-out coins, and then counter-marking to obviate spurious coinage that proliferated in Goa under such propitious circumstances.

As for the silver and gold coinage, it continued to be of presentable types but by 1841, when the last of the Portuguese gold coinage was issued in India, opinions were being expressed on the advisability of transferring the mint of Goa, from the inadequate quarters it was then housed in,[2] and soon after in 1842, through an order issued, the mint was closed and all its equipment and material sent to the newly designated place, the Arsenal of Goa.[3] Subsequently the mint was reopened in 1845,[4] and standard works on this subject express the opinion, that based on the documents in the interim period of 1843-44, no coins were issued, from the mint of Goa. However, during the last decade, exemplars appeared showing the mint to have been active to some extent.[5]

By then, a new reformed type of coinage was initiated, consisting of pieces with a more uniform shape and thickness and having weights in accordance to the standards adopted and proportional for various denominations. The introduction of improved mechanical systems is evident from the blanks cut and consistent die-axis[6] adopted for a series or a denomination in each year.

At about this time, the merchants of Goa who encountered difficulties in their transactions due to prevailing worn-out coinage along with counterfeit pieces in circulation, forwarded a petition to Governor José Ferreira Pestana requesting permission to allow them to exchange all the worn-out coins for new ones. This request was granted and the Treasurer of the mint gave instructions accordingly.[7]

With the mint fully active, the Treasury department, ordered a large quantity of coins to be struck in 1845 and 1846 thus putting a heavy burden on it, as can be judged from the recorded total of 274,120 *xerafins* equivalent in silver and 5,452 in copper issued during these two years.[8]

Since the overstruck coins now discovered are contemporary to those of Goa, the differences between the two issues are comparatively detailed in the following chart, along with photographs of specimens which enable one to verify their crude types, die-axis adopted in the process of striking and their excessive weights.

DATE	FACE VALUE	WEIGHT		ARMS		DIE-AXIS	
		GOA	O.S *	GOA	O.S *	GOA	O.S *
1845	4 ½ R	Average 3.0 g	7.3 G- 11.5 g			Vertical	Vertical
1848	7½ R	Average 5.0 g	9.6 G- 11.6 g			Hori-zontal	Hori-zontal

*Overstrikes

Overstruck coins

1845

4½ R.

1848

7½ R.

1848

7½ R.

Considering the notings in the above chart and as seen from the photographs we can observe that:

The dies used for overstriking were of a crude type and the coins show original native characters partly visible.

The crowned arms (*Escudo*) in overstrikes show 8 castles in all cases, instead of the correct 7 as in issues of Goa.[9]

In the overstruck specimens of 1848, the centre of the shield shows an arrangement in + form as compared to X form in the coinage of the same year and denomination from Goa.

Whilst positioning the obverse and reverse dies for striking 7½ *réis* in 1848, the axis adopted was vertical in overstrikes whilst for the same denomination and year it was horizontal for in the issues of the mint of Goa.

The overstruck coins both in 1845 and 1848 exceed by 2-3 times the legal standards of weight followed in Goa. (Observation nos. 1,2 and 3 can be verified from photographs and nos. 4 and 5 as stated in the chart).

Having a knowledge of contemporary facts and comparative details of specimens, what remains to be determined now is – where did the Portuguese overstrike native coins and what was the purpose?

The crude dies used with incorrectly depicted Portuguese arms, indicate another mint and untrained personnel, and a different die-axis adopted for the pieces of the same denomination in 1848, further strengthens this possibility.

The fact that native coins were utilised on both occasions, leads us to believe that such pieces must have been readily available for the purpose, and once again we shall rely on documentary evidence.

It is observed from the records that, of the three territories the Portuguese had at the time (Goa, Daman and Diu) it was only at Daman that various types of native coins were current. In fact, besides the Portuguese copper pieces of 60, 30 and 15 *réis*, the lower coinage in circulation there, consisted entirely of local ones from various states. The British who had their own extensive colonial coinage in India, with the purpose of having further commercial advantage, also struck at Surat local types of copper pieces which could easily pass for trade in other states including those of the Portuguese.[10]

Considering normal variations to be expected in thick unshapely pieces, and the wear due to circulation, we find that the overstruck specimens have weights closely corresponding to native coins denominated as "*Dirqui*" (Didqui) and "*Shiurai*" (Shivrai) both recorded as such, among the contemporary current coins at Daman.[11] What appears to have happened, is that either on orders from Goa or by a decision locally taken, the mint of Daman used local artisans to carry out the carving of the dies similar to those of Goa, and work was expedited by availing of local current coins of proper size but ignoring the excess weight. The fact that a consistent die-axis was adopted appears to signify that this mint was also equipped with some mechanical means, at least for the purpose of stamping.

As for the motive that led to such issues, there are many factors that may have influenced and we can only surmise them. For instance, as in Goa, there could have been a need to replace worn-out coinage in Daman. In the process, a similar pattern such as at Goa was adopted, so as to also substitute the local types, thus achieving both objectives. The denominations of 4½ and 7½ *réis* were convenient fractional values for the purpose of local transactions, but we also note the fact that the face value in *Réis* of the *"Dirqui"* and *"Shiurai"* which was more than the overstruck ones, could imply a sort of devaluation of existing currency thus bringing it more in conformity with that of Goa.[12]

There is a final aspect to be considered, which is about the specimens being counterfeit, as experienced in Goa. It appears that the possibility of the overstruck specimens being spurious or illegally made, could be excluded due to the intrinsic value of the metal, which is an important factor in such cases. The excess of copper used with the additional costs of preparing the dies and then minting would defeat the very purpose of a lucrative venture.

So it is with certain obvious facts, that we have arrived at the mint from where they must have originated whilst the motives for issue could at present only be surmised. As we mentioned earlier, the overstruck specimens have now revealed an unknown type of coinage issued from the mint of Daman, as a result of some legislative decision of the Portuguese government, that is not to be found in available records.

NOTES AND REFERENCES

1. F. Rebello, "Unpublished Silver Issues of Chaul-Bassein", *Numismatic Circular*, London, June 1998, p. 205.
2. Portaria no. 2003, *Boletim do Governo*, Goa, no. 49 (1.11.1841), p. 313.
3. Portaria no. 1510, *Boletim do Governo*, Goa, no. 54 (29.11.1842), p. 327.
4. Portaria no. 118, *Boletim do Governo*, no. 9 (25.2.1845), p. 2.
5. R. Schulman, Amsterdam, Cat. 1989 (no. 1042) ½ *pardau* of 1843; F. Rebello, "Peça inédita da Oficina de Goa (4½ *R.* de 1843)", *Numismatica*, Lisbon, 1998, pp. 15-16.

6. Axis is considered to be vertical or horizontal depending on whether the two dies are positioned in one direction or opposite whilst striking.
7. *Boletim do Governo*, no. 24 (29.4.1846), p. 159.
8. F. Neri Xavier, *Boletim do Governo*, no. 73 (18.9.1866), p. 634.
9. In the coinage of Portugal (1521-1557), there are also instances where the number of castles vary in silver issues – A. Gomes– Cat. A5-37.03 onwards and in gold Cat. J3-82.01 and 104.01.
10. P. L. Gupta, *Coins*, New Delhi, 1968, pp. 153, 157.
11. *Boletim do Governo,* (28.8.1846), pp. 250-51.
12. The equivalent of '*Dirqui*' being 10,59 *réis* and '*Shiurai*' 9 *réis* of Goa, at that time *Boletim do Governo* (28.9.1846).

4

Trade in Goa during the 19th Century with Special Reference to Colonial Kanara

N. SHYAM BHAT

From the arrival of the Portuguese to the end of the 18th century, the economic history of Portuguese Goa is well examined by historians. But not many works are available on the economic history of Goa during the 19th and 20th centuries, which witnessed considerable decline in the Portuguese trade in India. This, being a desideratum, it is not surprising to note that a study of the visible trade links between Portuguese Goa and the coastal regions of Karnataka[1] is not given serious attention by historians so far. Therefore, this is an attempt to analyse the trade connections between Portuguese Goa and colonial Kanara in the 19th century.[2]

The present exposition is mainly based on the administrative records of the English East India Company government such as *Proceedings of the Madras Board of Revenue, Proceedings of the Madras Sea Customs Department, Madras Commercial Consultations*, and official letters of the Collectors of Kanara. These documents are used for the first time in the study of Indo-Portuguese history. These sources present clear trading relations between Portuguese Goa and colonial Kanara and refer to the various items of trade, both imports and exports.[3] Of these, however, one could see repeated and striking references to the import of salt from Goa to Kanara and export of rice from Kanara to Goa. This basic, historic and essential link between the two colonial pockets is striking and calls for a study. I have tried to examine this problem in the wider historical context of western colonialism in India, particularly the Portuguese and the British, and in the context of the world system. The British empire in India and their imposition of unequal treaties on the Portuguese in India cannot be ignored by any study of this kind.

Buchanan[4] and Blair[5] opined that there was a revival in the external trade of Kanara after 1799-1800. On the basis of the available sources the trade of the Kanara coast may be described as an entrepôt trade. Except for the already existing trade with Arabia, Goa and Malabar, Kanara, during the period of our study, acted more as a transmitter of trade than the direct feeder to England. The ports of Kanara were the trade links between the indigenous, interior lands and foreign dependent markets. This was very similar to the role the country played in the 18th and 19th centuries when her merchants acted as the conveyors of spices collected from areas of production and distributed them to the countries of Asia and Europe. "India was then, the central, the focus or fulcrum for Indian Ocean trade".[6] Kanara traded in many products of Malabar, Mysore, Coorg and even those brought from outside like Bombay, Arabia, Travancore, Sind and Gujarat. It was, in fact, a spatially widespread and broad-based commercial phenomenon in which the port of Mangalore acted as an entrepôt. The same could be said of Portuguese Goa as regards a few products, for example, textiles and the trade with Africa and Brazil.

A dominant feature of the sea trade of Kanara of this period was that it was export-dominated, and that too, in merchandise. The excess of exports over imports was also the characteristic of the trade dealing of India in the 18th and 19th centuries. In fact, this single character, foreign trade was the problem of most of the underdeveloped colonial countries. As M. N. Pearson observed, "the problem of third world countries then is not their poverty; for often they are naturally rich; the problem is that its wealth ends up in the metropolis."[7] The fluctuations in trade were dominated largely by the interplay of several factors like vagaries of weather, the piratical threats, political upheavals like internal rebellions in the trading countries, the natural calamities like famines or droughts in the dependent areas, a change in the tariff policy of the government, unforeseen commercial causes, etc. Some of these factors played a crucial role in the trade of Goa and trade dealings between Goa and Kanara.

Rice and other items of trade

Some of the important ports on the coast of Kanara in the beginning of the 19th century were Bekal (Kasaragod), Kumbla, Manjeshwar, Mangalore, Mulki, Padubidri, Kaup, Kundapur, Baindoor, Shirur, Sadashivgad, Honavar and Kumta.[8] Sir Thomas Munro described the trade of Kanara in 1800. He wrote that about one-third of the rice exported reached Arabia and the rest, Malabar, Goa and Bombay. Arrack and gin were imported from Goa. Salt was imported from Goa, Bombay and Muscat.[9] In fact, a letter of Munro to the Madras Board of Revenue dated 29th April 1800, mentions an advance to the tune of 4000 *Bahadury pagodas* (Rs. 16,000) to the Captain of Frigates sent by the Governor of Goa to enable the Captain to purchase rice from Kanara.[10] Buchanan also described rice as the grand article of export which was sent to Muscat, Bombay, Goa and Malabar.[11] John Sturrock also considered rice as next only to coffee in point of value. He observed that more than half of its exports went to Malabar, about one-third to Goa and only a small quantity to foreign countries such as Arabia and Zanzibar. Exports were made from all the parts of the district but the rice trade with Goa was chiefly on at Hangarkatta and with Persia, Arabia and Zanzibar at Kundapur (Gangolli) and Mangalore.[12] The difference in the proportion of the rice exports to the same places alluded to in the two records, one of Munro and another of Sturrock, is noteworthy. These two records, in fact provide the two time limits, one at the beginning of the 19th century and the other at its fag end, between which the fortunes of rice trade fluctuated before it yielded its prime position. By 1850s, coffee in the southern division and cotton in the northern division of Kanara had taken over as prominent items of trade.

As far as Kanara was concerned, three-fourths of its sea-borne trade was carried on at Mangalore while the rest was shared by the ports of Kundapur, Hangarkatta (Barkur), Malpe (Udupi), Mulki, Kasaragod, Kumbla, Manjeshwar and other ports. Kundapur, Hangarkatta, Mulki, Mangalore and Bekal were the main rice exporting ports. The ports of Mangalore, Hangarkatta and Kundapur exported mainly three varieties of rice, namely, the first, 'Muscati', the name received from the Arabs who took it in large quantities to Muscat, the second, 'Rassy', a coarse variety of rice exported to Goa and Malabar, and the third, 'Ersalah' to Kutch.[13]

From 1802 to 1804 there was excessive demand for Kanara rice from Bombay, Goa and Malabar markets and as such the export of rice at Mangalore to Arabia was prohibited and rice was exported to the places of demand.[14] A few Portuguese and French records of this period refer to the import of rice from Kanara to Goa. It is said that in the beginning of the 19th century, rice cargoes would arrive at Goa from Kanara especially from Basrur, Mangalore, Honavar, Kalianpur and Ponani.[15] Vitalji Kamat, Keshav Parab Cawandy, Vithoji Sinai Dhempe and the Mhamai brothers of Goa were some of the well-known merchants involved in the flourishing rice trade on the west coast of India.[16] Brown and Dineur, a Mahe-based firm, often consigned rice cargoes from Mangalore and Ponani to the Mhamais for sale in Goa. In 1805 when there was a shortage of Mangalore rice, Brown and Dineur informed the Mhamai brothers that the export of Ponani rice would be resumed as there had been a good harvest.[17] It is interesting to note that in Kanara also the Gowda Saraswat Brahmins or Konkanis played a crucial role as traders of the region. This fact is supported by Buchanan[18] (in the beginning of the 19th century) and John Stokes[19] in 1830. In 1809, Alexander Read, the Collector of Kanara, wrote to the Board that the export of rice to Goa should not suffer as the troops at Goa were more than that of the previous year, and that settlement could procure its supplies from no other quarter but Kanara.[20] In 1822-23 the exports from Kanara to Goa by sea valued Rs. 1,68,000.[21]

Many regions contributed to the overseas trade of Kanara. Rice, the staple of the region, was exported mainly to Arabia, Muscat, Bombay and Malabar. Because of the enormous supply of rice to Arabia and north western parts of India, Kanara was regarded as the granary of the western coast and of Arabia.[22] The following table (see next page) gives a comparative statement of the quantity of rice in *muras*, (a *mura* is equal to about 39 kilograms), exported from Kanara to various places, namely, Arabia, Bombay, Goa, French ports, Malabar and others.[23]

The only two foreign settlements in India with which the Kanara coast had trading connection were Mahe and the Portuguese settlement of Goa. A document belonging to the year 1845 reveals that the trade with Mahe was meagre, not exceeding Rs. 6,000 a year, but with Goa it was more than Rs. 1,60,000.[24]

Mangalore was the most important port in Kanara. In 1809, Alexander Read considered it to be the emporium of Kanara. Rice was the chief article of export from here. It imported salt from Goa.[25] The principal port of Barkur was situated at Hangarkatta. It was a busy port till the end of the 19th century. It concluded a large export trade in rice and paddy, principally to Goa. In fine season, as many as a hundred native craft were seen there loading for Goa and the ports of North Kanara.[26]

From Mangalore there arrived in mid-1812, in Goa, a shipment of 9 horses priced at 300 *xerafins* each, thereby possessing a total value of 2,700 *xerafins*.[27] Besides merchandise, in Kanara, treasure too was imported and exported from and to the neighbouring regions like Mysore, Coorg, Goa and the Maratha states. Goa exported salt to Kanara and imported paddy, rice and wheat from Kanara by land.[28]

In 1836, C.R. Cotton,[29] the principal Collector of Kanara, reported

Official Year	Arabia	Bombay	Goa	French Ports	Malabar	Sundry	Total
1838-39	4,55,986	6,83,873¾	1,35,727¼	7319 ½	75,116	3744 ½	13,61,767
1839-40	3,96,532	4,38,168	1,11,492½	4079	35,393 ½	4353	9,90,018
1840-41	3.78,046	4,71,062	1,26,591¾	1715	41,416	763	10,19,593 ¾
1841-42	4,26,315	5,13,342½	84,356½	5976	65,918 ¼	280	10,96,188 ¼
1842-43	4,87,567	5,44,704½	1,18,507½	2284	81,898 ½	707	12,35,668 ½
1843-44	4,78,192	5,24,484	1,63,809¼	6744	81,838	1295	12,56,362 ¼
1844-45	5,19,453	5,11,046½	1,20,094¼	5271	89.951	1972	12,47,787 ¾
1845-46	5,01,642	7,76,395	78,433	494	1,08,507 ¼	920	14,66,391 ¾

on the various articles of exchange between Kanara and Goa during 1828-29. Cotton's report clearly reveals that rice and paddy were major articles of export from Kanara to Goa. It indicates that dates, drugs, paper, dry grains, sugar, wines and spirituous liquors were also imported into Kanara from Goa. Further coir, drugs, dry grains, sandalwood oil, pepper, timber, etc. were exported from Kanara to Goa. A miscellany of the articles purchased by the Portuguese included sugar, iron, ginger, coir, saltpetre, wood, timber for masts and ship-building operations conducted at the Goa shipyard.[30]

During 1845-46, Goa exported to Kanara by sea, commodities like coconuts, dates, furniture, glassware, grain of sorts, spirituous liquors, wine, coir, dried fish, piece goods (silk), provisions of various sorts, salt (valued at Rs. 5,888), timber and sundry items. In the same period, Kanara exported by sea to Goa drugs of various sorts, tamarind, dry grain, paddy and rice (valued at Rs. 1,32,357), piece goods, cotton, silk, fish bladder, salt (pure), pepper, black wood, black timber and jungle timber wood.[31]

During 1851-52, rice exported from Kanara to Goa was 1696 *corges* and 33 *muras* and it shot up in the following year.[32] In 1852-53, Kanara imported the following items from Goa by land:[33]

Articles	Quantity	Value in Company's Rupees
Betel nut	cwt. 1,710	7,632
Catchu or Terraja Ponica	cwt. 415	2,489
Fruits – Coconut	nos. 25,01,238	37,518
Fruits – Dry	cwt. 3,192	13,768
Oil – Coconut	gals. 7,006	4,398
Provision Salted	cwt. 2,392	14,813
Salt (Goa)	cwt. 44,058	11,283
Sundries		5,281
	Grand Total	97,182

In the same year Kanara exported to Goa the following items by land:[34] (see next page).

In 1854, rice imported by Goa amounted to 71,312 *fardos*.[35] In 1855-56, Kanara exported by sea to Goa various items like cotton wool, cotton goods, coconut, rice (7107 quarters valued at Rs. 84,182), metal-iron bars and bolts, molasses or jaggery, cardamon, mace, pepper, timber and wood.[36] During the same period, 121 Portuguese craft arrived at the ports of Kanara and the tonnage was 1;747. In the same period, 122 Portuguese craft departed from the ports of Kanara and the tonnage was 1,693.[37]

Articles	Quantity	Value in Company's Rupees
Cotton Wool	lbs. 5,158	1,006
Cotton Goods-Piece Goods, Plain	Pieces 2,585	1,305
Gall Nuts or Analicoy	cwt. 3,200	3,207
Grain of Sorts	quarters 160	661
Rice	quarters 14,892	69,392
Wheat	quarters 1,590	17,529
Wak-Bees	lbs. 11,244	4,819
Sundries		6,689
	Grand Total	1,04,608

In 1858-59, Goa imported by sea, paddy (worth Rs. 43,339), rice (worth Rs. 59,836) and wheat (worth Rs. 5,796) from Kanara. These were imported along with other sundry items. In the same year, Goa exported salt worth Rs. 8,488 on government account and worth Rs. 364 on private account to Kanara. Exports from Goa included coconuts, chillies, provisions and other sundry items.[38]

In 1862-63, Goa exported to South Kanara items like cabinet ware, fire works, fruits and nuts (dates and others), glassware, spices, spirits (gin), wax and wax candles, wines and sundries. In the same year, one steamer and 160 native craft under Portuguese colours (2,909 tonnage) were sent from Goa to Kanara and 156 native craft (2,895 tonnage) under Portuguese colours departed from Kanara to Goa. Along with other commodities, they took mainly rice to Goa.[39] In 1869 rice imported to Goa from South Kanara was 16,198 *khandis* of 16 *mãos* and the import of paddy was to the tune of 19,868 *khandis*.[40] These details show the magnitude of trade that existed between Kanara and Goa during the period under study. Statistics reveal that there was considerable fluctuation in the quantity of rice and salt traded between these two regions. It could have been due to the various reasons stated earlier. As the British had a better bargaining power, the balance of trade was in their favour.

Tariff Policy

The changes in the tariff policy and the occasional restrictive measures adopted by the Company government in Kanara affected the trade between Kanara and Goa. Thackeray, in 1807 while writing on the production of rice and its export said: "... the peculiar climate and situation of Canara make it the granary of the Western Coast, and in spite of a heavy duty it must continue to supply the Arabian, Bombay and Goa markets."[41] In 1813-14, the double duty imposed (as per the Regulation of 1812) on goods imported and exported under Portuguese colours acted nearly as a prohibition, and would have put a stop to the export of rice to Goa altogether but for the decision of the Madras Board of Revenue to withdraw it.[42] The diminished export of rice to Goa in 1816-17 was caused by a reduced demand on account of the imposition of a tax on its import to Goa from the British ports, to the extent of 4% which with the 10% export duty payable to the Company government proved a disincentive to the Goa trade. This was, in fact, done in retaliation of the 16% duty imposed by the British government on all articles imported under the flag of Portugal into the British territories.[43]

Salt Trade

On account of the salt monopoly introduced in Kanara by the Company government in 1807, the inhabitants of the region had to depend on the government supply. Even the licensed manufacturers were unable to meet the demands of the region, and, as such, a large quantity of salt was imported from Goa by land on payment of a customs duty of 12 annas per *maund* which was considered to be equal to the profit on the manufactured salt of the district.[44] Salt occupied a place of considerable importance in the trade dealings of the period. In spite of its long sea coast, Kanara did not produce sufficient salt to meet its own demand.[45] Hence it was imported from Goa and Bombay. In 1838 the supply from Goa failed and the contractor was allowed to bring 120 *garce* of salt from Bombay.[46] The partial failure of the manufacture of salt in North Kanara and scarcity of the article in Bombay and Goa in 1858-59 compelled Kanara to get its supplies from the eastern coast.[47]

The salt sold at Buntwal in South Kanara was of three varieties- of Kanara, Goa and Bombay. The Company government purchased salt at the following rates:[48]

	Pagodas	Fanams	Coins/Per Garce
Kanara Salt	8	--	50
Goa Salt	8	21	--
Bombay Salt	11	21	--

As the last two, that is, Goa and Bombay salt were superior in quality, they were mostly sold and the stock of the first variety remained. To set this right, the Collector of Kanara recommended the monopoly price of the three varieties as follows:[49]

	Pagodas	Fanams	Coins/Per Garce
Kanara Salt	20	--	--
Goa Salt	22	--	--
Bombay Salt	24	--	--

The Collector opined that as soon as the Goa and Bombay salt were sold, the merchants would bring that of Kanara.

The high monopoly price and the consequent sufferings of the people and the continuous suppression of the home manufacture by the Goa salt in the northern part of Kanara and the Bombay and Arabian salt in the south caused embarrassment to the Collectors. One of them as a solution proposed that the monopoly be substituted by an excise. The admission of the Goa, Bombay and Arabian salt at fixed duty was recommended by the Collector of Kanara in 1851 to establish equality in different varieties of salt that entered Kaṇara.[50] The salt imported from Goa into Kanara was further shipped to the Amindivi Islands.[51] In 1857-58, as there was failure in the manufacture of salt in Kanara, Kanara's import of salt from Goa was to the tune of 92,750 *maunds* which valued about Rs. 16,803. And in 1858-59, it was 42,325 *maunds* the value of which was Rs. 13,342.[52] From the *Report of J. J. L. Ratton* (1873) it is clear that Kanara imported salt from Goa and in 1862-63, the amount of salt imported into Kanara was 726 *maunds* at an average rate of Rs. 25.70 per *garce*. In 1863-64, it was 2,09,280 *maunds* at an average rate of Rs. 46 per *garce*.[53] The reason for this great variation in the price and quantity of salt traded in such a short period as one year is not clear.

In Portuguese India, till the middle of the 19th century the emphasis was on trade in luxury goods. But by the middle of the century when the trade declined, it was restricted to essential commodities. Notable items of export included coconut, salt, areca-nut, poultry and fruits. Among items of import, rice and timber were very prominent. Among the trading communities, the Gowda Saraswat brahmins and Gujarati vanias played a major role. Mormugao emerged as a rendezvous of trade in Goa.

The Portuguese commercial interests clashed with those of the British in India. The British made determined efforts to curb the Portuguese through their tariff policy and unequal treaties. As discussed earlier, in Kanara they tried to protect their colonial interests through their tariff policy which proved disadvantageous to the Portuguese. The flourishing clandestinely conducted Portuguese Malwa opium trade was disrupted by the British transit system introduced in 1831, which sought to protect the English East India Company government's opium monopoly.[54] In the same way, the British tried to do away with the Portuguese slave trade across the Indian Ocean by the treaty of 1847. Further, England also compelled Portugal to sign treaties to open up its ports to cheap British textiles. This caused considerable damage to the Portuguese Indian textile commerce.[55] Besides, the Anglo-Portuguese treaty was signed in 1878. The idea that a railway link between Portuguese Goa and British India would help to restore the shattered economy of Goa did not materialise through the provisions of this Treaty. The British salt monopoly and the *abkari* system under the Treaty left the Goan economy in shambles. This unequal treaty clearly revealed and established the British supremacy over the Portuguese in India.[56] Nevertheless private traders, private trading network and trade in essential commodities continued to exist in Goa during this period and later.

The foregoing analysis throws fresh light on the trade relations between Portuguese Goa and colonial Kanara in the 19th century. It delineates some of the lesser known aspects of the trade relations between the two European colonial settlements on the western coast of India. Our study shows that Kanara existed as the granary of the west coast and Goa suffered as a grain-deficit region. Export of salt and coconuts from Goa to Kanara, and import of rice and paddy from Kanara to Goa, are striking. Though there was the absence of 'big trade', there was considerable 'small trade' which enabled the Goan economy to move towards the 20th century. The developments in the world system, the superior political and economic position of capitalist Great Britain affected the fortunes of the Portuguese in India.

NOTES AND REFERENCES

1. The coastal regions of the present Karnataka State, then known as the Province of Kanara and Sonda, came under the control of the English East India Company government in 1799 and remained so until 1858 and from 1858 to 1947 formed part of the British empire in India. With its annexation in 1799, Kanara was absorbed into the broader colonial network which the English had developed in India. Presently these regions constitute three districts of Karnataka and one district of Kerala namely, (1) Dakshina Kannada,(2) Udupi, (3) Uttara Kannada (all in Karnataka), and (4) Kasaragod in Kerala.

2. It may be noted that the political, economic and cultural relations between these two regions on the western coast of India had been studied by historians, particularly by B.S. Shastry. His works, "The Portuguese in Kanara 1510-1763", unpublished Ph.D. thesis, University of Bombay, 1969 and *Studies in Indo-Portuguese History*, Bangalore: IBH Prakashan, 1981 and other published articles throw light on these relations from 1510 to 1799. This period saw the rise and fall of the rulers of Vijayanagara, Keladi and Mysore in Karnataka.
3. We are aware that a detailed study of this theme is not possible unless the relevant Portuguese sources and other records of the period are thoroughly consulted and interpreted.
4. Francis H. Buchanan, *A Journey from Madras through the Countries of Mysore, Canara and Malabar* (hereafter *Journey*), (3 volumes), Madras, 1870, vol. III, p. 58.
5. H. M. Blair, *Report on the Modification of Beriz in Kanara, 1842,* Mangalore, 1897, para 7. Blair was the principal Collector of Kanara.
6. M.N. Pearson, *Before Colonalism: Theories on Asian-European Relations 1500-1750*, Delhi, 1988, p. 62.
7. *Ibid*, p. 6.
8. Sir Thomas Munro to the Madras Board of Revenue (hereafter MBR), 28-6-1800, in *Proceedings of the Madras Board of Revenue* (hereafter *PMBR*), 28-8-1800, vol. no. 261, pp. 7490-7505. Munro, the famous architect of the Ryotwari System, was the first Collector of the Province of Kanara and Sonda.
9. Munro to the MBR, in *PMBR*, 28-8-1800, vol. no. 261, pp. 7492-97.
10. Munro to the MBR, 29-4-1800, in *PMBR*, 21-4-1800, vol. no. 51, pp. 4070-73. In the same document we get a letter written by I. Uhethoff, perhaps a British representative in Goa to Munro in Kanara. See *Appendix - I.*
11. Buchanan, *Journey, op. cit.*, vol. III, between pages 4 and 5.
12. John Sturrock, *Madras District Manuals, South Canara*, vol. I, Madras, 1894, pp. 218-19.
13. *Ibid.*, pp. 203-04.
14. *PMBR*, 9-11-1801, vol. no. 302A, pp. 13, 280-84; *PMBR*, 30-10-1806, vol. no. 435A, pp. 7008-09.
15. Xavier Centre for Historical Research (XCHR), Mhamai House Papers (*MHP*), (Portuguese), document dated 8-2-1809; *Historical Archives of Goa* (*HAG*), *Registos Gerais de Fazenda* (*RGF*), 7709, fl. 373, quoted in Celsa Pinto, "Portuguese India in the Late Eighteenth – Early Nineteenth Centuries" (Unpublished Ph.D. thesis, Goa University, 1992), p. 347.
16. Pinto, , *op. cit.*, p. 348.
17. XCHR, *MHP* (French), vol. 6, fls. 79-80, quoted in Celsa Pinto, *Trade and Finance in Portuguese India: A Study of the Portuguese Country Trade 1770-1840*, New Delhi: Concept, 1994, p. 217.
18. Buchanan, *Journey, op. cit.*, vol. III, p. 271. Buchanan opined that the

Konkanis emigrated from Goa and the rest of Kanara, were found in large numbers in Buntwal, Manjeshwar and Mangalore towns. He noted that they had fled from Goa to escape the Portuguese persecution and proselytisation.

19. John Stokes, *Report on the Revision of Assessment, and on the Disturbances known as Koots in Kanara, 1830-31*, Mangalore, 1885, p. 9, para 33. Stokes wrote in 1830 that "all the merchants in Kanara are more or less educated and seem to be sufficiently expert and assiduous as men of business; and the Concanis, in particular, are characterised by acuteness and intelligence. It is not surprising that men of this stamp in the general struggle for wealth should be successful competitors with the simple and ignorant farmers with whom they have to deal."
20. Alexander Read, the Collector, to MBR, 22-2-1809, in *PMBR*, 2-3-1809, vol. no. 485, pp. 1424-25. In volume no. 485 mentioned above, we get statistics regarding the rice exported from Kanara to Goa and a few other stations during this period. For details see *Appendix II*.
21. *Proceedings of the Madras Sea Customs Department* (hereafter *PMSCD*), 26-2-1824, vol. no. 50, p. 283.
22. Walter A. Hamilton, *A Geographical Statistical and Historical Description of Hindoostan and the Adjacent Countries*, (two vols.), vol. II, London, 1820, p. 256; *PMSCD*, 25-11-1847, vol. no. 104, p. 511.
23. T. L. Blane to the BOR, 10-7-1846, in *PMBR*, 4-3-1847, vol. no. 2070, p. 4174, Blane was the Collector of Kanara.
24. T. L. Blane to the BOR, 8-11-1847, in *PMSCD*, vol. no. 104, 25-11-1847, p. 513.
25. *A Gazetteer of South India*, 1855, p. 550.
26. Lt. H. S. Brown, *The Handbook to the Ports on the Coast of India between Calcutta and Bombay including Ceylon and Maldive and Laccadive Islands*, Mangalore: Basel Mission Tract Depository, 1897, p. 257.
27. Celsa Pinto, "Goa-Based Coastal and Overseas Trade: 18-19th Centuries", in T. R. de Souza (ed.), *Goa Through the Ages*, vol. II, New Delhi: Concept, 1990, p. 193.
28. *Report on External Commerce for the year 1813-14, Board's Miscellaneous Consultations*, (hereafter *BMC*), Sl. no. 256, p. 51; also see Buchanan, *Journey*, *op. cit.*, vol. II, p. 243.
29. C. R. Cotton to the BOR, 26-2-1836, *PMBR*, 10-3-1836, vol. no. 1494, p. 4262. See *Appendix III*.
30. Celsa Pinto, "Goa-Based...... etc.", *op. cit.*, p. 193.
31. *Report of W. E. Underwood, Reporter, External Commerce, 1846, from Imports into Canara by Sea and Exports from Canara by Sea, in the year 1845-46*, pp. 160-67.
32. F.N. Maltby, *Settlement of Land Revenue of South Canara District for Fasli 1261*, p. 4. *Fasli* means revenue year or financial year. Add 590 to convert a Fasli year into Christian Era. In this case it is 1851-52.
33. *Statement showing the Imports into Canara by Land in the Official Year 1852-53*, Fort St. George, p. 130.

34. *Ibid.*
35. A. Lopes Mendes, *A India Portuguesa*, 2 vols., New Delhi, 1989 (reprint), vol. I, pp. 47-48.
36. *Report of W. Fisher*, Collector of Canara, 1856, from the Statement exhibiting the Quantity and Value of Exports by Sea, from the Port of Canara, to Foreign Ports and to Indian Ports not subject to the Madras Presidency from 1st May 1855 to 30th April 1856, pp. 96-97.
37. *Report of W. Fisher*, Collector of Canara, 1856, from the Statement of Ships and Tonnage (Square Rigged and Country Craft) Arrived at and Departed from the Port of Canara, not subject to the Madras Presidency from 1st May 1855 to 30th April, 1856, pp. 138-39.
38. W. E. Underwood, Reporter External Commerce, Fort St. George, 1st May 1859, *Statement exhibiting the Quantity and Value of Imports by Sea* into the Port of Canara from Foreign Ports and Indian Ports, and Exports by Sea from the Port of Canara to Foreign Ports not subject to the Madras Presidency, from 1st May 1858 to 30th April, 1859, p. 164 and 228.
39. *Reports of W. Hudleston, Secretary, Revenue Board Office, on Imports and Exports of South Canara,* Fort St. George, 20th June 1863, pp. 149-51 and 29th June 1863, pp. 242-45.
40. A. Lopes Mendes, *op. cit.*, pp. 47-48.
41. William Thackeray's "Report on Malabar, Kanara and the Ceded Districts, 8th September 1807", para 68.
42. *BMC*, Sl. no. 266, pp. 87-88.
43. *PMSCD*, 1-11-1818, vol. no. 37, pp. 918-20.
44. James C. Melwill, *Reports etc. of Several Comissioners on Public Works at Bengal, Madras and Bombay 1851-52: of the Minutes of the Members of the Government thereon; and of any orders of Despatches of the Court of Directors relating thereto, 27 May 1853*, p. 28; Also *PMBR*, 28-8-1800, vol. no. 261, pp. 7490-505.
45. K. Abhishankar (ed.), *Karnataka State Gazetteer, South Kanara District*, Bangalore, 1973, p. 765.
46. *Appendix to the Report of the Commissioners upon Manufacture and Sale of and Tax upon Salt in British India*, p. 143.
47. *Administrative Reports of the Madras Presidency for the year 1858-59, Revenue Department*, no. 2953, pp. 1-2.
48. Malathi K. Moorthy, "Trade and Commerce in Early Colonial South Kanara 1799-1862" (Unpublished Ph.D. thesis, Mangalore University, 1992), p. 279.
49. *Ibid.*, p. 280.
50. Extract from the letter of F. N. Maltby, Collector of Kanara, to the BOR, 3-9-1851, *Appendix-E*, no. 15, *Appendix to the Report of the Commissioner*, p. 324.
51. The northern group of the Laccadives known as Amindivi Islands on the Arabian Sea formed a part of the Province of Kanara during the period of our study.

52. W. Fisher, Collector of Canara, "The Report on Land and Extra Sources of Revenue for *Fusly* 1268 (1858-59)", 12-10-1859, no. 182.
53. J. J. L. Ratton, *Report on the Manufacture of Salt in South Kanara*, 1873, pp. 20-22.
54. Celsa Pinto, *Goa, Images and Perceptions: Studies in Goan History*, Panaji: Rajhauns, 1996, pp. 46-47.
55. *Ibid.*, p. 47.
56. For details on the Treaty and its consequences on Goan economy, see Teresa Abuquerque, "The Anglo-Portuguese Treaty of 1878: Its impact on the People of Goa", in *Indica*, vol. 27, no. 2, September 1990, Bombay: Heras Institute, pp. 117-24; J. B. Amancio Gracias, *Subsidios para a História Económico Financeira da India Portuguesa,* Nova Goa, 1909; B.S. Shastry (ed.), *Socio-Economic Aspects of Portuguese Colonialism in Goa: 19th and 20th Centuries,* Belgaum: Yarbal Offset Printers, 1990.

Appendix I

To
Captain Thomas Munro,
Collector in Kanara.

Sir,

There being reason to apprehend a scarcity of rice within the Portuguese Territories during the approaching rainy season, the Governor has requested that I would solicit your good offices toward obtaining supplies of that necessary Article from the Kanara country, the Quarter from which the Portuguese Territories are usually supplied. I could have wished to consult with you on this subject prior to any measures being adopted at this place, but the season is now so far advanced that it becomes necessary to take some measures immediately for obtaining supplies of Rice – accordingly, the Governor is now about to despatch a Portuguese Frigate with five or six very large boats to bring Rice hither from the Ports of Mangalore, Cundapore and Barcoor. The quantity required is from twenty five thousand to thirty thousand Robins, and the Governor requests that you will afford your countenance support, and assistance toward his obtaining this quantity and likewise that you will provide the requisite funds for it the Governor will repay the Amount to me here, which will be a good mode of securing funds, for the use of the British troops stationed here, should you, as seems probable, have obtained by the time you receive this letter, the sanction of Government to supplying this station with cash; but should you not have yet received the decision of Government on this point, which is now under reference through the Resident in Mysore, I still beg leave earnestly to request that you will provide the requisite funds for the supply of rice, for which, and for every other part of my present application I hold myself officially and personally responsible.

I have the honour to be, Sir,

Your most obedient humble servant,

Goa, April 21, 1800. Sd. I. Uhethoff.

Source: PMBR, 21-4-1800, vol. no. 251, pp. 4071-73.

Appendix II

A comparative statement of the quantity of rice exported from Kanara from the opening of the two seasons, i.e., 1807-08 and 1808-09 to January 31, 1809

	Total		To Arabia		To Bombay		To Goa		To Malabar		All other Ports inclusive	
	Corges	Muras	Corges	Muras	Corges	Muras	Corges	Muras	Corges	Muras	Corges	Muras
31st Jan. 1808	5466	-11 ½	1407	38	485	12 ¼	1925	7	767	35 ¾	880	2 ½
31st Jan. 1809	7286	19 ½	3670	16 ¾	277	26 ½	2267	22 ¾	446	20 ¼	624	17 ¼
Difference	1820	8	2262	20 ¾	207	27 ¾	342	15 ¾	321	15 ½	255	27 ¼
Export to 15th Feb 1809	3153	36 ½	1152	34	128	23	1580	35 ½	271	40	19	32
Add Export to 31st Jan 1809	7286	19 ½	3670	16 ¾	277	26 ½	2267	22 ¾	446	20 ¼	624	17 ¼
Total	10440	16	4823	8 ¾	406	7 ½	3848	16 ¼	718	18 ¼	644	7 ¼
Export of 1806-07	20723	14 ¾	2993	34	3456	1	6781	1 ¼	3019	33	4772	29 ½
Balance remaining for export from 16-2-1809	10282	40 ¾										

Source: Alexander Read, Collector, to the BOR, 22-2-1809, *PMBR*,_2-3-1809, vol. no. 485, p. 1427.

Appendix III

Table showing the quantity and value of some of the articles imported into Kanara from Goa during 1828-29:

Articles	Quantity	Value £-S-D
Dates – bwt.	1-1-14	0-12-0
Drugs - bwt -	23-1-0	10-6-0
Dry Grains – bwt -	763-18-0	26-16-0
Paper – reams	302-0-0	211-8-0
Sugar soft bwt.	0-1-3 ¾	0-12-0
Timber - Guz	1875-0-0	18-14-0
Wines and spirituous liquors – doz..	29 ¼	24-6-0

Table showing the quantity and value of some of the articles exported from Kanara to Goa during 1828-29:

Articles	Quantity	Value £-S-D
Coir - bwt.	48-0-0	15-8-0
Drugs - bwt	0-2-21 ½	0-16-0
Dry Grains - bwt	532-0-28	151-8-0
Oil Sandalwood - bwt	0-0- ¼	0-2-0
Pepper - bwt	2-2-22 ¾	5-8-0
Piece Goods - pieces	4-0-0	1-16-0
Rice and Paddy - bwt.	92,816-3-24	17,300-18-0
Sandalwood - bwt	1-1-0	2-0-0
Timber – Guz	50-0-0	0-10-0
Turmeric - bwt.	1-2-3 ½	Not available
Wak-Bees-bwt	5-3-12¼	28-2-0

Source: C.R. Cotton to the *BOR,* 26.2.1836; *PMBR,* 10.3.1836, vol. no.1494, p.4262.

5

Iron Ore Rush and The Quality of Life in Goa 1947-1961

FÁTIMA DA SILVA GRACIAS

The Second World War contributed to a world-wide tide of decolonisation. The freedom struggle in British India culminated in its independence in 1947. Portugal was disturbed with the happenings around Goa, particularly because the Indian Union began to make claims to acquire Goa.

In order to please the local populace, the Portuguese government under the dictator Salazar tried to ameliorate the conditions of the people from the late 1940s. They promoted rapid expansion of the mining industry in Goa. The territory had rich deposits of iron, manganese and other ore, which were not scientifically explored. In the 1950s mining became the mainstay of the Goan economy. The impact of mining industrialisation is seen in various aspects of life of the Goans including economic, health, environment, transport and movement of population.

Historical background

The New Conquest areas of Goa from Naibagh in the northwest to Saligini in the southeast are endowed with rich deposits of mineral ore. Ore deposits were found at Bicholim, Satari, Ponda, Quepem and Sanguem talukas, in places such as Velgem, Surla, Pale, Maina, Sirigao, Darbandora, Kosti, Netorlim, Kodeli, Kurti, Sancordem, Rivona, Colomba, Barazan, Potrem, Bati, Vilian and Kurpem. The richest deposits of iron were located in north Goa.[1] About 60% of iron ore came from Bicholim mines in north Goa.[2] In the south, talukas such as Sanguem and Quepem had rich iron and manganese deposits.

There are references to ore deposits from early times. The Dutch traveller Linschoten, who visited Goa during the second half of the 16th century, noted the existence of ore in close proximity to the famous city of Goa. According to him, some Italian alchemists were interested in digging for copper and gold but the Portuguese ruler and the Viceroy did not permit it due to fear that reports of such treasure might attract the enemies.[3] Again, an early 17th century Portuguese report refers to iron mines not far from the city of Goa that could be used in the manufacture of artillery and cannon balls.[4] Ore was manually extracted in small scale throughout the Portuguese period to meet the local needs.

In the early 19th century the British during the Napoleonic wars, occupied Goa. A report of the time showed that there were iron mines at Ponda. However, the Portuguese government made no efforts to conduct a survey and encourage large-scale extraction of ore until the fag-end of their rule.

In the 20th century, a foreigner Agy Ismail Mirsa Bagdad, an 85 year-old Turk from Constantinopole, was one of the first to obtain a manifest. He was granted permission at the end 1905 to extract ore at Domingod-Molem in the village of Colem in Sanguem taluka.[5]

A few foreign firms, including a French one, made attempts to extract ore in north Goa during the second decade of the 20th century. *Compagnie de Mines de Fer de Goa*, made in 1910 initial attempts to extract manganese ore.[6] It obtained mining concessions, carried out a survey, bought heavy equipment and even proposed a plan to build a 30 kms. long railway connecting Bicholim to Margao via Sanquelim, Ponda, Raia, Loutolim and few more areas.[7] The French Company gave up its plan to explore mines in Goa on account of World War I. Some of their manifests might have been taken over by their Goan employers and sold later.[8] Surveys were also conducted during this period by the British Geological Survey of India.

A revival of interest in mining, particularly in manganese ore, was noticed in the 1920s. About four mining concessions were granted between 1929 and 1931. Iron ore was consistently extracted at Siolim, Surla in the north and Khandepar neai Ponda. Some foreign companies, including the ones operating from Bombay and Calcutta, showed interest in mines of Goa. Certain events in the rest of Asia during this period might have contributed to the revival in this interest. A naval base being established at Singapore required iron ore. Secondly, Manchuria and the Pacific Islands which were regular suppliers of ore to the Far Eastern countries could not send supplies due to the political crisis.[9] During this period, some eminent Goans also expressed the need to develop mining in Goa. There is reference to the export of manganese ore in small quantity to U.S.A. in the 1920s.

The 7th *Congresso Provincial* held in Goa, in the third decade of the 20th century, discussed various issues concerning mining, including the need to regulate the grant of concessions only to those who fulfilled the necessary requirements.[10]

Much before large-scale extraction of ore was started in Goa, ore for local use was extracted by a tribe known as *Dovolos,* the majority of whom lived in the village of Navelim and some other villages of Salcete in south Goa. This tribe migrated annually in the month of October to the New Conquest territories (mainly in south Goa) to extract iron ore. The extracted ore was then taken for melting to places such as Panchvaddy.

In 1939, the first sample consignment of iron ore was exported to Japan by Mitsui & Co. This was done under the supervision of Vishwasrao Chowgule. However, it was only after British India gained her independence that the Portuguese encouraged the development of mining industry in Goa. The purpose was to keep Goans contended by improving their quality of life and making it better then the rest of India.

A new phase began in the life of the Goans. The government without much trouble granted concessions in order to encourage local entrepreneurs. The Portuguese laws were such that they made it easy to grant concessions. In 1947, about 17 concessions were granted by the State to various individuals. This number rose to 42 in 1950 and 144 by 1953. In 1960, the State granted around 596 concessions to various companies and individuals.

Some events in post World War II in the Far East and in Europe helped the growth of mining in Goa. There was a global hunger for iron ore. Post World War II Germany and Japan were going through a period of reconstruction of war effects and large-scale industrialisation. Ore was required to rebuild and to expand steel industries. The stocks of iron ore in the Philippines, one of the usual suppliers to Japan were exhausted. Japan could not get supplies from Manchuria too. Further, Japan had broken links with Britain, so she preferred to import iron from Goa rather than from British India which was the earlier supplier of ore to Japan.

Iron ore could be extracted cheaply in Goa. From a logistic point of view, Goa was close to Japan, therefore the transportation was cheap. Furthermore, the *laissez faire* policy adopted by the Portuguese also helped the export of ore from Goa. The government in order to encourage mining activity in Goa granted mine owners some concessions. There was no foreign exchange regulation; they were free to do business in any currency, anywhere in the world. A nominal import duty on mining machinery was levied.

Mine owners in Goa took advantage of the opportunity offered by Japan, Germany, Italy, Holland and others to export iron and manganese ore. The regular export of iron and manganese ore started in 1947. V. D. Chowgule & Co. sent the first shipment of ore (manganese) to Czechoslovakia in 1947 . In 1950, the Chowgules were also the first to send iron ore to Japan.[11] In the course of time, the Chowgules had many firsts to their credit.

The ore industry of Goa was export-oriented. It brought foreign exchange and good profits. Mine owners exported ore from the mines owned or leased by them and at times ore bought from small mine owners. The early years were a period of prosperity for the mine owners. Until then Goa did not have any major industry worth the name. In 1948, about 5,464 tonnes of iron and a little over 4,500 tons of manganese ore were exported and in 1953 the one million mark was touched. The export figure reached 6.5 million tonnes by 1961.

The largest contribution to the State income in the 1950s came from mining. In 1951, Goa was the first in the list of exporters to Japan. In the 1950s, the three big consumers of Goa's iron ore in Japan were Yawata Iron and Steel Works, Fuji Iron and Steel Works and Nippon Kokan.[12] In addition to Japan, the next important buyers of ore from Goa were Italy and Germany.

Mining in the early stages was primitive, being essentially manually-operated. There was a lack of equipment and transport facilities. Little efforts were made to carry out the systematic exploration of the deposits for assessing their grade-wise reserves. A few mine owners were careful to screen ore for its size, weight and quality while others paid scant attention to the screening of ore. Therefore, foreign buyers at times were suspicious and reluctant to buy ore from Goa. Mine owners from Goa had to face competition also from other countries including Brazil and Australia where their respective governments encouraged mining by giving tax and other concessions. Even though active mining of iron ore started in Goa soon after World War II, the systematic prospecting for iron ore in the territory began only in the late '50s by a couple of firms.

In 1953, for the first time mines were mechanised in Goa. Chowgule & Co. mechanised their Sirigao mines. The mechanisation was possible due to the collaboration of Nippon Kokan Co. and loans provided by Japanese Export Bank. Mines were mechanised with the view of securing for Goan iron ore a place in the competitive world market. On the occasion of the inauguration of their new machines, Vishwasrao D. Chowgule said in his speech that such mechanisation was necessary to develop mining industry in an efficient manner and to reduce the cost of production. It was expected that mechanisation would bring down the cost of production of ore to the lowest extent so that the industry could survive irrespective of boom or slump periods. The mechanisation of the Sirigao mines laid the foundation for the export of bigger quantities of ore from Goa. As a result their annual target of 500,000 tons produce went up to 2,000,000 tons.[13]

The boom period was over by 1953. The ore market faced problems due to a shortage of buyers overseas. However, within a short period of time the industry recovered. In 1958, once more the exports of iron suffered a setback. The following year the first full-fledged Mechanical Ore Handling Plant was set up by the Chowgules at Berth no.6 at Mormugao harbour. This plant was the only one of its kind in the whole of southeast Asia.[14]

Since mining was export-oriented, Goan industrialists signed long-term contracts with buyers in Japan, Germany, Italy and other countries. A small number of spot contracts were also done in case of small consignments. The world famous steel mills of Ruhr used iron ore from Goa. However, major quantities of ore were exported to Japan.

Measures to regulate mining activities

At the fag-end of the 19th century, the Portuguese government had issued legislation to regulate mining activities in its colonies. In 1906, it felt the need to revise the existing regulation on the model of the one in British colonies. By this decree those who wished to explore mines had to seek a written permission from the government. Concessions were granted in perpetuity and the government alone had the right to exercise supervision over the extraction of ore.[15]

The first attempts towards mining exploration on the part of the Portuguese government were made in the early 20th century. In 1907, the government opened a section of Geology and Mines attached to General Administration Department and finally to come under the Department of Land Survey. This section was given powers to conduct surveys and to licence new industries. However, nothing much was done in this direction until the last decade of the Portuguese rule in Goa. In 1935, mining came under the Public Works Department. In 1957, the Directorate of Economic Services was created and later the Land Survey and Mining was placed under its control. The mining section looked after mining ore and the execution of the mining legislation.

In 1949, the government decided to regularise the export activities and the sale of ore in Goa. The Governor General of *Estado da India*,

Fernando Quintanilha Mendonça Dias decreed that those who desired to sell ore or export the same required permission from the government. For this purpose, the concerned persons had to petition with all details to the government through the Public Works Department.[16]

Impact on Goa: Towns

The ore rush in the late 1940s and 1950s brought about significant changes in the lifestyle of the people in Goa. Among these changes was the development of towns around the mining areas such as Vila Nova de Curchorem (as part of Sanvordem was known), Sanquelim, Bicholim, Ponda and Mormugao. Since the end of the 19th century, Curchorem was known mainly for its railway station but it developed only in the 1950s due to its close proximity to mining areas of Quepem and Sanguem.

The above-mentioned towns had their own schools in Portuguese, English and Marathi medium, modern houses, shopping areas with showrooms, theatres, children's park and a few other amenities which were not always available in some other talukas. Many of the facilities, such as showrooms and cinema halls were made available by the mining industrialists themselves. They distributed the latest films. Mobile vans at times carried films to remote areas. These were sources of entertainment for the people, especially for the mineworkers who visited the cinemas at least once a fortnight if not oftener. The shops catered to the needs of a floating population.

A variety of goods imported from Europe, Japan, China, the rest of India and other places found their way all over Goa. There was an increase in imports to cater to the demands of all kinds of luxuries. Durable goods brought to Goa in the 1950s, consisted of watches, pens, electronic goods such as radios from Japan, gold, crockery, cutlery and cars. In addition, a variety of cosmetics including famous French perfumes, textiles, footwear, western style clothes, victuals like rice, wheat, sugar, oil, tea and coffee were imported. Butter, cheese and other milk products came from Holland, Australia, England and Denmark. Fish and meat preserves, olive oil and wines were imported from Portugal, Holland, France and the rest of Europe. Fruits and vegetables came from various parts of Europe and Asia including from nearby Pakistan. There was also good demand for imported chocolates, cigarettes, beverages and alcohol which were cheaply available. A bottle of good Scotch whisky could be bought for Rs. 10.

Goa during this point of time had very few industries worth the name. Goods were imported more than required for a few lakhs of the population.

A large number of goods were later smuggled into the Indian Union, where imported goods were banned.

Weekly bazaars were held in these towns where the workers came in trucks from mining areas to shop. In these bazaars, village artisans and farmers brought in a variety of commodities for sale and in return purchased factory-made goods from Europe, Japan and other countries.

Mine owners, labourers and auxiliary services

Mining activities resulted in the rise of two new classes – the class of mine owners and mine workers. The former was in small number but in the course of time it became an important and powerful class. Most of the mine owners had modest beginnings while others came from already well-established families. However, within a short period of time they came to play an important role in society and government since the mining industry was the mainstay of Goan economy and ore the chief item of export.

V. D. Chowgule & Co., V. M. Salgaocar & Irmão, V. S. Dempo & Co., Bandodkar Pvt. Ltd, Sesa Goa Ltda, Timblo e Irmãos were some of the early mine owners who were involved in the export of ore to foreign countries. All mine owners were not from Goa. Some like Chowgules came from outside Goa and a few others from Italy and Germany. The Chowgules were pioneers in large-scale mining business in Goa.

Dempos sent their first consignment of 20,000 tons of ore in 1950. They exported ore mainly to Japan and at times to Germany, France and Holland. V. M. Salgaocar e Irmão made their first shipment in 1952 and exported in that year about 50,000 tons of ore. In 1957, Salgaocars exported one million tons of ore, which was 18% of Goa's ore production.

From mining, the mine owners diversified their activities to other lines. Foreign exchange earned from sale of ore was used to import goods from Europe, America and other parts of Asia such as China and Japan. Goa never produced much and depended for a large part of her requirements including victuals on the rest of India and countries overseas .

The mine owners sold a variety of imported goods from abroad directly or to wholesalers and retailers in major centres of Goa. For instance, the Salgaocars imported a variety of products including essential goods such as sugar and good quality flour from U.S.A. They imported Darjeeling tea, liqueurs, household goods, toiletries, cosmetics, fountain pens such as Parker pens, wristwatches from Switzerland, industrial goods, a range of mining equipment, automobile spares, American caterpillars, pencils from Karachi and others goods.[17] They built also in a later period a transhipper. Furthermore, Salgaocars were involved in ships-clandering, barge-building, construction and hotel industry. They were the first to introduce life insurance in Goa.

Before switching to mining, Dempos already owned vast ancestral land where they grew rice, betelnut, coconuts, cashew and mangoes. Coconut oil, copra, pepper were exported by them to British India. Vasantarao Dempo had acquired a stevedoring licence as early as 1942. The Dempos imported food grains for the government.[18] In the 1950s, they imported a range of goods in Goa such as cigarettes, perfumes including the famous French ones from the House of Dior, liquor, chocolates, trucks, motor cars like Austin, Chrysler and the Japanese Prince.

In the 1950s Japanese brand of cars were available for as much as Rs. 2,000. There was no great demand for Japanese cars. Japanese products were considered second-rate.

Chowgules imported also a large number of goods. In fact Chowgules like some other mine owners were already in import and export business before starting their mining business. Chowgules started exports with scraps left over after the manufacture of tins needed by Burmah Shell. Coal, wood, cowhide, silk, fancy articles, cigarette paper, coconut oil and bamboos were sent by the Chowgules to Middle East during World War II. Exports during the war years were helped by the fact that Portugal being a neutral country, it was easy to buy goods there and send them to other countries. For instance, the Chowgules bought tons of cigarette paper in Lisbon and sent it to Jordan. Rolex watches, John White footwear and other goods were imported into Goa by the Chowgules.

The Salgaocars and Shantilal Gosalia Pvt. Ltd. were involved in entertainment business too. They bought, leased theatres and distributed films in bulk. Dempos, Chowgules and Salgaocars secured the agencies of international maritime houses and handled the loading and unloading of ships in Mormugao.

A few industrial houses like the Chowgules, Dempos and Salgaocars were also involved in the educational field during the later period. They established schools and colleges. In some areas they acquired the sole distribution rights for a variety of consumer goods, mines and construction equipment. Many mine owners had their own petrol depots in mining areas and nearby towns. Mine industrialists were also in barge-building, construction, ships-chandelering and publishing, to name a few. Chowgules in the post-colonial period turned to the manufacture of pellets, textiles, producing beer, fish processing and pesticides.[19]

Mine owners made huge profits in boom times. Profits were invested for further profits. They built big offices, luxurious houses, bought movable and immovable properties and provided good education to their children. Profits were also invested in the acquisition and employment of technology for producing more and better quality ore, trucks, and ocean-going ships and so on.

Mining provided employment for Goans as well as for people from neighbouring areas in the mines and ancillary units. The conditions of the mine labourer in the early period left much to be desired. Mine workers were normally simple peasants who earned now more then they earned previously in their agrarian activities. They migrated every season from November to May with or without their families to the mining areas. During the rainy season, many returned home to their villages to carry on their agrarian activities. A gang of contractors took mine workers to mining areas. Their womenfolk worked also in the mines to carry baskets of ore load from the mines to the dumping grounds, trucks and country crafts. Workers operated in shifts.

Impact on environment

The mining industry has left a considerable impact on the environment of Goa and in particular around mining areas of north and south Goa. In the 1950s, the mining activities were responsible for deforestation, land degradation, mining dumps and heavy pollution of mining areas due to mining rejects, dust, grease, and petroleum.[20] It has also led to the breaching of protective bunds, erosion of khazan lands and inundation of paddy fields.[21] Mining rejects were dumped into the rice fields affecting the cultivation of crops.

Large areas where the mining activities were carried out were forest areas. Forests were cleared for mining activities. Unscientific deforestation led to the loss of species of botanical, medicinal and genetic interest. Deforestation has led to the loss of rodents, lizards, sucker birds and insects. Use of explosives for mining killed both flora and fauna in the mining area. Increasing trucking activity around the mining areas has facilitated further deforestation for prized timber and firewood.

The mining industry was also responsible for producing mining rejects and muddy water which was pumped from pits. These rejects or effluents were washed down during the monsoons in rice fields and rivers, thus ruining fertility, contaminating sources of water and food production. Trucks were washed in many of these rivers. Oil and grease from the trucks polluted the water. Until recently a majority of people particularly from the New Conquests consumed this contaminated water from the rivers.[22] In the absence of better alternatives, even today people drink water from the rivers. Dumping of the rejects in the river contributed to the decrease of shellfish production in some rivers.

Movement of trucks carrying ore was responsible for dust pollution. Much dust flew in the air at the dumping site or when a truck moved carrying ore.[23] The movement of barges caused bigger bow waves and destroyed bunds, flooding fields, salt pans and coconut groves along the riverbanks. These barges and country craft which moved to the port town of Momugao contributed to oil and grease pollution of the rivers.

Impact on Health

The sudden spurt in mining activities in Goa during late 1940s and 1950s caused overcrowding and pollution of mining areas. This was responsible for some chest and water-borne diseases.[24] Dumping of waste in the rivers contaminated water, which was later consumed by the people.

There was lack of health care and hygiene in the early period. The conditions in mining areas were somewhat primitive. The workers who came from different parts of Goa and from across the borders were not provided proper living facilities. These migrant labourers were responsible for bringing in diseases from across the border where many diseases existed in epidemic form.

There was no legislation to control health problems caused by mining activities. However, regular check of the mine workers by health officers of talukas was carried out. Some mining areas had their own medical clinics. In the late 1950s, the government started eight sanitary posts in charge of male nurses in mining areas. The state established also during this period some cottage hospitals in towns situated near mining areas. In the fag-end of the 1950s, B.C.G. programme was started. T. B. and B.C.G. vaccines were brought every fortnight from Portugal.

Movement of population

Goans have been migrating out of Goa through the ages.[25] In addition, there was seasonal migration within Goa from the early 20th century or even earlier at the time of harvesting, sowing or when certain groups of people moved to the New Conquests to extract ore.

The emergence of mining in the late 1940s and 1950s contributed to a shift of population from within Goa as well as from the rest of India. Workers from the Old Conquests and even from the New Conquests migrated to the interior of Sanguem, Quepem, Bicholim, Ponda and Satari talukas where the mines were situated. Normally, it was seasonal migration from November to May. During the monsoons mining activity came to a halt due to flooding of pits and other problems caused by the rains. An increase of 44.6%, 26.95%, 27.05% and 17.05% of the population was noticed in Sanguem, Bicholim, Quepem and Satari respectively.[26] A corresponding increase of population was also experienced in the Mormugao port region.

Until the 1950s, the above-mentioned talukas had more women than men. This could be due to the fact that agriculture being the main occupation of the people, employed greater female labour and also on account of migration of the male population. This trend changed in the New Conquest talukas due to the development of mining industries as more men worked in mines. In addition, due to the shift of local population to mining areas there was migration from neighbouring areas of the Indian Union. Hundreds of workers migrated from the rest of India to work in mines and related trade. Mormugao showed also an increase of population due to port activity on account of loading and unloading of ore. Export of mining needed also lengthening, widening of quays, levelling of dumping sites, dredging and deepening of mooring points. All this work required the services of a variety of people who were brought to the port town from different parts of Goa and the rest of India.

Transport and Communication

Transportation of ore from the mines to Mormugao harbour was not easy due the lack of transport facilities. Transport facilities were somewhat primitive. There were no proper roads to most of the mining concessions. In the late 1940s, ore was transported by trucks from the mines to river points or railheads to be loaded into wagons for the journey to Mormugao harbour. At other times, ore was sent directly by trucks to the harbour in old army trucks, which had been sold to private individuals. Transportation by truck was prohibitive due to high cost of fuel. Diesel was not yet used. Since the trucks were old, they were prone to constant breakdowns. Repair facilities were not easily available. In the early years of mining development, trucks were hired from owners/drivers on a daily or weekly basis. Trucks were always in short supply and most truck drivers were unreliable. The hire rates fluctuated almost daily. During the later period, the mine owners had their own trucks to transport ore. This made them set up workshops to repair trucks. Roads were bad. Trucks had to travel over makeshift roads, which damaged the tyres and the trucks as well.

Due to the short supply of trucks, mine owners depended on river transport to carry ore to the harbour. Goa has innumerable rivers and streams, some of which run close to mining areas. Among these rivers are the Mandovi and Zuari rivers. These inland waterway systems were a boon to the mining industry in Goa. It not only facilitated the speedy movement of ore from the mining areas to the port town but also provided cheap means of transport. To begin with, country craft were used to carry ore to the harbour. In 1953 for the first time barges were used for this purpose.

— The mining industry was the largest industry in Goa during the last decade of Portuguese rule. It was regarded as the backbone of the Goan economy. Although concessions were granted to a large number of individuals, mining was essentially in the hands of a few big industrialists. Since it was export-oriented, it brought in a large amount of foreign exchange which has helped to sustain the Goan economy.

— Mining generated growth in many ways. A fair amount of employment opportunities was provided to thousands of Goans and non-Goans in the mines and subsidiary services at a time when job opportunities were scarce. Till the end of the 19th century, agriculture was the main occupation of the Goans. The majority of people could be called poor. However, from the second half of the 19th century, Goans began to migrate in considerable numbers and remittances became the chief means of subsistence for many Goans particularly from the Old Conquests. Mining improved the quality of life of Goans who were involved in the mining and ancillary industries.

— It provided a boost to local ship-building and other related industries. Mining opened up transport right into the interior from the main urbanised centres. It helped the rural population to carry on small farming activity in distant areas and to sell their products in towns through motorable roads. On the other hand, mining had also adverse influence on agriculture as in the early stages labourers left farming and other related work and migrated to mining areas to earn higher wages. However, the benefits of this industrialisation were limited to a section of the population.

— The foreign exchange earned by the exporters of ore helped to buy plenty of luxury and other goods from different parts of the world. It created an impression of self-reliance. Availability of luxury goods kept the upper classes happy.

— Due to mining, the per capita income of the territory went up. It contributed to the improvement of the standard of living to an extent. Education, health and a few other facilities were expanded during the period under review. A better standard of living, availability of medicine, improvement in medical facilities helped the decline of the mortality rate especially among the vulnerable group of mothers and children.

— Mining had its negative impact too. It has harmed the ecology of Goa. It was responsible for large-scale deforestation, land-degradation, noise, air and water pollution. Mining which was the mainstay of the Goan economy for almost 50 years is today going through a period of recession.

NOTES AND REFERENCES

1. S. M. Rege, "Iron Ore and Manganese Ore of Goa - Present position and future position", *Earth Resources for Goa's Development*, Hyderabad, 1985, p. 89.
2. Armando Gonsalves Pereira, *India Portuguesa*, Lisbon, 1953, p. 213.
3. A. C. Burnell and P. A. Tiele (eds.), *The Voyage of John van Linschoten to the East Indies*, vol. I, New Delhi, 1988, p. 183 (Reprint).
4. M. N. Pearson, *The New Cambridge History of India - The Portuguese in India*, 1990, p. 154.
5. *Boletim Official*, no. 2 (5-1-1906).
6. J. B. Amancio Gracias, "Caminho de Ferro e Porto de Mormugao", *O Oriente Portugues*, series II, no. 28, Bastora, 1940, pp. 334-335.
7. *Ibid.*
8. Mario Cabral e Sa, *Song of the Golden Gateway - 100 years of the Port of Mormugao and the Peninsula*, New Delhi, 1985, p. 58.
9. "Belezas e riquezas de Goa", *Boletim Geral das Colonias*, XXV (no. 287), May 1949, p. 159.
10. *Congresso Provincial da India Portuguesa: Subsídios para sua História*, vol. IV (7th Congress), Panjim, 1929, p. 86.
11. M. V. Rajadhyaksha (ed.), *An Architect of Modern Goa*, Bombay, 1975.
12. *Ibid.* In 1970 all these three companies were amalgamated to form Nippon Steel Corp.
13. Speech delivered by Vishwasrao Dattaji Chowgule on the occasion of the inauguration of the mechanisation of Sirigao mines on October 31, 1953.
14. V. D. Chowgule, "Problems of the Goan Mining Industry with particular reference to Mormugao Port" (A note submitted to the Planning Commission, Govt. of India).

15. In 1987, the Indian government tried to abolish mining concessions granted before 1961. However, the move was challenged by the mine owners
16. *Legislação Relativa ao Estado da India*, 1949, Panjim, 1950.
17. Frank Simoes, *Fare Forward Voyager - A Tribute to the memory of Vasudev Salgaocar*, Bombay, 1990.
18. Dom Moraes, *A Family in Goa*, Bombay, 1976.
19. *An Architect of Modern Goa, op. cit.*
20. *Fish Curry and Rice - A Citizens Report on Goan Environment*, Ecoforum Publication, p. 157.
21. Nandakumar Kamat, "The Role of Inland Waterways of Goa: Catalysing the Export of Mineral Commodities. Some Observations for the Period 1946-1996" (paper presented at history seminar, Goa University).
22. Fátima da Silva Gracias, *Health and Hygiene in Colonial Goa*, New Delhi, 1994, p. 71.
23. Recently the High Court issued an order banning trucks carrying ore in Curchorem area from moving without covering the ore with tarpulin to prevent dust pollution.
24. *Health and Hygiene, op. cit*, p. 110.
25. Fátima da Silva Gracias, "Goans Away From Goa – Migration to the Middle East" (paper presented at the 3rd International Meeting of Lusotopie – Portuguese-Speaking space in Asia, Goa, 1999); Silva Gracias, "Women and Migration" (paper presented at history seminar, Goa University); *Health and Hygiene in Colonial Goa, op. cit.*, p. 38.
26. *Census Report 1900-1961.*

6

The Organisation of Water Navigation in Portuguese Goa (1934-1961)

XAVIER M. MARTINS

Goa, the capital of the *Estado da India* is endowed with a fine network of seven rivers which drain the major part of it.[1] The rivers Mandovi and Zuari constitute two principal inland waterways of Goa with a navigability of 105 kms. and 64 kms. respectively.[2] As these two rivers bifurcate the Ilhas (Tiswadi taluka) from Salcete and Bardez, the movement of people largely depends on the availability of adequate water transport. The Portuguese authorities issued a number of orders, taking into consideration the local conditions, to streamline water transport.

The present study is based on the two decrees issued in April and July 1934, regulating the water navigation in Portuguese Goa. They deal with issues such as the registration of seamen, classification of the vessels, the syllabus and the examination system for the crew. These regulations remained in operation even after 1961 with some modifications. The office of the Captain of Ports was the controlling and superintending authority with jurisdiction over Goa, Daman and Diu.[3] Registration of seamen, registration of ships, classification of vessels, conduct of examination for the crew, were the duties assigned to it. All nationals residing in the State of Goa, Daman and Diu and engaged in the maritime profession were required to be enrolled at the office of the Captain of Ports and the maritime sub-office in a special book termed "*Registration of Maritime Enrolment*".[4] It contained the number and date of enrolment, name, name of one's parents, date of birth, place of birth, residence, photograph, signature or thumb impression, class in which one entered, academic qualifications both technical and non-technical, signature of the enrolled person if he could write, his knowledge of rowing and swimming, clinical record, etc.[5] Exemption was granted to those who worked on board ships belonging to the ministries of Navy and War. Persons who were declared unfit and retired were debarred from enrolment as seamen. A minimum age limit was fixed for enrolment. Those below 14 and above 40 years were debarred from enrolment as seamen. Persons above the age of 40 were enrolled when they furnished proofs that they had already practised the maritime profession before being enrolled. The certificates of enrolment were checked, dated and initiated by the maritime authority once a year between the months of October and December, without any fees. Dual registration was not allowed.[6] Besides the registration in the office, every vessel was required to maintain an enrolment register of its crew. However, ships belonging to the ministries of Navy and War were exempted. Similar exemptions were also granted to cruise vessels, vessels of local traffic, local fishing vessels up to 8 tonnes, coastal vessels up to 5 tonnes, flat-bottom ships, passenger vessels up to 2 tonnes, and fishing boats with nets of less than 300 metres.[7]

The vessels of Portuguese India were grouped into the following categories: Ships of local traffic; coastal vessels; recreation vessels; large coastal vessels; vessels owned by the State and ocean-going vessels, respectively.[8] The Regulations of 1934, added to this, the tug-boat, auxiliary vessels and mixed vessels – of passenger and cargo. The ships of the local traffic could sail within the limits of the port of Goa.[9]

The command of the vessels was confided only to Portuguese citizens. Those commanding coastal sailing vessels were called *tandels,* while those commanding local traffic sailing vessels were known as coxswain. Similarly, those commanding steam-driven or motor-driven vessels were known as coastal masters of local traffic.[10] Apart from this, a fireman on all steam-propelled vessels was a must. The Order of 1934 stated that the *tandels*, coxswains, drivers of motor engines, engine drivers and the firemen should have requisite technical qualifications including the pre-course technical experience.

Any enrolled seaman who wished to appear for the examination was required to have the following qualifications: normal eyesight, no double-sight or colour blindness, normal auditive acuteness in both the ears, at least five years of service on a coastal vessel to be eligible to appear for the examination of *tandel*, at least three years of service on a coastal vessel or four years of service on a vessel of local traffic, of more than 5 tonnes to be eligible to appear for a certificate of coxswain or master of local vessels of more than 5 tonnes. Similarly, a candidate desiring to appear for an examination of coxswain or master of vessel of local traffic of

2 to 5 tonnes of passenger vessels was required to have a minimum of two years experience on a coastal vessel or three years on a local coastal vessel.[11]

The syllabus for the examination of *tandel* or master of coastal navigation included: necessary knowledge of the sailor's art; the technique of handling cables; towing of a ship in any condition and the mooring and unmooring of a vessel; general knowledge of the coast and the area of the coastal navigation relating to sandbanks, currents, tides, light houses, canals, sandbars and rivers; regulating signals for vessels navigating or anchored and rules for avoiding collisions; knowledge of all the navigational aids and terms like mariner's compass, plumb-line, orientation, deviation and declination; sufficient knowledge of meridians and parallels, and general rules of the office of the Captain of Ports pertaining to vessels and seamen.[12]

The person choosing to be a *tandel* or coxswain of the local traffic vessel was required to have the same knowledge of the subjects prescribed for the *tandel* or master of coastal vessels. In case of a *tandel* of the vessel of local traffic applying for permission to sail between the extreme parallels of the territory of Goa, he was required to possess a certificate of coastal services.[13]

The syllabus for the engine driver consisted of: knowledge of machines and different types of boilers, generally used on-board; nomenclature and uses of all their parts and accessories; description, use and nomenclature of the auxiliary machines and conduction of boilers; knowledge of manometers and safety valves; knowledge of the main combustibles used on board and the level and the verification of the water level in the boiler; and causes of explosion and measures to avoid them.[14]

The syllabus of the examination of the explosion and internal combustion of the motor-engine included: knowledge about the structure, nomenclature and functioning of the motors of explosion used on board; information about the various combustibles used and the storage of the same; rules and precautions to be taken before and during the operation of the motor; and maintenance of the motor engine including lubrication and cooling during the operation.[15]

The syllabus of the fireman covered the following: description and the types of boilers used on board; preparation of the boilers for lighting, conducting fire with solid, liquid and mixed combustibles; to light and put out engine fire; conduction of fire in sudden or prolonged halt; cleaning of furnaces while navigating or anchored; the formation and projections of water in the boiler; knowledge about the incrustations and corrosion on the lid-sheet of the boiler and tubes and the techniques to avoid them; a general awareness of the functioning of the main feeding pumps and the auxiliary ones; use and reading of thermometers and salinometers; and knowledge about the handling and storage of coal and other inflammable material.[16]

Conduct of the Examination

The Captain of Ports was authorised to hold the examination for the *tandels*, coxswain, engine drivers, drivers of motor engine and firemen. The sub-office was required to furnish the names of the candidates in advance to the office of the Captain of Ports. The maritime officers of Daman and Diu were required to prepare and submit the list of candidates by July 31 every year.[17] The purpose was to enable the Captain of Ports to arrange an examination panel and to fix the venue and time for the same. The examination board was headed by the Captain of Ports. The other members of the panel included the maritime officer of Mormugao and the Chief Master. The panel also included an interpreter who enjoyed the confidence of the Captain of Ports.

A similar examination was conducted for seamen in Daman and Diu. Here, too, the panel was headed by the Captain of Ports, who was the presiding authority. The other members were the maritime officers of Daman and Diu.[18] A detailed report about the proceedings of the examinations held at the sub-offices at Daman and Diu was prepared and forwarded to the office of the Captain of Ports. A candidate who failed the test was allowed to re-appear for the same after a gap of six months.[19] No change was allowed without prior authorisation.

The seamen were given practical training in different trades. In-service seamen were given an opportunity to improve their qualifications and were placed accordingly. The Captain, Master, *tandel*, coxswain or the person in-charge who held back in his possession the certificate of any seamen, was liable for penal action.

NOTES AND REFERENCES

1. *Goa, Daman & Diu Techno-Economic Survey*, New Delhi: National Council of Applied Economic Research, 1964, p. 129.
2. *Ibid.*, p. 130.
3. *Regulamento da Capitania dos Portos do Estado da India* (Hereafter *RCPEI*), Panjim, 1913, p. 124.
4. *Ministerial Order*, no. 8031, dated March 1935, p. 1.

5. *Ibid.*, p. 4.
6. *Ibid.*, p. 5.
7. *Ibid.*, p. 7.
8. *RCPEI*, *op. cit.*, p. 14.
9. *Anuário da Estado da India Portuguesa*, Panjim, 1929, p. 122.
10. *Decree Law*, no. 23, 764 (13.04.1934), Panjim, p. 8.
11. *Ibid.*, p. 9.
12. *Ibid.*, p. 11.
13. *Ibid.*, p. 11.
14. *Ibid.*, p. 12.
15. *Ibid.*, p. 12.
16. *Ibid.*, p. 13.
17. *Ibid.*, p. 10.
18. *Ibid.*, p. 10
19. *Ibid.*, p. 14.

7

Tourism in Goa

Risks and Opportunities

ÓSCAR G. PEREIRA

My paper aims at studying present-day tourism in Goa, with a short analysis of its economic, socio-cultural, environmental and moral implications. I intend to present alternatives that could go to meet the solutions based, on the one hand, on government tourism policies and, on the other, on the programmes and proposals of the Centre for Prehistory and Archaeology, Tropical Research Institute, and non-governmental organisations (NGOs) that aim at blocking a greater influx of tourists. These organisations find themselves, obviously, in opposition to the tourism policies of the government.

In the introduction, I touch on tourism in its global structure, because I believe there is an inter-connection between this global structure and tourism in India, where Goa is naturally inserted.

According to the World Trade Organisation (WTO), an organisation linked to the United Nations, in 1978, 269 million tourists traveled around the world. In 1996, this number had doubled. This organisation foresees that by the year 2020 there will be 1.6 billion tourists.

Summing up, one can say that tourism is today, an irreversible social and human phenomenon, never before known in these dimensions and that results from the freedom of movement, easy mobility at economically accessible prices, a greater purchasing power by the lower and middle classes, more free time and the spirit of adventure as well as the desire to learn of new worlds and enjoy to the fullest, one's free time. This is, without doubt, the spirit of our age.

The liberalisation of the international economic market, through the international economic agreements like the General Agreement on Tariffs

Translated from the Portuguese by Charles J. Borges

and Trade (GATT) ratified in 1993, placed the tourism industry in this structure. This agreement made it possible that international capital could be invested without great limitations in large tourism projects influencing the politics in area and limiting the autonomy of governments that find themselves dependent on tourism earnings.

This situation creates a global hierarchy where the large tourism companies can dictate their conditions with the aim of getting fiscal advantages or avoiding the responsibilities and demands linked to the environment. The tourism industry has turned into a global problem due to its social and economic facets, placed in an international context. This globalisation, as we see, does not level out the situation between rich and poor, neither in the political nor in the economic and cultural sectors. The horizontal mobility, that is, the space that tourism allows, does not lead to social mobility, or rather, to the betterment of one's personal level. Tourism in the Third World, where Goa also finds itself, is understood without doubt, in these terms.

The privileges of globalisation benefit exclusively the industrialised nations. France, for example, is the first destination on the world scale, with 60.584 million tourists, followed by Spain and the United States of America.[1] According to international revenue statistics, the U.S.A. was the country that gained the most profit in 1996. About 60 billion dollars in all, followed by France with about 30 billion and Germany in the fifth place with about 13 billion.[2]

India registered in 1996 a figure of 2.287 million tourists with an income equivalent to about 20 billion US dollars. According to Mr. Ashok Pradhan, director-general of Tourism (India), the income for 1996-97 was Rs. 100 billion equivalent to 4% of world tourism and 2% of the income at the same level in this sector.[3] In 1988, 76,400 Germans visited India and in 1994 this country was visited by 85,300 persons which represents a growth of 12%.[4]

On the world scale, Portugal was the 33rd country to spend on tourism, a sum of 1.013 billion US dollars.[5] On the other hand, in 1997 only 630 Portuguese tourists came to Goa which was a percentage of 0.2 of the foreign tourists. By way of comparison in the same year, 124,348 English tourists and 25,190 Germans visited Goa.[6] Contrary to what is said in Lisbon, it appears that Goa lies, in fact, very distant from Lisbon (See the statistics in the Annexure).

The exploration of the tourism industry in the Third World is another facet of this theme. It is a result of the international economic policy in which governments look for a way out from the economic crisis in which they find themselves and get solutions for their budgetary deficits. The tourism policy of Goa in this sense, in short, is to increase the maximum influx of tourists in order to obtain the maximum foreign currency although it is detrimental to the socio-ecological interests of the state.

Due to pressure from the International Monetary Fund, from the mid-1980s, the Indian rupee has been devalued many times. Although in 1993, India could accommodate 36% more tourists than in 1981, the balance in foreign currency did not improve. According to the U.N. statistics, every tourist in India spent 45.3 US dollars a day in 1981 and in 1990 only 27 as a result of this devaluation.[7] Although in 1996, 31% (131 million US dollars) may have been spent in the Third World countries, the economic reality is completely different, if we divide the total amount by the number of inhabitants. Thus, the Bahamas, for instance, obtained a per capita income of 5.640 US dollar's. India only 3.[8]

It is in this context that the tourist industry has evolved in India as well as in Goa, a state of the Indian Union.

In the ancient culture of India, the tourist was highly privileged and placed on a high moral level to whom the name *atithi* or guest was given. All foreigners whether they were travelers or pilgrims got a very respected and exclusive status, that of *atithi devobhava* (heavenly guest). In Goan history, however, due to the geographical situation and cultural heritage, the rulers believed that the tourist industry in Goa could be easily tapped. Already during the 2nd Provincial Congress, Roberto Bruto da Costa proposed that a department of tourism could be set up to study better possibilities in this area. He believed that tourism would come to be the most lucrative and compatible with the complacent Goan.[9]

During the last stage of the Portuguese administration in Goa in the 1950s, the department of Information and Tourism in Panjim was not able to establish the tourism industry on a grand scale, firstly, because the border with India had been closed, and secondly, in my opinion, because the Portuguese policies of the time feared the influx of new ideas that mass tourism, inevitably, would bring with itself.

With the liberation of Goa on December 19, 1961, its future, which till then had a western connotation, passed abruptly to being oriented according to the structures of the Indian subcontinent.

Since that date until its recognition as a state in 1987, Goans fought not only for the autonomy of the state but also for the imposition of Konkani as the official language. In this context I would like to make a reference to the Opinion Poll of 1967 by which Goans decided to remain as a Union territory and against merger with the neighbouring state of Maharashtra.

While Goans were immersed in these internal political fights between 1966 and 1977, the so-called "hippies" discovered Goa as a small paradise fit enough to spend a large part of their time and thus to flee from the stresses of the countries of their origin. The Indian administration saw that this was a group economically without profit for Goa and a nuisance to the local population as a result of their behaviour. The administration managed to make their entry to India difficult by imposing huge restrictions on the granting of visas and reducing thus a large part of their influx.

It was also at this time that there arose (today very well-known and appreciated) the music which in Europe is called "Goa Techno or Psychedelic" because it is associated with the consumption of drugs.

Tourism in Goa under the commercial but not official aspect, had its origin in the 1970s with the start of the charter flights from Germany. Very soon, Goans became aware of the many disadvantages of mass tourism, with opposition groups opposing government tourist policies. The protests multiplied, and I make a reference here to the agitation of the fishermen of Baga and the toddy tappers of Agonda, respectively. I mention also, the organised protests of the Jagrut Goenkaranchi Fauz (Vigilant Goan Army) against the charters of the German company, Condor in 1987, when the incoming passengers receiving posters with the words "If you love Goa, give up coming to Goa" and in the same way in 1989 against the charter flights of England. Before the dimension reached by the uncontrolled development of tourism, Goans saw for themselves the immediate and imperative need of an active front against this uncontrolled expansion. They saw that there was no other Goa waiting for them close to Lisbon or to New Delhi.

On May 30, 1987, Goa was made the 25th state of the Indian Union. On June 1, the government of the new State, took the decision to make tourism an official industry in order to grant investors exemption of taxes for five years, besides a 50% reduction on stamp duty and subsidies for the development of projects, investments and works dependent on electricity.

At the same time, the government of Goa announced that it intended to impose the regulation of Land Acquisition to enable it to take over private properties for public interest, or rather, in the present case, in favour of the interests of the big investors for tourism projects. I do not want to miss the opportunity to put my doubts, regarding the validity of this legislation vis-a-viz the democratic Indian constitution. The government decision provoked a big discussion in the local press. With this official ruling, there began a process in Goa which consisted in hosting a large number of foreign and national tourists, and inviting investors with the aim of creating adequate infrastructures for this end. It started for this purpose important negotiations with Japanese industrialists.

The 1987 statistics indicate that Goa hosted already 861,448 tourists in all, they being 766,846 Indians and 94,602 foreigners, a rise of 3.3% more than the previous year. The 25 chartered flights of that year brought 5,419 passengers. In comparison, in 1998 there were already 350 charted flights with 88,817 passengers [11] totaling 1,228,259 (953,212 Indians and 275,047 foreigners), more than the local inhabitants (1,169,793 according to the 1991 Census).[12]

To understand the dimension of the tourism movement in Goa, I want to stress that of all the chartered flights bound for India, 50 % are destined for Goa[13] while only 10% of the total regular flights are to that State.

In 1987 there started in Goa, for the tourism industry, an express movement. The Central government placed a model for tourism expansion and the local government tried to further this plan. On May 25, 1987, the then union minister, Mr. Mohammad Sayeed, declared that more than 14 five-star hotels were going to be built till 1990, or rather, within a span of three years. The legislation that banned constructions within an area of 500 meters from the line of the break-waters of the high tide, in order to protect the coastal environment, was ignored, allowing thus the construction of tourist homes closer to the sea, and encouraging investments in this way.[14]

In July 1987 the government published the Master Plan for Tourism Development in Goa, this being the first governmental study, which besides analysing the situation, made a long-term projection, of the consequences of tourism in Goa. This plan, gave rise to enormous controversies, and ended without being official. Jagrut Goenkaranchi Fauz, which protested vociferously against the setting up of five-star hotels, considered the project an insult to Goan culture.[15]

The problem of the tourism industry, touched thus, alarming proportions both on the national and international map, due to ecological, economic and social implications. At the international level, this situation alerted various organisations which were thought to be able to solve these problems.

Thus the declarations of the Letter of Lanzerothe (1995), the Declaration of Male (1997) and the Declaration of Berlin (1997) are seen in this context as demanding the protection of an environment and in the same way the protection of the inhabitants. These declarations, well meant, are, without doubt, utopian, in the sense they do not demand an immediate limitation of the influx of tourists and the respective rating to the short and long terms. Even under this aspect, one can cite a study made by the WTO in 1998 which projected Goa to have possibilities to accommodate 8 million tourists in 2001 or better 16,000 tourists per day if adequate infrastructures were created for this purpose.[16]

The Indian Association of Tour Operators (IATO) and the Travel Association of India demand a greater tourist development in India arguing that Spain with 40 million people hosts 50 million tourists, and India has hardly 0.4% of world tourism. For this reason, India could easily touch 10 million tourists.[17] They forget in the meanwhile that Spain has infrastructures capable of accommodating a number of tourists, more than her own inhabitants because of her "carrying capacity," or rather her socio-economic capacity which is substantially different from that of India.

In Goa, many non-governmental organisations started with the aim of opposing the governmental tourism policy and to conscientise the Goan population of the pressing need to fight against its growth, and of its fatal implications for the country. It is my wish to mention the Goa Foundation, Nirmal Vishwa, Goa Fishermen's Union, Peaceful Society, Bailancho Saad, People for Animals, Bailancho Ekvott, INSAF, Indian Heritage Society (Goa Chapter), Jagrut Goenkaranchi Fauz, and the sub-committee of the Diocesan Pastoral Council, Goa. The Catholic Church, as it could not quit being itself, pledges also to draw the attention of the government to this fact.

The NGOs have managed to conscientise the Goans, of the catastrophic implications of mass tourism, and to publicise this abroad. For example, it is my desire to cite the statement of Ms. Albertina Almeida, of the feminine group, Bailancho Saad, which draws attention to the problem of the shortage of water due to the excessive consumption by the hotels and its dramatic results for the housewives.[18]

Those groups demand that the tourism policy of the government ought to be the subject of an extensive public debate, by the fact that few known details of the plan for the promotion of tourism, are more than sufficient to create an atmosphere of fear.

Government policies and some aspects of its economic implications.

The main plank of the Goan economy rests on the exploration of minerals – iron and manganese and on the tourist industry. While these are the principal sources for the coming of foreign currency, yet it is strange they go purely and simply in favour of the central government. It is clear that it helps with great interest these two segments of the Goan industry. In this regard it is good to remember that while the per capita income in Goa is Rs. 16.148, in India the average is only 8.282.[19]

While agreeing with the chart of 1996 with reference to the tourist income of about 49 million US dollars, we have to consider the sum as fairly modest. The explanation is very simple. It is that a majority of the foreign tourists make their payments for journeys and hotels in the countries of their origin. (See graph in Annexure)

The second reason for the shortage of foreign currency derives from the inflationary problem of the rupee. Thus, there being more tourists in Goa, unfortunately the receipts in foreign currency go down. As was said earlier, India benefited in 1993 from a tourist increase of 36%, only that in 1981 each tourist spent 45.3 US dollars a day and in 1990 only 27.6. Thus the rush in favour of investments and a greater influx of tourists can be seen in this context. The focus of government policy in the tourist industry is extremely risky because it is very vulnerable. A simple political crisis or a small local disturbance immediately causes the moving away of tourists. Besides this, the tourist industry is highly subsidised. From 1984 to 1987 the government gave the tourist industry a subsidy of Rs. 3.5 billion. 50% of this amount continues in the open, waiting for, as is obvious, the payment of the contributor.

The ex-chief minister, Dr. Wilfred de Souza in response to a question made in the State Assembly said that the estimate for 1997 corresponded to an entry of Rs. 650 million and that the amount with reference to 1995 had touched Rs. 425 million. He mentioned also that there were in Goa 33,000 posts in the tourism sector of which 20,000 were directly linked to the hotels, 10,000 to food catering and the remaining 3,000 to other sectors.[20]

The government of Goa promotes tourism having participated in international fairs, sending prospectus, supporting conferences and seminars with organisations in charge of the tourist department of Goa, the Chamber of Commerce and Industry and the Goa Institute of Management, for instance, at the International Centre at Dona Paula on August 21, 1997. The government involves itself in giving information, which is very positive with reference to the tourism of Goa.

To encourage tourism during the monsoon the government of Goa invested about Rs. 3 million. This investment resulted in an increase in tourists, being 13,121 in 1990 it touched 20,004 in 1997. The Konkan Railway helped the growth of the industry in the interior of the State and the present policy of the government has as its objective decentralisation, taking tourism from the coast to the interior. An unbalanced growth of tourism without a social component can provoke in the long run the limits of tourism in Goa. One may ask, as a result, who would be the beneficiaries of the system.

Government policies and some aspects of environmental implication.

The government policy of Goa has not been defined for short, middle and long terms. Its interests exist, however, to safeguard the ecological system of many negative implications. Already in 1982 there was a project of an ecological plan known as "Eco-development plan for Goa" whose objective was to make recommendations in the areas of planning of transport, exploration of minerals, architecture, housing, agriculture and industry.

The "Environment Protection Act of 1986" did not allow the construction of complex touristic homes of a height greater than that of the coconut trees of the neighbouring lands, as well as at a distance less than 500 metres from the break-water line of the high tide.

Though the "Master Plan for Tourism Development" in Goa had been conceived in July 1997 it included various points referring to ecological protection. In April 1999, the Goa Tourist Department had in mind the study of a new Master Plan for tourism which covered the following 25 years. For this purpose, at present various organisations involved in this problem have been approached.

A major problem in Goa is that of water shortage. While the luxury hotels consume 250,000 litres of water daily for maintaining swimming pools and lawns, as well as for having running water for their guests, the inhabitants are on the other hand are obliged to rationing during some hours of the day, mentions Albertina Almeida. From Baga to Sinquerim there are 50 swimming pools which are 300 metres from the Arabian Sea. The owners of big hotels bore within the reserved zones of 500 metres from the line of the high tide introducing thus salt water into the underground reserves. The excessive consumption of water by the tourist industry caused the Assonora river to dry and because it was meant for irrigation of agricultural areas, the government saw the necessity of fixing water pumps in the Amthane river in order to maintain the inflow in the Assonora river.

For the construction of hotel chains, the sand from the dunes is used, keeping the coastal villages unprotected, which has caused the increase of the ecological disaster. The government, well-intentioned, but soft, contributes by this way for the disaster, pretending on the other hand, to have a policy of environmental defence.

Government policy and some aspects of the implications in the socio-cultural and moral scope.

The occupations of Goa in the past, like those of fishing, toddy-tapping, and agriculture have moved to a dependence on the needs and services of the hotel industry. Thus, and in relation to the agricultural production of other states in India, Goa falls in the modest percentage of 30%. The consumption of drugs, especially among young circles, has increased due to tourism. Prostitution and pedophilia, as happens in the Philippines and in Thailand, are today bitter realities that occur directly due to the tourism influx.

While nudism in Europe is accepted as an absolutely vulgar phenomenon, it has for the Goans a negative significance. The sexual liberty as well as the imitation of western habits as a model of conduct, result for the Goans a loss of their own values.

Proposals

One can deduce from this portrayal, that the implications of tourism as has been seen are complex, and even more so are the proposals for a solution. The tourism policy, the people of Goa, the tourists, the immoral capital that aims at profitability alone, are the components of this complexity. Each element in itself, supports its own interests and the only form of the solution is the agreement of these adequately.

The simple moral appeal is utopian, given that the behavior of the tourist is the expression of the society in which he lives, and one cannot demand a change of behavior during the time of holidays. The solution, under this head, would be a process of school education, where the students would deal with the critical aspects of tourism. The students of today are, in reality, the tourists of tomorrow!

The Goa government will have to define a tourist policy for a short, middle and long term, so that the institutions and persons concerned may be able to plan the needed adaptations.

So that the NGOs could be able to have an influence on the government tourism policy, there would be the necessity of having political party representation. This seems only possible with the setting up of a party that may have an ecological programme favorable to tourism, as for example, the Green Parties in Europe.

As happens in the various neighbouring countries, tourism in Goa is without doubt and in its present dimensions, disastrously arranged. For this reason, there is a pressing and demanding need to impose a cut on the number of tourists. In 1998, Goa was visited by 953,212 Indian tourists and by 275,047 foreign tourists, a total of 1,228,259. In percentages, this signifies that 22% of this equation, are foreign tourists.

In a democratic country like India, one cannot curtail a free movement of its citizens, within one's own country. As a result, the only hypothesis to avoid the disordered influx of foreign tourists, is the imposition of an annual quota of entries. For this, the government of India, has at its disposal, a fairly efficacious method: granting of visas. These could be granted only in well-defined circumstances.

To sum up, I wish to quote a saying much used in Asia: "Tourism is like a small flame, enough for cooking a meal or for burning a house".

I hope that Goans may know how to use this flame to be able to continue to cook a good curry.

NOTES AND REFERENCES

1. Samir Ahluwalia, "Tourist arrivals decline worldwide", *Business Times*, New Delhi, January 27, 1996.
2. *Ibid.*
3. Ashok Pradhan, *Herald Review*, Panjim, August 15, 1997.
4. *Herald,* May 29, 1987; *WTO Statistical Yearbook 1996*, Hammelehle, 1995.
5. *Asiaweek Almanac*, New Delhi, April 21, 1993.
6. *Tourist Statistics, Goa India*, Dept. of Tourism, Govt. of Goa, Panjim, 1999, p. 2.
7. Christian Stock, "Ein traumhafter Dollarkuh", *Travel im Paradies*, p. 30.
8. *Ibid.*
9. *Ibid.*
10. Frank Wilmink, "Studienarbeit an der Universitat Dortmund", 1997.
11. *Tourist Statistics, Goa India*, 1999, p. 3.
12. *Ibid.*
13. http:/www/goacom/info/economy
14. *Herald*, 1987.
15. Jagrut Goekaranchi Fauz, "The Five Star Master Plan: a case for concern in Goa", Goa, 1987.
16. *Herald*, September 26, 1998.
17. C. Stock, *op. cit.*, p. 30.
18. Albertina Almeida, "Die Gier der Hotels nach Wasser", *Paradise, Tourismus in die dritte Welt*, ed. C. Stock, Freiburg/Breisgau, 1997.
19. Economic Development Corporation of Goa, "Environment in Goa".
20. *Herald*, March 27, 1997.

BIBLIOGRAPHY

Aderhold, P., Lassenberg, D., Stäbler, M., & Vielhaber, A., "Tourismus in Entwicklungsländern", Hrsg. Bundesministerium für wirtschaftliche Zusammenarbeit und Entwicklung, Entwickungspolitik Materialien, no. 88, Bonn, 1993.

Arbeitsgemeinschaft Tourismus mit Einsicht, *Tourismus mit Einsicht*, Munich, 1992.

Bailancho Saad, *In the Name of a Game: The Stakes in Golf*, Goa, 1993.

Bailancho Saad, *Tourism - its Effects on Women in Goa*, Goa, 1987.

Bruto da Costa, Roberto, *O Turismo. Uma Indústria lucrativa*, Congresso Provincial, no. III, Goa.

Survey of Potentialities of Tourism in Goa, Panaji: Bureau of Economics, Statistics and Evaluation, Government of Goa, Daman and Diu, 1972.

Chandrakala, S., *The Impact of Modern Tourism on India's Environment*, Bangalore, 1989.

Chopra, S., *Tourism and Development in India*, New Delhi, 1991.

Contoms, Panjim, Goa, 1988.

De Sousa, Desmond, *Tourism as Pilgrimage: Tourism as Pilgrims?*, Goa, 1989.

Draft Report, *Master Plan For Tourism Development in Goa*, Goa, 1987.

EDC, Goa - Environment in Goa, 11.09.1999. http://www.edc-goa.com/goa-env.htm

Goa Foundation, *The Coastal Regulation Zone Notification in Goa*, Goa 1996.

---------, *Sand Mining, Beach Resorts and the destruction of the sand dune system in Goa*, Goa, 1989.

---------, *Feasibility of setting up a Free Port in India*, Goa, 1992.

---------, *The Green Goa Tourist Guide*, Panjim: Maureen, 1999.

---------, *Master Plan for Tourism in Goa: Statement of Objectives and Recommendations*, Goa, 1997.

Goa Today, Panjim, 1988.

Jagrut Goenkaranchi Fauz, *The Five-Star Master Plan. An assault on Goa's culture*, Parts I-II, Goa, 1987.

Gomantak Times, Panjim, 1989.

Hammelehle, Jürgen & Plüss, Christine, "Alternative Techno-Trips in Goa", in *Trouble in Paradise, Tourismus in die dritte Welt*, ed. Christian Stock, Freiburg/Breisgau, 1997.

Herald, Panjim, 1998.

Tourism Workers' Seminar, ITF-IUF-FIET Asia/Pacific, Penang, 1995.

Lobo, Urban in *Fish Curry and Rice*, Goa, 1993.

May, S., *Tourismus in der Dritten Welt: Von der Kritik zur Strategie. Das Beispiel Kapverde*, Frankfurt a. M., 1985.

Naisbitt, J., "Der Tourismus: Die Globalisierung der größten Industrie der Welt", in *Ders. Global Paradox*, Düsseldorf, 1994.

Navhind Times, Panjim, 1997.

Newman, Robert S., "Goa: The Transformation of an Indian Region", Australia, 1983.

Noronha, Frederick, "The Church and Tourism", Goa, 1992.

O'Grady, A., *The Challenge of Tourism. Ecumenical Coalition on Third World Tourism*, Bangkok, 1990.

Pereira, Óscar, "Goa in Vergangenheit und Gegenwart", in *Zeitschrift zur portugiesischsprachigen Welt*, 1 (1994).

Selvam, M., *Tourism Industry in India*, Bombay, 1989.

Srisang, Koson, *Churches and Tourism*, Goa, 1990.

Stock, C., *Kosten und Nutzen des Tourismus in der Dritten Welt*. Eine kulturgeographische Analyse am Beispiel Indiens, Freiburg, 1995.

Tourism in Goa, Sub-Committee of the Diocesan Pastoral Council Goa, 1988.

TOURIST MAP OF GOA

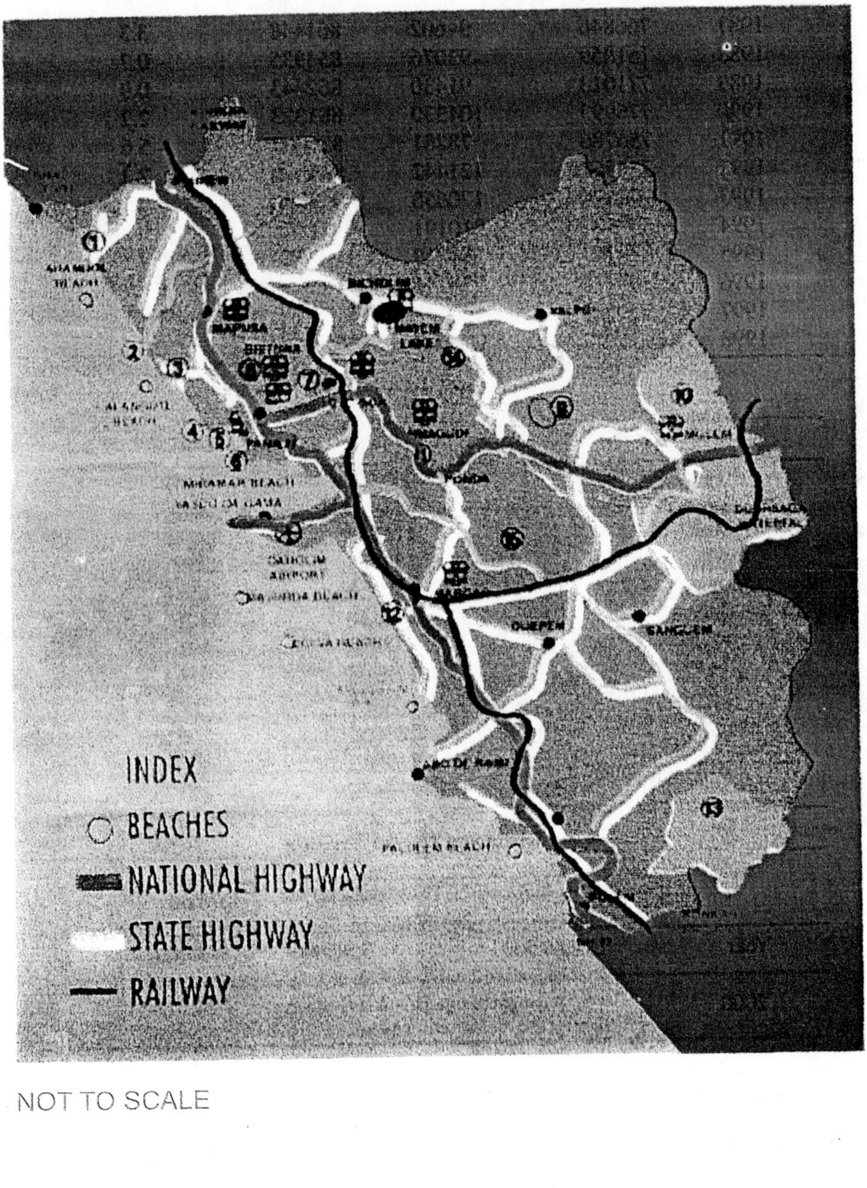

NOT TO SCALE

Goa Tourist Statistics Arrivals

Year	Domestic	Foreign	Total	Annual growth
1985	682545	92667	775212	-
1986	736548	97533	834081	7.6
1987	766846	94602	861448	3.3
1988	761859	93076	854935	- 0.7
1989	771013	91430	862443	0.9
1990	776993	104330	881323	2.2
1991	756786	78281	835067	- 5.6
1992	774568	121442	896010	7.3
1993	798576	170658	969234	8.2
1994	849404	210191	1059595	9.3
1995	878487	229218	1107705	4.5
1996	888914	237216	1126130	1.7
1997	928925	261673	1190598	5.7
1998	953212	275047	1228259	3.2

Foreign Tourist Arrivals 1998

Month	India	Goa
January	245706	41463
February	222089	38102
March	215534	36458
April	174204	23214
May	137868	8256
June	140810	4019
July	175322	3315
August	173095	7194
September	160369	7644
October	203903	25948
November	239919	37958
December	272415P	41476
Total	2361234P	275047

Estimated Tourist Arrivals

Year	Domestic	Foreign	Total
2000	10,50,000	3,50,000	14,00,000

Average Duration of stay

Domestic	5 days
Foreign	9 days

Arrivals by Charters. Season (October to May)

Year	No. of flights	Passengers
1985-86	24	3568
1986-87	26	4401
1987-88	25	5419
1988-89	83	9705
1989-90	107	9266
1990-91	41	5815
1991-92	121	17102
1992-93	259	39871
1993-94	299	58369
1994-95	313	59881
1995-96	337	75694
1996-97	282	73172
1997-98	350	88817

Foreign Tourist Arrivals (Nationalitywise break-up 1997)

	Actuals	Percentage
U. K.	124348	47.5
Germany	25190	9.6
Finland	10233	3.9
Switzerland	9506	3.6
Sweden	3386	1.3
Italy	4454	1.7
Austria	1412	0.5
France	8924	3.4
U.S.A.	7725	3.0
Canada	2969	1.1
Australia	3345	1.3
Japan	2673	1.0
Holland	2305	0.9
Denmark	2885	1.1
New Zealand	1435	0.6
Greece	388	0.2
South Africa	530	0.2
Russia	391	0.2
Portugal	630	0.2
Others	48943	18.7
Total	261673	100.0

Arrival by Charters (October-April)

Month	1997-98 flights	Tourists	1998-99 flights	Tourists	%
October	21	6520	8	2375	- 6.4
November	57	15108	55	15510	2.7
December	53	14663	58	15537	6.0
January	64	17179	72	19930	16.0
February	52	13996	58	15699	12.2
March	55	13718	57	13816	0.7
April	48	7633			
Total	350	88817			

Domestic Tourist Arrivals

Month	1997	1998	% Change
January	94797	96822	2.1
February	70595	72426	2.6
March	60326	64439	6.8
April	69872	70765	1.3
May	102114	102401	0.3
June	71944	72396	0.6
July	53071	56559	6.6
August	58160	62903	8.2
September	59125	60435	2.2
October	88963	90613	0.9
November	98675	100155	1.5
December	101283	103298	2.0
Total	928925	953212	2.6

Foreign Tourist Arrivals *

Month	1997	1998	% Change
January	40836	41463	1.5
February	36774	38102	3.6
March	35336	36458	3.2
April	20320	23214	12.5
May	5832	8256	41.6
June	2806	4019	43.2
July	2893	3315	14.6
August	6869	7194	4.7
September	7436	7644	2.8
October	25461	25948	1.9
November	36923	37958	2.8
December	40187	41476	3.2
Total	261673	275047	5.1

Star Category	3489	Rooms
Other Hotels	8542	Rooms
Paying Guest Houses	2500	Rooms
Grand Total	14531	Rooms

*Reference: Department of Tourism, Govt. of Goa, Panjim.

PART II

VILLAGE COMMUNITIES AND GOAN LIFE

8

The Village Communities

A historical and legal perspective

CARMO D'SOUZA

Introduction

The village communities or *Gaonkaria* were local institutions that evolved from the customary law in pre-Portuguese times. After the entry of the Portuguese in Goa, several legal provisions were promulgated concerning the functioning of these village communities. These legal provisions throw light on the prevailing social structure, as well as on pressures, claims and demands interplaying in that society. The present paper attempts to use those laws on the village communities in order to construct the image of the social structure of those days. Fortunately, these legal provisions practically cover the entire period of the Portuguese rule in Goa, starting with the Charter of 1526 (*Foral*) and ending with the Code of Village Communities of 1961.

Importance of the topic

A village community or *Gaonkaria* occupied a central position in that society and the agricultural life of the village revolved around it. It possessed and owned large lands which it leased to the tenants at auctions, thus controlling the village agriculture. For a society with an agricultural foundation, this control over lands gave it prominence in the society. Besides, the village communities protected the village lands to prevent erosion and denudation caused by the tidal waters and exercised sanitation and welfare functions compatible with the times. They also enjoyed judicial attributes to settle disputes at a local level, which were totally abolished in 1836. Some authors referred to village communities as autonomous units, depending on the sovereign only for functions such as defence, etc. Hence, the legal provisions of village communities are a gold mine for the material on the social structure of that society. While it is possible to reconstruct the image of the village life from the various legal provisions governing the village communities, one has to be cautious while using the material. The legal material should be supplemented by other historical sources.

Methodology and contents

The present paper probes the legal provisions promulgated from 1526 to 1961 in order to construct the social life in the villages of Goa, during that period. The paper, however, does so in a general way, to serve as an example of this technique. A deeper analysis of those laws would add to the richness of the history of the village communities. The present paper analyses the law of the village communities under the following sub-headings.

A) The *Charter of 1526*
B) The *Regiment of 1735*
C) The *Laws* of village communities of the 19th century, and
D) The *Codes* of the village communities of the 20th century.

A) The Charter of 1526[1]

The *Charter* was considered by many as a *Magna Carta* for the village communities. In this piece, great care was taken to outline the relationship governing these institutions with the sovereign, especially the revenue aspect. The *Charter* was applicable to the 31 villages of Tiswadi and consisted of 49 clauses.

Principle of common responsibility: Each of the 31 villages of Tiswadi had to pay a contribution to the sovereign, termed by the Portuguese draftman as rent (*renda*), irrespective of gains and losses suffered by the village. However, losses resulting from a war were to be taken into account when considering the contribution to the sovereign. The members of the eight principal villages[2] were responsible to pay the dues in case a village defaulted payment. The defaulting village could be leased at an auction. Interestingly, when a village was leased temporarily, the members did not totally lose their *Gaonkaria* rights and they could terminate that lease by paying the full dues.

System of "nems" and meeting: The *Charter* referred to the general meetings of the chief members of the village communities and their method of taking decisions and accords in the presence of a *thanadhar* and the head clerk by a particular system of assent called "*nems*", which required the clerk to read the resolutions aloud. The *Charter* also permitted the chief *thanadhar* to call the members or representatives of all the villages or of a particular village to elect a body called *Gaonkaria*. The above was some kind of democratic process in its functioning.

It is to be noted that status was given due consideration in the meetings of these communities. The *Charter* outlined the manner of writing names of members for a meeting which had to be as per status. In fact that status was given prominence in the agrarian setup and can be seen from other provisions discussed separately under the heading status.

The System of lapse: One of the very interesting provisions which is relevant in constructing the image of that society concerns the system of lapse. When a member of a village community died without a male issue, inspite of having parents and ancestors, his property lapsed to the king. An exception existed when the property was held jointly by the father and the son (*herança mistica*) in which case the property passed to the father. This system seemed harsh on the wife and daughters who were thrown at the mercy of society. Similarly, the separate property of a brother who converted to Islam or became a yogi, passed to the king. There were procedures of auctioning the property that lapsed to the Crown. One can understand those harsh measures if one perceives the social pressures of those days for a male issue. A male was needed in order to perform the last rites as well as to keep the continuity of the family god. These provisions are very important for understanding the Hindu customary law.

Leasing of lands: One of the important functions of a village community was to lease its land. It was a system which, while generating income to itself, provided agricultural opportunities to the villagers. The members of the village community together with the clerk decided on the contribution to be paid by the tillers. Every year rice-fields not reserved for particular individuals, were to be leased on auction. Such a lease could be made to residents of other villages only if custom permitted it.

Also leasing of land free of charge to outsiders, was prohibited as a rule, a part of "closed-door" policy followed by the village communities. While leasing some vegetable gardens, palm-groves and rice-fields, a fixed amount had to be paid irrespective of the losses suffered by the tenant while in case of others the rent could be waived off in case of losses. Yet other lands, were to be given free of charge. Uncultivated and barren lands on the border of the village could be leased on payment of a certain rent, which after twenty-five years would entitle the lessee to a kind of ownership. This helped in the agricultural development of the village.

Lease of land in lieu of service: The villages of those days were self-sufficient units with agriculture as a base, having less demands and requiring few indispensable services. The village communities could grant land in favour of its officials as well as its labour staff whose services were required in the village. For instance, such leases could be granted to the brahmin of the temple, the clerk of the village, the door-keeper, collector of revenue (?) (*sacador*), the washerman, the shoemaker, the smith, the menial labourer (*faraz*) who served in the temple, and the concubines attached to the temple. They could be given land in lieu of service. The above specified professions can help us build an idea of the village life and its requirements in those days. Once the donation was effected, it was a grant in favour of sons, grandsons and heirs, who were obliged to continue rendering those services. Thus certain services were assured of continuity in the village. This aspect re-enforces the hereditary nature in professions expected in those days, as a part of the continuation of those skills in the village.

Permission for sale of shares: The *Charter* laid down that if a member of the village community desired to sell his hereditary rights in the village, he needed permission of other members. Similar permission was required to buy shares in the village community. Sale or purchase in contravention of the above rule was null and void. The sale of hereditary rights was to be signed by the seller and all the heirs, the minors through proxy, failure of which could result in the sale being set aside. The buyer could recover the purchase price, however losing the money invested for additional improvements. Perhaps this could be a reflection of the Mithakshara co-parcenary in Hindu law, in which a father, son, grandson and great-grandson shared rights in a co-parcenary property. The mention of man's hereditary rights fits in the concept of co-parcenary.

Evidence and witnesses: The *Charter* laid down that the proof of hereditary rights or immovable assets was by way of documents (*escripturas e conhecimentos*) or through the books of the village. Evidence given by witnesses was not acceptable as a rule, on this point. If however, the above were not available or the book of the village was lost, one was permitted to swear on the temple called *Uzoo*. Minors of sixteen years and under, drunkards, the deaf, dumb, ruffians, daily-wage workers, gardeners, sons of prostitutes, infamous men, recognised as such by judicial authorities, were not to be accepted as witnesses.

Law of debts: The principle of "*damdaput*" followed in the Hindu customary law of debts, found a reflection in the *Charter*. In case of certain loans,[3] if one failed to demand them, due to one's negligence, within the time limit agreed, one could not recover at one time, the accumulated principal and interest together, exceeding twice the amount loaned.

Succession rules: Succession was from father to son and grandson *et al.* in a descending manner and from son to father and grandfather *et al.* in an ascending manner. Perhaps this reflects the Mithakshara co-parcenary principle of the Hindu law.[4] Succession took place only through males and never through females. The daughters did not succeed either their father or mother. The *Charter* mentioned the shares in case a male was married to two wives. The sons of the first wife took half the property and the sons of the second wife took the other half. Later in around 1534 in the case of the Sinay brothers,[5] it was stated that there was a second custom, too, of equal partition (per capita) among the sons which had escaped the notice of Afonso Mexia. In case of voluntary partition by the father, he could follow any one of the customs. The concepts of voluntary partition again appears to re-enforce the concept of Mithakshara co-parcenary.

Status: Certain members of the community enjoyed eminence over others. On festive occasions, it was the privilege of the chief member of the village community to take certain items (*betre, pachoris, joia*) first, others following in an order of prominence. Similarly, the chief had the privilege of sowing or reaping his field first and covering his house with palm leaves before others. The above-mentioned activities must have been very important to the village life then. Perhaps those activities had a ritualistic aspect which does not figure in the *Charter.* Similarly, during the festivities, the dancing men and women had to perform their arts first at the house of chief gaonkar. If such a right did not exist in certain villages in favour of chief gaonkar, then it could be sold to anyone interested, otherwise the honour went to the clerk of the village. The above is an interesting provision. Also it was not permissible to carry (*tocha, andor, sombreiro*) unless with the permission of the Governor, or if such a privilege was enjoyed as a hereditary right. Those items show the status symbols used by the society which could be claimed as a hereditary privilege.

Cleaning the city of Goa: As per the *Charter*, the village communities were obliged to provide workers at their own cost to clean the city of Goa, to cut down the grassfields and forest growth and to clean the walls of the city. Perhaps, it was easy for the agricultural based community to provide manpower which might have been difficult for the city to obtain.

Stolen property: The *Charter* mentioned that stolen property was to be returned to the owner, irrespective of the uses and customs by which ownership passed to the king. This is an interesting point on the customary jurisprudence of ownership and requires a deeper study.

Reaping ceremony at Taleigao: The village of Taleigao enjoyed the privilege of the first reaping ceremony among the villages of Tiswadi. This privilege could have been granted by the Portuguese in recognition of the help received from the village, during the conquest of Goa. The corn was to be presented to the Portuguese officials, after taking it to the Sé, the main church of the city of Goa.

Food for officials: When the *thanadar*, factor and clerk were on official duty, the village had to provide them with food as per the custom. This perhaps was necessary as such facilities might not have existed in the village, forcing one to depend on the village hospitality.

Conclusion: The *Charter* of 1526 contains valuable information on the customs and usages of those days which can be an important source in reconstructing the village life. However, one has to take due care to see whether some of the practices were modified by the Portuguese.

B) The Regiment of 1735[6]

The *Regiment* of 1735 was formulated to regulate the government and organisation of the chambers of the village communities of Ilhas, Bardez and Salcete. It maintained autonomy in the functioning of the village communities, while it made the members and other officials responsible and accountable to prevent fraud. It contained 46 articles (*capitulos*).

Officials: The *Regiment* mentions arbitrators, revenue collectors (*sacadores*) and the village clerks and referred to the proceedings that could be taken against them for illegal and unauthorised entries. The mention of arbitrators is relevant as it gives a hint to arbitration proceedings,[7] a system well recognised in the Indian customary law for settling disputes, unlike the one-way justice system of the west. The Collectors had to collect the dues from the tenants to whom land had been leased at auction on a yearly or periodical basis. The *Regiment* outlined the qualities expected from a village clerk, ordinarily, a life-time post. Similarly, it laid down the qualities expected from the elected representatives to the agrarian chamber.

Inquiries and accounting system: The judge of the Crown and the King's revenue had to inquire into the administration of the communities once every three years. To make the accounting system effective, time was prescribed for general accounts, for accounts of Collectors and there were provisions requiring entries to be made in the same accounting year.

Loans for repair of bunds: Urgent repair of bunds was often necessary to protect properties from being damaged by overflowing rivulets. The *Regiment* had restrictions on the use of money by village communities. However, this restriction was relaxed in case of urgent repairs of bunds. The above provision reveals the role of village communities in the repair of bunds and the importance of urgency in their maintenance, in those days.

Sale of shares: The *Regiment* referred to the sale of shares (*jonos*), the entry of which had to be made on the relevant books. The above is an interesting provision.

Meetings and books: The *Regiment* required the minutes of the decisions to be written in appropriate books. There was a total prohibition against participation of Europeans in the meetings of communities. This was to prevent the influence being exercised by the white race in the local units. It had provisions for extraordinary deliberations of the general agrarian chamber.

Treasury: In those days it was necessary to keep money safely in cash boxes. The *Regiment* laid down that the cash boxes had to have three keys, which were to be kept in the possession of three distinct officials.

Police: The *Regiment* throws some light on the policing system existing in that society. The village communities proposed three names for the post of head constable and the chief *thanadhar* nominated the most suitable among them to hold office for a period of three years.

The lower police were nominated by the captain with the approval of the chief *thanadhar.* The head constable had to submit a list of vagabonds, thieves and loafers to the chief *thanadhar*. In case of war, all able-bodied men between the age group of fifteen and sixty were to be enlisted for the war operation. In case of robberies, the head constable with the aid of the people had to deal with the situation, arresting, hurting or even killing if necessary. The measures appear harsh in the modern day in the light of the human rights philosophy. Soldiers and warriers passing through the village were obliged to show their licenses.

Inter-caste feuds: The *Regiment* referred to the village communities having equal number of votes shared by the two warring castes i.e. brahmins and chardos, which caused problems during the elections of officials. It was laid down that the two factions had to contest alternatively for the posts holding the position for three years as per the law of Viceroy Fernandes Cezar de Menezes. This provision throws light on inter-caste disputes in society, at that time.

C) 19th century provisions of the village communities

In the 19th century there were interesting provisions for the village communities. To begin with, the decree of 1836 on provisional judicial organization,[8] abolished the post of the judges of village communities and ended all the judicial attributes enjoyed by this institution. It is clear that the village communities enjoyed judicial powers earlier and the jurisdictional aspect was discussed in 1786 in *Assento da Relação,*[9] which resolved the conflict between the judge of matters of the Crown and Revenue and the judge of the village communities. The decree of 1836 in article no. 12 stated that the judicial cases relating to the village communities were within the jurisdiction of the district judge and consequently the post of chief *thanadhar* and the judges of the village communities stood abolished.

The *Regiment* of 1871[10] contained just eight articles and was concerned with the organisation and functioning of the village communities. Later came the decree of 1880[11] which had an interesting introduction on the beneficial functions of the village communities. It stated that the beneficial functions extended not only to associates and shareholders but even to the public in general. It referred to the contribution of these institutions in times of crises and epidemics as well as its contribution towards construction and maintenance of public works in the village. The decree of 1880 dealt with the types of members or associates of the village communities (*goankars, culacharins, joneiros, cuntenkars, interessados*), the governing body of each community at the village level and the agrarian chamber at the provincial level. It also regulated some important aspects such as auctions, leases and collection of revenues.

Extensive regulations were made in 1886[12] for village communities containing around 465 articles. It referred to the various functions of the personnel and officials concerned with the administration of the assets of the village communities. It also regulated the functions of the government officials when they exercised their powers on the village communities. The regulations laid down procedures for incurring expenditure, recovery of debts, on sale and mortgages. It also dealt with appeals to the Administrator of the district or the Governor or the Provincial Council, rules on accountability, records to be kept and registration to be entered in the village communities' books figured in the *Regiment*. Hence an in-depth analysis of the 19th century laws on village communities can assist one in learning about the social structure of society in those times.

D) Codes of the village communities of the 20th century

At the turn of the 20th century, the *Code* of village communities containing 750 articles was enforced from January 1, 1905.[13] It stated that the purpose of legislation was to secure development of vast properties as well as to achieve the welfare of the population. This can be understood if one keeps in mind the background of the functioning of the village communities. As the village communities leased lands for agriculture through auctions, these institutions played a central role in the agricultural growth of the village. Besides it had certain welfare attributes, welfare as understood in the terminology of the time.

The *Code* enforced in 1905 referred to the promises and assurances of Afonso de Albuquerque after the conquest of Goa. It abolished the agrarian chambers (*Câmaras Agrárias de Goa*) and passed their attributes to administrator of village communities. The *Code* was reframed in 1933 in a legislative piece containing 873 articles.[14] Later another *Code* was promulgated in 1961,[15] containing about 660 articles. A few observations on this Code can serve as a source for history of the time.

Code of 1961 and its annexures: The *Code* of the village communities of 1961 has annexures consisting of maps, forms and price or fee tables which are very important in constructing the image of that society. For instance, the first annexure (relevant to art. no. 2) gives the list of village communities in the talukas (*concelhos*) of Goa, Salcete, Bardez, Mormugao, Ponda, Bicholim, Pernem, Quepem, Sanguem and Canacona. Annexure no. 2 (relevant to art. no. 127) gives the number of personnel working in the village communities such as administrators, technical personnel, secretaries, clerks, servants and so on, and the salaries to which some of them were entitled. The third annexure gives the emoluments and salaries which can be useful for an economic study. Annexure eight (relevant to art no. 1 [3]) gives the process of establishing annual dividends, which varied from one village community to another and is very useful and provides information on the various weightages given to *jonos* and *acções* in a particular village communities. Besides, the annexures contain various forms to be filled, registers to be kept, certificates to be issued and they yield a rich source for a study.

Types of members: Articles nos. 3 and 20 of the *Code* refer to the members (*componentes*) of the village communities such as '*jonoeiros, accionistas, jonoeiros e accionistas, participantes*'. One gets a clarification on the concept of '*jonoeiro*' and '*accionista*' and can understand the principle of male dominance with regards to those who enjoyed '*jonos*' as only descendants through male lineage were considered in this setup.[16] The above concepts reflect the social setup of the times.

Meetings: Articles nos. 33-38 of the Code refer to meetings of the communities. There were to be four ordinary meetings in a year, to be held in the first fortnight of the months of March, April, May and December and extraordinary whenever required. The meetings were to be preceded by public announcement (*pregões*) through different wards of the village and with notices placed on the door of the house of sessions and the doors of all the religious temples existing in the village. The meetings ordinarily had to be held in the village itself in the house destined for the purpose and were to be public. One can understand the importance of these meetings in the village life of those days.

Loans: Art. no. 64 (5) refers to loans which could be given at 4% interest whenever there was disposable money available in the cash box. Loans were to be given on security of gold, silver or shares of the village community (*acções*) to the tenants of the fields. They were not to exceed a certain limit prescribed and were never to exceed a period of six months. Loans could also be given to other village communities of the same taluka. This throws light on the village economy.

Other matters: It is not possible to cover in this paper all the interesting matters that figure in the *Code* of the village communities of 1961 that can be useful in interpreting the social history of the time. For instance, one can get an idea on leasing of properties, maintenance of bandhs in *khazana* lands, on introduction of salt or sweet water in paddy fields, on usurpation of properties, on reversion of unused properties back to the village communities,[17] on the value of shares (*acções*) and so on. An in-depth study of this *Code* would yield a rich material for social history.

Concluding remarks: The present paper serves a limited purpose of demonstrating the use of legal provisions in village communities in the construction of the social image of village life. Fortunately, the legal provisions on village communities cover almost the entire Portuguese period in Goa starting with the *Charter* of 1526 to the *Code* of 1961. Hence, these legal provisions are very useful in writing the history of village communities during the Portuguese period.

NOTES AND REFERENCES

1. Cunha Rivara, "Foral dos usos e costumes dos Gauncares e Lavradores desta Ilha de Goa e outras annexas a ela", *Archivo Portuguez Oriental*, fasc. 5, pt. I, doc. 58, 1865, pp. 118-133.
2. The eight villages mentioned are: Neura o grande, Gansim, Ella, Azossim, Calapor, Morobim o grande, Carambolim and Batim.
3. Loans i.e. *prestar dinheiro sobre conhecimento*. For the rule of *damdupat* see, Paras Diwan, *Modern Hindu Law*, Allahabad Law Agency, 1998, pp. 435-437.
4. See *ibid.*, pp. 234-266 for the Mithakshara joint family system.
5. Cunha Rivara, *Archivo Portuguez Oriental*, fasc. 5, pt. I, doc. 72, 1865, pp. 155-159.
6. F. N. Xavier, *Collecção das Leis Peculiares*, pt. I, doc. 64, 1852, pp. 92-118.
7. See Carmo D'Souza, *Legal System in Goa, Judicial Institutions (1510 – 1982)*, vol. 1, 1994, pp. 39-40.

8. Decree of December 7, 1836. See *Constituição Política de Monarchia Portuguesa,* Panjim: Imprensa Nacional, 1839, pp. 38-44.
9. Xavier, *Collecção das Leis Peculiares*, pt. II, doc. 62, 1855, pp. 137-142, dt. January 30, 1786.
10. *Boletim* no. 40, dt. May 26, 1871, pp. 213-214, law dt. May 25, 1871.
11. Decree dt. September 15, 1880, *Boletim* no. 118, dt. October 23, pp. 703-707.
12. Regulations approved by *Portaria* no. 591, October 30, 1886; *Boletim* no. 246, dt. November 10, 1886, p. 1005 and the following numbers.
13. *Portaria* no. 315, dt. December 1, 1904, approved the *Code* of village communities. Also decree dt. January 12, 1908 from Portugal approved the *Code* of village communities of 1904. See *Boletim* no. 63, dt. August 14, 1908, p. 765.
14. *Boletim* no. 40, dt. May 20, 1933, supplement.
15. See *Codigo das Communidades*, Panjim: Impresa Nacional, 1961.
16. *Os que tenham jono, quer per capita, quer per stripes, e os descendentes varões por linha veronil, legitimos, legitimados, perfilhados e adoptivos, seja qual for o seu numero* (art. no. 20 (I).
17. O *terreno aforado que não for aproveitado* (art. no. 341).

BIBLIOGRAPHY

Boletim do Governo do Estado da India Journal Official (Boletim), Panjim. December 7, 1837, weekly, later irregular. Title varies after 1879, *Boletim Official do Estado da India.* Also *Government Gazette.*

Constituição Política da Monarchia Portuguesa, Panjim: Imprensa Nacional, 1839.

Codigo das Communidades, Panjim: Imprensa Nacional, 1961.

D'Souza, Carmo, *Legal System in Goa,* vol. I (1994), vol. II (1995).

Souza, T. R. de, *Medieval Goa: A socio-economic history,* New Delhi: Concept Publishing Co., 1979.

Xavier, F. N., *Bosquejo Histórico das Communidades.* pts. I-IV, Panjim, 1852. Edited as 2nd ed. in vols. I-III by J. M. de Sa, Bastora, 1903-7.

Xavier, F. N., *Collecção das Leis Peculiares das Communidades,* pts. I-II, in *Gabinette Litterario,* Panjim, 1852-5.

Xavier, F. N., *Collecção de Bandos e outras differentes providencias que servem de Leis Regulamentares para o Governo Económico e Judicial das Provincias Denominadas das Novas Conquistas,* Panjim: Imprensa Nacional, 1840.

9

Village Communities in Goa and their Evolution

JOSEPH VELINKAR

"Local Government," Prof. Sidney Webb once wrote, "is as old as the hills." India more than any country is extremely fortunate in having preserved its ancient system of local self-government, though with some changes. Although the administration varied from village to village in fine points and minute details, there was a regular and rigorous observance of principles and main features, the chief purpose being related to the village economy, defence of life and property, promotion of all-round development and finally prevention of crime.[1]

Emile de Laveleye in a study on this subject has shown that the system of village communities which existed in Goa has close affinity to the "primitive and universal regime of agrarianism" which existed as *mir* in Russia, *marco* in Holland, *allmend* in Switzerland, *almaenig* in Sweden and Finland, common property in France and Belgium and ancient property in Scotland, U.S.A, the Iberian peninsula, Italy, Japan and the Celt countries.[2]

It has been conjectured that the *kuddumbys* or *kunnbis* were the earliest colonizers of the land of Goa. They came with their sheep and cattle, but especially cows, from which the land on which they settled got its name Goparashtra or Govarashtra and the capital was called Gopakpur or Govapuri. A writer of the 16th or 17th century, probably relying on an old tradition, has stated that "the Neiquebares were descendants of the first colonizing families ... the family of the Giis, descendants of the first colonizers, were lords of the Province of Salcete... The ganvkars who actually reside in Salcete are not, whereas the Giis and Neiquebares are, the ultimate possessors and descendants of the first colonizers..."[3] So we can conjecture that the local self-government of the time was very simple certainly not as complex as it became in the 16th century.

After quite a period of time, an influx of sudras from the Karnataka region started pouring into the territory. They were admitted as helpers, some working as village herdsmen, called *gauddes, gaudde* or *gaullis,* and leading the cattle to pasture on the border of villages or hills. We have no information about their village administration. But it could not have changed very much, chiefly because they occupied a very low position in society and were subsidiary to the *kunnbis*. The *Vocabulário* describes the sudras as being between the *kunnbis* and *chandorins*. We are therefore led to surmise that the village administration remained essentially the same.

After many years (some centuries?), the Marathas came to Goa. They were warriors, seemingly from the north. They occupied parts of Goa as defenders of the earlier inhabitants or as a martial group to ward off attacks from outside.[4]

The brahmins, among the last of ancient Goan immigrants according to F.N. Xavier, came at the beginning of the Christian era when they entered the southern half of India and occupied parts of Karnataka and Malabar. Dr. G. M. Moraes holds the view that the "aryanisation of Goa must have started centuries before their advent during the Mauryan period, the formation of Konkan being one of the results of this process".[5]

Dr. K. A Nilakanta Sastri holds that the aryanisation of South India probably began about 1000 B.C. and was completed by the 4th century B.C. (Mauryan period).[6] The affinity of Konkani with Magadhi, the language of Magadha, which was the centre of Buddhism and emperor Ashoka's rule, confirms the time of the aryanizing influence in Goa.[7]

From all this we can conclude that during this period (B.C.), the structure of the village community must have changed and developed over the years. The brahmins and kshatriyas were given prime land to build temples to various deities and played an important part in the villages where they predominated, the former becoming a necessary part, as scribes and preservers of village records, of many village communities.

After the advent of the brahmins the lands were distributed anew, the low-lying *neli* (Kannada: paddy) lands of the village being set aside for the temple, its ministers and its attendants. It was also given to the village administrators in lieu of wages and used for raising funds for the community. The second type (medium quality land) was granted for temple needs or to village servants as land grants (*namassis*). Some of it was reserved for public utility works like roads, tanks, village offices, etc. The last type (low quality land) was rented out in perpetuity either on a fixed (*cutubana*) or variable (*vanty*) tax.[8]

The control of the village rested within the community. For all land tilled or fallow, with the exception of some tracts which were reserved for outsiders, a tax-like tribute was paid by the village.

The village community had become, according to an ancient system of village autonomy in India, "self-governing and self-supporting" like a small independent republic. It had its own statutes or rules about agriculture, production and loss. Each conqueror respected these statutes, claiming only a part of the produce and imposing extra taxes only in times of grave public need.[9]

The statutes (*mandavoli*), with awards and fines attached to certain cases, were drawn up by the village community members in mutual consultation and agreements and meant exclusively for their internal use. All agriculture (even its insufficiency) and distribution of produce were regulated by a system of shares or units (Konkani: *zonn*), which varied in details from village to village but were basically uniform.

With the advent of the Portuguese, the Comptroller of the Treasury, Afonso Mexia compiled these statutes in 1526 into the now famous document *Foral dos usos e costumes dos Gancares e Lavradores*. This was followed by another *Foral dos foros e contribuções* dealing with taxes, drawn up by Fernão Rodrigues e Castello Branco in 1541. Both these charters were made applicable to Salcete and Bardez about 30 years later.[10]

It is from these two documents that we begin to have a clear view of village administration for the first time. Village affairs were managed by a group of people's representatives or hereditary officers, each of whom was called *ganvkar*, or *gramapurusha* (in Maharashtra *vatandar*). The Council of *ganvkars* (*ganvkari* or *ganvpann*) was the village council. Each councillor represented a clan (*vangod*) in the village at the time of its founding. The clans were classified as first, second, third clan, etc.[11] according to the importance of the production made by them in favour of the village. The village council therefore varied according to the number of founding clans, one village (Verna) having as many as 48 and another (Chicolna) as few as 3.

Mexia in the first article of his *Foral* gives the origin of the village council, as he learnt it from his contemporaries (villagers): "In ancient times four men set about cultivating an island. They tried the same on another, barren though it was, and succeeded so well that people flocked to it and called the first settlers ganvkars because of their excellent government, administration and harvest..." Each word of the legend need not be taken *ad pedem litterae*, but the whole story does afford an insight into the manner and motives that went into the origin of the village council *(comunidade)* system in Goa. The main qualities of the founding fathers and their families were their capacity for hard work and organization. F. N. Xavier opines that the ganvkar system of Goa originated during the 8th and 9th centuries A.D or earlier.[12]

The village council was divided into wards (*vaddos*, *bairros*) and the land of each ward into first and second quality soil. A senior and respected person headed the council as president and chief councillor. He presided over the meetings and may have been a member of the mahal or regional council (*Câmara Geral*). When a pair of representatives was sent from a 'privileged village' to the regional council, both were called chief councillors (*ganvkars*) of the village, though the president of the village council was probably the senior of the duo.

The chief councillor was honoured at regular intervals in the village. Some modes of honour have been laid down in the last articles of Mexia's *Foral*. At a feast or function, each chief councillor received betel-leaf or a scarf (or headcloth). Before the onset of the monsoon, his residence had to be protected first against the rains. In the sowing season, his field was ploughed first and at harvest time was reaped before the others. When male and females dancers went to perform at a village festival, they began the celebrations by dancing near the doorstep of his house.[13]

The meeting of *ganvkars* can be called either "a primary assembly", in which all founding-family male members met, or a village council on which only one male adult represented each clan.[14] People of the same clan stayed together in one or more wards of the same village. It was therefore easy for the *ganvkars* of certain clans to meet together or separately at short notice. The council met in a suitable place under a spreading tree, usually a stout banyan.

The president called the meeting and the village clerk (*kulkarni, escrivão)* was present at each session in the open air or in a room or hall (*chauddi*). Nearby, the village records were stored and preserved.[15] The village clerk had probably been called in quite early in the village community history and enjoyed much freedom and tax exemption. He was originally appointed by the headman, but in course of time the office became hereditary and was usually a brahmin, except perhaps in some kshatriya villages. He drew up the deeds (*namoxims, namassis*), kept the records in order, did all the writing and kept the accounts. In *kunnbi* villages, the clerk held a superior position and did much of the head-work. Though he might disagree with the president, his presence was probably a *sine qua non* for the meeting, just as the regional council clerk was for the regional council meeting,[16] but he had no right to vote. At the end of the meeting, he read out the resolution (*nemo*) agreed upon. If there was no amendment, the resolution was considered carried and ready for execution.

Two other officials mentioned in the records are *porteiro* (door-keeper) and *porteiro da dita aldeia* (gate-keeper). What their duties were is not clear. *Variku* was the official-in-charge of the sluice valves and *tarlu*, the watchman, who guarded the boundaries and served as justice official, public messenger and guide.

The tax collector (*potecar, sacador*) or bailiff used to collect the actual payments of each family and carry them to the store-house or treasury (*potha*). Baden-Powell opines that he may been an outsider, who got the post by bidding lowest when the post was auctioned. How long ago was the tax collected in kind is not known. But the amount payable was determined by an assessment (*zaebhasa*) of land and the village council resolution about it entered in the village register (*vahi*). During the Portuguese rule, tax was paid in cash and regional taxes collected in coins. Yet quite a few families were asked to pay their tribute (in full or part), according to the incidence of the tax, to the village temples in kind.

J. H. da Cunha Rivara has adverted that this contribution to the Treasury has been called a "real tax" (*foro, renda*) by the Portuguese. Caetano de Figueiredo in his article "*As Communidades de Goa*" holds that this is a village contribution and not a tax, as stated in the *Foral*, "because from this usage originated the erroneous opinion that the villages had lost the ownership of the land."[17]

Before the coming of the Portuguese the tribute imposed was heavy and disproportionate to the income of the people. The village assembly or council had to stand surety for its payment. In order to avoid confiscation of property for non-payment of dues, the villagers devised a system of units (*tangas de cunto*) into which the total loss or gain of the village was divided.

Over and above the system of the *ganvkar* and his descendants getting the *jono*, there came into existence in the New Conquests, a new system of shareholders who received a 'dividend' on the net income, and a limited number of 'participants', who also received a certain amount from the net income of the community.

The village council consisted usually of male adults, one representing each clan. According to article no. 14 of Mexia's *Foral*, the chief *thanadhar* was empowered to convoke a village council (or island council, for each island of Tisvadi) meeting. All councillors were obliged to attend the meeting or to assemble together to determine his successor or choose a person, if one was lacking. If a person did not attend the meeting, he incurred a penalty determined by the village council.[18]

At the meeting each councillor had one vote (*mata*). All resolutions had to be passed unanimously. A *nay* (*naka)* effectively became a veto. In the face of one *naka,* the rest of the councillors had to compromise or shelve the issue. A single person could block the decision of the rest. Only on November 10, 1745, the veto power was abolished and resolutions could be passed by a simple majority. Quite understandably, the powerful councillors were called *mhazana* and their status graded according to their influence, habits and caste.[19]

Over the years, the assembly and council drew up a set of rules for the internal government of the village with a system of rewards and fines in certain types of cases. Everything was regulated: from ploughing to distribution and deficit through the system of units in order to make good any loss. The special concern of the council was public utility works which improved the people's state of living: roads and funeral paths, drainage channels, tanks for ablution and drinking water for cattle, dams and water conduits, bridges over rivulets, schools in which *shenois* and travelling sadhus taught, pillars (*davarne*) for laying down head-loads on and planting trees by the road to shade the weary traveller.[20]

By erroneously interpreting the word *foro* to mean tax in Mexia's *Foral*, the Council of Landed Properties (*Conselho da Fazenda*) by its resolution of July 5, 1649 considered the State as direct lord (owner) of the community lands and declared that the village councillors cared for them only as tenants. Thus the old principle on which Afonso de Albuquerque had made an agreement with the people of Goa (islands), Bardez and Salcete was infringed, marking the beginning of continuous and overt interference in village affairs.[21]

In the 17th century a new class of interested people rose among the rulers. As I have said before, the people paid a certain fixed, unchanging contribution on land, with a right to participate in the losses and gains of the crops. This contribution or tax was called the *foro corrente*. Not forming part of the community's lease or regular control, the outer or pasture lands could therefore be more easily alienated together with the *foro corrente*. Some time later because of various needs of the government and payment of proportionate tax according to the growing needs of the economy, the village council was obliged to part with the surplus, and separated from the land to which it was connected. It is the beginning of other taxes: *tangas, melagas, arequeiras* and *covas.*

The owner of such pasture lands could not take part in the administration of the communities, nor embark on the auction of fields. He received only a certain portion of the surplus and had to pay to cover any deficit. Of the intermittent disputes between the village councillors and other interested parties the government took note and recognized the latter as participants in the rights and obligations of the village councillors. In 1735 the communities were given an *Instruction* (*Regimento*), a detailed exposé about the administration, according to which the supervision in each mahal would be managed by a judge of the communities, substituted much later by a mahal administrator, and in the Old Conquests, from 1870, by a special administrator in each mahal. From 1880-97, sporadic efforts were made to adapt to the new circumstances. In 1880 a decree was passed, which became the fundamental document by which the communities and their economies were governed.

In 1889 a committee was set up to make suggestions to better the village as an institution and to codify the existing laws. As a result, a report on the village community *Code* was prepared and approved four years later by the government.

Between the village and the government was another organization, the mahal council. From times long ago, groups of villages had got together to form larger units, each of which was called mahal or *tanadaria.* The mahals had been formed on the basis of geography, social interchange and commerce. F. N. Xavier holds that the mahal council was formed before the village communities became independent and each established its own functioning. [22] When exactly they were formed is difficult to say. Some think it must have happened after the arrival of the brahmins in Goa because the mahal organization and administration were channeled through the mahal council which was represented by eight villages (in Tisvadi) and twelve villages (in Salcete) in which brahmins predominated.[23]

After the conquest of Tisvadi in February 1510, Albuquerque took charge of Salcete, Bardez, Ponda and other areas on the mainland "which were all *tanadarias* subject to the City and Isle of Goa, their capital..."[24] Salcete and Bardez were called *tanadarias,* each under the jurisdiction of a *thanadhar,* at the outpost (*thana* or *thane)* of which the chief and his men were stationed. A *thanadhar* was a police or military chief who guarded an area under his care with a possé of armed guards. At first his duty was to defend the territory, maintain law and order and collect taxes. Albuquerque in a gesture of trust had appointed Mir Kasim with Diogo

Fernandes to collect the taxes and defend the people against roving gangs that molested and robbed the people. But the system of a *thanadhar* being in charge of areas like Salcete and Bardez was in use long before and continued to be in use after that time.[25]

Soon the defence of Goa and the nearby mahals became so strenuous and urgent that an army captain had to be appointed to supervise the defence of the villages or each mahal. Slowly defence became the responsibility of the captain and finally only the task of collecting taxes remained to the *thanadhar*. By 1560 the *thanadhar* was usually referred to as *recebedor* (mahal tax gatherer), but the mahal continued to be referred to as *tanadaria*. About 150 years later, the terms *tanadaria* and *comarca* were used to denote mahal.

The mahal was governed by a council called *Câmara Geral* or *Gancaria Geral*. The Salcete mahal council was composed of 25 persons, 2 representatives from each village on an average and a secretary (*nadakarni*).[26] At this meeting too every member had a vote of equal weightage, but even one '*nay*' was a veto. The interest of every village was represented in the mahal council. No village interest could be brushed aside or overlooked.

After the liberation of Goa, the village communities being found stagnant, the Agricultural Tenancy Bill was passed to provide security to and reduce the rent burden on the tenant cultivators. The tenant was also freed from the absentee landlord's exploitation and kept in direct contact with the State.[27]

In fine, it is apparent that the village community organization was based chiefly on agrarian land and its cultivation. Round this was built the whole religious, social and economic life of the people. The village administration gave wide scope to improve cultivation and expand the economy. No wonder many *grampurushas* were worshipped and revered in the temples which they helped build or maintain. But the State slowly usurped its authority over the years!

Another section dealing with Town Administration would complement this paper, but that calls for a separate study.

NOTES AND REFERENCES

1. A. Lopes Mendes, *A India Portuguesa (IP)*, vol. II, Panaji, 1923, p. 375.
2. *Ibid.*, pp. 393-94.
3. *Arquivo Nacional de Torre do Tombo*, Mss. *Cartorio dos Jesuitas*, masso 89, ff. 21, 23.

4. Filippe Nery Xavier, *Bosquejo Histórico das Communidades (BHC)*, vol. I, 1st ed., Panaji, 1852, pp. 77-83.
5. G.M. Moraes, "Dr. José Gerson da Cunha 1844-1900" in *Journal of the Asiatic Society of Bombay*, vols. 39-40, 1964-65, p. 26.
6. Nilakanta K. A. Sastri, *A History of South India*, Chennai, 1958, p. 75.
7. A. B. de Bragança Pereira, *Etnografia da India Portuguesa*, I, Bastora, 1940, p. 436.
8. *BHC*, I, pp. 27-29; Teotónio de Souza, *Medieval Goa*, New Delhi: Concept Publishing Co., 1989, pp. 74-75.
9. *IP*, p. 374.
10. *BHC*, vol. II, pp. 1-4.
11. *IP*, vol. I, Lisbon, 1886, p. 142.
12. *IP*, vol. II, p. 181; *BHC*, vol. II, p. 6; J. Velinkar, *India and the West: The first encounters*, Mumbai, 1998, p. 124.
13. *IP*, vol. II, pp. 196-97.
14. Francisco de Souza, O *Oriente Conquistado a Jesus Christo ...*", I, conq. I, div. 2, n. 56, Bombay, 1881, 2nd ed.
15. *O Oriente Português*, vol. VI, p. 318; S. R. Dalgado, *Glossário Luso-Asiático*, vol. I, pp. 268-69.
16. *BHC*, vol. I, 2nd ed., pp. 72-73.
17. *IP*, vol. II, p. 378.
18. *Ibid*, pp. 187-88.
19. *Ibid*, p. 196, art. 41.
20. *Ibid*, p. 408.
21. *Ibid*, p. 378.
22. *BHC*, vol. I, 1st ed., pp. 94-102. *passim*.
23. *Ibid*.
24. *Ibid*.
25. João de Barros, *Décadas da Asia*, II, pt. I, 2, bks. 5-8.
26. J. Velinkar, *op. cit.*, p. 129.
27. Gazeteer of the Union Territory Goa, Daman and Diu, Pt. I, Goa, 1979, p. 668.

10

Peasantry and the Colonial State in Goa 1946-1961

PRATIMA KAMAT

> "Whatever befalls the earth befalls the sons of the earth. Man did not weave the web of life, he is merely a strand in it. Whatever he does to the web, he does to himself."
>
> - Amerindian Chief Seattle
> of the Duwamish tribe of Washington, c.1800 [1]

The problem to be investigated

The institution of land has since time immemorial played a significant role in shaping the course of human history not only as a primary condition for human existence, but also as a basis of human interaction. Agriculture, being integrally linked up with land, underlies the equations of power and status inherent in land in all their socio-economic and political overtones.

My researches into the resistance offered by the Goans to the colonial regime in the 19th and early 20th centuries revealed to me the stagnant nature of the Goan economy, especially the depressed condition of the agricultural sector that provided sustenance to a majority of the local population. These voices of agrarian anguish and suffering are rather poignantly reflected in the repertoire of Goan oral tradition of the tillers of the land.

Why did this pain fail to translate itself into the power of protest during Goa's struggle for freedom from 1946-1961?

My related readings on Goa's struggle for freedom failed to provide me with a satisfactory answer to this question. Although there is a considerable body of published knowledge on this topic, it is largely a collection of personal reminiscences of freedom-fighters, accounts of the important events leading to liberation, publications on the "Operation Vijay" itself, discussions on the genesis of the Goa Problem and India's foreign policy. There is, in fact, a dearth of published literature that attempts an analysis of the struggle through a more people-oriented, broader issues-based interpretation of the three component units of the term, Goa's Struggle for Freedom, that is,

- who, rather than what, constituted GOA,
- what was the nature of the STRUGGLE, and
- what was meant by FREEDOM? Was it a mere snapping of political ties with the colonial regime or did it visualise a comprehensive agenda for the development of land and the emancipation of its people?

The failure of the leaders to mobilise the contemporary agrarian discontentment for the cause of Goa's struggle for freedom and instead, their over-dependence on the Indian Prime Minister, Pandit Jawaharlal Nehru, to do the honours of liberating Goa, tickled my academic curiosity enough to take up a research project on the theme of "Peasantry, the Colonial State and the National Question in Goa, 1946-1961." This ongoing project is based on archival source material, contemporary newspapers and publications, as well as on oral sources, on interviews with the peasants, *bhaattkars* and *mundkars*, members of the *comunidades* belonging to the pre as well as the post-Liberation generation and also freedom-fighters. Similarly, oral tradition, in particular the folksongs of the exploited peasantry constitute an additional methodological input into this project.

When the invitation to this Conference came along, I at once thought what an ideal forum it would be to present the preliminary findings of my research with a view to elicit a scholarly feedback. In keeping with the theme of the Conference, "Goa and Portugal: History and Development," I thought I would posit the historical evolution of the Goan peasantry, fashioned as it was by the considerations of the colonial state, with the issue of development and then proceed to locate the agrarian question in the context of Goa's struggle for freedom.

The role of the peasantry in India's struggle for freedom has been the subject of intensive scholarly research in recent times. However, in any discussion on the nature of agrarian change in India under colonialism, the case of Portuguese Goa is invariably ignored. A comprehensive and analytical inquiry into the relations between the peasantry and the state in colonial Goa during the course of this territory's struggle for freedom, when the issue of the mobilisation of an impoverished and disgruntled peasantry loomed large on the canvas of the nationalist movement, is, therefore, a desideratum.

The time-frame has been selected with an objective to examine the agrarian question within the context of the larger socio-political canvas of Goa's anti-imperialist struggle, for which the opening salvo was fired on June 18, 1946, and it lasted till December 19, 1961 when Goa was liberated from the Portuguese rule and merged with the Republic of India. In this connection, the dynamics of Goa's freedom-struggle has been probed with the help of the methodological tool of oral tradition employed in tandem with archival sources.

The paper attempts a critical evaluation of the agrarian question in Portuguese Goa for the period following T. R. de Souza's *Medieval Goa* (1979) which has not yet been comprehensively undertaken. It studies the colonial transformation of Goa's land system and inquires into the impact of the two world wars, of the intervening international economic crisis of the early thirties as well as the emergent mining industry, on the status of the individual cultivator. It attempts to define the nature of agrarian stratification, status and power in an atmosphere of stifling dictatorship at home, on the one hand, and independence, democracy and socialism taking roots in the neighbouring Indian Union, on the other. Further, the study investigates the interaction between the rural Goan and land, discerning the local land tenurial patterns, especially the systems of *bhaattkari mundkari* and *comunidade*. An inquiry has been made about the largely inequitable nature of the contemporary agrarian structure, the condition of rural indebtedness, the contribution of the alien regime to the existing socio-economic disparities in the countryside, and the nexus between the land owner and the foreign ruler. Besides tracing the development of colonial feudal capital in the Goan countryside, the agrarian 'reforms' introduced by the Portuguese on the eve of their departure from the Goan shores as a reaction, though much belated, to the territory's struggle for freedom, have also been taken up for review.

The paper has addressed itself to some fundamental questions about the role of nationalist organisations in mobilising the peasantry; about their attitude towards the land question; and the inability of the immediate agricultural producer to struggle in an organised manner against the shackles of exploitation. A major issue that has been raised in this paper is the near-total absence of any agrarian question on the agenda of the nationalist organisations in Goa despite the existence of an economically depressed peasantry.

The paper addresses itself to questions such as:

- Why did the freedom-fighters fail to muster support for the struggle from within?
- What was the role of the nationalist organisations in mobilising the weaker sections of the agrarian sector?
- What was the attitude of the nationalist leaders and organisations towards the land question?
- Why was the immediate agricultural producer unable to struggle organisedly against the shackles of colonial exploitation?

In the light of the above questions, an examination of the extent of exposure of the peasantry to and its role in the freedom struggle reveals the failure of the techniques of mobilisation, if any, that were employed by the nationalist organisations. The question that must be asked is whether they were unable to translate the disgruntlement of an impoverished peasantry into a mass movement for liberation and therefore, preferred to depend on the government of India in this regard; or, whether the independence of India prompted them to wait for the 'imminent' liberation of Goa and hence they did not work towards mobilising the peasants into mass action.

This study, it is hoped, will generate knowledge not only on the complexities of the land question in Goa on the eve of the territory's liberation from colonial yoke, but it will go a long way in improving our understanding of the dynamics of Goa's struggle for freedom, in particular about the techniques of mobilisation employed by the nationalist organisations.

With regard to the current debate on the *mundkarato* and the *comunidade* systems, this study aims at providing a much-needed historical understanding of the genesis and evolution of these issues. It seeks to explain the process of agrarian transition that took place in Goa during the colonial rule which is of fundamental importance in understanding the agrarian question today. The merger of Goa into the Indian Union was a significant agent of change in the agrarian society, especially regarding its institutional and ideological superstructure. A brief examination of this aspect constitutes the final component of this paper.

The first part of this paper aims at providing a better understanding of the evolution of the peasant society in colonial Goa within the development paradigm, and the second, examines in detail the exposure of the peasantry to and its role in the territory's struggle for freedom.

The Historical Evolution of the Agrarian Question

The Goan economy down the centuries has been predominantly an agricultural one. The primary occupation of the Goans during the period of study was agriculture, accounting for 64% and 58% of the total working population of the territory in 1950 and 1961, respectively. Let us now trace the historical evolution of the agrarian question in Goa.

Goa has been gifted by nature with a verdant, undulating landscape which is criss-crossed by a fine network of rivers and streams and long stretches of golden beaches. Physiographically, Goa can be divided into the three zones of the Eastern Sahayadris, Central Uplands and the Western Coastal Plains. It possesses a rich natural resource base of biotic as well as abiotic, exhaustible and inexhaustible, and developed as well as potential natural resources. Its strategic location, entrepot status and rich natural resources had made Goa a cynosure of Deccani rulers and European maritime powers at different times in its history. Hence both seaward (to be understood within the *Goa Dourada* image from the 16th century onwards) as well as 'Ghatward' (the *Goa Indica* image) influences have played an important role in shaping the developmental profile of this territory.

The etymology of the place-name 'Goa' contains reference to a fertile land well endowed with agricultural and faunal wealth, as is indicated in the pre-Sanskritic *guwi* (arecanut) and *goen-bab* ("an inclined ear of paddy" with the adjective 'inclined' denoting prosperity) to the Sanskritic Gomantak ("the land where cows abound") and the Luso-Indian *goemoat* ("a fertile and refreshing land" according to Diogo do Couto). Further, the 'Paradise of Indra' of the *Suta-Samhita*, the Kadamba '*kalyan gude*' ("abode of welfare") and *Sunaparant* ('golden land beyond') are some other appellations by which this land was known in ancient times.[2]

Gaonkari and Ghar-Bhaatt

The Goan economy down the centuries has been predominantly an agricultural one. The Parashuram legend symbolises the process of the creation and the agricultural development of the unique ecosystem of Goa, the low-lying, reclaimed coastal *khazans*, through the agency of the brahmins. The brahmins established their hegemony over the economic resources and socio-ritual practices of the coastal society. The *khazan* lands were developed through the institution of the *bous* controlled by them and they also administered the temples and their assets through managing committees or the *mahazanias*. The temples were served by artisans and professionals who enjoyed a reciprocal right (*namoxin*) in the cultivable lands. The 'Parashuisation' of this society enabled the brahmins to establish their hegemonic control over the institutions of land and the temple, typifying sustenance and faith.[3] Thus, as *gaonkars* and *mahazans*, the brahmins controlled the *gaunponn* and *devasthan* (temple) and thereby displaced the *gavdas*, kunbis and *velips* who were the original settlers of this territory.

Gaonkari

The most important characteristic of the pre-1510 Goan economy was the institution of the self-sufficient, quasi-autonomous village community known as the *gaonkari*. The reclamation and development of the fertile *khazans* had created a regional coastal society where the cultivation and administration of the village lands was being undertaken by coparcenary co-operatives, the *gaunponns*. A *gaon* is a village, a *gaonkar* a villager who, by virtue of being the descendent of an original settler of the village, is a freeholder; a *gaonkari* is an association of villagers formed to hold the lands of the village on a co-operative basis; and the *gaonponn* can be literally translated as the village administration. The *gaonkars* had framed a set of rules and regulations called the *mandavoli* that served as the basis for the local administration. Thus a *gaonponn* was the traditional "economic organisation of co-proprietors."[4] The Portuguese termed these *gaonkaris* as *comunidades* (communities) because "the *gaonkars* jointly held, administered and enjoyed the village lands."

The *gaonkaris* were thus "little village republics made up of villages of the same clan who came over the *ghats* and settled in the fertile low lands of the Konkan." Hence the ownership of land was vested not in the individual but in the entire community which operated as an interdependent self-contained unit. In the village communities, land was owned in common by the *vangodds* (clan lineages) of *gaonkars* (descendants of the original settlers of the village). The profits accruing from the co-operative coparcenary cultivation of land were divided among the *gaonkars* as *jono* which even today (or rather, especially today, in the context of the surfacing *goenkar/bhaylo*, Goan/non-Goan, tensions) is an important constituent of the Goan identity.

The social stratification of a multi-caste *comunidade* was done along casteist, occupational and hierarchical lines. This indicates the heterogenous nature of the village society subjected to a casteist occupational differentiation operating within a homogenous economic framework. The distribution of the village lands reflected this hierarchical division of the rural Goan society.

The superior lands were split into three sections: one part was kept as the exclusive preserve of the priestly class; the second division that was meant to be used by the *gaonkars*, was sub-divided into two sectors, that is, the houses of the villagers, circumscribed by small plots that were used to grow fruits and vegetables; and secondly, the plots that were cultivated by the *gaonkars* on a collective basis. After deducting the tribute paid to the king and defraying the expenses for the general maintenance of the village, the surplus was divided amongst the *gaonkars* as *zonn*. Thus, *gaonkars* enjoyed a proprietory right in the produce and not in the land as such. The final component of the fertile sector was cultivated with the help of hired labourers known as *kulacharins* who received payment in kind, as a certain portion of the total produce. The less fertile lands were devoted to the maintenance of the servants of the village community and for building roads, to serve as pastures, etc. A third part of these inferior lands were leased out to either *gaonkars* or non-*gaonkars*.

Ghar-Bhaatt (The *Bhaattkar-Mundkar* System)

Within the frame-work of the age-old institution of the village community, Goa possessed the traditional *ghar-bhaatt* (homestead farm) organisation which exhibited the *bhaattkar-mundkar* relationship. The *bhaattkar* is the landlord in whose landed property the *mundkar* lives. "The *mundkar* or a hereditary dweller is an individual who resides with a fixed dwelling in the rustic property of others specially for the purpose of agriculture or watch-and-ward duties, be the dwelling constructed on account of the *bhaattkar* or landlord receiving or not from the latter any assistance in cash or kind for its contribution or establishment."

The relationship between the two was a contractual one. In exchange for the offer of residence, the *mundkar* and his family had to generally guard the *bhaatt* and serve its owner in a domestic as well as an agricultural capacity. The *mundkar* was compensated for the services that he rendered to the *bhaattkar* in kind, generally in terms of parboiled rice.

It was probably the right enjoyed by the *gaonkar* to reclaim land and hold it as his private property that gave rise to this system. Later the introduction of feudalism and the institution of land grants to individuals gave a further boost to the *mundkar* system. The Adilshahi, Vijayanagari as well as the Portuguese rulers promoted feudalism, landlordism and monopoly capitalism in land at the cost of the traditional self-reliant village economy. They disputed the claims of the descendants of the original soil-clearers to the ownership of the village lands in favour of their ruler and thus injected feudalism into the body-politic of this territory.[5]

The Colonial Transformation of Goa's Land System

The following paragraph attempts to briefly dislose the colonial transformation of Goa's land system and also escapsulates the socio-economic characteristics of the colonial regime with a view to highlight the agrarian policy pursued by the alien government.

In order to make an assessment of the nature and impact of the colonial regime in Goa, one may adopt the *Goa Dourada-Goa Indica* model of the image of Goa.[6] The *Goa Dourada* ('Golden Goa') component of this image essentially stresses on the much-touted thesis that Goa is culturally and emotionally Lusitanian: "The transplantation of the West into Eastern lands, the expression of Portugal in India".[7] The Indian base of the land and its people, on the other hand, can be summed up in the *Goa Indica* paradigm. *Goa Dourada* is an outward-looking, seaward image, symbolising the thalassocratic and the 'extended *reconquista*' nature of the *Estado da India* of distinct Eurocentric, Lusocentric and Christocentric dimensions.

The historical evolution of the development profile of Goa can be understood within the *Goa Dourada-Goa Indica* paradigm as well as with reference to the denationalisation thesis[8] as will be apparent from the following paragraphs.

The image of prosperous Goa found acceptance in the Portuguese terminology of *Goa Dourada* or 'Golden Goa.' From its previous images associated with abundance of food and cash crops as well as pasture lands, Goa now came to be famous for the lucrative commerce centred around the 'golden' port. This prosperity, which enabled the City of Goa (present-day Old Goa) to wear a rich urban look and its *fidalgos*, to sport a leisurely, aristocratic lifestyle, was derived from the warehouse nature of the port which paid scant attention to the development of the hinterland (how 'golden' was Goa to the Goans who now found the economy of their homeland in a condition of stagnation?) Even the rich agricultural base of Goa suffered neglect and, at times, damage in the form of violent local reactions to the conversion policy of the Portuguese. This resulted in the import of rice into Goa from the 16th century onwards.

Immediately after the Portuguese conquest of Goa, Albuquerque, in a bid to win over the loyalties of the Hindus of Goa, assured them that their customs and usages would be respected. The land tax was also reduced. However, as the Portuguese strengthened their hold over Goa, the later administrators freely interfered with the local customs and institutions. They legislated sweeping changes in the administration and the functioning of the *comunidades*, which dealt a severe blow to their autonomous and self-sufficient nature. The Portuguese preserved the institution of the *gaonkari* through a major overhauling of its internal mechanism as will be dealt with a little later.

The colonial administration gave encouragement to the institution of private property. The following factors were responsible for the emergence of individual proprietory rights in land:

- In the wake of the Portuguese campaign of frenzied evangelisation, lands belonging to destroyed temples were either gifted to the church or leased out to individuals;
- The lands of those *gaonkars* who had stoutly resisted the pulls and pressures of evangelism met with a similar fate. Such lands were confiscated from the *gaonkars* and transformed into church or private property;
- Those who helped the government in suppressing a rebellion or performing any such 'meritorious deed' were rewarded in terms of land;
- In a bid to create a loyal Luso-Indian progeny that would further the interests of the Portuguese seaborne empire, Afonso de Albuquerque encouraged inter-racial marriages. He assigned plots of land to the *casados*, the Portuguese soldiers who had wedded local women.

Another impact of the colonial rule was the shift in the emphasis of the economy from agriculture to commerce. Seaborne trade dominated the economy of Goa in the first one and a half centuries of the Portuguese rule in this territory. The tremendous wealth and the resultant ostentatious lifestyle of the elite of Goa earned for the land the envious (though misleading) epithet of 'Golden Goa.' During this period agriculture was ignored in favour of the more lucrative external commerce. Even after Goa lost its commercial lucre the government failed to adopt agriculture as a thrust area for development.

With the decline of Portuguese trade centred around the port of Goa, the economic condition of the territory deteriorated further. The aetiology of the widespread economic stagnation that characterised the Goan economy in the 19th century refers to the contribution of the following factors: increased taxes, frequent outbreak of violent revolts, expenditure incurred by the state on crushing these uprisings, integration of the people living in the 'New Conquests', ignorance of local resources, adventurous experimentation with the *comunidade* system, lavish expenditure on buildings and monuments and most importantly, the British factor.[9]

Let us first examine in brief the reaction of the peasantry to the socio-economic policies of the *Estado da Índia.*

The Peasant-as-a-Rebel:

In the early centuries of the Portuguese rule in Goa, the Lusitanised brand of evangelisation, advanced through coercive methods, led to the emigration of the peasants, the 'flight' of their deities and direct resistance offered by them, through non-payment of taxes and the use of violence.[10] This policy of religious persecution had also invited a Hindu response of "everyday resistance" and "avoidance protests" even when they had ostensibly succumbed to the pressures of proselytism, by accepting baptism or emigrating. There was thus another kind of resistance that was offered by the Goans to the Lusitanian cross through syncretic practices followed by the convert community.[11]

In the 19th century as the *Estado da Índia* consolidated its gains in the territories of the 'New Conquests' of Goa and proceeded on a neo-imperialistic spree in Africa, new areas of conflict emerged from within - the revolts of the Ranes and mutinies of the *sipais*.[12] The latter who belonged to the impoverished peasantry of the sub-*Ghat* region unfurled the banner of mutiny as "a desperate gut-reaction ... without clear-cut strategy or aim" every time they were threatened with unemployment or an overseas posting without adequate financial benefits for themselves and maintenance for their families.

The Ranes were feudal lords who had rebelled against their overlords, the Portuguese, and before them, the Sawants of Wadi, in defence of their feudal privileges. Initially, the Portuguese used the Ranes as a '*contra*' force against both the Marathas as well as the Bhonsles. However, as the threat from the Indian rulers dimmed in the 19th century, the Portuguese did not shy away from encroaching on the feudal privileges granted to the Ranes, either independently or at the instigation of the Nadkarnis, the brahmin rivals of the feudal Ranes for the best lands of Sattari and who were to some extent the indigenous beneficiaries of the colonial rule, and the European commercial interests, in the lands and the forests of Sattari.

This led to the outbreak of the revolts of the Ranes which were eulogised in most post-1961 writings as 'glorious' attempts to 'liberate' Goa from the clutches of the colonial regime. In recent times, however, attempts have been made to "deconstruct" the myth of the Ranes as freedom-fighters by arguing, at times, in favour of the "freedom-struggle" waged against them by the Nadkarnis who have been portrayed, rather erroneously, as representing "the traditional village interests." The 19th century revolts of the Ranes throw up issues pertaining to two types of peasants: the rich peasants who functioned as rural local bosses, seeking to preserve their feudal privileges and if possible extend the same; and the pauperised peasants who were the worst hit by the colonial rule. However, both the Ranes and the Nadkarnis, who had stakes in the land, were involved in furthering their own interests in the name of the welfare of the *ryots* and *gaonkars* of Sattari who continued to live a miserable, hand-to-mouth existence. Since the Nadkarnis managed their "freedom struggle" from within the colonial system, the Ranes had to fight against the Portuguese regime. In the revolts that ensued, the *ryots* and *gaonkars* of Sattari whose interests both claimed to uphold, were forced to emigrate into British Indian lands as the border records indicate.

Then again, in the context of the revolts of the Ranes, one perceives a number of "freedom-struggles": in particular, that of the Ranes against the Portuguese authorities in defence of their feudal rights and privileges; that of the Nadkarnis and the other brahmins against the Ranes in defence of the lands that they had acquired through manipulation and in active or tacit collaboration with the Portuguese administration; and that of the British railroad and timber interests against the *ryots* and the *desais* of Sattari with active support from their Lusitanian neighbours from across the Ghats. If one applies the analytical framework of Kathleen Gough, the revolts of the Ranes exhibit features of restorative rebellions, social banditry and at times, mass insurrections for the redress of particular grievances.

The history of peasant resistance in Goa is therefore quite disjointed: conflicts tended to remain localised and confined to particular grievances and hence could not constitute a consistent and formidable challenge to the colonial state. Rather, it remained, to borrow a phrase from David Hardiman, "a collection of histories of local relationships and struggles."

Anglo-Portuguese Treaty of 1878 and the increased pauperisation of the peasantry:

In the 19th century, Portugal, whose king had once assumed the grandiose title of the Lord of the Conquest, Navigation and Commerce of Ethiopia,

Arabia, Persia and India, was elbowed out of the European imperialist race for India as Britannia came to rule the eastern seas. Survival now became the dominant *weltanschuang* of the *Estado da Índia,* even if it meant readjusting its equations with the British in a submissive-dominant, dependant-protector relationship as is indicated in the Anglo-Portuguese Treaty of 1878. This treaty subjected the Goan economy to the dual colonial control of both Portugal as well as England. It witnessed the linking of Goa with British India through a railway line and the development of the port of Mormugao, and thereby, increased Goa's dependence on the Indian sub-continent in terms of both imports and exports.

As a result of this treaty the means of transportation, linking Goa with British India, underwent considerable improvement and extension. But this was regarded as an attempt on the part of the British to extend their hold over Goa, not politically, as they had long since desired, but economically, by converting Goa into a dependency of theirs. The treaty resulted in the outflow of salt and other commodities from Goa into the British territories of India through the cancellation of customs duties and the railway link. The *mandde* (popular songs associated with the Catholic community of Goa), *Tratad feringuean kelo/Ingles Goiant ailo* (A treaty has been signed by the foreigners/ ushering the English into Goa); *Soglea sounsarak khobor/segredan kelem munn contrato* (Everyone knows that the treaty was signed in secret) and *Chintuleari caliz fafsota*, express this feeling very lucidly in the following lines. "*Te aileai goinkarank khauchaco*" (they have come to eat the Goans) and "*Povak marlo chepunum*" (they have trampled the Goans to death). Similarly, another *mando, Chintlem na re konnem* (nobody had thought about it), discusses three separate events of the 19th century – the extinction of the army in 1871; the Anglo-Portuguese treaty of 1878 and the demolition of the churches and convents of Old Goa in the early decades of the 19th century. The common factor binding these three incidents is the element of destruction. Thus, the treaty of 1878 is denounced vehemently as an attempt on the part of both the European powers, the British and the Portuguese, to fleece them, the former, by draining the commodities from Goa and the latter, by increasing the taxes so as to compensate for the loss of revenue incurred by the Government on account of the British drain.[13]

The treaty enriched the exchequer, hit the producer and, in the final analysis, ruined the country by subjecting it to the "two-fold British and Portuguese imperialistic exploitation," as has been stated by T.B. Cunha. Trade deficit and mass emigration constituted its most serious consequences. As J.B. Amancio Gracias puts it, "Its (Goa's) commerce has fallen systematically from its old grandeur to the point of reaching levels of absolute poverty and misery." Widespread economic stagnation ushered in by the treaty was responsible for the large-scale emigration of Goans, which in turn produced a remittance-based economy in Goa particularly in the coastal sub-region which contributed to the bulk of the emigrants. Remittances constituted the most important component of the state income in the first half of the 20th century till mining came to contribute substantially to the fledgling economy from the 1950s. The remittances not only brought about an improvement in the quality of the Goan's life but also helped to prop up the dwindling finances of the *Estado da India.*

The Peasant-turned-*Émigré*

A majority of the first generation international emigrants from Goa came from a peasant background. The stagnation of the Goan economy had forced them to migrate into the urban centres of British India especially Bombay, Calcutta and Karachi. While in the earlier centuries they had emigrated in defence of their faith, now they did so in search of sustenance and better employment opportunities. They were absorbed on ship and on land as waiters, butlers, cooks, servants, tailors, musicians and governesses. In 1900, 29% of the Goan emigrants in Bombay were serving as cooks, butlers and governesses, 21% as servants and 20% as clerks, while in the 1950s, 18% of them were cooks and waiters, 8% clerks, tailors and governesses, 2% musicians, 37% seamen and 18% unemployed.[14]

The Goan Catholics, on account of their Lusitanian background, far outnumbered the Hindus in the emigration statistics and came to be gripped by an intense climate of mobility.[15] In 1900, when Goa had a population of 4.86 lakhs, 6% of the population of Bardez and 11% of the residents of Salcete had outmigrated with Bombay serving as their most favoured destination. Two decades later, out of a population of 4.69 lakhs, 2 lakhs had settled in British India (which received about 50,000 migrants), East Africa, West Asia and Burma. By the mid-20th century the number of emigrants stood at 1,80,000 with a lakh in India (of which 80,000 lived in Bombay), 30,000 in Pakistan, 30,000 in Kenya and Uganda and 20,000 in the Persian Gulf. Inspite of this heavy flow of international migration the *émigrés* sought to maintain their Goan identity through clubs and associations in their adopted cities like the famous village and often also caste-based *kudds* of Bombay.[16]

The development of mining in Goa in the 1950s failed to check the outmigration of those Goans who sought professional jobs, educational facilities or an escape from the stifling Salazarist dictatorship. Although Goa had been open to the Indian Ocean littoral since pre-Portuguese times, the flood in international migration of Goans in the 20th century, prompted by the condition of "a moribund economy presided over by a bankrupt state",[17] was characterised by large numbers, wider geographical dispersal and occupational mobility. This was fuelled by the Portuguese Goan educational system which, instead of providing Goans with requisite skills to improve the local economy and their position in it, offered instruction in the English medium with a view to facilitate emigration.

"International migration became incorporated as a socio-economic alternative in the Goan social system".[18] The families of the emigrants improved their lifestyle with the help of the remittances and also the internationally marketable skills of the next generation already cast in the potential emigrant mould. Emigration had led to the further neglect of the agrarian sector. There was a reduction in rights to the comunidade lands and only a microscopic amount of the remittances were ploughed into agriculture which had witnessed a sharp rise in tenants and hired labour. On account of simultaneous internal migration of Goans to the coastal talukas, mechanisation or commercialisation or feminisation of agriculture did not occur as it had been experienced in other countries where large-scale emigration had taken place. Emigration denuded the Goan village of its active and capable human resource leaving behind those who clung on to 'the idiocy of village life' with an "apathetic indolence" and frequently with an assurance of migrant remittances.

In the post-liberation period emigration to the oil-rich Persian Gulf countries has been the dominant theme - almost an obsession - with the Goans. The "Gulfies" in turn have promoted a highly materialistic, leisure-luxury *nouveau riche* pattern of development in their homeland with real estate, tourism and 'commercial complexes' receiving a considerable boost. The recent decades have also witnessed the immigration of people from other states of India like Maharashtra Karnataka, Kerala and Andhra Pradesh, the *ghanti* (one who has come from across the Ghats) immigrants who initially came in search of the least appealing menial and semi-skilled jobs and later took roots in the state, bringing their relatives as later settlers. The '*bhaylo*' (outsider) phenomenon in Goa's development process has increased to such an extent that today the non-Goan is being resented by the *niz goenkar* (original Goan) for having 'infiltrated' into Goa and grabbed a large chunk of the 'fruits' of development thereby depriving the *goenkar* of the same, be it in real estate, commercial centres, hospitality concerns or in acquiring luxury bungalows in upmarket, beachfront residential areas which an average Goan can only dream of.[19]

The Portuguese rule therefore led to the transformation of a fairly viable subsistence economy into a defective and crippled peripheral economy which was incapable of (1) feeding the Goans with local agricultural products, (2) integration of the mass of population productivity into the economic production process, (3) innovative and transformative ability which would invent and manufacture local means of production, and (4) structural differentiation.[20]

Nature of Agrarian Relations

The present study seeks to examine the nature of agrarian relations in the colonial regime on the basis of an analysis of the distribution of cultivated land, the extent of tenancy, the payment of rents by the agriculturists and the state of agriculture.

Distribution of cultivated land: The taxes indicating the distribution of cultivated land in Goa in 1960 gives ample evidence of the inequalities present in the agricultural sector. In that year, 14% of the farms larger than two hectares each (no. 3983), occupied 85% of the total land. On the other hand, farms with an area of more than two hectares accounted for 86% of the total number of farms and constituted about 15% of the land.

Size of the Farm: The disparity in the distribution of the farmland is further emphasised by the fact that the size of an average big farm (above two hectares) was 13.8 hectares and that of a small holding (below two hectares) was just 0.37 hectare. On the whole, the land holdings in Goa were small, scattered and generally unviable economic propositions. These figures also reflect on the existence of income inequalities in the agrarian sector.

Pattern of Land Tenure: The land tenurial systems in Goa which define the fundamental relationship between "man and land and owner and tenant" have considerably influenced the lifestyle of a major section of Goa's population, that is, those engaged in agriculture. In order to investigate more deeply into the interaction between the rural Goan and land, a brief description of the local land tenurial patterns is discussed below.

The multi-dimensional land tenurial system of Portuguese Goa contained forms of proprietory ownership of land ranging from the government and the private person to the religious institutions and the *comunidades*. This pattern of ownership of land indicates that the government was the single largest owner of land, accounting for 31.7% of the total, while private individuals constituted the largest collective owner of land holdings (54%) and the village communities followed next (11.2%) with Hindu temples and Christian religious associations occupying the last position (3.1%). The holdings of the municipalities, the charitable institutions and those in litigation constituted a negligible percentage of the total land holdings in Goa.

The emergence of private property in land created a new set of socio-economic relationships at the village level, especially the *comunidades* and the *ghar-bhaatt*, the two principal forms of land tenure that came to characterise Portuguese Goa.

Comunidades:[21] The *gaonkaris*, referred to above, soon shed their original character and tended to become profit-sharing organisations under the Portuguese regime. The *Foral dos Usos e Customes dos Gauncares e Lavradores das Ilhas de Goa* of 1526 had restricted many of the traditional privileges of the *gaonkars*. By this *Foral*, the *gaonkars* were converted into 'renters' of the land whose ownership was now claimed by the king of Portugal. The *koxivorodo* continued, but as a compulsory tax. The *gaonponn* was stripped of its political, judicial and religious functions, to serve as a mere agrarian company whose administration was controlled by the government. The appointment of the president of the *comunidade* council now rested with the government and not with the villagers themselves.

In accordance with the new legislation, the *gaonkars*, who enjoyed the hereditary right of cultivation of the village lands by virtue of being the descendants of the original settlers of the village, came to be transformed into shareholders and newcomers were even included as members of the *comunidade*. The *accionistas*, for example, were non-*gaonkars* who had bailed the *comunidade* out of a financial crisis and had thereby acquired a share in the village produce. By the decree of 1882 all hereditary services were abolished by the state. The working of the *comunidades* was further regulated by the state in 1933 by the Code of the *Comunidades* which underwent several amendments before it was re-enacted in 1961.

These changes discouraged the *gaonkars* from undertaking the task of improving the yield of the land that they tilled. Such a lack of motivation dealt a body blow to agricultural productivity in Goa, although agriculture continued to remain the biggest source of employment to the Goans.

Mundcarato (*Bhaattkar-Mundkar* System)[22]:

Under the colonial rule this system, that had its origins in mutual dependency, now deteriorated into an unjust and exploitative one that was detrimental to the interests of the *mundkars* and their family from whom free service was demanded by the *bhaattkar* under the threat of eviction. This only served to aggravate the existing socio-economic disparities in the countryside.

The nexus between the *bhaattkar* and the *paklo* (a *Konkani* term used to describe the foreigner) rendered the *mundkar* helpless. It was only in 1910, that in response to a representation made by several *mundkars* against their landlords, the Portuguese government framed a set of rules that sought to define the *mundkar*'s relationship with the *bhaattkar*. The royal decree of Augsut 24, 1901 which was considerably modified by the Legislative Diploma no. 1952 dated November 26, 1959 aimed at protecting the *mundkar* from the arbitrary excesses of the *bhaattkar*. The order of 1901 has specified that a *mundkar* could only be evicted by applying to the administrator of the taluka at least six months in advance. In 1959, the laws of eviction were tightened by declaring that the *bhaattkar* had to have a just cause for evicting the *mundkar*.

Denied a political forum, the poor agricultural workers and tenants took refuge in the medium of the folksong to give vent to their frustrations and fears. The *kunbi* song usually hauntingly portrays the toil and exploitation to which they have been subjected. Some of their songs are tirades against the libidinous activities of the landlord's son and the Portuguese soldier against whom the *kunbis* are helpless as the former enjoy the protection of the colonial government.

Payment of Rent: This yardstick, that can be used to understand agrarian relations, reveals high rents of upto 50% of the gross product, accompanied by insecurity of tenure and an absence of an assurance of a profitable yield from the land which adversely affected the standard of living of the cultivators. Such a system was obviously not conducive for the development of agriculture.

State of Agriculture: Stagnation - In 1961, agriculture was the most important and the least productive economic activity in the state. This has been evident by the fact that while agriculture absorbed about 3/5th of the total labour force of Goa, it contributed to only about 1/6th of the total income of the state, although land revenue was an important direct tax.

The colonial government failed to increase agricultural productivity despite favourable natural resources. In fact, faulty governmental planning and neglect had resulted in the import of foodgrains worth Rs. 3 crores into Goa on the eve of its liberation.

Although it had been the backbone of the Goan economy through the ages, agriculture remained a backward sector in the 1940s and 1950s on account of: lack of mechanisation, absence of adequate irrigation facilities, reduction in soil fertility, unavailability of chemical fertilisers, frequent outbreak of diseases and pests, neglect of modern techniques of cultivation and superior quality seeds, migration of agriculturists to the mining sector in search of improved prospects, inequitable nature of land tenure and governmental neglect.

Goa "slumbered on" till the Second World War, when in the wake of worldwide decolonisation in general, and Goa's struggle for freedom in particular, Portugal made a belated effort to develop Goa through a Development Plan in 1952 (which boosted mining activity, expanded education and improved sanitation) and an Agricultural Mission was sent to Goa in 1955. However these efforts were too few and came in too late to be effective.

The economic blockade imposed by the governement of India in 1954 on Portuguese Goa as a strategy to hasten the liberation of this "colonial pimple," awakened the colonial regime to the need to improve agriculture. The Agricultural Mission of 1955 suggested methods to improve the productivity of this sector and identified insecurity of tenure as the major hindrance in this regard. An agricultural front was established to develop agriculture along scientific lines.

The Second World War gave a boost to mining which weaned agricultural labourers away from their traditional occupation. The consequent labour-vacuum in agriculture persuaded the then governor-general, Col. José Cabral, to introduce reforms in this ailing sector. Attempts were made to transfer control of the paddy fields of absentee landlords to the tillers of the soil; rice was purchased from the local peasants at controlled prices; and a financial scheme of 50% (initially 30%) subsidy and 50% loan was introduced in order to enable the peasants to undertake the construction of permanent improvement works.

However, these reforms failed to take off in an appreciable way because of the inefficient implementation and apathetic attitude of the peasantry who failed to understand the propaganda of these schemes that was carried out by the government in the Portuguese language.

Impact of Mining: Besides having an adverse impact on the fertility of the soil, mining also created a labour crisis in agriculture. The stagnated nature of this economic sector forced the struggling cultivators to migrate in search of more lucrative sources of employment. In the first few decades of the 20th century, the large-scale emigration of Goans produced an acute scarcity of manpower in the countryside. By the middle of this century, the mining fever gripped the low-wage agricultural labourers. During the monsoons, when heavy rains forced the mines to work at a reduced capacity, these farmers practised sustenance-agriculture. Initially, the shortage of labour led to the mechanisation of agriculture to some extent, however, when the mining industry mechanised itself, the surplus labour returned to agriculture causing a sharp fall in the wage-levels there.

Having inquired into the largely inequitable nature of the contemporary agrarian structure, the contribution of the alien regime to the existing rural socio-economic disparities and the nexus between the landowner and the foreign ruler, let us now proceed to the second aspect of the problem.

Agrarian Question and the Liberation of Goa, 1946-1961

In the second half of the 19th century and the opening decades of the 20th century, the exploited and the stagnant nature of the Goan economy provoked prominent Goan political leaders like Francisco Luis Gomes, Fr. A. F. X. Alvares and Luis de Menezes Bragança to raise their voices in protest. These leaders, through the might of their pens and the power of their oratory, tried to infuse a love and concern for their homeland amongst the people. At the same they offered concrete suggestion for the nationalist revival of the Goan economy. They strongly advocated economic self-reliance, based on a strong, productive agrarian sector with agro-based industries, and spread of education as a primary condition before any demand for political independence could be made.

Francisco Luis Gomes devoted his work, *Liberdade da Terra e a Economia Rural da India Portuguesa* (1862), to a study of Goan agriculture, especially its systems of land tenure. The preface of this work is in itself a scholarly exposition of the impact of the colonial policy of Portugal on Goan agriculture. He expressed his disappointment over the fact that the ideals of the French Revolution, liberty, equality and fraternity, had failed to touch land which continued to be governed by a system of privileges. Gomes had strongly championed the cause of liberating the land from the collective control of the *comunidade*. The *Liberdade da Terra ...* campaigned against the *comunidade* for being no longer suited to the exigencies of the time and instead called for its replacement by individual and tenant ownership. He stood for individual ownership of land and asked for every farmer the right to own and dispose off one's land. Gomes also advocated the sale of all public lands as well as those that belonged to religious institutions.[23]

In order to increase the income of his motherland and make it as self-sufficient as possible, Fr. Alvares advocated the optimum utilisation of its existing natural resources. He also spoke of the introduction of new, high-yielding crops in Goa and at the same time called upon the people to expand and diversify the existing home-based industries. He made a special appeal to the Goan youth to renounce merry-making which was indulged in on feast days in the name of saints and instead take up the laborious, yet rewarding cultivation of the crop, *mandioca*. Fr. Alvares felt that "this would channelise the superficial pleasures of dancing and feasting into the true joys of work, sweat and sacrifice." As the yield of *mandioca* per acre was six times that of rice or wheat, he urged the people to take up the cultivation of this crop which would not only increase their personal income but would also improve the finances and food stocks of their motherland. Citing the examples of Trichinopoly whose prosperous economy had been built on its arecanut and banana plantations, this *swadeshi*-minded prelate censured his fellow countrymen for ignoring the lucrative commercial potential of the local coconut and mango plantations. Goans were urged to export coconuts, coconut oil, cashew nuts, jackfruits, tamarind, mango pickles and sweets to the chief metropolitan cities of British India. [24]

The liberal and secular promises made by the Republican government (established in Portugal in 1910) remained unfulfilled as the dictatorial regime of António d'Oliveira Salazar assumed power in Lisbon. The *Estado Novo* of Salazar was an authoritarian, corporate political organisation which imposed severe curbs on the civil liberties of the people of Portugal of its colonies, with the latter being also subjected to the humiliating *Acto Colonial*. In Goa, political parties and public meetings were banned, newspapers were severely censored and nationalist literature was confiscated. "The unchecked sway of the Portuguese imperialism over us implemented by an indifferent and callous bureaucracy, takes no account of the people's voice and needs, and represents an anachronism in the midst of progress and emancipation," commented a group of eminent Goans in Bombay.

On June 18, 1946 the opening salvo of Goa's anti-imperialist struggle was fired by the veteran socialist leader, Ram Manohar Lohia, when he publicly challenged the Portuguese government's ban on civil liberties in

Goa. The Indian National Movement had by then arrived at a critical juncture. British Indian newspapers reaching Goa were full of particulars of the ideology of the movement and the courage and determination of its top leadership. Their contents fired the nationalist sentiments of the Goans and gradually the idea of launching a similar struggle in Goa took shape in the minds of the local people.

As the struggle for civil liberties transformed itself into a movement for the liberation of Goa, new politically conscious organisations sprung up in this territory. These were primarily interested in "the attainment through peaceful means, of freedom from foreign rule and the entry of Goa into the Indian Union on the basis of self-determination." Most of them had not applied themselves to the land question from the long term point of view. Their approach was more emotional, based on the Gandhian principle of land to the tiller without fully examining the modalities of this economic problem.

There were, of course, exceptions, like T. B. Cunha, whose speeches and writings aimed at enlightening the people about the economics of the Portuguese rule in Goa. One of his most notable works in this regard was an analysis of the government's extortionist policy entitled *The Rice Problem in Goa.*

Inspired by a contemporary resolution of the Indian National Congress on the issue of land reforms, Madhav Bir, a freedom-fighter from Goa, organised a *kisan sangh* or a farmers' association in the village of Nerul in 1942. This association aimed at organising the peasants into a co-operative farming unit and popularising amongst them modern techniques of cultivation that were in tune with the local conditions. A literacy campaign was also initiated amongst the peasants.

Ram Manohar Lohia, the eminent Indian socialist leader who had flagged off the 18th June 1946 struggle for the restoration of civil liberties in Goa, had addressed a letter to the Goans in which he had appealed to them, especially the villagers, to organise themselves and adopt strong measures, like the boycott of the payment of taxes, till their difficulties were removed. Lohia advised the Goans to revive village industries, such as the manufacture of *khadi* or hand-spun cloth, and establish new ones. He also championed the cause of co-operative farming. However, these reforms were to follow the restoration of civil liberties and the attainment of liberation from foreign rule.

In the 1930s and the 1940s, nationalist organisations were operating within Goa in the guise of socio-cultural associations like the *Goa Seva Sangh*, the *Gomantakiya Tarun Sangh*, the *Vidyarthi Congress*, the Goa branch of the *Rashtriya Seva Dal*. They aimed at generating political awareness amongst the youth and the villagers. The *Goa Seva Sangh* was concerned with spreading the message of Gandhian nationalism in Goa. Its workers held spinning classes, sales of *khadi* cloth and handicrafts and moved from village to village in order to propagate nationalist ideas. These house-to-house contacts proved to be invaluable in harnessing support for the cause of Goa's anti-imperialist struggle. Such organisations and individuals tried to infuse a feeling of patriotism amongst the villagers through the medium of *bhajans* and *jalsas*. Nationalist plays like *Jalta Gomantaka* were staged at frequent intervals within and outside Goa. Sakharam Barve, a noted playwright and *keertankar*, sought to arouse the patriotic sentiments of the Goans through dramas and *kirtans* which he frequently performed in the border areas.

The poems composed by patriotic poets testify to the discontent of the Goans and the repressive and exploitative nature of the Portuguese colonial administration. In one such tirade addressed against the governor-general, Bossa, the poet vividly describes the prosperous condition of the *bhaattkar* ("the paunches of the landlords grow bigger") and adds that "still the 50 % rent that they collect from their tenants is not sufficient." This condition of plenty was being enjoyed by the landlord at a time when the poor were finding it very difficult to make both their ends meet due to low wages, corruption, black marketeering and governmental indifference to their plight. In all of their patriotic compositions, the nationalist poets of Goa generally made a special mention of the underprivileged *kunbi* and the *gavda* communities to which the agricultural labourers and the *mundkars* belonged.

The nationalist organisations like the National Congress (Goa) possessed village committees that were formed to gear up nationalist consciousness in the countryside. The manifesto of the *Azad Gomantak Dal* identified land reforms as one of its objectives. However, the first priority of these organisations was the independence of Goa from colonial rule. To the freedom-fighters, the extension of the alien rule was the first step towards the amelioration of the socio-economic disabilities under which the Goans had suffered for so long.

The marginal farmers, *mundkars*, tenants and agricultural workers were considerably affected by the ongoing struggle against imperialism. They were full of admiration for their fellow countrymen and women who braved the Portuguese bullets and offered themselves for arrest at great personal sacrifice. Ram Manohar Lohia, in a letter addressed to the Goans, had mentioned that he was approached by a villager from the northern taluka of Goa, Pernem, who admired Lohia only for having defied the Portuguese authorities and consequently suffered imprisonment on two occasions. The man, writes Lohia, was only vaguely aware of the ongoing struggle for freedom. Lohia had explained to him the ideals for which the struggle had been launched and requested him to spread the message in and around his village.

The participation of the agricultural workers was generally at two levels, some of them were emboldened enough to join nationalist organisations like the *Azad Gomantak Dal*. Here they received military training in order to enable them to work actively for the cause of Goa's liberation. Others served as couriers and supplied the freedom-fighters with food, clothes and shelter. Besides agricultural workers, the shepherds (*dhangars*), milk-vendors (*gavlis*) and the village artisans also frequently lent a helping hand to the freedom-fighters.

However, the nationalist organisations like the *Azad Gomantak Dal*, the National Congress (Goa) and the Goan People's Party preferred to wait for the government of India to free their homeland of colonial rule. This happened on December 19, 1961 with the success of the Indian Army's "Operation Vijay." Goa now joined the national mainstream of planned development at the time of its liberation in 1961. Liberation brought with it a revolution of rising expectations and close to four decades down the road its economy has performed well and is surging ahead of other states of the Indian Union with respect to socio-economic indicators such as birth and death rates, per-capita income, urbanisation, levels of literacy and education and bank deposits. Goa's manufacturing sector has attained a commendable rate of growth, and the state is in the process of switching over from the pre-liberation import-oriented economy to a post-liberation production-oriented economy.

The Goa Government aims to usher Goa into the next century with "sustainable physical and socio-economic development" based on the twin principles of conservation and development and "protect and produce", by resolving the various gaps and structural bottlenecks that have so far cropped up in the realisation of the ideal of balanced regional growth. It therefore drew up a Regional Plan for Goa, 2001 A.D. which aimed at achieving

1. rationalisation of intra-regional disparities in development,
2. integrated resource utilisation,

3. balanced provision of urbanised opportunities and choices,
4. integrated rural development,
5. environment conservation and
6. improvement of quality of life.

In addition to such a strengthening of the intra-regional socio-economic and functional unity, the Regional Plan seeks to develop the vital relationship with the surrounding hinterland. This is proposed to be achieved through "a systematic land utilisation strategy, spatial articulation of economic activities and development of a hierarchy of interconnected rural and urban settlements."[25]

However, with the year 2001 A.D. just around the corner, agriculture has become a casualty of the tourism industry-oriented development that characterises Goa today. Fields are being filled up to erect apartment blocks and the rural population prefers white-collared jobs and tourism-related employment. *Comunidades* and the issue of the *mundkars* are still subject to a lot of discussion and debate in various public fora and in the letters-to-the-editors columns of the local dailies.

> "In human affairs, the logical future, determined by past and present conditions, is less important than the willed future, which is largely brought about by deliberate choices - made by the human free will."
>
> \- René Dubois[26]

NOTES AND REFERENCES

1. Vab Matre & B. Weiler (eds.), *The Earth Speaks,* Warrenville, Ill.: Institute for Earth Education, 1983, p. 117.
2. Pratima Kamat, *Farar Far: Local Resistance To Colonial Hegemony In Goa, 1510-1912*, Panaji: Institute Menezes Braganza, 1999, pp. 6-8.
3. *Ibid.,* p. 40.
4. Rui Gomes Pereira, *Goa*, II, *Gaunkari -The Old Village Associations,* Panaji: A. Gomes Pereira, 1981, p. iv.
5. T. R. de Souza, *Medieval Goa,* New Delhi: Concept Publishing Co., 1979, p. 71.
6. Caroline Ifeka, "The Image of Goa," in *Indo-Portuguese History: Old Issues, New Questions,* T. R. de Souza (ed.), New Delhi: Concept, 1985, pp. 181-195.

7. A statement attributed to Salazar, in T.B.Cunha, *Goa's Freedom Struggle,* Bombay: Dr. T. B. Cunha Memorial Committee, 1961, p. 455.
8. The thesis propounded by T.B. Cunha in his treatise, *The Denationalisation of the Goans.*
9. B. S. Shastry (ed.), *Socio-Economic Aspects of Portuguese Colonialism in Goa: 19th and 20th centuries,* Belgaum: Yarbal Printers, 1990, p. 14.
10. Pratima Kamat, "No Taxation without Cessation of Religious Persecution! Agrarian Protests against the Colonial Religious Policy in Goa, 1559-1583," in *Agrarian India: Problems and Perspectives,* E. K. G. Nambiar (ed.), Calicut: Association for Peasant Studies, Univ. of Calicut, 1999, pp. 23-38.
11. Pratima Kamat, "The Politics of Conversion and Collaboration of the *Estado da India* and the Hindus of Goa, 1510-1789," in *Vasco Da Gama and India,* T. R. de Souza & João Pedro Garcia (eds.), Lisbon: Fundação Calouste Gulbenkian, 1999.
12. Pratima Kamat, *Farar Far,* chs. 5-7 and Conclusion.
13. The *manddes* are from the personal collection of Mr. Agapito Miranda, Margao. Please refer to Pratima Kamat, in "Political Life of Nineteenth Century Goa as reflected in its Folksongs," *Goa: Cultural Trends,* P. P. Shirodkar (ed.), Panaji: Directorate of Archives, Archaeology and Museum, Govt. of Goa, 1988, pp. 229-242. Also see Celsa Pinto, "Goa Under the Anglo-Portuguese Treaty of 1878: A Phase in Portuguese Colonialism", *Socio-Economic Aspects of Portuguese Colonialism in Goa, 19th-20th Centuries,* B. S. Shastry (ed.), 1990, pp. 46-63.
14. M. N. Pearson," The Portuguese in India," in *The New Cambridge History of India,* Gordon Johnson (ed.), Cambridge: Camb. Univ. Press, 1987, p.156.
15. T. R. de Souza (ed.), *Goa Through the Ages - An Economic History,* II, New Delhi: Concept, 1990, p. 247.
16. M. N. Pearson, *op. cit.,* pp. 155-156.
17. *Ibid.,* p. 105.
18. *Ibid.,* p. 158.
19. Pratima Kamat, "Crítica a algumas das principais questões de desenvolvimento da Goa de hoje," Rosa Maria Perez (ed.), *Histórias de Goa,* Lisboa: Museu Nacional de Etnologia, 1997, pp. 125-143
20. Richard Merrit & Bruce M. Russet (eds.), *From National Development to Global Community,* London: George Allen & Unwin,1981, p. 286.
21. António de Emilio, *As Comunidades de Goa,* Lisbon: Bertrand, 1890; Maximo Menezes, *Breves Notas sobre a História das Comunidades de Goa com Diversos Mapas Anexes,* Goa: Tipografia Nacional, 1961; Filipe Nery Xavier, *Bosquejo Histórico das Comunidades de Goa,* Bastora: Tipografia Rangel, 1804.
22. Report of the Goa Land Reforms Commission, Panaji: Govt. Printing Press, 1964.
23. Deepa Kolwalkar, *Francisco Luís Gomes: His Contribution to the Growth of Political Consciousness in Goa,* M. A. dissertation, Goa University, 1991.

24. F. X. Alvares, *Mandioca,* Bastora: Tipografia Rangel, 1916, p. 17. On the title page of this pamphlet Alvares exhorts "The people of Goa to rise and work" ("*Povo de Goa: Surge e Trabalha*"). Pratima Kamat, *Farar Far*, ch. 4.
25. *Regional Plan for Goa, 2001 A. D.,* Panaji: Town and Country Planning Department, Govt. of Goa, 1988, pp. 292-3.
26. John L. Seitz, *The Politics of Development*, Cambridge, Mass: Blackwell Inc., 1988, p. 170.

11

Land Tenure and People in Daman

Past and Present

LÍVIA BAPTISTA DE SOUZA FERRÃO

When they arrived in India, the Portuguese rulers following a policy of friendship and understanding did not care to antagonise their Indian subjects and so they adopted most of their rules and customs.

In the *Regulations* dated March 5, 1505 given to Viceroy D. Francisco de Almeida, King Manuel I expressed his wish that, in those first years of the Portuguese presence in the Orient, it was important " ... *to bestow favours and not to harm the Indian people* ... ".[1] Three years later, in his instructions to Diogo Lopes de Sequeira he ordered him to honour and protect them in every way in his capacity.[2]

We must then assume that the first Portuguese conquerors did not impose new customs or even a foreign system on their Indian subjects. It is clear that they observed a continuity of the local institutions as they accepted some portions of their system which they adapted as time went on, to meet changing needs.

In the kingdom of Gujarat, it seems that grants were freely given by the king and that land concessions or assignments were common.[3] For practical reasons, as we will refer to the agrarian system established by the Portuguese Crown in Daman at the end of the 16th century, we will distinguish between small and large assignments both of which will be described as *iqtas*[4] and both of which implied liability to military service.

By small assignments we mean the lands which were given to military men who were obliged to present themselves with horses and arms whenever they were called up for service or in times of war.[5] These tenants could apparently settle down quietly in a village and enjoy the revenue it yielded and we assume that the peasants accepted this arrangement without much difficulty. The life in these villages went on as before as the only difference for the peasants was the revenue collector who came to live in it with the authority of the king behind him. The larger assignments were given to men of rank. These concessions involved liability to personal service and also the maintenance of a body of troops to serve the king when he needed it.

There were also reserve lands or Crown lands but, in this case, these lands were administered directly by the revenue officials for the benefit of the Treasury. Therefore the Maratha chieftans were able to collect revenues from two main sources: the income derived from the assignments and the rents collected from Crown lands.

This was the agrarian system the Portuguese found when they arrived in Daman. So, they adapted several social, political and economic aspects of the Indian institutions and established in the North Province as well as in other regions in India, the *prazo* system.[6]

Due to the similarity of a number of details pertaining to the agrarian system established in this region at the time, it is understandable that the *prazo* system was well accepted by the Indians.

Initially, most of the *prazos* or villages as they were called in Daman, were bestowed by the viceroy in the name of the king. The Portuguese *foreiros* as a remuneration for their services to the kingdom were granted a portion of land and the income from this source described as their right or perquisite was intended to suffice for their maintenance. As time went on, all governors as well as captains of fortresses had also the power to grant favours to these *foreiros.*[7]

D. Constantino de Bragança, at the time of his conquest which occurred in 1559, found Daman[8] divided into provinces while the villages were grouped into 8 parganas[9] - Naer, Poarim, Calana, Sangens, Loaça, Barem, Tarapor, Maim[10] and Danum [11]. The jurisdiction of Daman included more or less 300 villages, small landholdings, palm-groves, *mandovis*[12] and *pallitas.*[13]

In order to provide for the defence of Daman, the viceroy issued an order of bestowal on D. Diogo de Noronha, the first captain-general of the fortress, to give and divide the land as he thought best for the welfare of the people and for the service of the king providing that the payment of a *foro* or tribute was agreed upon. Naturally, all transactions pertaining to the lease of the lands were subject to the sanction of the viceroy.

These *foros* were stipulated according to the revenues got from the lands already tilled and they were paid either in cash or kind[14] or in terms of agricultural implements[15] sometimes acquired with great difficulty by the tillers. As the landlord had to settle in the fortress on account of its defence, he had to have hired labourers cultivating the land under the supervision of a tenant or a patel and, at a stipulated time, he had the right to demand from his tillers the payment of the rents.

Besides this payment, the Portuguese *foreiro* (who was in fact the landlord) had to fulfill certain obligations such as improving the land and defending it against its enemies, living in the fort with his family as well as " ... *not sell, divide or give away the land without the approval of the viceroy* ... ".[16] He had also to support a number of armed men, either Portuguese or Indian, as well as one or more Arabian horses. The duty of this small army paid by the *foreiro* with the income of the village, was to be permanently ready to face the raids made by king Assarceta's men. These incursions which occurred mainly during the harvest season, were always due to the collection of a tax, the *chouto*, which the Portuguese *foreiros* had to pay to the king of Cambay, but which they rarely did.

At the main fortress, there was the factor with the troops maintained by him and there were also smaller centres of authority.[17] In the villages, there were the tenants to whom the factor turned for the revenue. If the tenants rebelled, or refused (as they often did) to fulfill their obligations regarding the supporting of men, arms and horses or if they did not pay the revenue, the Crown could reclaim their lands as well as their *comedias.*[18]

Each *prazo* or village had its own troops which in times of war, would join the main forces at the fortress of Daman, the headquarters of the political and administrative power. It was with this advanced guard which received no financial support from the Crown that these *foreiros* were able to maintain the North Province until the end of the 18th century.

The settlement of the people in the territory under the jurisdiction of Daman as well as inside the fort, was another priority of the Portuguese Crown. Therefore, Viceroy D. Constantino de Bragança in order to help the Portuguese as well as the Indians to settle in the fortress, issued an order to the captain of Daman to distribute small portions of land among the people. These small concessions concerned small landholdings, *terras salgadas,*[19] *hortas,* [20] *palmares,*[21] and *pallitas.* The large assignments concerned whole villages as well the rents derived from parganas, *mandovis* and *cassabes*[22] and were granted, to "*pessoas de merecimento,*"[23] that is, to men of position and rank who had to live in the fortress with their families as well as who had to make improvements on the land and defend it against the enemy.

In Daman, except for the case of the fort of Danum which included all its villages, custom house and *cassabe*, whole parganas were seldom granted. Danum was assigned to Francisco Paim de Melo, the captain of the fort, under the obligation that he would live there with his family, earn no wages, and support a small army of soldiers and servants.[24]

Most of the *prazos da coroa* were leased for the duration of two or three *lives*, whilst others, the smaller ones and therefore with less income, were assigned *in perpetuity*.

For reasons related to the defence of the fortress, only the sons of *foreiros* were allowed to inherit the land. Later on, by warrant of Viceroy D. Antão de Noronha, and at the request of the people of Daman, women were also allowed to succeed their fathers in the tenements.[25] However, if the women could not carry out their engagements they had to hire a tenant willing to carry out in their place the duties which they themselves were unable to perform.

From time to time, the conditions of the tenure were reassessed and the *foreiro* was granted another *life*, besides the ones he had already been granted, as long as the amount paid by his successor was raised by one quarter.

In addition to the revenues yielded by the villages, the *Fazenda Real*[26] could also raise income taxes collected from other sources: the custom duties paid on all merchandise in the *mandovis* of Daman, Poarim and Tarapor;[27] the *durupagem* tax; the duties paid for all the fish and timber entering the *mandovi* of Daman and the selling of oil, cotton, figs and Indian cane in the parganas of Tarapor and Maim, amongst others. The payment of these income taxes were made with local coinage - in *pardaus de ouro*, in *mamudes* and in *ducaras*.[28]

It is clear that the Portuguese did not change the system of collecting the revenues of the villages. It continued as it was during the reign of the Maratha chieftains, that is, through a collector who played the role of middleman between the government and the peasants. He was, in fact, the patel, the head of the village. It was the patel who declared the crop production for the year and his assessment was always accepted by the Portuguese administration. So, we may conclude that there was no direct communication between the farmers and their rulers. Whatever contact there was, was always through the head of the village.

This situation would lead to the exploitation of the farmers, as the Portuguese administration was concerned mainly with the collection of revenues and the forest products from the forests of Nagar Haveli.[29] On the other hand, most of these patels with the authority conferred on them by the king, showed no mercy to the farmers and made them pay more than they had to. We have not found details bearing on the life of the farmers or on their relations with their chiefs at the time except that they must have led a very hard life.

The land was never or at least very seldom farmed directly by its owner. Each landlord had his own tenants who in turn employed tillers and labourers to cultivate the land. These workers had to pay a rent to the landlord which in some villages (Calicachigão or Damão de Cima) was paid in cash but more often in kind. The landlord usually kept for himself one third of the crop production.

In the second half of the 19th century due to several misfortunes in Daman and Nagar Haveli[30] the inhabitants migrated to neighbouring areas. Furthermore, the village chiefs who were, as was mentioned earlier, the only link between the government and the labourers, were given a free hand by the landlords to settle all matters related to the lands. So, their greed increased and they started to demand money, fuel, food items and other products from the tillers. When these unfortunate farmers could no longer fulfill their demands for goods and money, the patels took away their lands.

The situation was intolerable. Therefore, the Governor of Goa in order to improve the revenues of the Treasury, informed the Portuguese authorities in Lisbon of the developments which were taking place in Daman and Nagar Haveli and advised them on the necessity of having direct relations with the local people. The system of patels was then abolished and the farmers and tillers who had fled the country started coming back to their villages. No doubt they were still poor but then they knew that the land they cultivated was their own. Only then did the production increase and this resulted in an improvement in the collection of revenues. So it may be said that it was in fact the peasantry which supported the kingdom by the revenues they furnished.

Prior to the independence of Goa, the district of Daman included two *concelhos*: Daman and Nagar Haveli. The *concelho* of Daman had two *freguesias* - Damão Grande or pargana Naer and Damão Pequeno or pargana Calanã. The *concelho* of Nagar Haveli comprised the *freguesia* known as pargana Nagar Haveli whose headquarters were at Silvassa and which was occupied by the Indian government in 1954.[31]

The district of Daman at present has 22 revenue villages, 8 panchayats, one town which is the taluka of the district, and one municipality. It comprises a total area of 72 kms. of which 66.40 kms. are rural and 23.36 kms. are urban, having a total population of 62,101 inhabitants.[32]

Notwithstanding its climate and soil, the economy of the district is based mainly on agriculture - more than 60% of the workers are engaged in agriculture and allied occupations - although fisheries, salt-pan exploitation and commerce are also very important activities. The main crops of the district are rice (pedi), wheat, pulses and millet besides vegetables and other crops such as fruits, coconuts and sugarcane which are cultivated within 2,500 operational agricultural holdings intercepted throughout the district.[33]

Prior to the independence of the district, there were mostly large landholdings pertaining to a very small number of owners while the actual farmers remained serfs of the landlords. Some of these large properties were former tenements; others were acquired by purchase either from former *prazos da coroa* or from farms which were abandoned by families who had left the country.

When in 1961 Daman became part of the Union Territory of Goa, Daman and Diu, the government of India in view of an agrarian reform in these districts published a number of regulations concerning the abolition of proprietorship of villages. These norms were passed in order to abolish the intermediaries and put the tillers in direct relationship with the government. The rules were also made to simplify the collection of the land revenue and the tenure of land held by the farmers. Furthermore, the government in order to provide for regulations of the terms of tenancy related to agricultural lands in the Union Territories published the *Agricultural Tenancy Act and Rules* which included directives to be followed by tenants in cultivating lands held by them as well as the special rights and privileges granted to the tenants and the protection of these rights. As a result of the agrarian reforms established in the villages, the former proprietors were removed and a great number of farmers were made occupants.[34]

In the subsequent years, many applications from the former landowners were directed to the government demanding compensation from eviction as well as asking for resumption of his property. If the landlord was able to furnish adequate proof of his ownership as well as the extent, identity and other relevant particulars of the land and provided that the landlord required the land to cultivate it personally, the mamlatdar would authorise the resumption of the land.

The landlord had the right to terminate the tenancy of any tenant in his land if he or a member of his family did not live in the village in which the land was located or in a village nearby during the agricultural seasons. He was also not allowed to cultivate any other land and the income from the cultivation of the land he wished to resume work on, had to be the main source of income for his maintenance. Furthermore, he was not entitled to take possession of more than 2 ha. of paddy land in the case of *khazan* or *kher*[35] lands and 4 ha. in the case of *morod* lands.[36]

The rent payable to the landlord by the tenant had to be paid within 30 days from the date of each harvest and could not exceed one-sixth of the total produce of the land.[37] It had to be paid in cash or in kind at the discretion of the landlord or from an agreement between the landlord and the tenant but could never include the rendering of any personal service or labour.

Besides the payment of the rent, the tenant could not transfer by sale, exchange, gift, mortgage or lease any land purchased by him without the sanction of the mamlatdar unless the land was mortgaged in favour of the government for the purpose of a loan for undertaking improvements on the land.

In recent years, due importance was given to increase the agricultural production and so a number of programmes have been devised by the administration to meet the needs and the demands of the farmers. Therefore, several schemes, namely the multiplication and distribution of seeds, manure and fertilisers, plant protection, horticulture, agriculture engineering and farmer training, have been implemented by the directorate of Agriculture. Furthermore, the government has succeeded in increasing the productivity of the land substantially by providing fertilisers and bullocks and lending implements to the farmers during the harvest season.

In Daman (as also in Dadra, Nagar Haveli and Diu) the majority of the tribal population depends for its livelihood on agriculture. However, its farming methods are still very primitive and the practice of shifting cultivation of forest land has not as yet been adopted. Nevertheless, small plots in the reserved forest area in Nagar Haveli were granted to the tribal families on a yearly lease basis for farming by the erstwhile Portuguese government. It was locally known as *teram* cultivation and the practice still continues.

Today, in order to improve the social as well as economic conditions of the local tribal families, grants of subsidy and loans for agriculture projects as well as training courses are given not only to scheduled castes and scheduled tribes but also to small and marginal farmers.

Under the financial assistance of the government of India which has set up a fund to further several developmental plans, the administration of the Union Territories has undertaken the implementation of a number of social and economic programmes.[38]

The achievements of the administration of the Union Territories which have been remarkable were directed mainly to fields like the creation of additional irrigation potential, tree plantation, the allotment of surplus land and house sites, assistance for the construction of houses for the poor; adult education and the setting up of small-scale industries.

Through developmental programmes, agriculture, forestry, animal husbandry, transport, industries and health services are reaching socio-economically backward areas. Besides these programmes, other social and community services which are also being planned, will lead the Union Territories of Daman, Diu, Dadra and Nagar Haveli into a new age.

NOTES AND REFERENCES

1. In his Instructions, the King stated among other things " ... em quaisquer terras onde os houver vos recomendamos muito que favoreçais em tudo quanto puderdes e os honreis e façais honrar e tratar em todas as cousas ... ".
2. Instructions of the King to Diogo Lopes de Sequeira on February 13, 1508.
3. On this subject see B. H. Baden-Powell, *The Land-Systems of British India*, New Delhi, 1988.
4. *Iqta* is the land tenure of Muslim India similar to *emphyteusis*, the Portuguese agrarian system.
5. These men who had to live in their villages as if they were owners, however, later on, they put forward claims so that the holdings could be grants and not assignments. Therefore, the king of Gujarat passed orders on these claims resuming the assignments of those unfit for service and giving them small pensions in cash while the assignments were given to men who were able and willing to perform their duties.
6. The *prazo* was essentially a portion of land which was granted by the king as a recompense for services rendered to the Crown provided that its owner paid annually a tribute to the Crown.
7. The rents and privileges were bestowed by Viceroys D. Constantino de Bragança, D. Francisco Coutinho, D. Luis de Ataíde and D. Antão de Noronha, among others as well as by the captain of the fortress of Daman, Garcia Rodrigues de Távora.
8. This administrative division also occurred in the kingdom of Gujarat. Gujarat was in the 16th century an important province but unfortunately the Portuguese chronicles say very little about this region.
9. *Historical Archives of Goa, Tombo de Damão*, codex no. 7599. In 1996, this *Tombo* was detailed in a paper "Tenants, Rents and Revenues of Daman in the late 16th Century" and presented at the VII conference on Indo-Portuguese History. This register of landholdings includes a large number of manuscripts from the 16th century and are of a great historical value for the reconstitution of an important period of the economic as well as social evolution of this country.
10. Maim as well as Tarapor ceased to be in the possession of the Portuguese Crown in 1739.
11. In *Tombo de Damão*, fl.160, two other *parganas* (Boticer and Gortogar) were also mentioned. However, we will not concern ourselves with the tenements of these *parganas* because while they were leased to Portuguese *foreiros* as they belonged to the Portuguese Crown, they continued, nevertheless,

in the possession of the king of Cambay who in fact collected the revenues derived from them.

12. Custom houses.
13. Lands given by the king of Cambay which had to pay a special tribute, the *salamy.*
14. In Portugal, for instance, we find a great variety of products such as honey, cattle, poultry, sheep, pigs, wine or cereals.
15. As was the case in Nagar Haveli, in the 18th century.
16. *Tombo de Damão*, codex no. 7599.
17. The other territories under the jurisdiction of Daman.
18. That is, the income yielded by *emphyteusis*. Warrant from Viceroy D. Antão de Noronha dated October 18, 1567.
19. Seashore lands.
20. Vegetable gardens.
21. Palmgroves.
22. Administrative unit.
23. *Tombo de Damão*, fl. 162.
24. *Ibid.,* fl. 96.
25. *Ibid.*, fl.162v.
26. The Royal Treasury.
27. These custom houses were usually rented for a three-year period.
28. However, other coins were also used as was the case of the *pardaus de 4 mamudes* and *meio o pardau* or *tangas de prata,* ancient silver coins, currently used in the kingdom of Cambay, also known as *chaparizes.* These coins were worth 10% more than *pardaus de larins* (*Tombo de Damão*, fl.160v).
29. To ensure the military support of the Portuguese against the Muslim rulers and their feudatories, the Marathas decided to give away the territories of Dadra and Nagar Haveli as well as the right of passage to the Portuguese troops from Daman to the Maratha territory. The Treaty was signed on December 12, 1779 but the Portuguese only occupied Dadra in 1783 and Nagar Haveli in 1785. The revenues from these villages yielded Rs. 12,000 each year.
30. After a terrible drought in Nagar Haveli in 1859, the farmers abandoned their homes and lands and left the area. The landlords and the patels taking advantage of this situation, claimed all these lands as their own. But the villages continued to be abandoned and the fields were left uncultivated.
31. From 1954 to 1961 Nagar Haveli was a separate Union Territory. It later became part of the Union Territory of Daman, Diu, Dadra and Nagar Haveli.
32. According to the Census of 1991 – 26,905 lived in urban areas and 35,196 in rural areas.
33. Data forwarded by the Directorate of Agriculture in Daman, in 1997.
34. Besides, the acts, rules, orders and notifications covering tenancy and proprietorship matters, the government realising the injustice done by the *sahukars* and the landowners in Nagar Haveli, created a committee to assess the situation. Through this committee, the lands were surveyed and measured

and the landlords and *sahukars* were asked to release them. The lands were then given to the farmers.

35. *Khazan* land means any low land situated near riversides. *Kher* land is land which has adequate irrigation facilities.
36. Any other kind of land.
37. If a second crop was raised by the tenant during the same year, the raised quantity was not to be included in the gross produce unless the crop was raised with the financial or other assistance of the landlord or if there was a tradition of paying rent in relation to the second crop.
38. Namely, the *Integrated Rural Development Programme*, the *National Rural Employment Programme*, the *Rural Landless Employment Guarantee Programme* as well as the *Health Programme*, the *Maternal and Child Welfare Programme*, the *Family Planning Programme*, among others. On this subject see, *Gazetteer of the Union Territory*, pt. 2: Daman, 1979, pp. 105-108.

12

Kenaf, An Annual Plant for the Paper Industry

Its Viability and Potential Interest for the Economy of Goa

AUGUSTO FÉLIX FRANCISCO RODRIGUES

Introduction

The widely-growing tropical and subtropical Kenaf plant (*hibiscus cannabinus L.*), was used since ancient times in India, the Sudan and Egypt as a producer of textile fibres. It is referred to in Sanskrit literature of ancient India in a document about its cultivation, at the end of the 7th century in Calcutta. It was also equally known in ancient Greece and Rome.

There is a certain controversy about the place or places of the genetic origin of this species. Due to its great geographical spread, it is held that it could have had its origin in East Africa, Asia, Australia or tropical America.

Within an enormous variety of other textile fibre-producing species, jute deserves special mention due to the exceptional quality of its fibre. It occupied a place of importance in the international market, reaching the second position in production behind cotton, the textile fibre *par excellence*.

However, due to the special conditioning of the ecological order, jute is cultivated only in very restricted areas of the world, the major part of production being concentrated in Bangladesh, China, India and Pakistan.

At the beginning of the 1940s, due to the conflicts during World War II and which affected some Asian countries, the production of jute suffered a very significant decrease and its price a notable increase. As a result of these facts, it was necessary to have an alternative for jute and the choice

Translated from the Portuguese by Charles J. Borges

fell on kenaf. Effectively, this plant, showing a greater ecological plasticity, proved to be a good substitute for jute and has been cultivated with success in many tropical and sub-tropical countries.

With the reappearance of the jute fibre in the international market and with the advent of synthetic fibres, more resistant, lasting and cheap, the interest for the kenaf fibre for some time went into a decline. With the passing of time, kenaf production meant mainly for the sack-making industry, came to see better days again.

It is estimated that the production of the kenaf fibre in the world is between 1.3 and 1.5 million tons per year. It is presently cultivated in many parts of Asia (India, China, Thailand, Japan, Korea, Saudi Arabia, Iran, Indo-China, and some countries of Central and Southern America - Mexico, Guatemala, San Salvador, Cuba, Peru and Brazil, and of Africa - Nigeria, the Ivory Coast, Zambia and Tanzania). However, it is in Thailand that cultivation has reached the greatest spread along the River Mekong.

The plant in question, traditionally used for the rope, sack and rough-cloth industry, as earlier referred to, is today raising a new interest in many countries and is assuming a notable importance in the paper industry showing its fibre to be of high quality for the making of cellulose paste.

The cellulose fibres show high resistance and durability and have a high capacity to absorb water even in humid states, and the natural fibres of cellulose do not lose their resistance. It is the combination of this characteristic with that of flexibility which gives cellulose the right for the manufacture of paper. In principle it is possible to get cellulose pulp from any annual plant. However, the technological characteristics required by paper and the economic aspects condition the choice of plants as potential suppliers of the raw material.

At present the major source for the raw material which feeds the cellulose industry is the wood of the forest variety. However, in many regions of the world with a deficit in forest resources, the paper industry is very much dependent on annual plants which stand as a good alternative to the expensive import of pulp for paper. Many annual plants, grasses in particular, have been experimented upon with a view to the production of pulp for paper.

Taking, however, as a term of comparison many plants already studied for the production of paper pulp, the kenaf merits special attention. Effectively as a result of an exhaustive study started in the 1950s in the U.S.A and which covered a large number of annual plants with a view to increase the spectrum of plants potentially suppliers of raw material destined for the paper-pulp industry, kenaf showed special characteristics which point to it as a privileged fibrous variety for the purpose.

Kenaf, as a plant of textile fibre, reached its height of success in the 1970s but after that went into a decline. Presently on discovering its new vocation, it will be able to be a preferred complement of arboreal species for the production of cellulose fibres meant for paper-pulp, a strategic product with growing consumption worldwide and in relation to which India is highly deficient.

The kenaf plant has many uses in the exploitation of its different parts since besides the textile fibre and the paper-pulp, it can be used for fodder, for extraction of oil, for husk and protein, for the making of panels, and for the production of energy, etc.

Materials for writing till the advent of paper

Till the advent of paper, man used a variety of materials as a means of expression of his culture. The invention of paper dates back to the year 105, and is attributed to Ts'ai Lun, a military attaché of the royal Chinese court, who produced paper using Liberian mulberry fibres along with fragments of fishing net, old rags and wastes of hemp. From China the knowledge of the art of producing paper reached Korea only in 600, Japan a few years later, Samarkhand, in Central Asia in 751, and 40 years later Baghdad in the golden period of Islamic culture. From Baghdad, this art went to Egypt around 900 and in 1100 established itself in Morocco. It was from Fez (Morocco) that Europe, through Spain, received this technology in the middle of the 12th century. From Spain it spread to the New World the first factory being set up in Mexico in the third quarter of the 16th century. The market for paper was however, limited. The perfection, of the art of printing by Gutenberg in 1450 allowed a substantial development of the printing press and led to a great demand for paper. This demand grew more during the Renaissance in the 15th and 16th centuries, during which time, literary and scientific works had a wide circulation.

During this period, the main raw material was made up of rags of flax (hemp), and cotton or their mixture. The search for new raw materials was the object of an intense research throughout the 18th century and fell primarily on yearly plants, namely, hemp and jute, and later on, on wood of the forest variety.

The methods of production of paste from wood, namely through the use of chemical products, were first developed in the U.S.A. and in Sweden. As a consequence of this, there was a great boom of factories of paste and paper in Europe and more so in the U.S.A. The pulp industry for paper, due to its peculiar production characteristics, is fairly complex, there being more than 5,000 types of paper.

The production and consumption of paper and cards

The worldwide production of paper and cards in 1997 came up to 299,042 x 103 tons with the U.S.A., Japan and China in first, second and third places with 28.92%, 10.37% and 9.17% of the total, respectively. India, with the second largest population in the world, stood in 20th position with 3,000 x 103 tons, a production that corresponds to 1% of the total.[1]

As regards the annual production, imports and exports *per capita* of paper and cards, the statistics for the year 1997 show that the three countries that were placed the best were U.S.A., Finland and Belgium with 335, 332, and 301 kgs., respectively. India does not figure and the last country to do so in 30th position is Malaysia with a consumption of 87 kgs.

Yet with relation to the consumption of paper, at the beginning of this decade, the U.S.A. already showed the most consumption *per capita,* in the region of 310 kgs. a year, followed by the Scandanavian countries with 225 kgs., the countries of the European Union with 158 kgs. and Australia with 125 kgs. Those with a smaller consumption are the East European countries, with 35 kgs. and smaller still are Latin America with 27 kgs., Asia with 20 kgs., Africa with 7 kgs., there being some countries where the *per capita* consumption has not reached even 500 gms. Goa publishes seven daily newspapers, one fortnightly, one monthly magazine in three languages, English, Marathi and Konkani. The newspapers alone consume annually 5,700 tons of paper with a value of Rs. 119,700,000 which is equivalent to about US $ 2,850,000.

The forecast of a growing worldwide population, the growth in consumption in industrialised nations, and the perspectives of improvement of life in developing countries, inevitably, will lead to a greater demand for paper.

In many cases, the consumption of paper takes on a restrictive character, not because of the lack of internal demands, but due to the limits on imports which for many countries is an intolerable loss of foreign exchange.

Kenaf plant, its botanical characteristics, edafo-climatic demands and cultivation practices

Kenaf (*Hibiscus cannabinus L.*), an annual herbaceous sub-ligneous plant, belongs to the Columnifera order and the Malvaceae family. The genus *Hibiscus* includes nearly 200 species of which a large part is cultivated in tropical and sub-tropical regions.

The kenaf is endowed with a notable ecological adaptation and is cultivated in a wide range of edafo-climatic conditions, reaching heights of 3 to 4 metres and producing high bio-masses, around 80 to 130 tons of green material (aerial part). As regards the soil, the plant prefers those of medium texture, well-drained, having a good proportion of organic material and with pH between 5.5 and 7.

As regards the climate, it needs high temperatures, is very sensitive to frost, does not resist intense cold and does not bear strong winds. During the vegetative cycle, the mean temperature should be not less than 16°C with the optimum between 25° and 28°C bearing high thermic oscillations. The night mean temperature should be between 18° and 24°C.

The formation of capsules and the maturation of the seeds after the beginning of the flowering period, need two to three supplementary months of vegetation and daily temperatures of over 15°. In its reaction to photoperiodism, the cultivated varieties of kenaf act mostly as plants of short days, varying their vegetative cycle from long to short. Regarding water needs, in areas of low precipitation in the dry season, the kenaf plant needs to be watered to the tune of 240 to 490 mm, with a good distribution for the whole cultivation cycle.

The cultivation benefits with an adequate preparation of the soil, avoiding the infesting plants at the beginning of the growth of the plants. The density for the sowing ought to be relatively high, i.e. between 40 to 60 plants per sq. metre in order to obtain plants without branches and uniform, of not a very large diameter, in order to provide a larger percentage of long fibre.

Regarding the mineral fertilization, nitrogen is the principal element responsible for the obtaining of high bio-masses, though phosphorous and potassium are also complementary for the fertilization. The harvesting over large areas ought to be done mechanically. In small areas it can be done manually using a simple sickle.

The Kenaf fibres

The stalk of the kenaf contains two types of fibres. In the cortical layer, long fibres of 2.5 to 4.5 mm. in length are seen and in the ligneous layer, there are short fibres of 0.45 to 0.75 mm. in length.

One can work on the whole stalk or process separately the fractions with long fibres and the short ones which give rise to different types of pulps and consequently different types of paper. The separate processing

Kenaf Flower

Kenaf Plant

of these fractions make a better valuation of the raw material. There exists already equipments which allow the separation of fibres to take place with efficiency.

Mechanical harvesting

The harvesting operation at the end of the whole cultivation process will be lucrative to the farmer only if all the other operations, beginning with the preparation of the soil, have been followed. There are various methods of harvesting which have been utilised already in many countries. These are:

a) cutting the plants in pieces,
b) cutting the whole plant by splitting the stem, and
c) cutting the whole plant tied in bundles.

The viability of the cultivation of Kenaf dependent on pedo-climatic conditions of Goa

The climate of Goa is well marked by the monsoon season. The water cycle encompasses three processes: evaporation of the waters of the ocean and evapo-transpiration of the continental part, precipitation under liquid form and draining of the waters to the sea through various rivers, from Tiracol in the north to Galgibaga in the south. The most rainfall occurs only in the months from June to September, and there is a long dry period of about eight months, with its negative effects on the productive potential of agro-ecosystems. The annual mean rainfall is in the region of 3,000 mm. The relative humidity which has a mean annual value of 75.6% reaches in the monsoon 97%, a level extremely high which affects the well-being of the people. The maximum temperatures reach 34°C and the minimum descend to 20°C.

The annual hours of sunshine are 2791.1, corresponding to a percentage of 64.2 which can be considered mean when compared with other areas of the world. However, it is very low in June (19%) and attains its highest value in February (89.5%). According to the classification of Thornthwaite, Goa shows the following climatic type: B3 A' w2 a' (humid, mega-thermic, a big deficit of water in winter and non-existent or little thermic efficacy in summer).

With reference to the pedological matters, Goa has largely soils of natural ferralitic nature (about four-fifth of the total area) characterised

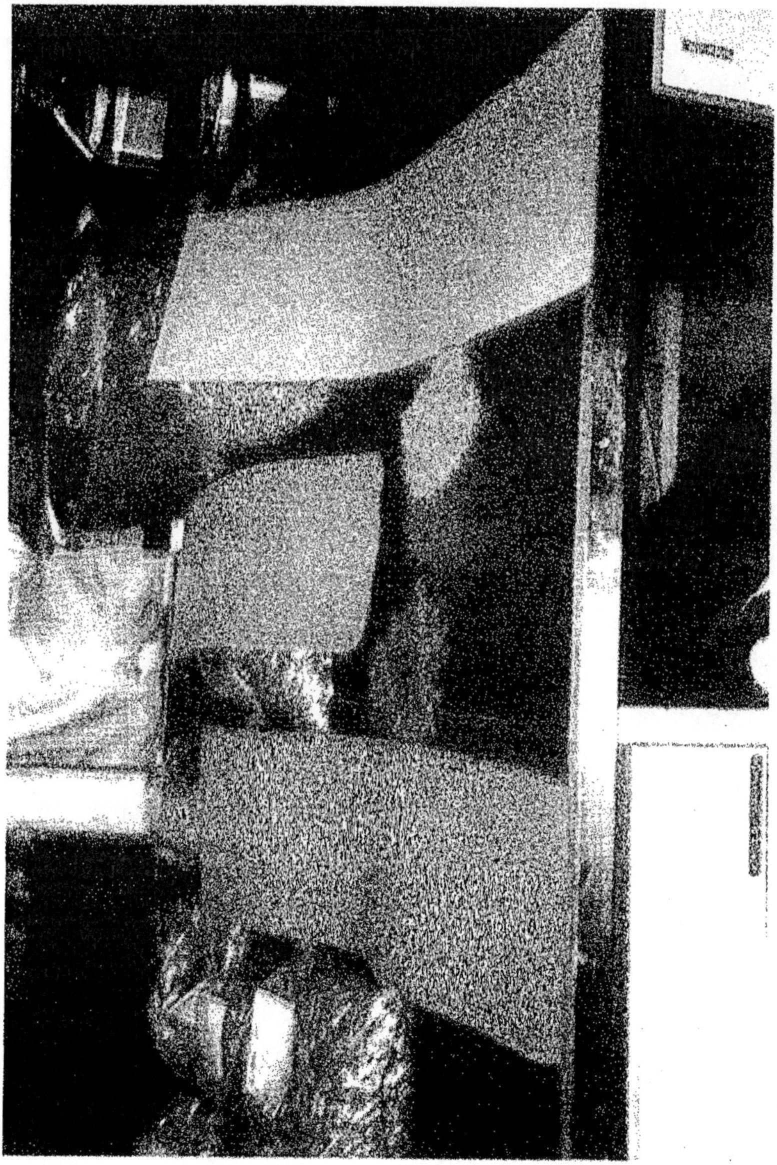

Paper produced by eucalyptus and Kenaf pulp

by high limits of iron oxide and alluminium. The soils are relatively poor in some macro nutrients and by being subject to high temperatures and large lixiviation in the monsoon they become unprovided by the organic material. There exist also hydromorphic soils which correspond to 5% of the total area of the state.

As has been seen, the kenaf plant is mega-thermic and as a result the temperatures that occur in Goa go along perfectly for its cultivation, relative to this climatic parameter. On the other hand, being a plant showing some rusticity, it does not need very fertile soil for Goa has many marginal lands which can be marked for the cultivation in question.

In relation to the water needs, if cultivated from October to February (rabi season), the State offers two infra-structures for irrigation, one in the north and the other in the south, which could provide the necessary water. Although, *a priori*, the edafo-climatic conditions appear viable for cultivation in question, its launching will have to be based on the previous experimentation as indicated hereafter.

The economy of Goa and the launching of a new agro-industry

The economy of Goa receives its support from its two main pillars, i.e. iron ore and tourism. The exploration of iron ore started already during the Portuguese regime and has shown a great increase, amounting to an export of 182 million US dollars in 1995-6. The main countries of destination were Japan (56%), China (13%), and South Korea (10%). Some European countries also figured among the importers, namely, Italy (7%), Romania (6%), the Low Countries (4%), Belgium (2%) and Turkey (1 %).

Tourism has also evolved very significantly. Thus, of the total 200,000 registered visitors in 1975, it crossed more than 1.1 million in 1977, of which 15% were foreigners. The projection for the year 2000 is about 2.5 million tourists, national and foreign. In reality, Goans are pacific, they do not know crime, they live in perfect religious harmony, are cheerful and hospitable, love to organise festivals and prepare exotic cusine. These human qualities, which characterise the Goan, combined with the natural beauty of the land with a large and rich flora and fauna bio-diversity, with extensive beaches bathed by warm waters, with a legacy that encompasses old monuments among which are the churches of the 16th century and Hindu temples of great architectural richness, constitute an agreeable attraction for the tourists who come from very distant places.

Fishing comes third among the products of exports and provides work for a significant segment of the population. Goa has also small and medium scale industries that supply the internal needs and make the export of the excess possible.

Goa is equally gifted with good infra-structures like roads and railways. These are now extended with the functioning of the Konkan Railway, river navigation and an airport for large aircrafts. It is also well-equipped in other areas like electric energy, water supply, telecommunications, and banking.

While suggesting, the introduction to the kenaf plant in the cultivation pattern of Goa, we think that it would strengthen the agro-industrial slope. The farmers could obtain a better yield of the land, and the businessmen would have an opportunity to invest in an industry whose final product, paper, has more and more demand and is more and more scarce.

Proposal for lines of investigation and development

Experience shows that not all the agricultural techniques which are known can be transfered with a guarantee of success, since each species reacts differently with regard to the environment where it is planted. In fact, for each ecological region, the productions are subject to the interaction of a multiplicity of factors, that cover three categories: heredity, environment and cultivation techniques.

The research into a plant meant for use in industry, will have to encounter also the problems of agronomic and industrial components. There will have, then, to be established a straight cooperation between these two areas, one, the upstream and the other downstream, which will have to complement, so that the final product in view may be possible with better technological characteristics, and as a result, become competitive in the market of similar raw materials.

Thus, in relation to the agronomic slope, we propose the carrying out of the following lines of investigation:

1. The establishment and study of a collection of germ plasma of the *Hibiscus cannabinus L.* variety
2. Comparative study of genotypes
3. Times of sowing and harvesting
4. Density of population
5. Control of infesting plants
6. Mineral fertilization
7. Efficient use of water for irrigation
8. Mechanical harvesting

9. Control of plagues and diseases
10. Regulators of growth and production of seed.

Final Considerations

Kenaf stands out among the annual plants for the production of cellulose, growing naturally in areas between 30° latitude to the north and 30° latitude to the south, an area that covers Goa.

The cellulose industry based on annual species gives off less pollutants than traditional ones that use as raw material wood species material, and have the advantage of using less energy. These two issues - the protection of the environment and the economy of the consumption of energy - ought to be more and more present in the launching of new industries.

The introduction of kenaf in the cultivation system of Goa, technically and economically viable, will give farmers a good source of income and put at the disposal of the cellulose industry a better raw material for the manufacture of certain types of paper.

It is our conviction that the plant in question after being studied under various conditions will be beneficial for the agro-industrial sector of Goa. We end quoting the words of M. O. Baghy on the future foreseen for this plant: "... a sleeping giant waiting for the stimulating splash of a major pulp and paper conversion facility. The giant is beginning to stir".[2]

NOTES AND REFERENCES

1. *Boletim Estatístico da Indústria Papeleira Portuguesa (CELPA)*, Lisbon: Associação da Indústria Papeleira, 1998, p. 69.
2. *Tappi Pulping Conference on Kenaf: Development for Commerce*, Bk. 1, Toronto, 1990, p.175.

BIBLIOGRAPHY

Berger, J., *The world's major fibre crops*, Zurich: Centre d'Étude de l'Azote, 1969, pp. 227-231.

Boulanger, J., "Choix d'une varieté d'hibiscus textiles en Afrique", *Garcia de Orta, Est. Agron.*, 10 (1-2), Lisbon, 1983, pp. 169-174.

---------, "Production de tiges de kenaf sur la bordure de la Mediterranee destinées a la fabrication de pate a papier", *CEE-DG XII/F1, Workshop on fibres*, Scotland, May 17-19, 1989, 21 pp.

Boulanger, J. & Gramain, E., "Comportement des hibiscus textiles dans le Sud de la France", *Cot. Fib. Trop*. Paris, 34 (3), 1979, pp. 331-327.

Candilo, M. & Faeti, V., "Kenaf: Caratteristiche, importanza e indicazioni di techniche colturali", *L'Informatore Agrario,* Verona, 46 (25), 1990, pp. 47-50.

Edmonds, J. M., "The distribution of *Hibiscus L.* Section Furcaria in tropical East Africa", *International Board for Plant Genetic Resources*, Rome, 1991, 60 pp.

Esteves, J. D., "Plantas produtoras de fibra", *Gazeta do Agricultor*, série B, no. 12, Lourenço Marques, 1958, pp. 5-15.

Exell, A.W. & Wild, H. (eds.), *Flora Zambesiaca,* vol. I, pt. II, 1961, pp. 434-472.

Geus, J., "Fertilizer guide for tropical and subtropical farming", Zurich: Centre d'Étude de l'Azote, 1967, pp. 257-258.

Hofman, J., *Arbustes décoratifs,* Paris: Gründ, 1969, 134 pp.

Hunter, D., "Paper and other writing materials", *Collier's Encyclopedia*, vol. XVIII, 1969, pp. 415-420.

"Notiziario Enea", *Renagri/Agricoltura e Innovazione*, no. 10, 1989, Rome, pp. 80-81.

Leitão, A. B., "Do Kenaf e da sua produção", *Gazeta do Agricultor,* 15 (171), Lourenço Marques, 1963, pp. 261-269.

Martin, J. & Leonard, W., *Principles of field crop production,* New York: Macmillan, 1967.

Menarini, M., Baschieri, T., Filippini, P. & Maccaferri, G., "Kenaf: Produzione e transformazione industriale", *L'Informatore Agrario*, Verona, 46 (25), 1990, pp. 54-58.

Mignoni, G., "Kenaf, a new potential source of raw material for Europe: agronomic experience in the Mediterranean area", International Conference on Biotechnology & Agriculture in the Mediterranean Basin, Athens, 1986, 29 pp.

--------, "Utilizzazione delle piante annuali da fibra ad integrazione dell'attività degli zuccherifici ed a salvaguardia del patrimonio forestale: il caso Sardegna", International Conference on Kenaf, Rome, 1992, 30 pp.

--------, *Il kenaf, non solo una nuova materia prima cellulosica*, Roma, 1994, 127 pp.

"Paper and Paper Production", *The New Encyclopaedia Britannica*, 15th ed., vol. XIII, 1980, pp. 966-977.

Peeler, C., "Production of kenaf and other soft fibres in Kenya", *East African Agricultural Journal*, 33 (2), 1967, Nairobi, pp. 139-144.

Petrini, C., Foschi, G. & Belleti, A., "Indagine conoscitiva su una collezione di kenaf", *L'Informatore Agrario*, Verona, 48 (8), 1992, pp. 97-99.

Rodrigues, A. F., "Kenaf (*Hibiscus cannabinus*) L., uma planta anual para a indústria do papel. Proposta de linhas de investigação no domínio da fitotecnia", Oeiras, 1996, 96 pp.

Semences Agricoles et Horticoles, Rome: FAO, 1961.

13

Indo-Portuguese Furniture and Its Evolution

PERCIVAL NORONHA

While the different facets of the Indo-Portuguese history are being studied in its minute details, it would appear that little attention is devoted to the study of the history and development in the range of crafts or useful arts in Goa, which is very wide.

Interweaving the rich history of the Goan way of life, the late Goan scholar, Jorge de Andrade, in a series of 17 articles in the erstwhile Portuguese daily, *A Vida*[1] based in Margao (Goa), made an intriguing narrative embracing the study of the so-called Indo-Portuguese furniture. This narrative written prior to 1947, was based on sources of foreign authorities in the field, mainly that of the French scholar, A. Jacquemart, the author of *History of Furniture* wherein he describes India as the "land of no furniture". In fact, many other authors have commented that the contribution for the chapter of the history of furniture in the golden period of Hindu civilization and even up to the arrival of the colonisers, had been extremely poor. In this regard, due acknowledgement must be made to the pioneering works of Ananda Coomaraswamy, Stella Kamrisch, K. Khandalawalla, Pupul Jayakar and others. Their works refer to generalised aspects of various arts and crafts in India, including furniture. Also, the magnificent volumes of the *Journal of Indian Art and Industry*, dealing with the various aspects of the aesthetics, designs and craftsmanship of Indian arts and crafts, contain a wonderful record of achievements of the people of India in the above fields. From these studies, we are now aware that India too had a wide range of furniture. So, the assertion of Jacquemart could be conveniently corrected, due to strong evidence to the contrary, through the most valuable sources that we find on the wall paintings of Ajanta (6th century A.D.), in the sculptures of Nagarjunakonda (3rd century A.D.), Amravati and others.

But all this furniture was restricted for use in the royal courts and in the palaces of the nobility of the epoch, while the masses, stricken by endemic poverty, contented themselves with a simple and unassuming living. For the poor, a mat upon the floor or simply a floor of mud and cow-dung smoothed flat, had to serve for seat and bed alike. However, the general mode of sitting was by spreading the mat, carpet or even a piece of skin on the floor. Over these, the traders or well-to-do people, used long pillows or bolsters, or even cushions as rests. But this simple way of life is not restricted to Indians alone. The Arabs are among those who customarily squatted on the ground. Even many Arabs who lead today most luxurious life in their cities, still follow the old ways, sitting and sleeping on rugs and pillows. The Japanese are another who, until recently, usually knelt or squatted on the floor. Yet, many of them retain today a room exclusively for relaxation and for the tea-making ceremony without the use of any furniture. The Chinese were the first in Asia to adopt pieces of furniture in their homes. Chairs first appeared in that country in the 2nd century A.D. They were probably transported all the way from Greece or Rome across the deserts and mountains of the northern trade route.[2]

In the ancient literature from Rig Vedic times, reference is made to *asanas*. These were the moveable equipment of a room, made or used for sitting and resting. The average citizens who could afford such furniture were in a very small percentage. The most antique piece of furniture in vogue in India was the *paat*, which is current even today. It is a slightly raised board for sitting on, or rather a plank generally of 60 cms. x 45 cms. size, without legs but with narrow strips fixed at the sides to provide a little elevation (5 cms.) from the ground. It is generally carved on sides, with light carvings on the border of the upper surface. This item is part of the dowry given to the bridegroom and used for sitting while taking meals. The other items in vogue were: the *charpoy*, a light four-legged stool; *chowkies*, a bit low, but larger and heavy four-legged stools. When longer on one side, they could be used as cots. *Mancha*, is a seat-cum-bed piece, while *vidala manchaka* is a chair with arms. *Bhojana manchaka* is another type of stool but quite low in height. Children used to sit in *addha-pallanka* (half seats). Swings were popular and were a common feature since very ancient times in the affluent society. Ornamental brass chains and carved wood-work often provided decorative motifs for the swings.[3]

To the above restricted use of furniture, there is one notable exception for the throne which is noticeable from the earliest historical period. This object served both as physical support and as a symbol of authority. The throne was the tribute of gods and kings. In the earliest Buddhist reliefs in India, around the 2nd century B.C., the throne is seen in various forms. Some have a flat rectangular seat, supported on four legs with perhaps an upright back and no arms. Later, the Buddha is shown upon a throne of flat seat type supported on animal legs.[4] The kings' seats had special names and were called either *rajasana* or *rajapatra*. These were stately units with large ornamental backrest, arms and legs. If the main motif was the face of a lion, then the chair was named as *simhasana*. If the motif reflected a peacock, it was called *mayurasana* or a peacock seat.[5] Elaborate cane or bamboo chairs seem to have been well established in southern India by the 2nd and 3rd centuries A.D.[6]

The frescoes and sculptures of Buddhist and Gupta periods, reveal the use of furniture of gorgeous styles. Most of the legs of this furniture were not only lathe-turned, but also finely chiselled with carved legs either straight or curvilinear, with floral and animal motifs.[7] Another development in the style of furniture is revealed from the illustrations in a Jain manuscript, *Prasana Vyakarana*. The model 'cabriole leg' which appeared in Europe in the 16th century is but a concept of the model of metal pedestals utilized in the Jain temples of the medieval epoch.[8]

Several decorative motifs were adopted by Indian craftsmen in the carving of furniture. The most popular is the lotus motif (fig. 1). The lotus (*Nelumbo nucifera, Nelumbium speciosum*) is a water plant. The flowers, ranging from white to deep pink and red, grow well above the water level and are large with each petal being concave and veined. The seed heads of the lotus are like the nose of a watering can, embedded in a swollen receptacle. In Hindu mythology the lotus is the cradle of the universe.[9]

Another popular motif adopted is that of the pipal leaf (fig. 2) drawn from a design found in Mohenjo Daro (circa 3rd millennium B.C.). The pipal tree (*ficus religiosa*) is a very large one. The leaves are heart-shaped tapering at the apex into a long tail. Considered a sacred tree, the pipal is seldom cut. It is associated with the triad, the roots being Brahma, the stem Vishnu and each leaf being the seat of a minor god.[10]

The palm leaf motif known locally as *tala-parna* (fig. 3) was adopted from a design found in the Bodh Gaya temple. After the Muslim invasions, the new occupants made lavish use of this motif during the time of the Mughal emperor, Akbar (1542-1605).[11]

A large number of panels of cupboards, side-tables or even doors of wall cupboards in Goan homes, present one of the oldest motifs created by Indian wood-carvers. The *surajmuki* or sun-faced panels (fig. 4) are found in place of the fluted designs and cartouches of the Renaissance period.[12]

The Indian craftsmen were accomplished in the art of carpentry, joinery, carving and other crafts too. The marvellous furniture manufactured in the palaces and manorial houses of kings, rajas and nawabs, is due to the great skill of the Indian craftsmen. From earliest times, Indian craftsmen were organised into craft guilds. Membership at first was not restricted to any one caste but to those who followed one trade. In time, however, the vocation became synonymous with caste and the hereditary basis of craft organisations became firmly established. Exposed to the living tradition, the son of the artisans, consciously grew familiar with forms, patterns and techniques. Thus, knowledge was communicated from father to son, from master to disciple. Within this great artisan tradition there was also the element of classical patronage rendered by the rulers to the craftsmen who congregated for work under one roof and where the craftsmen produced for the master. Ajanta frescoes and Amravati sculptures prove that wood was widely used for making furniture. The 6th century work *Brihati Samhita* of Varahamihira, enumerates different species of wood suitable for furniture. The following species of wood have been listed and the process for seasoning timber has also been explained: *Asana* (*Pentaptera tomentosa*); *Syandana* (*Dalberiga ogeinensis*); *Chandan* (*Santalum album*, sandalwood); *Haridra (Mesua ferrea); Suradaru (Pinus deodara); Tinduki (Diospyros glutinosa); Sala (Shorea robusta); Gambhar* or *Kasumari (Gmelina arborea); Anjana (Michaelia champaca); Taka (Tectona grandis*, teak); *Sinsapa, Sissum* or *Sisso (Dalbergia* sps., or Bombay blackwood); *Tun (Cedrela toona)* and *Phanas* or *Ponoss (Artocarpus integrifolia* or *Artocarpus heterophyllus*, jackfruit tree).[13]

Around the 12th century, the Muslim invasions would come in a continuous wave to impose its hegemony on the great Indian sub-continent. As a consequence, new ethnic and religious groups appeared on the scene to aggravate further its mosaic condition of races and religions. The clash of two peoples of different religions, profoundly disturbed the socio-political and cultural structure of India. However, in the long run, the latter did gain with the new Muslim culture, which contributed to the remarkable advancement and expansion of ornamental arts. Later, at the end of the 16th century, in north India, independently from Portuguese influence, there was a great flowering of ornamental and well-designed carved furniture obeying Muslim styles and fashions. The Muslim art was in essence, an extension of Arab. Turkish and Persian traditions, which became most popular in all the regions where they ruled, like, India, Persia (Iran), Afghanistan, Anatolia (Asia Minor), North Africa, Sicily, Spain and Portugal. By that time, there started entering into the great Indian sub-continent, original elements and motifs of geometrical decoration, typical and unique of Muslim world. Among all the useful arts, the cabinet and furniture making took a new turn during this period with new designs introduced by the newcomers. Intarsia, the craft of using wood inlays made its way into India. Almirahs and chests made of carved wood, and inlay work, formed part of the furniture. Chests were fitted with brass corners and ornamented with metal rosettes and knobs. These formed very decorative and at the same time useful articles of furniture. Likewise, the concept of divan and dressing tables was introduced in India.

In the epoch of navigation and conquests when the Portuguese were the masters of the seas, several settlements were established on the western coast of India with Cochin as its headquarters. In 1510, Goa was conquered by Afonso de Albuquerque and in 1530 it was selected as the capital of their eastern empire, one of the biggest colonial empires of those days. But Goa of that time was small in size, a microscopic point on the western coast comprising the present talukas of Ilhas, Bardez and Salcete (with Mormugao). In fact, the Portuguese conquests at that time in Goa, had not gone beyond those settlements having hardly an area of 575 sq. kilometres. This small area was one of the most interesting spots in the Indian peninsula in the middle of the 16th century. Here, the alliance between the sword and the cross was a close one. While the military might was being maintained on the land and the sea, the religious policy of the State was a forward one. It placed at the disposal of the ecclesiastical authorities all its resources. Now, various religious orders landed in Goa, and started erecting noble and expensive churches, chapels, monasteries, convents and colleges. While construction activity of large religious buildings was going unabated, a zealous campaign for the Christianisation of the local population was being relentlessly pursued. After the first clash of two different cultures which appeared to be antagonistic, the equilibrium was maintained and the conquerors at once discovered in this people a wealth of potentialities for their policy of fusion.

One of the measures, which produced the most far-reaching influence on Goan life and Portuguese administration, was the establishment of parochial schools, colleges and seminaries by various Religious Orders who also introduced Goans to western taste and modes of life. As we see, Goans were the first in this part of the world to have come into direct contact with the western civilization.

In Goa, as in the rest of the country, the traditional crafts were also wrought by members of a particular caste following one trade. Thus, we have the *kumars* (potters); *shetties* (goldsmiths): *charis* (blacksmiths); *suttars* (carpenters, joiners); *chittaris* (lacquer work artisans); *kansars* (brass and copper artisans); *mahars* (basket weavers); and *chamars* (shoe makers). The *charis* were later performing also the art of carving and even that of idol-making. When the Portuguese landed in India, these particular artisans were called *santeiros* as they shaped and carved images of saints and other artistic images of symbols of Christian art. This class of artisans was also known under the name of *Zo*.

The local artisans with their receptive minds, proved themselves capable of easily assimilating the symbols and culture of western civilization. In the field of useful arts, a great flowering of craftsmanship among Goan artisans created fame and pieces of art decorate today some of the museums and manorial houses. In particular, the work of blacksmiths and the art of carpentry, carving and joinery, flourished in Goa to the point of exhibiting a high degree of perfection, so much so, that Albuquerque soon after the conquest of Goa in 1510, wrote in one of his letters to King Dom Manuel I of Portugal not to send caulkers and carpenters as in "Goa there are more and better than seen in those kingdoms,"[14] and in another letter, he was praising the Goan gun-makers who in his opinion were manufacturing guns similar to those of "Bohemia with rifling and with a good finish."[15] Nevertheless, in order to accelerate the development of the art of furniture as well as that of the armoury and even of other crafts, a grand stimulus was extended with the opening of various workshops at different cities of the East, from Goa to Malacca. Similarly, the Portuguese craftsmen accompanying the conquerors, in close contact with their Indian counterparts, spread lavishly the new techniques acquired during their sojourn in the eastern lands. Another factor that greatly contributed towards perfection in the art of furniture making was the Arsenal of the Navy in the old city of Goa.

From the training the Portuguese craftsmen received in India and from the works of Indians at Lisbon, by an imperceptible process, quite slow, resulted this artistic hybridization, the so-called Indo-Portuguese furniture, with such a unique and distinct personality, a *sui generis* type, very rare in the vast art gallery of world furniture. On this type of furniture, let us have the authoritative opinion of Andrew Ciechanowiecki : "The

FIG.1

FIG.2

FIG.3

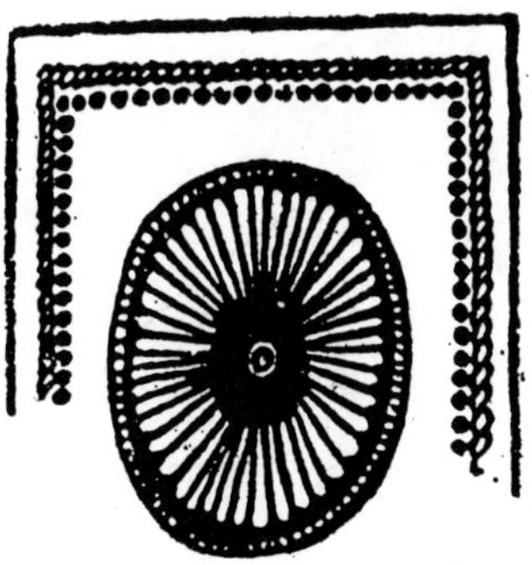

FIG.4

FIG.5

FIG.6

FIG.7

FIG.8

FIG.9

so-called Indo-Portuguese furniture was produced on the west coast of India at Diu, Daman, Goa and Calicut for the Portuguese living in India and also by Indian craftsmen working in Portugal, mainly in Lisbon. At the end of the 16th century, Goa became one of the richest towns in the world".

"Graced with the same civic privileges as that of Lisbon, its population wanted good furniture, not only imported from home, but made locally from fine wood such as teak, ebony and rosewood. The shape of these pieces is usually European while the decoration is oriental. Most of the chests, tables, rare chairs and many cabinets are of teak, inlaid with ebony, imported Brazilian dark wood and sometimes with bone and decoration. The later ones are covered with an intricate inlay of circles, studded with ivory and ebony. Sometimes purely Indian decorations appear. The legs of the stands or tables are shaped like mermaids, crude figures of natives, birds or scrolls with stylised birds' heads. Indo-Portuguese furniture is also recognisable by its large elaborately pierced lock plates and other brass mounts. This furniture, impervious to European stylistic changes can only be dated on the basis of the inlay and the decorative mounts. Both become increasingly colourful and elaborate, with a loosening of formal discipline. Among all the colonial furniture, it was the products of Goa, brought back by trading ships, which became most familiar in Europe."[16]

As mentioned earlier, the members of Religious Orders were responsible for introducing several symbols of western ornate especially of the Greek school. A conventionalised representation of the acanthus leaf was popularised in its different forms and formats (fig. 5).

Availing of the skilled tendencies of Goan craftsmen, it was possible for them to create artistic combinations, which can be seen on the altars, pulpits and other furnishings of the church paraphernalia. Also motifs of local fruits like cashew, caju (*Anacardium occidentale Linn.*), churna (*Z Rugosa, Lamk.*) find place not only in the church decoration, but also in the décor of local furniture. With the interaction of Portuguese artisans, motifs of fruits like grape (*Citrus paradisi*, bearing this fruit) were also introduced. Otherwise, in North India where grapes are produced in abundance, the artisans there made use of this fruit as a motif in their carvings.

All the work in the churches was wrought in teakwood (*Tectona grandis, Linn.*) while *sisso* or *sissum* (*Dalbergia sisso, Roxb.*) was partly used for making furniture. For the home furniture, besides the *sisso* wood, large scale use was made of timber of *ponoss* (*Artocarpus Integrifolia,*

Linn.) and that of *bendi* (*Thespesia populnea, Correia*). The Jesuits when they took charge of the Christianisation of Salcete and Mormugao in the 16th century, soon realised that teakwood was the best for the needs of the churches. In order to prevent its use by the local population, people of those areas were highly motivated by the Jesuits not to utilise teakwood in the houses as it was responsible for T.B. and other pulmonary diseases. It is for this reason that up to the end of the 18th century i.e. till the suppression of the Jesuit Order in 1759, no use of teakwood was being made in Salcete and Mormugao talukas by the locals, either for construction purposes or for furniture making.

During the first three quarters of the 16th century presence of Portuguese in India, most of the furniture was meant for the churches and their monasteries and colleges. Their furniture was made locally under the direction of members of Religious Orders. In the early days, the essential furniture for the use in the churches and convents was restricted to benches, chairs, chests and tables. The thought of cupboards never arose, as in the old convents etc. Cupboards were built into the walls like the built-in furniture of today's tiny modern flats.

Much in use then was the 'bench' -- a simple four-legged long-seater of medieval concept, used variously for sitting, sleeping and even for storage. Later, for comfort's sake, the back and arm rests were added when it was called 'settle'. It is found in various models either plain or with little ornate. Few typical benches of the early period have survived and can be seen today in the Sé Cathedral (outside the sacristy) and in the interior of the Rosary Church on the Holy Mount (*Monte Santo*), both in Old Goa. In the course of time, with the Baroque and the Rococo movements that were taking place, the bench, without losing its identity gave way for more sophisticated models. An interesting combination worked out by Goan craftsmen with Indian motifs and those used by Portuguese masters in Europe, resulted in a wonderful piece known as *canapé* (settle) (fig. 6). These pieces were very popular in the Augustinian complex in Old Goa. Today, such models are very rare and a few have been identified in Aldona in Bardez taluka. The introduction of benches in the churches for the use of the congregation was a feature of the late 19th century. Prior to this, benches were utilized only by the members of Religious Orders and nuns in the churches, convents, etc.

The early typical chair which made its appearance in Goa, after the Portuguese arrival and much in vogue in the churches and monasteries of Old Goa is the *cadeira de breviario* (breviary chair) (fig. 7) because it was used very much by the priests while reading the breviary. The type under reference, was made out of multiple battens and carved on exterior surface with seat and back-rest of leather or cane. Some specimens of these chairs have survived the ravages of time, and are seen today in few old churches and even in old private residences.

Decree no. 17 of the 1st Provincial Council held in 1567, restricted the use of chairs of high backrest inside the churches for the use of church dignitaries and other high-ranking government officials only. The congregation at large, were made to squat on the ground. However, Goan families of high social status, the ladies in particular, could make use of stools. The restriction imposed by the same decree was lifted after the abolition of Religious Orders in 1834. In many manorial houses, in Salcete and Bardez, there are still artistic stools of Indo-Portuguese style of the bygone era, which the members of the landed gentry used to carry for sitting in the churches. In Europe, unlike in India, stools never had any projection in the vast gallery of furniture. The reason is that the westerners made little use of stools and concentrated their efforts on improving the stability and comfort of the chair. The stools in vogue in Portugal were most of them of the folding type and utilised by ladies while sewing, stitching and while working at embroidery.

Heavy chests of large dimensions (1.20 x .65 x .60 metres) for storage of documents, linen or even golden treasures were very much in vogue in the 16th century as part of church furniture in Old Goa. Almost all the churches of the Old Conquests also had such pieces (fig. 8). Most of them were devoid of any ornamentation and were shielded with heavy corners and strips of iron or brass. Some of the models present vaulted lids. Few chests of the distant era are found in the Sé Cathedral and may be seen in other churches also. In the late 17th century, more elaborate chests of drawers of very large size (6.50 x 1.50 x 1.50 metres) for keeping high mass vestments, were made of intarsia art and with decorative mounts of brasswork. The sacristy of the Basilica of Bom Jesus at Old Goa presents a wonderful sight of such furniture pieces.

The setup during the first decades of the Portuguese administration in Goa, followed the patterns of Lisbon. Besides the viceregal palace, *Tribunal de Relação* (Sessions Court), the Treasury, *Câmara de Goa* (Municipality) and, later, the establishment of the Inquisition (1560) and many others must have certainly had some furniture. At least, there is a mention of a chair of the Inquisition in the article "Sic Transit ..." written by the late chief of the High Court of Goa, António Floriano de Noronha.[17] Besides, the Sé Cathedral itself was the scene of altogether five Provincial

Councils. Also, 316 decrees relating to ecclesiastical disciplines were passed. Definitely, well-fashioned tables mixed with other plain, uncarved but functional pieces must have been in existence in that distant epoch. A specimen of an antique table was spotted in the premises of the Sé Cathedral that suggests it belongs to the 17th century. The legs are conically shaped and spirally turned.

At the end of the 17th century with the raising of several religious institutions in Goa, the material demand for furniture increased considerably and more sophisticated pieces of current models were added. Up to the time of the abolition of Religious Orders, the vast range included chairs, armchairs, benches, tables, stools, tabourets, cupboards, chests, tabernacles, lecterns, highly decorated candlesticks, confessionals, etc. These are seen in different styles, with accentuated Portuguese influence from Gothic to Renaissance and Baroque to Neo-classic, while Regency, Rococo and other influences are also found among the specimens. The armchairs of high backrest with gilt decoration from where the ministers of the church used to address the congregation (old liturgy), are veritable pieces of art. These chairs are exhibited in almost all churches of Goa and are objects of curiosity among visitors. Chests for keeping vestments, some with fine inlay work (marquetry) or of intarsia art, with different type of wood, ivory, bone, metal or mother-of-pearl, constitute a rich repository of Church heritage in Goa from 16th to 19th centuries. In the sacristy of the Basilica of Bom Jesus, one can notice a rich repository of chests of fine inlay work of different sizes and shapes and also a set of in-built cupboards on the wall.

Already by the end of the 17th century the impact of western civilization was noticeable on the Goans. Several families of the landed gentry were leading a life similar to that of the colonisers. Most of their houses displayed diverse styles, revealing Indian influences, blended in a peculiarly interesting way with the architectural aspects and tastes imported from the distant West – a quaint, but all the same fascinating mixture of the eastern and western concepts. Obviously, the occupants felt the need of owning artistic furniture in keeping with the environment in which they lived. Today, these houses mostly spread through the villages of Old Conquests (Bardez, Ilhas also known as Tiswadi, Salcete and Mórmugao), display a vast array of curiously heterogeneous furniture such as tables, benches, chairs, *cadeiras de balouco* (rocking chairs), *cadeiras a Voltaire*, (easy chairs), stools, sofas, beds, day-beds, *canapés*, divans, machilas, oratories, cupboards, cabinets, chests with a variety of inlay work – a real treasure trove of the so-called Indo-Portuguese furniture, that are the pride of the rich cultural heritage of Goa.

An active trade spread this type of furniture throughout Europe and many outstanding pieces are being exhibited in several European museums and stately houses.

While the Portuguese were taking most of the furniture for their own use as objects of art, its trade got intensified when the British set their foot in India. Apart from Indo-Portuguese furniture, the British trade got extended even to ordinary pieces of furniture. The main reason was cost. Lord Sir Dudley North put it plainly in a book written in 1691: "As much labour or manufacture may be had in India for two pence as in England for a shilling (twelve pence)."[18]

The production of the Indo-Portuguese furniture entered into a frank decline in the second quarter of the 20th century. The new trend of modern style – a type of monotonous furniture of plain and flat surfaces – made its appearance in Goa with all the adverse consequences, very symptomatic of the negligence, partly of our craftsmen and partly of our people with the consequent downfall of its production so vital in the domain of our artistic activity. Nevertheless, the artistic impact of such furniture continues to subsist on the spirit of many Goans so much so that of late the appreciation of antique furniture has become more pronounced and many families are trying to restore the antique pieces in their possession, to their pristine glory while others who can afford such luxuries, indulge in ordering replicas of old models. There are still others who engage themselves in research for maintaining the general outlook of this type of furniture but by reducing its massiveness and curves with the aim to economise in the utilisation of costly wood which today is becoming quite scarce (fig. 9).

But the above trend is not restricted to old furniture alone. In fact, a consciousness of the aesthetics of the traditional arts and crafts of Goa is being revived among the masses. Unfortunately, those craftsmen who wrought those artistic pieces with great ingenuity, originality and splendour are no more. Today, artists are working on their own, and are finding scope for their talents. This is a departure from the traditional organisation of craftsmen.

With this dynamic approach, Goa continues to be a unique and rich store place of Indo-Portuguese furniture, which is displayed in our churches, in private residences, and even in government departments.

The topic on Indo-Portuguese furniture is a valuable area of study in the domain of useful arts though its listing (including photographic documentation), classification and dating will be a tremendous challenge to any scholar in the field.

NOTES AND REFERENCES

1. Jorge de Andrade, *A Vida* (I – 13.8.1946; II – 28.8.1946; III – 12.9.1946; IV 1.10.1946; V – 16.10.1946; VI – 3.11.1946; VII – 14.11.1946; VIII – 7.12.1946; IX – 30.1.1947; X – 14.2.1947; XI – 28.2.1947; XII – 9.3.1947; XIII – 11.4.1947; XIV – 30.4.1947; XV – 23.5.1947; XVI – 5.6.1947; XVII – 14.6.1947).
2. J. C. Giblin, *Be Seated,* Harper Collins Publishers, pp. 2-3.
3. Kamala S. Dongerkery, *Interior Decoration in India – Past and Present,* Bombay: D. B. Taraporevala, p. 48.
4. Anthony Christie, *The Middle East, India and South East Asia in World Furniture,* London: Hamlyn, p. 287.
5. Dongerkery, *op. cit.*, p. 51.
6. Anthony Christie, *op. cit.*, p. 287.
7. Dongerkery, *op. cit.*, p. 52.
8. *Ibid.*, p. 52.
9. Maneka Gandhi & Yasmin Singh, *Mythology of Indian Plants,* Calcutta: Rupa & Co., 1991, pp. 151, 157.
10. *Ibid.*, p. 135.
11. Dongerkery, *op. cit.*; p. 56.
12. *Ibid.*, p. 55.
13. G. C. M. Birwood, *Industrial Arts of India,* London: Chapman & Hall, pp. 202-3.
14. Afonso de Albuquerque, *Cartas*, vols. I-VII, Lisbon: Imprensa Nacional, 1903-35.
15. *Ibid.*
16. Andrew Ciechanowiecki, *Spain and Portugal, in World Furniture,* London: Hamlyn, p. 106.
17. António Floriano de Noronha, "Sic Transit ...", in *A Patria, Revista dos Novos – Literária, Científia e Artística* (ed. Ramachandra M. Rau), Panjim: Tip. Rau & Irmãos, 1924, pp. 70-75 .
18. J. C. Giblin, *op. cit.*, p. 39.

Note: Illustrations were taken from the following publications:

1. Figs. 1-4 from Kamala S. Dongerkery, *Interior Decoration in India – Past and Present*, pp. 55-56.
2. Fig. 5 from Maria Helena P. de Abreu & J. A. Ferreira Antunes, *Compêndio de Desenho*, Lisbon: Ministerio de Educação Nacional, p. 218.
3. Fig. 6 from *O Nosso Mobiliário, Enciclopedia pela Imagem,* Oporto: Lello & Irmãos, p. 36.
4. Fig. 7 from Maria Helena Mendes Pinto "Sentando-se em Goa", in *Oceanos: Indo-Portuguesmente,* nos. 19/20, September/December, 1994, Lisbon, p. 46.

14

Emergence of A Goan Elite of Intellectuals (1820-1926)

PIA DE MENEZES RODRIGUES

Introduction

In the early 18th century, sons of the Goan soil were not given the same honour, privileges and prerogatives enjoyed by those born in Portugal. The liberal ideas of French philosophers, Voltaire, Condorcet and Rousseau had laid the foundation of liberalism and espoused the doctrine of equality, liberty and fraternity which had its repercussions in various countries of the world. The American War of Independence and the French Revolution are the direct outcomes of liberalism. The great statesman, Marques de Pombal, was instrumental in introducing liberal ideas in Portugal and in the colonies. During his tenure, the *Act of 1761*[1] was promulgated whereby, all Portuguese subjects born in India or in the Portuguese Asian possessions who were Christians and not suffering from any legal disability, were to enjoy the same honours, privileges and prerogatives as enjoyed by those born in Portugal, without any discrimination whatsoever. According to Carmo de Souza "this law was a milestone in Goan legal history. It served as an ego booster to the spirit of Goans for a long time to come. It also influenced later policies of Portugal towards Goa".[2]

Constitutionalism

The French invasions in the first decade of the 19th century paved the way for a constitutional movement in Portugal. After the revolution in 1820 the constitutional rule established in Portugal introduced a liberal regime. The news of the change in government in Lisbon, reached Goa through the medium of the press published in British India. On receiving the news, many Goans and some Europeans approached Governor-General, Conde de Rio Pardo, to enforce the constitution in Goa too. As he refused to do so, he was deposed on September 16, 1821 and the administration was handed over to a provisional *Junta.*[3] The functioning of this *Junta* created much discontent mainly because the chief physician, Dr. Lima Leitão, was not included as a member of the *Junta* and also because of other measures favouring the Europeans as regards promotion, and dissolution of some regiments of the battalion of Bardez.[4] As a result, after the arrival of the new Governor, D. Manuel de Camara, the *Junta* was overthrown by a new revolt, and a second *Junta* was installed on December 3, 1821 with Viceroy Camara as its president.

As an outcome of the constitutional regime, Goans enjoyed the right to elect their representatives to the Portuguese Parliament. The first election was held in Goa on January 14, 1822. Dr. Bernardo Peres da Silva, Constancio Roque da Costa and Dr. António José de Lima Leitão were elected members of Parliament. Since Dr. Leitão was a member of *Junta de Governo,* a fresh election was held to fill the vacant seat in the *Junta.* However, there was a strong protest as regards the co-opted member Joaquim Mourão Garcez. The protests were specifically from the people of Bardez who revolted under the leadership of Fr. Pedro António Ribeiro of Pilerne and Lt. Col. José de Assa, respectively.[5]

The government did not pay any attention to their protests and tried to silence the people. As the support to the revolt caused much upheaval, later on, on the recommendation of the army, the government expelled from the territory all those who had engineered the revolt. This act resulted in more protests culminating in the assassination of Luis Prates de Almeida Albuquerque, the editor of the *Gazeta de Goa*, a staunch supporter of the liberal movement, who had protested against the action of the army.

After the transfer of power from the liberals to the absolutists in Portugal, on October 18, 1822, Governor Camara dismissed the *Junta* in Goa and assumed full control of the government as Viceroy. He set free all the political prisoners, and imprisoned the Ranes for causing disturbances in Satari. After the death of the Viceroy in 1825, the government was entrusted to different officials and only in 1827, D. Manuel de Portugal e Castro took charge of the government. Many improvements were introduced in Panjim. Bridges and public and private buildings were constructed. The greening of the area leading to Gaspar Dias (which from that time was called Campal) was undertaken for which he was accused of incurring unnecessary expenditure. He also started five primary schools, reorganised the army, and established the public library of Goa.[6] Meanwhile, the liberals regained power in Portugal in 1827, and the Liberal Charter was sworn in Goa on October 18, 1827, although it had to be abolished consequent upon the rise of the absolutists in Portugal.

In 1834 the liberals came to power again in Portugal and the Goa-born Bernardo Peres da Silva, a staunch liberal was offered the post of Prefect of *Estado da India.* The Prefect did not prove to be an able administrator and he could rule for 17 days only from January 14, 1835 to February 1, 1835.[7]

D. Manuel de Portugal e Castro took charge again, tried to restore peace and order, and later handed over the government to Marechal Correia da Silva Gama who was the first counsellor of the Prefect. Gama tried to bring back Peres da Silva which was strongly resented by the army who revolted on May 3, 1837, with the support of the military Governor. Till November 1837, there was no stable government in Goa and the period was marked by much violence and a reign of terror. The Governor, Simão Infante de Lacerda, Baron of Sabrosa, after taking the charge of the government in 1837, strove to establish peace and introduce judicial and administrative reforms.

During the period from 1840–1882 there were many other important developments. Education was reorganised, courses in engineering artillery and infantry were introduced in Escola Mathemática e Militar, the Military Hospital was transferred from Panelim to Panjim, a school for Marathi and primary schools for girls were started, the Escola Médica Cirúrgica de Goa was established with courses in medicine and pharmacy, the course of Escola Normal was recast and the Liceu Nacional de Nova Goa was created.[8]

Furthermore, postal stamps were introduced and the postal system was reorganised. The Instituto Vasco da Gama, a literary and scientific institution, and the Instituto Profissional were established. Again, the first part of the Mormugao railway, the construction of which was begun on March 22, 1880, was inaugurated on October 31, 1882, and a steam launch was introduced as a means of water transport. However progress was affected by the revolt of Ranes and that of the army. Rafael de Andrade (1895–96) who substituted Governor Viscount of Ourem, took strong action against Fr. Francisco Xavier Alvares for attacking some European officials through the columns of his paper. The European community succeeded in convincing the Governor that the locals were behind the sedition caused. So, the Governor took action against Goan officers, who were either transferred to Mozambique, Daman or Diu, or dismissed from service. Extreme measures were also taken, such as appointing a Council of War which imprisoned all those who participated in the revolts and the sedition. The publication of all newspapers was suspended and the circulation of the Bombay-based papers was banned.[9] The Goan population succeeded in convincing the Portuguese authorities about the importance of the press for defending the rights of Goans. Joaquim José Machado (1897-1900) after taking charge of the government declared an amnesty to the revolters, revived the press and took every measure to restore peace in the territory. The telephone lines from Panjim to Ponda and from Sanquelim to Valpoi were exploited and Bardez was covered by a network of roads. During the tenure of Eduardo Augusto Rodrigues Galhardo (1900-1906) several steps were taken to put an end to the disturbances in Satari by suspending constitutional rights in the New Conquests and by imprisoning all those who were involved in the disorders. Primary and secondary education was reorganised. He also took various measures to control contagious diseases. Rules for civil registration for non-Christans were published and a census of the population was carried out. Comissão de Arqueologia Permanente da India Portuguesa (Permanent Archaeological Commission of Portuguese India) was also constituted.

The year 1905 marked the beginning of the exploration of manganese mines for which an office of mines was established. During the government of José Maria Souza Horta D'Costa (1907-1910) the provinces of the New Conquests were covered by a network of roads, several bridges were constructed and works related to improvement of agriculture were taken up.[10]

On October 5, 1910, the Republic was introduced in Portugal and a new constitution was proclaimed in 1911, which gave a boost to educational, cultural and literary activities in the territory. In 1926 the army overthrew the democratic regime and put an end to the constitutional liberties enjoyed by the people. Summing up, the period from 1820–1926 was marked by much progress in the fields of education, communication, commerce and urbanization. Peace and tranquility were affected by the frequent revolts by the Ranes, the Maratha soldiers and military personnel.

Emergence of a Goan elite of intellectuals

The introduction of a constitutional regime, and developments in the field of education and communication, would be singular factors which contributed to the emergence of a Goan elite of intellectuals.

Constitutional development: According to Carmo D'Souza, the constitutional era in Portugal in the post-1820 period opened the floodgates of individual rights and guarantees which were much influenced by the legal thinking of western European countries.[11]

The Constitution of 1822 guaranteed liberty, security and the right to property for all Portuguese.[12] It regarded the Portuguese nation as a union of all Portuguese wherever they might be and provided for a legislative house to be known as *Câmara dos Deputados,* which was to be elected by citizens eligible by age and professing the Catholic religion. It also envisaged a Council of State with representation from its overseas provinces, and an elected municipal chamber. This Constitution was in force for a very short period, from September 1822 to June 1823.

The Charter of 1826 which was introduced in Goa in October 1827,[13] enumerated the territories that composed the kingdom of Portugal and Algarve, in Europe, Africa and Asia. Hence by considering Portugal and her colonies as one nation, the Charter did not differentiate between Portuguese citizens of Portugal and those of its overseas provinces. Under the Charter, Parliament consisted of two houses., viz., *Câmara dos Deputados* and *Câmara dos Pares.* A Portuguese citizen was entitled to contest as a member of *Câmara dos Deputados* from any electoral circle, irrespective of whether he was born, resident or domiciled in the electoral circle. The Charter assured freedom of thought and expression and the freedom to move in and out of the country, although these rights could be suspended in cases of rebellion, invasion and uprisings. The concepts of commercial and professional freedom were included in the section on individual rights. Furthermore, the right to secrecy of letters, the right to public help, assurance of free primary education, were enshrined in the Charter. It made provisions for local bodies to look after the economic and municipal administration.

The decree of December 7, 1836[14] introduced certain changes in the administration of overseas territories. It provided for a consultative body next to the Governor and called the government council. This consisted of heads of departments from the judicial, military, fiscal and ecclesiastical sections, two or more councillors to be chosen by the Governor from a list of four members elected by *Junta de Província.* He could invite experts to the meetings of the council and take decisions in consultation with it.

With the aim of giving information to the public, the decree made provision for the publication of the *Official Bulletin* under the supervision of the Governor-General, giving details about the orders, decrees, official work, current information, statistics and other features of public interest.

The decree of 1869 brought further changes in the administrative institutions, introduced by *Carta Organica.*[15] The Governor had an advisory body called *Conselho do Governo*. Besides, there were bodies like *Junta Geral de Provincia* and *Conselho de Província* which had official as well as elected members. After the overthrow of the monarchy, the Constitution of 1911[16] envisaged a unitary state model with a democratic machinery with great emphasis on the individual. It secured the guarantees concerning the individual rights of liberty, of personal property and security and of freedom of conscience and belief. It guaranteed civil and political equality to all religious cults and freedom from persecution for religious motives. The legislature consisted of two houses, *Câmara dos Deputados* and *Senado*. It made provision for decentralisation of power and it stated that the special laws meant for the overseas territories, were to be adequate for the stage of civilisation of each Portuguese possession. It is a pity that due to political instability, the Constitution did not grow and evolve.

From the foregoing it can be seen that the Constitutions and legal provisions of the 19th and early 20th centuries made provision for individual rights, and enabled the people to participate in government through their elected representatives. Awareness about the functioning of government was brought among the people through publications.

Education: The knowledge of European languages imparted in the Lyceum and other courses, exposed Goans to western science and culture. The knowledge of history and civics made Goans conscious of their right to freedom, inculcated in them the spirit of fighting for individual rights and liberties. The Lyceum also provided a good cultural scientific foundation enabling students to take up medical education or to proceed for higher studies to Europe. Seminary education not only prepared the students for the priesthood but also implanted in them a sound general culture based on the humanities. The Medical School was intended not only to prepare one for a medical career but also to acquire a new orientation, the scientific spirit. *Escola Matemática e Militar* also imparted knowledge of sciences. Though there was no formal education in law, Goans could take to the studies of law privately and obtain the *Carta de Advogado* after passing a special examination. Many a times these courses were not opted for professionalism alone but, to acquire further education and a better social status.

In 1831 the government of Portugal also provided an opportunity to Goan students to take up medical studies in Portugal, and in 1840 a provision was made for higher education in sciences, arts, medicine and surgery in

Portugal, for 100 students from the overseas provinces. As a consequence, from 1833-1857, 48 students from Goa were sent to Portugal at the cost of *Fazenda Pública* and *Câmaras Agrarias.*[17] Moreover, some Goans migrated to British India for higher education and professional studies.

Communication Systems: Books, journals and newspapers played an important role in enlightening Goan society. It is through these sources of information that Goans were made aware of liberal movements in Europe, and socio-economic, political and scientific developments in different countries. The establishment of telegraphs, railways and roads further enabled Goans to have access to journals published all over the world. Facility in transport gave them the opportunity to meet and discuss personally, issues of relevance and importance. They were influenced by the European intellectuals, especially when they were in Portugal either for higher studies or as parliamentarians. Some European intellectuals like Tomas Ribeiro, a literary figure of merit, posted in Goa, also had an impact on the Goan elite. Eminent personalities from British India too influenced the Goans through the press and other means of mass communication.

Abolition of the Exército da India: With the suppression of the army in 1871,[18] the supremacy of Luso-descendants came to an end and Goans were able to take up the higher posts in the administration, which were earlier held mostly by the Luso-descendant community.

Goan Intellectuals: During the period under study, Goa produced eminent personalities in the fields of politics, journalism, sciences, languages and historiography.

Politics: Constitutional reforms enabled Goans to become members of Parliament and other elected bodies. Goa produced some distinguished parliamentarians who represented their people and the best interests of their homeland. They defended the rights of Goans with determination, vigour and enthusiasm. For the first twenty five years of democratic representation, the parliamentary representatives were concerned chiefly with greater autonomy in administration, the grant of civic rights and the removal of many of the irksome features of colonialism, whereas in the second half of the 19th century, they started asserting their right for self-government.

Goan intellectuals conscious of their heritage, their Indian tradition and history, looked upon their past with pride and they uttered their pledge against colonialism and their right for independence.[19] Bernardo Peres da Silva, Constancio Roque da Costa, Fr. Estevão Jeremias Mascarenhas, Francisco Luis Gomes and Cristovão Pinto are some of the Goan leaders well known for their distinguished contributions in the Portuguese Parliament.

Bernardo Peres da Silva (1775–1844), a Goan who completed his studies in the Medical School at Panelim, was a staunch supporter of liberalism and was elected a member of the first Parliament in 1822, and again in 1827. However, he could not function due to dissolutions of the house. He continued being in Portugal and worked hard for the restoration of constitutionalism. After the return of the Liberal government, in recognition of his services, he was appointed *Prefeito do Estado da India,* a charge he assumed on Jaunary 14, 1835. The post was equivalent to that of a Governor, but without military powers. He was the first and only Goan to hold such a position during the Portuguese rule. Some hasty measures favouring the locals irked the Europeans and absolutists, who revolted and brought his rule to an end. Bernardo Peres da Silva took shelter in Bombay and backed by his supporters went to Daman from where he administered the settlement of Daman, Diu, Dadra and Nagar Haveli. Owing to his popularity, he was re-elected to the Portuguese Parliament in three subsequent elections. In 1839 he was appointed a member of the standing committee for the colonies. In the Portuguese Parliament he defended the interests of Portuguese India and other colonies. In a speech entitled "*Aos Representantes da Nação Portuguesa*" delivered in 1840 he defended his measures and demanded an inquiry into the action of his adversaries. He also fought vigorously to do away with the military forces stationed in Goa.[20]

Canon Estevão Jeremias Mascarenhas (*1800–1857*) took a course in theology at the Seminary of Chorao and a diploma as advocate of the ecclesiastical court. He was elected member of the Portuguese Parliament in 1848 and retained his position in two subsequent elections. He was the first Goan parliamentarian to raise his voice to express the desire for independence. He realized that this was not possible as there was a probability of Goa coming under another nation. This he stated in a speech delivered in Parliament on May 24, 1853: "I would desire from my heart her independence, but I know that such circumstances do not occur. I am convinced that if she wishes to get out of the Portuguese dependence, she will necessarily fall into that of another nation, and in this alternative

I and my countrymen want to live united rather to Portugal than to England".[21]

He took a very active part in the Portuguese Parliament and proposed reforms like education of the youth in the mission lands, separation of the duties of the public notary from those of district judges, trial by jury, and extension of the jurisdiction of judges to Daman and Diu. Earlier, he had been a member of the *Junta Geral* from the Bardez district, as well as a member of the council of government.[22]

Bernardo Francisco da Costa (*1821–1896*) was another distinguished Goan parliamentarian. He was a multi-faceted personality who strove for the overall development of his land. He completed his studies in law privately, and then took a course in mathematics from *Escola Matemática e Militar.* He was elected member of Parliament on three occasions, in 1852, 1856 and 1869, respectively. Through his eloquent speeches in Parliament, he secured various benefits for his motherland. He succeeded in revoking laws which made distinctions between local and European priests. He secured funds from the central government for repairs of *Barra de Goa,* and fought for equality and against casteism by dropping out references regarding class and caste.

His activities were not limited to Parliament. He was also a member of the Municipality for two terms and Procurator of *Junta Geral do Estado da India, Caixa Económica de Goa* and *Seguros Mutuos da Vida.* He founded the theatre *Harmonia* at Margao for the development of dramatic art and he took the initiative of popularising European dance in Goa, and the habit of speaking Portuguese at home. He was also a pioneer of the private press in Goa.

Owing to the scientific studies which he had carried out while in Portugal, setting up his own laboratory at home, he was offered the post of professor of chemistry, physics and natural history at *Escola Médica de Goa.* He also introduced various reforms in the field of education e.g. by including the knowledge of living and non-living beings at primary education. In the last years of his life, tired of his political career, he dedicated himself to the agricultural and industrial development of Goa. He introduced the Indian plough, fruit canning industries, machines for extraction of oil and sugar cane juice.[23]

Francisco Luis Gomes (*1829–1869*), a physician by profession through *Escola Médica de Goa,* he represented Portuguese India in the Portuguese Parliament from 1861 to 1869 and took a seat with *Partido Regenador*, a party which stood for liberal ideas. He was proud of his Indian ancestry and said: "I ask for India liberty and light; as for myself, more happy than my countrymen".[24] He did not confine his sphere of action to his native land, but extended it to the entire world of Asia, America and Africa which was enslaved by the Europeans, He thus worked for the creation of a society based on the principles of liberty, equality and fraternity. He traced his philosophy of equality to Jesus Christ. He struggled to ameliorate the condition of his constituents and succeeded in placing colonial public servants on the same footing as public servants in Portugal. He laid down the principles of a Goan budget and purged it of several illegal items of expenditure.

Francisco Luis Gomes fought against slavery and defended the cause of the *Padroado*. He did not confine himself to political activities, as he too was a multi-faceted personality. He was a born writer and made contributions in the fields of literature, history, political economy and journalism. His novel, *Os Bramanes,* was much influenced by Victor Hugo. It centered on the militant love of liberty, justice and concern for the fallen, the weak and the destitute. His work, *Liberdade da Terra e Economia Rural da India Portuguesa,* is considered his *opus magnum* wherein he advocates colonial autonomy and a uniform system of colonial administration throughout the Portuguese empire and tries to formulate a scheme of economic and financial reforms which would rescue the country from the sloth of economic stagnation. In his work, *Essai sur la theorie de L'Economie Politique,* he challenged the theories of renowned European personalities and propounded his own views. It is one of the landmarks in the history of Portuguese economic thought recognised by learned European societies like Societe d' Economie Politique of Paris, Society of Medical Sciences of Lisbon and the Economic Society of Cadiz. An honorary doctorate was conferred on him by the University of Louvain. He also left historical works like *Le Marquis de Pombal, Os Brigadeiros Henriques Carlos Henriques* and *Joaquim José Xavier Henriques.*[25]

Francisco Luis Gomes was indeed "a universal genius who during his stay in Europe deported himself as an unofficial ambassador of India, drawing the attention of the learned public to the pleasing aspects of our culture and its abiding values".[26]

Christovão Pinto (1851-1926), a Goan parliamentarian took his studies in the Lyceum. He represented India in the Portuguese Parliament for four consecutive terms right from November 1889. He was elected a member of *Partido Indiano.* He introduced bills on education and local self government similar to those of British India. However, these were not passed in Parliament. He fought for the revival of Konkani as a vernacular language and as a medium of instruction.

Earlier, he had joined the Secretariat and held posts of senior official of *Direcção Geral do Ultramar* and *Inspecção Geral da Fazenda.* He was also a member of teaching faculty of *Escola Colonial de Lisboa.* He collaborated on political themes related to Portuguese India. He was conferred knighthood of the *Ordem Militar de Cristo.*[27]

Lamartine Prazeres da Costa (*1879-1949*), a Goan who after completing his studies at the Lyceum, completed a course in arts at the Faculty of Lisbon and later obtained his doctorate from the University of Sorbonne. After the implementation of the Republic he was elected member of the Constituent Assembly as a representative of Portuguese India. He was instrumental in raising the category of the Panjim Lyceum to that of a central Lyceum, in establishing two Municipal Lyceums, and a commercial institute in Panjim. He succeeded in transferring the metropolitan budget to meet the expenses connected with the Padroado and the Satari revolt, and in the substitution of the word *indigena* in the organic Charter by the word local. Later, he held responsible official positions in Portugal as well overseas and participated in various international conferences.[28]

Journalism

The freedom of expression granted by the Constitution stimulated Goans to express freely through the medium of the press, their thoughts and ideas so as to secure their rights and liberties, and to disseminate the spirit of freedom and equality guaranteed by the Constitution and thus contribute to the progress of their land and people.

After the introduction of the constitutional regime in 1821 the first official paper, *Gazeta de Goa* was launched on December 22, 1822. It had a political section which championed the cause of liberalism and constitutionalism. However, it had to be closed down in 1826, due to much dissension and misunderstanding which had been created. The need of a newspaper was felt again in 1835 to counteract the support to the cause of Bernardo Peres da Silva, and the attack on the government by the Bombay-based newspapers. *Chronica Constitucional* was started on June 13, 1835, but stopped publication on November 30, 1837, due to much discontent which had been created. Parliamentarian Bernardo Francisco da Costa, who was so impressed by the role which the press played in

Europe, that on his return to Goa, he was depressed to see that unlike the Europeans, the people of his birth-place did not have a publication through which they could raise their voices so as to alert the authorities and people on various issues and also keep the people well-informed about the progress in social, economic, political and scientific fields. To overcome this, he succeeded in publishing the first private paper, *O Ultramar* in 1859 and thus became the pioneer of the private press in Goa. The paper was the spokesman of *Partido Ultramarino*, a party to which he belonged, and which was constituted of individuals from the higher strata of Goan society. It was through the columns of *O Ultramar* that da Costa exposed the shortfalls of those in power and fought for the interests of his motherland and for the rights and privileges of the people. He succeeded in reducing taxes (*sizas*), and abolishing the tax on salubrity. The paper also acted as a literary school where the contributions of well-known literary figures of the time were published.

To counteract *O Ultramar* the rival party of *Partido Ultramarino, O Partido Indiano* started *A India Portuguesa* under the editorship of José Inácio de Loyola, who was a physician by profession, from the *Escola Médica*. The paper had a special section '*Para Portugal*' where it analysed the political and administrative situation in Goa so as to appraise the Overseas Minister of Portugal of the situation, in order that he might take necessary action to put things right when the situation so demanded. Both these papers being the voices of the two rival parties which were in the forefront of most of the political battles that were fought in the second half of the 19th century and early years of the 20th century, gave a fillip to creating a tremendous political consciousness among the Goans.[29]

Fr. António Xavier Alvares (*1837-1932*) is another Goan journalist who fought for the rights of Goan people. After his seminary education at Rachol, he was ordained priest in Bombay with dismissorials from the Archbishop of Goa. Due to his hostile relations with the Archbishop, he joined the Syrian Orthodox Church in Ceylon and he was given the title Mar Julius I. He protested against the malpractices prevailing in the Goan administration, through the columns of his papers *O Progresso*, *The Times of Goa*, *A Cruz*, *A Verdade* and *O Brado Indiano*. It was through the latter that he vocalised the need and the sentiments of the downtrodden. He criticised the bureaucrats for siphoning off a large portion of the state income for personal use because of which the sons of the soil were compelled to emigrate. Though his main aim was to increase the income of his motherland and make her self-sufficient, he was many times misunderstood and even charge-sheeted.[30]

Luis de Menezes Bragança (*1878-1938*) was one of the greatest journalists that Goa gave birth to. Although his formal education was restricted to that of the Lyceum, he was truly a self-made man having acquired knowledge from a rich collection of books including works of the French encyclopaedists. He was so influenced by this literature that much before the advent of the Republic in Portugal he defended the ideal of a secular republic through the columns of *O Heraldo, O Nacionalista* and *O Comércio.* Through the columns of his paper, *O Debate* which he started in 1911, he moulded the minds of readers with his concepts of free thought of religion, politics, nationalism, press and social relations. After bringing down the curtain on *O Debate* in 1920, he championed the cause of liberty of religious cults through the columns of *Pracasha* and *Pradeep*.[31]

Sciences

Scientific studies offered in Goa were limited to those of medicine and pharmacy. However Goans availed of the opportunities to acquire higher education in Portugal and other European countries.

Agostinho Vicente Lourenço (*1822–1893*) is one of the eminent scientists that Goa has produced. After completing his medical studies at *Escola Médica de Goa,* he proceeded to Portugal with financial assistance from *Câmaras Agrarias* and a subsidy from Portugal. Due to his keen interest in organic chemistry he worked in the laboratory of chemist Wurtz in Paris. After working for sometime in Gemany and London, he returned to Paris and took up a course in civil engineering and later obtained a doctorate in natural history. During the last phase of his life, he remained in Portugal, where after teaching for some time he carried out research on mineral water for which he was awarded a gold medal. He also did research on sulphuric water. A number of his research findings on the synthesis of monoatomic alcohols were published in research journals like *Jornal das Ciências, Fisicas e Matemáticas de Academia Real das Ciências.* He was a member of the Academy of Sciences of Lisbon.[32]

Dr. Caetano António Claudio Julio Raimundo da Gama Pinto (1853-1945) was a renowned ophthalmologist, who after studying at the Lyceum and the *Escola Mathemática e Militar* proceeded to Portugal to pursue further studies. After completing a medical course through the *Escola Médica do Porto* he worked with Dr.Wecker in Paris, later visited various universities in Germany and then specialised in ophthalmology. He was unable to take the charge of the professor's post at *Escola Médica de Goa,* for which he was appointed because of the offer he received from the University of Heidelberg to work as an assistant to Otto Becker at the latter's eye clinic. Later, he was in charge of the practical course of ophthalmology and practical eye surgery. He delivered lectures to most eminent ophthalmologists of various countries.

After returning to Portugal in 1882, he was appointed professor of ophthalmology in Lisbon and later founded *Instituto Optalmologico* which is named after him. He contributed to various journals and presented papers at various international conferences. He was a member of the International Society of Ophthalmology and the Academy of Sciences of Lisbon.[33]

Dr. Bossuet Afonso (1880-1957) is another Goan ophthalmologist who after completing his secondary education in English took up medical studies at various German universities. In 1900 he was awarded the degree of doctor at the J. M. University at Wurtzberg for his work on "Experimental study of the effect of X- rays on the eye lens". He was awarded the title of professor and later given a bronze medal for his meritorious research. He published several research papers and was corresponding member of the Society of Ophthalmology. He returned to Goa and devoted himself to ophthalmology and general clinic.[34]

Languages

Goa has also had eminent personalities in the field of linguistics.

Mgr. Sebastião Rodolfo Dalgado (1855-1922) is one of them who after completing his theological studies at the Seminary of Rachol, left for Rome where he obtained a doctorate from the University of St. Apolinarium. He was offered various posts, but he did not accept the same since his aim was to carry out missionary work. He dedicated himself to this career in which he came in contact with various Indian languages. For his great interest in his mother-tongue, Konkani, he compiled a *Konkani-Portuguese Dictionary*. Later on he worked on a *Portuguese-Konkani Dictionary* and proceeded to Portugal to complete his work. The Dictionary was published in Portugal in 1904. *Florilégio dos Provérbios Concani* is another Konkani work which was published by the Academy of Sciences, Lisbon.

Mgr. Dalgado's studies were not limited to the Konkani language. He has to his credit numerous works on Indo-Portuguese dialects spoken in

Asia, and some works on Sanskrit language and literature. His missionary work in various parts of Asia enabled him to take up a study on the influence of the Portuguese language on Asiatic languages, which was later published by Academia das Ciências, Lisbon. The work was hailed by the Portuguese intellectuals as a monumental work of importance for world culture. He was a lecturer of Sanskrit in Lisbon and an elected member of Sociedade de Geografia, Lisbon, corresponding member of the Academy of Sciences, Lisbon and honorary member of the Royal Asiatic Society, London.[35]

Vaman Ragunath Varde Valavlikar (*1887-1946*) alias *Shennoi Goymbab* did his Portuguese elementary education in Goa and proceeded to Bombay where he completed his matriculation. Dissatisfied with teaching and clerical jobs, he dedicated himself to the study of his mother-tongue, Konkani, after being convinced that this was the vernacular language of Goans. According to Fr. António Pereira, "research in the available libraries, reflection and meditation at home, daily perusal of ancient and modern Konkani literature, the close study of the language of gods, Sanskrit, made him one of our greatest linguists, the philosopher and the protagonist of Konkani language".[36]

In addition to a number of books on Konkani language, he wrote books in Konkani on different subjects including history, biography and fiction. *Bhurgeanlem Veakoronn, Albukerkan Goym koxem Jiklem, Abbe Faria* and *Goekaranli Goyam bhaili Vasnnuk,* are some of his works. He is indeed a great Goan linguist who brought about the renaissance of Konkani language and literature.[37]

Historiography

Among the Goan intellectuals, one finds those who devoted themselves to historical and archaeological writings and transcribed various archival documents. They were much influenced by Portuguese research scholars and bibliographers like *Joaquim Heliodoro da Cunha Rivara.* The latter was posted in Goa in 1855 as secretary-general of Portuguese India and carried out extensive research in the Goa Archives. The documentation collected by him relating to the 16th-19th centuries is published in *Archivo Português Oriental.*

Filipe Nery Xavier (*1801-1875*): After seminary studies at Chorao, he joined the Medical School of Goa. However, since he could not pursue his studies, due to some problems, he volunteered his services to the government Secretariat. His services were soon regularised and owing to his efficient and dedicated service and for the interest shown for historical and literary works, he was promoted to the post of senior officer. During the last phase of his life he held the post of director of the Printing Press. He carried out extensive research in the Archives, hence most of his works are supported by historical documentation. There is no aspect of Portuguese India that he did not cover, right from comunidades, personalities, different pieces of legislation, political history and various other issues. He was the first Goan corresponding member of the Academy of Sciences, Lisbon and various other literary societies. He was awarded knighthood of *Ordem de Cristo* and of *Nossa Senhora da Conceição de Villa Vicosa.*[38]

Miguel Vicente de Abreu (*1827-1884*), a senior official at the Secretariat where he served from 1843-1878, and a contemporary of Cunha Rivara, devoted himself to the study of history and published several books fully supported by archival documentation including Portuguese translations of some historical works. He was a provincial associate of the Academy of Sciences, Lisbon, and member of the Royal Asiatic Society, Sociedade de Geografia, Lisbon, and Instituto Vasco de Gama, respectively. He was also the recipient of the knighthood of the Order of Christ and *Nossa Senhora da Conceição de Villa Vicosa.*[39]

João António Ismael Gracias (*1857-1917*), a senior official at the Secretariat, is well-known for his writings on history, archaeology and bibliographical works. After completing the courses of Lyceum and of physics, chemistry and natural history at the *Escola Médica,* he took up a course in commerce at the Instituto Profissional. He joined the Secretariat, and due to his good record, he was promoted to the post of senior official (*Official Maior).* He was also offered other official assignments like those of teacher at the Lyceum, curator of Numismatic Museum, and director of Biblioteca Nacional de Goa. He was a member of the Junta Geral de Província, Conselho de Província, Tribunal de Contas, and the Conselho Inspector da Instrucção Pública.

He left a number of works on history, archaeology and literature. It was under his direction that the archaeological journal *O Oriente Português* was published. His contributions are also found in *Almanaques, Boletim dc Governo* and various journals from Goa, Bombay and Portugal. He was a member of the Royal Asiatic Society, Bombay, Sociedade de Geografia, Lisbon, and various other learned institutions world wide.[40]

Conclusion

After going through the period 1820-1926, one finds that there emerged a Goan elite of intellectuals who derived ample sustenance from constitutional provisions, developments in the field of education and communication. Among the intellectuals there was a group which excelled in Goa itself, and there was another which proceeded to Portugal either for higher studies or as members of Parliament and gained eminence there.

Goans who proceeded to Portugal either as parliamentarians or for higher studies were directly influenced by the European models in the socio-economic, political and scientific fields.

NOTES AND REFERENCES

1. C. L. Barbuda Monteiro, *Instrucções com que El Rei D. José I mandou passar ao Estado da India,* pp. 256-257. Ruling of April 2, 1761.
2. Carmo D'Souza, *Legal system in Goa*, vol. II, p. 115.
3. For more details see M. V. de Abreu. *O Governo do Vice-Rei Conde do Rio Pardo no Estado da India Portuguesa desde 1815 até 1821*, 1869.
4. M. V. de Abreu, *Relação de alterações politicas de Goa desde 16 de Setembro de 1821 até 18 de Outubro de 1822*, pp. 10-11.
5. A. A. Bruto da Costa, *As revoluções políticas da India Portuguesa do século XX*, p. 32.
6. M. J. Gabriel de Saldanha, *História de Goa*, vol. 1, p. 250.
7. Roberto Bruto da Costa, *A Hidra do nativismo*, p. 7.
8. The first primary schools for girls was started in 1841, Escola Normal e Ensino Mutuo in 1841, and the Escola Médica Cirúgica de Nova Goa in 1842. The course of Escola Normal was reset in 1844. Liceu Nacional de Nova Goa was created in 1854, Instituto Profissional was started after the abolition of Escola Matemática e Militar in 1871. For more details about these institutions see: Menezes Braganza, "Educação e ensino na India Portuguesa", in *India Portuguesa*, vol. II, 1923, pp. 1-206; P. S. Varde, *History of Education in Goa*, 1977.
9. Portaria no. 803, December 2, 1895 in *Boletim do Governo*, December 3, 1895.
10. M. J. G. de Saldanha, *op. cit.*, p. 306.
11. Carmo D'Souza, *op. cit*, p. 182.
12. *Grande Encyclopedia Luso-Brasileira*, vol. VII, p. 504.
13. *Carta Constitucional da Monárquia Portuguesa*, Panjim: Imprensa Nacional, 1880, pp. 1-19; M. J. G. de Saldanha, *op. cit.*, p. 252.
14. *Constituição Política da Monárquia Portuguesa*, pp. 32-37.
15. J. A. Ismael Gracias, *Carta Organica das Instituições administrativas nas Províncias Ultramarinas*, 1899, pp. 93-97.

16. "Constituição Política da Republica Portuguesa", *Boletim Official*, no. 72, dated September 11, 1911.
17. P. J. Peregrino Costa, *A expansão do goes pelo mundo*, 1956, p. 21.
18. Decree nos. 1 and 3 of November 1, 1871 in *Boletim Official*, no. 99, 1871.
19. Sarto Esteves, *Politics and Political Leadership in Goa*, 1986, p. 31.
20. António Anastasio Bruto da Costa, *Goa sob a dominação portuguesa*, 1897, p. 137; Miguel Vicente Abreu, *Noção de alguns filhos distinctos da India Portuguesa*, 1874, p. 36.
21. Quoted by Robert de Souza in "Political Consciousness among the Goans", *Navhind Times*, April 9, 1967.
22. Expectação Barreto, *Quadros biographicos dos padres ilustres de Goa*, 1898, p. 90.
23. For more details see J. B. Amancio Gracias, *Contemporaneos ilustres, esboço biographico de Bernardo Francisco da Costa*, 1896.
24. Francisco Luis Gomes, "Letter to Lamartine" dated January 5, 1861 in *Selected Works of Francisco Luis Gomes*, p. 369.
25. For more details see *Selected works of Francisco Luis Gomes,* with an introduction by A. Correia Fernandes & Armando Menezes, Centenary Committee Bombay; Mario Cabral e Sa & M. Lourdes B. Costa Rodrigues (eds.), *Great Goans*, vol. III, pp, 1-39.
26. George M. Moraes, "Francisco Luis Gomes as a historian", in *Francisco Luis Gomes Death Centenary Commeration Committee of Salcete Souvenir*, 1974, p. 129.
27. Roque Correia-Afonso, "Cristovão Pinto", in *Heraldo,* March 9, 1926. For bibliography of his works see Aleixio Manuel da Costa, *Dicionário da Literatura Goesa*, vol. III, p. 62.
28. Joaquim Rosa, "Tradição Prazeriana", in *O Heraldo*, June 4, 1949; "Projectos de lei e propostas apresentadas ao congresso da Republica e ao Governo", *O Heraldo*, May 24, 1949, May 26, 1949, June 3, 1949, June 10, 1949.
29. For more details see António Maria Cunha, "A evolução do Jornalismo na India Portuguesa" in *A India Portuguesa*, vol. II, pp. 503-594; Alvaro de Loyola Furtado. "Primordios da Imprensa e da Jornalismo em Goa e no resto da India", nos. 116 and 129, 1977, 1981.
30. Sertorio Coelho, *Uma Página negra para as annaes da história colonial Portuguesa,* 1895; Pratima Kamat, "Some protesting priests of Goa", in *Essays in Goan History*, ed. Teotónio R. de Souza, New Delhi: Concept Publishing Co., pp.103-117.
31. For more details see Luis de Menezes Braganca, *Prosas dispersas*, 1965; "Instituto Menezes Bragança homenagem pelo centenário do seu nascimento", *Boletim do Instituto Menezes Braganza*, no. 116, 1977.
32. Miguel Vicente de Abreu, *op. cit.,* pp. 12-14; *Grande Encyclopedia Portuguesa e Brasileira*, vol. V, p. 498.
33. *Grande Encyclopedia Luso-Brasileira*, vol. XII, p. 118.
34. Bailon de Sa, "Past Goan Scientists", in *Boletim do Instituto Menezes Braganza,* no. 176, 1996, p. 19; Aleixio Manuel da Costa, *op. cit*, vol. I, pp. 22-33.

35. António Pereira, *The makers of Konkani literature*, 1982, pp. 161-173; *Grande Encyclopedia Portuguesa e Brasileira*, vol. VIII, pp. 350-51.
36. Pereira, *op. cit*, p. 177.
37. Manohar R. Sardesai, "Modern Konkani literature" in *Boletim do Instituto Menezes Braganza,* no. 176, 1996, p. 29.
38. Amancio J. B. Gracias, "Esboço biografico de F. N. Xavier" in *Bosquejo histórico das comunidades*, pp. 1-55; Aleixio Manuel da Costa, *op. cit.*, vol. III, pp. 348-56. The following are some of the important works by F. N. Xavier: *Bosquejo histórico das comunidades,* 1852; *Nobiliarchia Goana*, 1862-63; *Resumo histórico da maravilhosa vida, conversão milagres de S. Francisco Xavier*, 1859.
39. D. M. Terreiro. "Representative Sons of Goa", in *The Indo-Portuguese Review*, vol. XI, 1928-1929, p. 100; Aleixio Manuel da Costa, *op. cit.*, vol. I, pp. 16-20. Some important works by M. V. de Abreu are: *O Governo do Vice Rei, Conde do Rio Pardo*, 1862; *Memória sobre os Livros das Monções do Reino*, 1866; *Noção de alguns filhos distinctos da India Portuguesa*, 1874; *Relation de L'Inquistion de Goa* by Gabriel Dellon (translation into Portuguese).
40. *Grande Encyclopedia Portuguesa e Brasileira*, vol. XII, pp. 655-57; Aleixio Manuel da Costa, *op. cit.*, vol. II, pp. 133-44.

15

Liberation and the Goan Ethos

TERESA ALBUQUERQUE

It is the history of a people that shapes its culture and moulds its ethos. This paper seeks to show also how sometimes the culture of a people even determines the course of its history. Goan culture is a unique blend of East and West due to a historical circumstance. Goan history was the result of this cultural divide – an old colonial ploy, probably. And ironically, it was this Goan culture created by the Portuguese, that ultimately chose the path of Goa's march to freedom.

Goan culture

The history of Goa predates the Christian era. From the 8th century A.D. there definitely existed the organised system of federated village republics, called *gauponn* (in Konkani). And to quote the late Goan historian, Prof. George Moraes: "The greatest monument of pre-Portuguese culture is the village community, an institution under whose aegis from the earliest times Goan youth has had its intellectual formation".[1] Down the centuries, in the face of constant change of rule, the *gauponn* remained and this stability caused local patriotism to tower above loyalty to king and country. Thus the village gave to the Goan his identity, a deep-rooted link that continues to bind the farthest emigrant to his native land.

When the Portuguese conquered Goa in 1510, they astutely chose to retain the prevailing pattern of village administration along with certain evils that had crept into it – like the caste hierarchy. By retaining this system, insidiously they perpetrated yet another divisive force among the local people. For, when the Portuguese missionaries converted the Hindus of Goa to Christianity during the early 16th century, the transformation seemed to be total. The converts discarded the vernacular for Portuguese religion, language, names, dress and way of life. So deeply ingrained was this change that these Christians became a new breed, a race apart from their own Hindu fellowmen around. And yet, this was a mockery. While professing the Christian concept of universal brotherhood and equality, ironically in practice the converts held on to their traditional castes and the barriers it rent within their own circles. The Church itself was even more guilty, reserving in the early days the Goan priesthood only for the high castes.

Religion to Indians has always been something very close to their heart. To the Hindu masses, who staunchly clung to their traditional beliefs, anything and everything Portuguese became repugnant. At one stage, a number of Hindus fled in terror to escape religious persecution and only when the wave passed did some return. However to survive under the new rule Hindus had to bear with fortitude religious discrimination; those in commerce kept good relations with the government, even propping it – to mutual advantage – when it was threatened. Due to these circumstances the Goan Hindu culture stayed largely untouched by alien influence.

Converts, on the other hand, embraced the new religion and clung to it. They became exposed to western learning. Basic knowledge was imparted to them at the church school, along with the rudiments of the Gregorian chant. They learnt to articulate through speech and writing in Portuguese and later in clerical seminaries acquired higher education in the arts and humanities, which slanted their horizon to the west. When medical and military schools were instituted, they availed of this training. Hence, apart from service as clerks and writers, some rose in the professions of law, medicine and military. Was it some snobbish inhibition, or due also to their "other world" Christian slant? Commerce and money-making did not attract and Christians converted by the Portuguese have never as a community been very affluent.

Because they became thus a privileged class under the new government, Goan Catholics began to adopt a rather supercilious attitude that clung to them, and later made them an enigma of ridicule to many. They were a curious hybrid of east and west, for though their outlook had turned western, in private they retained many features of their ethnic heritage. Hence, they considered themselves Goans, but not Indians.[2] They referred to Hindu Goans rather derogatively as *Konknos* (inhabitants of the intensive Konkan region), and quite often as *Indianos*.

Dissent

The Hindus of Goa were not complacent about the foreign rule, instances of revolt, being stray, only drew further repression. But early during the 16th century, seeing Jesuit attempts to proselytize as also a threat to the existing financial structure, an organized protest resulted in the well-known Cuncolim massacre of a group of Jesuit missionaries in Salcete.[3]

However, in time, rampant dissatisfaction infected even the favoured Christians. The Goan priests who were adequately qualified for positions of responsibility in the Church, bitterly resented that, despite their protests, the religious hierarchy continued to be composed exclusively of Portuguese who were natives of Portugal. Frustration motivated a number affiliated to the Portuguese *Padroado,* to opt for higher appointments under the newly-formed Roman *Propaganda* and serve in the mission field outside Goa. Besides, taking advantage of Pombal's recent liberal decrees which upheld the equality of Goan candidates for higher posts in church and State, in 1787 a group of disgruntled clerics resorted to what came to be known as the Pinto Conspiracy. Cruelly crushed by the authorities, resentment stayed under.[4]

Foretaste of freedom

However, the liberal tendency did pave the way for the electoral struggles that took place in Goa in the wake of constitutional reforms ushered into Portugal in the year 1820. The following year Goa was empowered to dispatch a few of her own sons as elected representatives to the Parliament of Portugal. This measure of political liberty strengthened the feeling of oneness and loyalty to the rulers, and because Goans were formally declared citizens of the Portuguese empire, the misguided notion that they themselves were Portuguese was reinforced. It may be noted that, generally speaking, except at the time of the Goa Inquisition, Portuguese offences against the people of Goa were more of omission than commission, and there certainly existed a definite empathy in the rapport established between these colonial rulers and their ruled.

Significantly, though only for a very limited period (1822-1925), Goans were given a foretaste of autonomy long before any other people in the Indian sub-continent. This bonded them within a Portuguese enclave that lasted for over 450 years, and at the same time isolated them from the rest of India. But voting rights were granted to a "a privileged few" just about 40,000 persons in a population of 550,000, only to those who had knowledge of the Portuguese language, and who paid a certain minimum of tax to the State.[5]

Moreover, the actual implementation of the liberal decree of 1820 in Goa resulted in bloody conflict which caused a number of political émigrés to flee to Bombay in neighbouring British India. From there they started in 1835 a campaign through the press which kept alive the spirit of resistance to imperialist injustice, both there and in Goa.

Simultaneously Bernardo Peres da Silva, the earliest elected Goan representative to the Portuguese Parliament, was making futile attempts to stabilize a constitutional government. Though deputed by Portugal as Governor-General of *Estado da India* in 1833, his efforts were thwarted by the local Portuguese authorities. In 1861 Francisco Luis Gomes made his famous fiery speech in the Portuguese Parliament demanding as a right political autonomy for Goa. Violence continued till 1890, but Goan elected representatives were still being sent to Portugal and they remained outstanding defenders of the Goan people as equal citizens of the Portuguese empire

The spirit of liberalism was slowly permeating although it was restricted mainly to the "privileged few" who alone were greatly exposed to the new ideas. In 1859 the press in Bombay found its echo in *O Ultramar*, the first product of private journalism in Goa. This opened the floodgates to numerous local newspapers which vociferously voiced the growing restlessness of the Goan intelligentsia. Stalwart free-thinkers like Luis Menezes Bragança, José Inácio de Loyola and others created an intellectual ferment, awakening Goans to the concept of self-determination and national awareness as was being promoted by Mahatma Gandhi across the border. Still the staunch loyalty to Portugal and the sense of oneness with it persisted in the very ethos of the Catholic Goan. There was as yet no thought of replacing the government of Portugal.

In 1926 the dictatorial regime of Salazar abolished constitutional government in Portugal and Goa too came under severe political repression.

Goan Diaspora

Goans were already moving out of their homeland, their culture facing further encounter. As we have seen, the earliest migration of Goans probably began during the 16th century when scores of Hindus fled with their religious deities to escape the rigours of religious intolerance under the Portuguese. Simultaneously, in an attempt to colonise and consolidate their recent conquests, the Portuguese transported a number of baptised

Goans as settlers to Mozambique on the east coast of Africa. They were even taken into the hinterland and ably assisted their masters to penetrate into the unknown interior and extend Portuguese influence. Subsequently the Goan settlers mingled with the Africans and by marrying into African tribal nobility and royalty, they became locally accepted and very powerful. During the 19th century this alliance came to identify Portuguese imperialism as the common enemy, and so jointly resisted it, thus preventing further Portuguese into the south. These pioneer Indo-African families are counted as heroes of the early resistance to colonial rule – a forerunner of the liberation movement, *Frelimo* of the later 1960s.[6] However, the Goan cultural impact on these communities was probably diluted and today it is not strongly in evidence.

Further dispersion

Towards the close of the 16th century, *Estado da India* suffered political and economic decline, being "reduced from the status of a giant to that of a pigmy", in the words of a contemporary observer Manoel Godinho. By 1687 this steady downward trend spurred ambitious merchants, both Portuguese and indigenous, to venture out into other parts of the country where other European powers were already on the ascendant. A number of Goan soldiers and sailors also accompanied the Portuguese to their flourishing possessions in Burma and the Far East, including Macau, and gradually settled there most comfortably.

In view of the situation, using Napolean's threat to make Goa a base from which to destroy their colonial power, in 1799 the British occupied Goa, evacuating their forces only in 1815. This period marks the start of unlettered Goans emigrating to Bombay as domestics in the entourage of British officers.[7] In Goa's deteriorating financial situation the common man was worst hit. Rather than drudge and be exploited by heartless landlords, some chose the hazards of travel on foot over the Ghats or the equally intimidating prospect of sea voyage in primitive country craft. With their exposure to western cuisine and music, they qualified as cooks and musicians, along the way some were absorbed in military bands in the Maratha Confederacy or neighbouring princely states. Some Goans found occupation as stragglers in those armies. A few even became renowned as officers in the Peshwa army.[8]

By 1818 British paramountcy in the western region was confirmed. On the other hand, *Estado da India* was hopelessly enslaved by an economy that had become precarious: export trade was nil but for the feeble exchange across the border, local industries narrowed down to salt and the local brew. The British, cashing in on Goa's vulnerability, manipulated the Anglo-Portuguese Treaty of 1878, a straw the tottering Portuguese government grabbed. However, but for its happy fall-out of remarkable improvement in transport and communication with British India by coastal steamer and railway, for the people of Goa the treaty created a grim struggle for survival. [9]

The twin results of the Treaty now forced on Goans no choice: it became *potak laghun* or the question of stark survival that drove them out of their homeland. Those who could, availed of ready transport facilities. By 1888 the exodus from Goa had carried away one-sixth of the population.

Facing the challenge

By 1860 emigration had created Goan enclaves around *Padroado* churches in the city of Bombay. What contributed in no small measure to the success of this up-hill venture was that never-failing Goa resilience. The gregarious pioneers initiated an economical "home away from home". A room *(kudd)* was hired and then shared exclusively with later entrants who kept on coming from the village. This launching-pad to better accommodation as one prospered, served also the temporarily unemployed, or seamen in transit. Incidentally the system of *kudd* survives till today in most Indian cities where the early Goan migrants settled.

Few Hindus ventured out at this phase. The Christians, with their westernised way of life, had already shed many inhibition, and could adapt fast and take what living came their way: cooking, tailoring, bread-making, coach-building, even domestic work; seafaring attracted many. Familiarity with the Latin script, at a time when hardly a Hindu or Muslim could decipher the Roman alphabet, enabled the more literate to enter clerical service with the British, as well as private firms in the growing city. Notably, it was not merely their expertise but their strong sense of honesty, integrity and dedication to duty which brought Goans marked respect and success.

Largely trusted and patronised by the British rulers as they had been by their previous Portuguese masters, Goans intensified their learning towards everything western and consequently their isolation from other Indians. Local Christian converts of Bombay had undergone a similar crisis of identity which proved detrimental later.[10] With deterioration of conditions in Goa at the fag-end of the last century, the landed gentry was drawn into the exodus. Most of them were well-educated, some with professional training. Respected as Goan leaders in Bombay they unceasingly promoted all-round betterment and advancement of the community through co-operative ventures.[11]

The Portuguese government imposed a tax on emigration and from 1918 Goans in British India were also subjected to the Bombay Disqualification Aliens Act which debarred them from the right to vote. In 1932 they could opt for domicile so as to retain service under the British or hold property.[12] These circumstances probably instilled a practical change in attitude regarding Goan loyalty. No longer birds of passage, those better placed – by now landed proprietors – felt a new sense of financial security which inclined them to shed their strong allegiance to the Portuguese and appreciate instead their new status and privileges as domiciled British subjects. They envisaged a future for their children and went all out to give them good English education. The British system, its values, manners and the English language now substituted Portuguese. A western outlook still, but more widened and receptive to change and progress.

Some Goans fanned out: finding work opportunities in Karachi and the Persian Gulf under the early British programmes of development, as well as in steamship companies that regularly operated along the East Africa coast. The establishing of rail links to the interior of East Africa drew a number of Goans who gradually were absorbed also in the clerical service of the British administration, and settled there in growing numbers. Led by their gregarious Goan instinct they formed clubs, but due to the lack of education, allowed caste to create internal factions. However, they prized education and, patronised by the Portuguese Embassy in Kenya which offered exclusive financial support to set up schools for their children, professional guilds, etc., these Goans renewed their loyalty to the Portuguese and designated themselves Portuguese/Goans, not Indians.[13]

Into India's freedom movement

When India's call for independence from British rule came, emigrant Goans were in a quandary and took time to respond.[14] As we have seen, they were deeply integrated with the west, imbued as they were with affinity to everything western; language, dress, music, etc. Moreover in British India, they had just achieved a new sense of financial security. Now on sufferance of the British government, could they shed all impunity and bite the hand that fed them? Yet another consideration held them back, from active participation in the national movement. Blind adherence to the dictates of the Church had become a habit right from the early days of conversion under the Portuguese; and now they were very much under the stranglehold of the British ecclesiastical hierarchy that instilled into the faithful an unshakable obedience to the ruling power.

As far back as 1909, the popular Bombay-based Goan organ, *Anglo Lusitano*, vociferously denounced the political apathy of the community, the lone voice in its wilderness being the local East Indian Joseph Baptista who was boldly advocating the national cause. But the Jalianwalla Bagh massacre in 1919 was an awakening. As one Goan intellectual Aloysius Soares stated: "things happened which roused in me emotions which turned me into an Indian... From a Goan I evolved into an Indian even though owing to a historical accident I continued to be an alien."[15]

Reading the signs of the times the Goan intelligentsia was faced with a dilemma: both, *the Examiner*, mouthpiece of the Church in Bombay and the local English-language press projected the British government viewpoint. The *Examiner* firmly exhorted Catholics to place their trust in the government, and leave the bishops to protect the religion should it be threatened.[16] Ultimately it was Soares' paper, the *Week* functioning since 1926, that fearlessly created a sense of national consciousness among Catholics until it was throttled by the government in 1932.

The *Examiner* frowned on Catholic participation in Gandhiji's Civil Disobedience warning the Church would suffer under an Indian government of the future. But as the struggle for independence mounted in 1930, the Catholic elite joined other Christians under the Nationalist Christian Party, defied the government and courted arrest. However, put on the alert by Gandhiji's adverse remarks on Christian proselytism by missionaries in India, safeguards for religious rights became a priority. Therefore in 1932 when Christians were invited to attend an All-Parties Conference to resolve the minorities issue, seeing this as an opportunity to relate with the Indian mainstream, most educated Catholics, including the elite section of Goans, promptly collaborated to project Indian Christian solidarity.

This unity added clout. In 1944, the Catholic Union of India, along with the All-India Council of Indian Christians, was appointed to study the question of fundamental rights and present its demands for Christian representation. In 1946 Christians, now in the Constituent Assembly, ensured that fundamental rights, religious safeguards were firmly engrafted into the Constitution - a commendable step that undoubtedly helped lay the foundation for a solid democracy. Their surrender of reservation of seats for Christians was much appreciated by the majority party and when independence was granted in 1947, Indian Christians proudly marched forward as rightful citizens into the national mainstream.

Towards the Liberation of Goa[17]

In 1928 during the struggle for India's freedom, Tristão Braganza Cunha, popularly known as 'Father of the Goan Freedom Movement', began an agitation in Goa, but his efforts were curbed by the Portuguese government and later he was deported.

On June 18, 1946, in Goa, Ram Manohar Lohia publicly called on Goans to break the shackles of foreign domination. Though in sympathy, in Goa itself, the long-oppressed masses were totally powerless to resist; they were stifled by the existing system of *barcari* under the prevailing pattern of village administration. The *bhatkars* (landlords) firmly supported the imperialist regime and held their tenants in thrall. If the latter showed the slightest defiance they would be evicted from their homes and stood to lose even their meagre sustenance. Lohia's arrest and eviction by the Portuguese fanned the flickering flame of freedom and in a programme of non-violent action, mass satyagrahis were launched into the Portuguese enclave from the Indian border furtively abetted by a few daring individuals within Goa. When the Portuguese countered with arrest and deportation, action shifted to Bombay. There, in June 1947 a "Quit Goa" resolution was passed by the Goan Political Conference, a mass meeting composed of prominent Goans, editors of Goan periodicals, representatives of Goan village unions and managers of Goan *kudds*. Notably the struggling Goan working class which still patronized the *kudds* took time to get involved and, long accustomed to western religious depiction, was even skeptical of the nationalist Goan, Cardinal Valerian Gracias, Archbishop of Bombay, who sported for public veneration an indigenous representation of the Virgin Mary.[18]

Even after India was free, Portugal refused to relinquish her hold on Goa. The government of India patiently hoped to achieve a change through diplomacy. Goan agitators, thrown on their own resources, could only focus a spotlight on Goa: keeping its spirit alive through periodicals and pamphlets in Konkani, Marathi, English and Portuguese, through revival of Konkani folk-song, dance and Goan folklore, by a grand Goa exhibition, and a Goan Information Bureau to counter Portuguese distortion of facts throughout the world.

When Portugal still did not yield to diplomacy by the Indian government, leading Goans of Bombay signed a formal manifesto drafted by Aloysius Soares "to free ourselves from the Portuguese rule and unite with India". Dispatched to Prime Minister Nehru with a plea for guarantees that the culture, religion and customs of the people of Goa would be respected by India, this elicited a specific assurance in Parliament. However, as is usual with Goans the world over, there existed some petty squabbling for leadership.[19] Adopting drastic action in July 1954, some political parties hoisted the Indian national flag in the Portuguese enclave of Dadra and Nagar Haveli which resulted in a fracas at the Hague.

Meanwhile Hindu chauvinism reared its head, and some Christian missionaries were attacked. Though the act was condemned by Nehru, a section of the Goans had strong misgivings about churches in Goa and the tomb of St. Francis being respected. Towards unity, Soares set up the Goa Liberation Council and in 1956 its organ *the Goan Tribune* to project the Goan question to the world at large.

Portugal still did not budge, even after the French withdrawal from India. Finally Nehru took up the challenge by African nationalists to lead the way to end colonialism. Uniting the various factions, Soares set up the Goan Political Convention, which actively participated in the 3rd National Conference of Afro-Asian Solidarity in Bombay in December 1960, which prepared the ground that finally led to military intervention. Operation Vijay launched on December 18, 1961 brought freedom to Goa.

For Freedom of Kenya[20]

The movement for Kenya's freedom went on for more than seven decades, but only gathered momentum with the struggle that ended colonial rule in India and Goa. A few Goans in Kenya played a most conspicuous role in the campaign but the vast majority under British employment, were too indifferent to risk the watchful eye of the authorities and vigorous opposition of the vice-consul for Portugal.

Pio Gama Pinto (Free Kenya's first martyr for freedom, widely acknowledged as a bridge between India and Africa) had actually participated in satyagraha at the Goan border and came to Kenya in 1948 to escape arrest for involvement in the Indian naval mutiny. To create awareness of Goa's problem, he started the Konkani newspaper, *Uzvad*, and in September 1955 was appointed secretary of the newly-formed East African Goan National Association. Also working for Kenya's freedom were two Kenya-born, British-qualified Goan lawyers who had been active members of the Indian National Congress in Nairobi: namely Joaquim Nazareth and Fitzeval de Souza. The Afro-Goan, Joseph Zuzarte Murumbi also played an important role.

In 1947, at the culmination of India's struggle, East Africa and India were linked by a common cause. After India's independence its government covertly encouraged further collaboration. In 1950 frustration at the threat of perpetuation of the policy of racial domination, sparked off the violence of *Mau Mau* terrorism and the call for *Uhuru* – total freedom. In 1952 an emergency was declared and Jomo Kenyatta, the popular African leader was arrested. The Kenya African Union – which included a few Indians and Goans – continued its nationalist propaganda. Pio Gama Pinto was at the helm, in the press and in the Trade Union movement, until his five-year arrest for involvement with *Mau Mau*. With material he provided, in 1953 Murumbi carried the sympathy campaign to India, Cairo and London.

At the famous trial of Kenyatta in 1953, Fitzeval de Souza featured prominently on his defence team. Though the trial was a travesty of justice, it attracted global sympathy for a morally legitimate cause. Meanwhile in 1958, in the newly created multi-racial Legislative Council, Joaquim Nazareth supported African members in their demands. After Kenyatta's release in 1961, Souza accompanied Kenyatta to the ensuing Lancaster House Conferences, that ushered change, and assisted him in drafting a new Constitution. In 1963 Kenya was finally granted *Uhuru.*

Conclusion

As we have seen, the Goan spirit is indomitable in the face of challenge, and at the turn of the last century, Goans were able, not only to keep their heads above high water, but to swim with the tide. Though Goans in great numbers, did not participate in movements for political liberation – for reasons which are obvious – their involvement was qualitative. They played a pivotal role in ensuring to the best of their ability that freedom was all-embracing. The spectacular success of this miniscule group could be attributed to the influence of their innate culture, strong sense of values, firm dedication, purposeful leadership, education, and consequently the ability to discern the path which promised the greatest good.

NOTES AND REFERENCES

1. G. M. Moraes, "Goan history and culture", *Souvenir of the Grand Goa Exhibition*, Bombay, 1947.
2. C. F. Saldanha, *A Short History of Goa*, Bombay, 1952, p. 101.
3. T. R. de Souza, "Why Cuncolim Martyrs", in *Jesuits in India: In historical perspective*, eds. T. R de Souza & C. J. Borges, Macau: Instituto Cultural de Macau, 1992, p. 38.

4. Saldanha, *op. cit.*, pp. 114-17.
5. B. G. D'Souza, *Goan Society in Transition*, Bombay, 1975, p. 275.
6. S. Sadiq Ali, "India and Mozambique: Past and Present", *Purabhilekh-Puratatva* (Panaji: Directorate of Archives and Archaeology), vol. VI, no. 1, Jan-June 1988.
7. Saldanha, *op. cit.*, p. 124.
8. *Biographia Goana*, Bombay, p. 109.
9. T. Albuquerque, "Anglo-Portuguese Treaty of 1878 – an impact on the people of Goa", *Indica* (Heras Institute, Bombay), vol. 27, no. 2, pp. 117-124.
10. E. Baptista, The East Indians, Bombay, 1967, p. 20.
11. T. Albuquerque, *To Love is to Serve*, Bombay, 1986, pp. 12-25.
12. *Anglo-Lusitano*, October 1, 1932.
13. J. S. Mangat, *A History of the Asians in East Africa*, Oxford, 1969.
14. T. Albuquerque, "Christians of Bombay in the cause of freedom. Part I: The National Movement", *Indica*, vol. 21, no. 2, pp. 97-113.
15. A. Soares, *Down the Corridors of Time*, vol. I, Bombay, 1972, pp. 92-3.
16. *The Examiner*, January 25, 1919.
17. T. Albuquerque, "Christians of Bombay in the cause of freedom. Part II: Goan Liberation", *Indica*, vol. 22, no. 1, pp. 71-8.
18. A. Soares, *op. cit.*,
19. *The Bombay Chronicle*, March 12, 1954.
20. T. Albuquerque, *Goans in Kenya*, Mumbai, 1999.

PART III

RELIGIOUS ISSUES

16

A Glimpse of the Hospitallers of Diu in the late 18th Century

ARTUR TEODORO DE MATOS

The brothers of St. John of God had settled since 1681 in Mozambique where they set up a convent and a hospital.[1] Four years later, they were already in Goa, Bassein and Diu.[2] In Diu they built, outside the fortress, a hospital which had a small church. The hospital and the convent were under the supervision of three or four friars and the Portuguese Crown granted them annually some financial support which was accounted for in the budget of the *Estado da India.*[3] In 1702 and 1711, a number of *prazos da coroa* as well as several rents were given to the brothers in order to help them meet the expenses of the hospital.[4] In 1705, the convent building which had previously belonged to the Carmelites, was given to them and they settled there until the 19th century when their brotherhood was no more.[5]

The Order of the Hospitallers at Diu was in the same state of degredation as many of the Religious Orders in the Orient. However, in 1878, D. Manuel de Santa Catarina, the polemic Carmelite archbishop who would end his term as bishop in the Algarve, set forth to reform the statutes of the Hospitallers as well as those pertaining to the convents of Daman and Mozambique of the same Order.[6] This archbishop, who was in fact the reformer and *Visitador Geral* of all Religious Orders in India, felt that in many Hospitallers "iniquity abounded" and that almost all the members of this Order no longer practised charity, the essence and main foundation of the Order. Furthermore, the province was without incorrupt friars capable of "keeping up" the reform. Besides, in his opinion, the king would certainly suppress these Orders if he knew the "great negligence" with which they lived.[7]

But the archbishop, so often obstinate and not cautious during his term as bishop, was determined to carry out a reform in order to change the improper situations and include rules which were, in his opinion, essential for the accomplishment of his duties and, as he himself wrote, "to strengthen what was weak, to cure what was corrupt and to bind what was broken" in order to redeem what was already irredeemable.[8]

In addition, Frei Domingos de São João de Deos, the commissary-general of the Order and the hospital orderly, in a pastoral letter sent to the convent of Diu and probably to other convents as well, criticised the members of his Order, mainly on account of the bad management of the convent property, the sale of servants belonging to the brotherhood, the mortgage of the church silver, the estrangement of furniture and property "with the false pretext of having no food". These transactions could be performed - if his allegations were true, which they were not – only with the authorisation of their superiors.[9]

This is the picture drawn by both the reformer and the commissary-general. A number of rules and regulations would then be prepared with the view of inducing the Hospitallers to practise charity, prayer and other duties prescribed by the statutes of their Order.

However much the reassessment of the reformer's determinations are important for the restoration of the Order and the welfare of the convent of Diu, we will, nevertheless, concern ourselves only with the deviation from the rules by the brothers of St. John in this northern fortress. If the inspection made by the commissary-general in the name of the archbishop gives us an account of the state of their financial affairs as well as of other irregularities in 1783 and 1786, we must reflect through the stated rules, on the misguidances and omissions of these Hospitallers.[10]

But, first of all, let us follow the most relevant details of their daily affairs which were similar to those of the brothers of the Royal Hospital of Goa.

At the sound of the bell, at three in the morning, and after the distribution of the medicine to the patients, they would go to the church to pray. After attending Mass, they returned to the infirmary to distribute water for the washing-up of the patients, made the beds and, afterwards, visited the so-called "House of the Weak," i.e. the hospital ward where the patients with terminal illnesses were kept. In this ward, they waited upon the sick and made the so-called "spiritual exercises" and, later, they returned to the infirmary in order to sweep the floors.[11]

Meanwhile, the physician or the surgeon would arrive. The monks assigned to assist him would minister the medication in their respective wards.[12]

At eleven, lunch was served to the patients and, afterwards, the friars would eat their meal in the refectory. While they ate in silence, they would hear the chronicles of the Order or some chapters of its Constitutions.[13] The following hours would be spent in silence, that is, resting, as the brothers carried out the profane custom of taking an afternoon nap which the climate warranted, tradition enforced and the hour granted.[14]

Once again the bell would summon the friars to their duties: of giving medication to the patients, washing the feet "of those to whom there was no inconvenience to do so" and giving them the afternoon lunch. At the end of the day, supper was served to the patients and afterwards to the brothers who would assemble at the chapel for their night prayers. Another distribution of medication was once again carried out and the patients were prepared for the night, after all the dormitories had been blessed.[15]

During the night, each brother would keep a three-hour vigil in order to watch over the patients in the wards as well as to give some broth and the medication prescribed by the physician.[16]

The members of the Order of St. John in addition to their duties as male nurses, had also to perform the religious obligations prescribed by their Order. Besides the morning and night prayers, there was the daily examination of conscience, the discipline and the abstinence from food every Friday,[17] daily masses with prayers invoking divine blessings, frequent confessions, spiritual exercises every ten days, etc.[18]

But of which malpractices were the Hospitallers of Diu accused?

If the rule of the cloister imposed on the regular members enabled them to practise the vows they were required to at the time of their profession as well as to allow for a better seclusion, it was, nevertheless, a way for them to withdraw from the outside world. However, as the brotherhood was devoted to the care of the sick and needy, it was therefore forced to have contacts with the local community not only through the patients who were admitted and through the relatives who visited them but also through the servants hired to perform the daily chores for the hospital. And, if women were not allowed inside the male convents, we know for certain that the Brothers of the Order of St. John hired African maids, probably slaves, to do the kitchen chores, to bake bread and, perhaps, to perform other services. The Reformer gave them an order to substitute these maids for local maids and to forbid the admission of any woman into the convent. We must not forget that a large part of the slaves came from Mozambique where the Hospitallers were looking after the Royal Hospital since 1681 and had an ancient tradition of trading deals with Diu.

Besides the women who could cause them to sin, relationships between members of the same sex, secular or otherwise, as well as visits to each other's cells, were also forbidden. They had to avoid - we do not know whether that meant repress - any kind of friendship with young males. Thus, the brothers were not allowed to have male servants and if any monk requested a servant because he was too sick or too old, the Superior of the convent would then choose one providing that he was not very young.

The excessive consumption of spirits like brandy, rum or wine, was naturally highly criticised and hardly recommended to the members of the clergy whose main activity was the care of the patients. The use of alcoholic beverages was, henceforth forbidden by the archbishop excepting when ministered as a treatment to the patients or served at the refectory on festive occasions. The archbishop felt that "the excessive use of liquor was a source of destruction for the clergy and for the province as well."[19]

Beyond reproach was indeed the "business" classified as "disgraceful" which was carried out by several Hospitallers on the local weavers: these brothers would order for suits but never paid for them or, sometimes, they would give in return "an amount which had no bearing on the work".[20]

But their condemnable behaviour did not end there. An inquiry into the accounts of the convent of Diu from 1783 to 1785 whose rector was Friar Estevão de Jesus Maria José, uncovered several irregularities under his management.

After having stipulated the terms of the contract for the leasing of his palm-groves, this friar demanded from the *colles*[21] a surplus of 3,000 coconuts which he sent as a present to the wife of Sebastião Franco. The somewhat suspicious transactions made by this member of the Order were many. In addition to an excessive acquisition of sugar - we do not know whether he intended to give it to someone related to him - grave errors in the account books were also found which meant a great loss to the convent. With the evidence of the malpractices found out, as well as of the external signs of wealth shown by this administrator, the Visitor stated: "with what money has this priest started to negotiate? where did his money come from? where did he find this mine and how did he manage to acquire such wealth?" And he added that Friar Estevão de Jesus Maria José arrived in Diu with no possessions, that he did not inherit a fortune from his family and did not benefit from earnings collected from the sermons, masses and other church services.[22] At the time of the inquiry, he was already living on the Mozambique Island but he had been told that his accounts had not been approved as they were "forged" and, consequently, a minute inquiry had been carried out.[23]

But many other procedures of the brothers of St. John were also condemnable mainly because they did not perform the religious as well as nursing duties which were assigned to them at the hospital at Diu. There had been a lack of religious conviction as well as a negligence in the reception of the main sacraments: confession and communion. Indeed, several monks went to confession and received communion once a year - on Maundy Thursday - when they should have done it every week.[24]

And, notwithstanding the fact that "hospitality has been the essence of our sacred religion" as the Visitor stated in 1787, several friars besides being careless in the discharge of their elementary duties, did not make charity one of their main virtues. Furthermore, they often did not give spiritual assistance to their patients as "many had died without receiving the sacraments" and they did not take enough care of the weaker patients. On many occasions, they made the slaves perform their duties, namely, the cleaning of the patients. The cleanliness of hospital wards was seldom satisfactory as the brothers very often forgot to sweep the floors.[25] Therefore, the commissary-general prescribed a number of precepts from which they could not exempt themselves - they had to take good care of all the patients and be charitable. They had to wash them, kiss them and feed them with their own hands. They had to fulfil exactly the engagements imposed on them by the archbishop.[26]

The corruption of the Religious Orders and the indiscipline inside the convents were matters which had taken place among the regular clergy in the Orient since the late 17th century but became even worse in the following. The Church was then obliged to appoint, in 1785, the archbishop of Goa, as the reformer of all religious congregations.[27] The events which occurred in the hospital and convent of Diu might not have been the most grievous ones. The important contribution of the brothers of this Order to the Military Hospital in Mozambique and in Goa - the self-denial and devotion with which they took care of the patients, many of them arriving in a critical state after a long and tiring journey, is well-known.

The observations issued from a number of documents concerning an inspection made of the convent of the Hospitallers of Diu may only suggest that this was the decline into which the regular clergy had fallen in the latter part of the 18th century. But the dedication of an Order such as the Order of St. John cannot be ignored because of the malpractices of a few members who did not do their duties in the manner in which the founder of the Order would have wished them to.

The territory of Gujarat in which the island of Diu was included, did not offer the best conditions for the performance of religious duties. The country was very poor, the climate adverse and there was only a very small Christian community living there. In addition, the number of brothers of the Religious Order of the Hospitallers in Diu never exceeded four and, during the most part of the 18th century, there were only three. Therefore, there might have been an accumulation of duties and consequently more work to be done. Nevertheless, who can claim that one is not liable to human frailty?

NOTES AND REFERENCES

1. António Alberto Banha de Andrade "Fundação do Hospital Militar de S. João de Deus em Moçambique," in *Studia* (1958), pp. 77-89.
2. *National Library of Lisbon*, codex 177, fls.171-172v, "Rellação do Cathalogo dos Conventos e Hospitais que tem na India a Religião de S. João de Deos; quam forão os seus fundadores, e o anno em que foy fundado cada hum dos ditos Conventos". Concerning the presence of this Order in the Orient, see also A. A. Banha de Andrade, "Os Hospitaleiros na India" in *Portugal em Africa*, XIV (1957).
3. Banha de Andrade, "Os Hospitaleiros de S. João de Deus na India", pp. 117-118.
4. "A Fortaleza de Diu" in *Arquivo Português Oriental*, ed. A. B. de Bragança Pereira, tomo IV, vol. II, pt. II, Bastorá, 1938, pp. 637-638.
5. *Historical Archives of Goa (HAG)*, *Monções do Reino*, no. 79, fls. 348-350, "Lista dos Conventos, e Hospitaes que administra a ordem de São João de Deos, no Estado da India Oriental, e a despeza que com elles fas Sua Magestade que Deos guarde, e principio que tiverão suas fundações, e numero de religiosos que nelles assistem".
6. *HAG*, *Convento de Diu*, no. 2566, fl. 45-48. "Copia do Decreto de Reforma que enviou o Sr. Frei Manuel de Santa Catharina dos Religiosos Carmelitas Descalços, por merce de Deos e da Santa Sé Apostolica Arcebispo Metropolitano de Goa, Primaz do Oriente do Conselho da Rainha Minha Senhora, e por ordem sua, e Authoridade Apostolica, Reformador, e Vizitador Geral de todas as ordens na India Oriental", Goa, dated July 3, 1787.
7. *Ibid.*, fls. 45-45v.
8. *Ibid.*, fl. 45v.
9. *HAG*, *Convento de Diu*, no. 2566, fls. 41v-43, "Rezisto da Pastoral que baichou o Nosso Reverendissimo Padre Comissario Geral Frei Domingos de São João de Deos neste convento de Nossa Senhora do Carmo da Ordem do Nosso Padre São João de Deos desta fortaleza de Diu", on the 4th of January 1788. This pastoral letter had to be read every month to the community and nailed on the choir door.

10. *HAG, Convento de Diu*, no. 2566. Inspection by the general commissioner, Frei Domingos de São João de Deos to the convent of Diu took place on October 13, 1787. This document is incomplete as its first part is missing.
11. *HAG, Convento de Diu*, no. 2566, "Copia do Decreto da reforma ... ", articles 14 and 15.
12. *Ibid.*, article 16.
13. *Ibid.*, articles 18 and 10.
14. *Ibid.*, article 18.
15. *Ibid.*, articles 18, 19 and 20.
16. *Ibid.*, articles 21 and 22.
17. During Lent it would also be on Mondays, Wednesdays and Fridays. *Cf. Ibid.*, article 5.
18. *Ibid.*, articles 5, 24 and 25.
19. *Ibid.*, article 1.
20. *Ibid.*, article 2.
21. Shudra caste. They depended for their livelihood on agriculture and fishing.
22. The intentions of the Mass were previously fixed by the prelate of the Order to whom all alms had to be addressed. The alms were included in the income of the convent. The priests could only celebrate Mass for the purposes chosen by them twice a week; they were then allowed to receive the alms which could be used "for their own private needs". *Cf.* article 13.
23. fl. 40v. Inspection of the convent of Diu on October 13, 1787.
24. "Copia do Decreto da reforma ... ", art. 3.
25. *Ibid.*, article 6
26. Visitation on October 13, 1787, fls. 41-41v.
27. On the reform of Religious Orders see Maria de Jesus dos Mártires Lopes, *Goa Setecentista: Tradição e Modernidade (1750-1800)*, Lisbon: Centro de Estudos de Povos e Culturas de Expressão Portuguesa, 1996, pp.155-163.

17

The Sisters of Santa Monica in the 18th Century

Details of Their Daily Life

MARIA DE JESUS DOS MÁRTIRES LOPES

At the beginning of the 17th century several changes had occurred in Goan society. The intensification of the Dutch attacks on this territory had created an ambience of war and uncertainty which had affected the families of the soldiers. Their wives and children found themselves in an acute state of poverty as well as abandoned. In order to relieve their problems, Archbishop D. Aleixo de Menezes had founded in 1605 two shelter homes (*Nossa Senhora da Serra* and *Santa Maria Madalena*). In the following year, taking advantage of a favourable political situation that had made him provisional governor of India, the archbishop established the congregation of Santa Monica which was the first religious congregation for women in Asia. He would in this way oppose the generally agreed policy of encouraging women to marry which resulted from the need to colonise the Portuguese territories in India.[1] We must remember that contrary to the policy followed by the Spanish government, the Portuguese did not favour the presence of women in India.

The foundation of the convent of Santa Monica took place at a time when there was a religious predominance in Goa and conversions to Christianity were intensified. With the Counter-Reformation in Portugal, a policy of religious imperialism had began to emerge which according to Luis Filipe Thomaz had the intention of "turning the Portuguese *Estado da India* into a powerful Catholic state and Goa into an important religious centre, a strong focal point of Christian culture."[2]

The ecclesiastical term of D. Aleixo de Menezes was marked by the application of the Tridentine reform in India, with the establishment of new religious institutions and by a stronger religious authority. In the 17th century, the religious congregations of European origin were joined by others, namely the Carmelites, the Theatines, the Hospitallers of St. John and the Goan Congregation of the Oratorians.

Built on the 'Holy Hill', the convent of Santa Monica, built between 1607 and 1627, became a royal monastery in 1636, when its rules were approved by Pope Paul V in 1613. It was meant to house around 100 religious women. It sheltered the wives and daughters of military men who were either absent or deceased in order to help them to attain an ascetic ideal. In 1609, it had 37 sisters and several novices and, in 1624, it had already around 100 religious members besides the young girls who were educated by them.[3]

Let us analyse some details of the life in this convent during the 18th century and try to characterize the daily life of these women, from their religious programmes to their other activities. However, we must ask ourselves several questions: What was the social universe of the monastery? Who were its members? What were its resources and what was its financial situation?

There were a number of social as well as religious categories in the convent – the lay sisters of the veil (*religiosas de véu*), the lay sisters (*leigas e conversas*), the girls, the servants and the slaves. The lay sisters needed to be about 20, healthy and strong enough to work at the convent. They were white women, either virgins or widows. However, "a local woman who was not black (African) and known to be virtuous and a virgin, could be admitted too".[4]

The lay sisters had "to be strong, have the necessary age, be virgins or virtuous widows ... and they could be either white or local women".[5] The young girls who were admitted had to be, at least, six years of age. The servants were girls "well-trained to undertake their domestic chores".[6] Women of the nobility, provided they were humble and devoted to religious life, or women of high rank who had no dowry, could also be accepted. As many military men came to India on account of the wars in the New Conquests, it is probable that throughout the 18th century and more so particularly during the second half of that century, many girls and women of the nobility entered the convent.

In order to do the various works in the convent, slaves could be bought. A certain hierarchy was however observed notwithstanding the statutes of the convent stipulating that no woman could be termed "mistress or my lady". In the second half of the 18th century, Indian women were allowed into the convent and the wearing of the white veil for the local women and the black for the Europeans, was abolished. The social reforms established by the Marquis of Pombal granting the same civil rights to the Goan Christians as to the Portuguese who came from the kingdom, certainly contributed to the allowing of women wearing the same veil.[7]

All women had to bring a dowry consisting of a stipulated amount of money as well as an amount requested for the maintenance of the Novitiate besides the habit, a bed for oneself and another for the hospital ward.[8] Many formal petitions of the 18th century show a certain lack of resources and many financial difficulties due probably to many factors, such as the number of servants against the requirements of the statutes, poor management, and loss of property in the North Province in 1739.[9] There were also several petitions requesting new rents, such as the revenues from the transit of ships at Agassaim, shops at Jua and Chorão and the landed estate in the New Conquests. These privileges were not always given as they meant a reduction in the revenues of the Royal Treasury.

Let us examine the occupations and activities which covered the schedule of the sisters of Santa Monica. Their religious schedule was their main occupation: Mass had to be attended by all the sisters and "in that the nuns had to excel themselves".[10] Besides this, mental prayer (an hour in the morning and another in the afternoon), visits to the Blessed Sacrament, frequent confession and communion as well as listening to sermons, fast and abstinence, completed their spiritual exercises.

The contacts with the outside world were severely supervised because, as a congregation in cloister, all lay sisters were strictly forbidden to leave the monastery.

There are a number of instances on how the women abided by these rules. Friar Lourenço de Santa Maria speaks of their devotion in the performance of their religious duties. We can also find information concerning their good behaviour in the letters exchanged between the authorities in Goa and the government. However, the visitations made by Archbishop Inácio de Santa Teresa between 1772 and 1731 mention several misconducts such as "strange precipitation", "talking during prayer" and "sitting while meditating".[11] But the accusations concerning their relationships with the Augustinians were more serious as they referred to "nodding, glances, letters, messages and clandestine presents". The religious inmates used to even use binoculars to look at the friars who lived in the convent on the other side of the street.[12]

Around 1730, the admission and presence of several Augustinian friars caused a number of serious occurrences which made the king order their removal and the substitution of the Augustinian confessors by secular priests. The visitation in 1730 refers to the large presence of monks for burials and forbids them from spending the night in the convent of Santa Monica after giving the blessing to the sisters.[13]

What were the other activities which filled the daily life of the sisters of Santa Monica in Goa? The statutes favoured undoubtedly their handiwork which adorned the altar, the vestry room, the hospital wards and the dinner refectory. Their needle work was done in a special room which was pleasant, bright and was of comfortable size. There, the sisters and the other inmates gathered to sew and adorn the curtains for the altars and the Blessed Sacrament, and to decorate the towels and other materials.

It is clear that the documents do not mention the anonymous work of so many religious inmates and the inventory of the artistic heritage pertaining to the churches in Goa has only just begun. However, even today, tradition mentions the artistic handiwork of the sisters of Santa Monica, namely the magnificent flag embroidered by them on the occasion of the Dutch attack on Mormugao in 1683.

The sisters were allowed to accept needle work orders for the Augustinian convent, some minor repairs for other churches and orders to make clothes for the Hospital of the Poor. However, they could not occupy themselves on unnecessary tasks.[14] The statutes strictly forbade the doing of any work in view of its sale except when it was necessary for the convent. The Archbishop D. Inácio de Santa Teresa, after his visitation to the convent in 1724 stated that "some embroidery as well as other similar handiworks were ordered by other churches."

The life inside the convent was sometimes enlivened by the celebration of religious services which was an expression of its faith and also of its cultural and artistic capabilities. Christmas, Easter, the feasts of the patron saints, St. Augustine and St. Monica as well as those of the popular saints, were very important. On these occasions the sisters made artistic Nativity scenes and, according to Friar Agostinho de Santa Maria, they adored the child Jesus with dance, songs and rhymes. Quatrains performed to the popular saints, in which Christian joy joined humour with artistic taste, were included in the literary repertoire of the sisters.[15]

The demands of the divine services led the sisters to lay emphasis on church songs and hymns, particularly on Gregorian chant and music. The statutes encouraged singing lessons as well as lessons for harp and organ given by an elderly music teacher. This musical knowledge helped the religious services and were used by the sisters of Santa Monica in their songs, hymns, quatrains and ballads dedicated to the prioresses, to certain religious inmates and to the Augustinian friars in a divine and profane mixture as is shown in a number of poems of the above-mentioned repertoire.[16]

As the convent welcomed girls who were six years old and above and who intended to take the veil, it was necessary to teach them to read and write according to the limits of women's education at the time. The mistress of these girls had to devote herself to teach them to write properly which shows the importance given by the sisters to calligraphy. In the convent of Santa Monica there was also a certain literary activity which was embellished by Portuguese and Spanish poetry having a rich Indo-Portuguese vocabulary and which potrayed some everyday scenes while disclosing their problems and fears.[17]

Besides the religious ceremonies, other special moments were celebrated with great solemnity in the convent of Santa Monica as was stipulated by the statutes. These moments occurred every time a novice entered the convent, or when a religious inmate took the veil or when the prioress was elected. As was common in other convents, the choice of one from three previously selected sisters to be the mother superior of the convent followed a number of carefully chosen requirements and was the result of a democratic vote by the sisters of the black veil, who had been instructed for more than a year.

We know that some elections were highly disputed. The Archbishop, in his letter concerning his visitation to the convent in 1728, cancelled a concession he himself had once granted – the liberty of the sisters to talk about the election on the day before it took place. He furthermore commanded that none of the sisters were allowed to write or speak with people outside the convent, not even with a religious member of the congregation, on matters concerning the election. But he ordered them to choose "with their eyes on God and free of personal feelings". One may then assume that the election of the prioress sometimes was discussed outside the halls of the convent and was influenced by the opinions of their religious neighbours. These elections were the theme of several poems which only reinforce their importance in the life of the monastery.[18]

A moment particularly important and crucial for the convent occurred between 1731 and 1735 at the time of the 'schism' which resulted in the division and departure of a large number of sisters, thus breaking their vows of cloister.

What were the reasons that had led the sisters to this schism? Notwithstanding the documents found concerning this subject, it is not an easy task to inquire into the true reasons. In order to understand it we must go back to the previous decade. In March 1720, the government had ordered that secular priests should be nominated as confessors of the convent instead of the Augustinians as had happened since then. The King made this decision after a complaint presented by the prioress and the prelate of the Augustinians stating that probably four Augustinian friars had once entered the convent of Santa Monica in a licentious manner thus making the inmates violate their religious vows.[19]

However, in 1723, the King would annul his order taking into consideration that it would go against the statutes of the convent which, later on, was confirmed by the papal documents of Popes Paul V and Gregory XV. Therefore, he ordered that what was stipulated in the statutes should be maintained. On the other hand, he forbade the Augustinians to interfere in the administration of the revenues and management of the convent as, according to the same source, this was a matter pertaining to the jurisdiction of the Archbishop.[20] The King had made his decision based on the letters of the sisters and he stated his reasons. The more important ones are as follows:

1. The *Graciano* priests belong to the same order of St. Augustine and therefore they have a better understanding of the sisters of Santa Monica. They are children of the same father.
2. They are better equipped to preach, guard and practise religious life.
3. Both monasteries are situated on the same hill. Therefore, these friars can help the sisters quickly at the time of death and in this way can take part in the remissions of sins of their congregation.
4. If they confess their sins to the priests of this order, they can enjoy the privileges granted by the papal document given by Pope Gregory XV.
5. The secular priests who do not live with the prelate are therefore not able to help the sisters quickly.
6. Among the secular clergy there is no good spiritual director who is needed for mental prayer, the pillar of religious life. Only in religion, harmony between the interior and active life can be practised. On the altar and in the sermon, they do not conform with the spirit of the congregation.[21]

Having these facts in mind, we analyse the rebellion of the sisters of Santa Monica on October 7, 1731, against the jurisdiction of the Archbishop and the departure of three or four sisters from their cloister. This issue concerned besides the King, other public and ecclesiastical authorities as well as the clergy, namely the Augustinians and the Jesuits and several important members of the realm. Thus, many letters exchanged can be found and a number of reasons were presented while the real motives were not mentioned.

Two groups of sisters were formed – one that was obedient to the jurisdiction of the Archbishop and the other, the rebel one. The rebels abandoned the convent three or four times and, as they outnumbered the obedient, they thought themselves to be the true community of sisters of Santa Monica. They blamed the Archbishop for the turn of events, from the unfortunate departure from their cloister to their other rights and to the schism of the two prioresses belonging to the same convent which was against the rules of the statutes.

The "obedient" blamed the others of breaking the vow of cloister as they continued to maintain social contacts with the Augustinians and of going against the vow of poverty as they continued to make expensive presents in order to give them to those who asked for them.[22]

The "rebels" demanded that the king order the Archbishop to return to Portugal and that meanwhile, he appoint someone to direct them; that he change the jurisdiction of the archbishops in the convent in favour of the provincials of the order, as otherwise the convent would be slack in the application of the statutes. They wanted Augustinian confessors because they belonged to the same order and had a better understanding of spiritual guidance than the local priests.[23]

These are the main arguments from the two parties and from which several conclusions can be drawn.[24] We will confine ourselves to assessing whether there were any excesses and the strengthening of sides in this issue which ended with the pastoral concerning the cessation of the jurisdiction of the convent of Santa Monica in 1733.

In a letter dated January 30, 1738, the Viceroy told the Secretary of State, António Guedes Pereira, that "after the election of the prioress they were already calm and united and the religious members of their order were their confessors" and he added "the Archbishop worked in this matter in such a way that the sisters told me that they were satisfied".

It must also be mentioned that the sisters of Santa Monica while being a cloistered congregation, had also an active interest in the problems of the State as they took an interest in events by their prayers and actions. Their intervention, for instance, was seen during the attack on Mormugao by the Dutch in 1683. The Portuguese soldiers encouraged by the banner having the Virgin Mary embroidered on it, fought valiantly and thus overcame the enemy. The Viceroys were also helped by the prayers of the sisters during their wars against the Dutch, the Adil Shah and Sambhaji.[25]

The existing documents concerning the sisters of Santa Monica give us many insights of their daily life in Goa. As this convent housed women who came from Portugal as well as Indo-Portuguese and Indian women, it also reflected the customs of the Goan society. We may then see the custom of putting *kajal* in the eyes,[26] of chewing areca nuts with betel leaves[27] and of sitting on mats made of matted grass. There are a number of references to the *carepo* (oyster) windows, a distinguishing mark of the houses in Goa that even today are mentioned in tourist bulletins.[28] In order to treat certain illnesses, the sisters on several occasions asked the help of the pandits (local doctors) as was the common practice to do in Goa.[29]

If some clouds overshadowed the horizon of the convent of Santa Monica in the 18th century with the misconduct of its inmates, the convent was nevertheless "a temple worshipped by the people of India and known for its virtuous life and customs" as stated in a number of chronicles of the time.[30] We must also remember that during the 18th century, several serious problems had arisen regarding the negligence in other Religious Orders, mainly in the Franciscan order which reduced itself on a certain occasion to a "sinister theatre of cruelties". Was it because the congregation of Santa Monica was the only religious congregation for women in Goa that it became the obvious scapegoat? Or was it because it was an example for virtue and sanctity that the ecclesiastical authorities tried to solve its problems?

The existing documents do not note the importance of the sisters to Goan society, teaching many young girls and women, the art of embroidery, of making pretty artificial flowers, of preparing delicacies and sweetmeats.[31] It is obvious that the artistic patterns imported from Europe sustained several local influences and new forms marked by religious and cultural syncretism were reproduced.

From what we have mentioned and from what we have failed to mention, it seems that we may say that in this religious community there was a significant cultural activity as well as manifestations of artistic sensibility which had a positive influence on the society of Goa.

NOTES AND REFERENCES

1. Carlos Alonso, *Alejo de Meneses, O. S. A. Arzobispo de Goa (1595-1612): Estudo biográfico*, Valladolid: Estudio Augustiniano, 1992. See also my paper "As recolhidas de Goa em Setecentos", in *O Rosto Feminino da Expansão Portuguesa, Actas*, vol. I, Lisbon, 1995, pp. 653-64.

2. *De Ceuta a Timor*, Lisbon: Difel, 1994, pp. 249-52.
3. E. R. Hambye, "Goa", *Dictionnaire et Geographie Ecclésiastique*, ed. R. Aubert, fasc. 121, Paris: Letouzey et Ané, s.d., pp. 326-27.
4. *Constituições do Mosteiro de Santa Mónica de Goa* (henceforth *Constituições)*, pt. III, ch. I, fls. 179-91.
5. *Ibid.*, fl. 185.
6. *Ibid.*, fl. 185.
7. See my *Goa Setecentista, Tradição e Modernidade*, Lisbon: Portuguese Catholic University, pp. 150-51.
8. The amount requested for regular maintenance was 200 *xerafins* and 100 *xerafins* for the maintenance of the novitiate (*Constituições,* fl. 182).
9. *Archivo Histórico Ultramarino* (*AHU*), *India,* maço no. 32 (289), letter from the Marquis of Alorna to the King dated February 21, 1750; *Historical Archives of Goa*: *Monções do Reino*, no. 123-A, fls. 140-42, letter from the King to the Marquis of Távora dated February 27, 1750.
10. *Constituições*, fl. 3.
11. *Arquivo Secreto do Vaticano*, *Visitas ad Limina-Goa*, "Visitações ao Convento de Santa Mónica de Goa (1722-1731)" (henceforth Visitações), fls. 1, 5-5v, 11, 18v, letter from the King to the Marquis of Távora dated February 27, 1750.
12. *Ibid.,* fls. 6, 8v, 12v, 13v-14: sentences, fls. 17-19.
13. *Ibid.*, fl. 19.
14. *Ibid.*, fl. 16.
15. These can be found in *Patriarchal Archives - Goa*; See Maria Carmen d'Assa Castel-Branco, *Na Diáspora Portuguesa: A Intervenção da Mulher em Goa (1750-1900*). Lisbon, 1996, p. 138.
16. *Ibid.*, pp. 138-39, 147-48.
17. M. C. Castel-Branco, "The Presence of Portuguese Baroque in the poetic works of the sisters of Santa Monica in Goa" (following article in this book).
18. M. C. Castel-Branco, *Na Diáspora...*, pp. 152-53.
19. *Biblioteca Nacional* (*BN*), box 1, ms. 1, 4^{2} bis, letter from the King dated March 11, 1720.
20. *Ibid.*, letter from the King dated April 11, 1723.
21. *Ibid.*, letter dated January 2, 1721.
22. *AHU, India*, maço no. 44 (42), letter from the abbess to the King dated December 31, 1734; *BN*, box 1, ms. 1, 4^{1} bis, letter from Sister Isabel de Madre de Deus to the King.
23. *BN*, box 1, ms. 1, 4^{1} bis, letter from the abbess to the king dated December 22, 1734; *BN,* box 1, ms. 1, 4^{12} bis, undated letter; *BN,* box 1, ms. 1, 4^{1} bis, letter dated January 22, 1735.
24. For a more detailed study see Leopoldo da Rocha, "Uma página inedita do Real Mosteiro de Santa Mónica de Goa (1730-1734), in *Mare Liberum*, 17, Lisbon, 1999, pp. 240-66.
25. António dos Mártires Lopes, *Velha Goa: Guia Histórico*. Imprensa Nacional, 1952, pp. 135-36, 139; Fr. Agostinho de Santa Maria, *História da Fundação*

do Real Mosteiro de Santa Mónica (...), Lisbon, 1699; *BN*, box 1, ms. 1, 4² bis, letter dated January 22, 1721.

26. Visitações, *op. cit.*, 1722, fl. 4.
27. *Ibid.*, 1724, fl. 11.
28. *Ibid.*, 1730, fl. 24.
29. *Ibid.*, 1730, fl. 26.
30. *BN*, box 1, ms. 1, 4² bis, letter dated March 11, 1720.
31. Maria de Jesus Mârtires Lopes, "As Especiarias na Culinária Goesa", in *A Epopeia das Especiarias*, Lisbon: Instituto de Investigação Científica Tropical, 1999, p. 139.

18

The Presence of Portuguese Baroque in the Poetic Works of the Sisters of Santa Monica in Goa

M. CARMEN D'ASSA CASTEL-BRANCO

It has been with great admiration and pleasure that I have dedicated myself to a study of the life of the Sisters of the Royal Convent of Santa Monica at Old Goa. Perhaps for this reason, I have asked myself what could be the reason for the great interest of thinkers, poets and of Indian men-of-letters, from the more dedicated to the more modest, to this same theme.

Perhaps the fact of their existence may have given rise to a reality which hangs on the frontiers between the real and the myth and this, like it or not, is the source of my thinking, for this attracts me and seduces me so much. It seems that it belongs to the sphere of myth, in which it is unthinkable that the sisters in the fullness of their infancy or adolescence exchanged the toys and childish fun for the seriousness and austerity of convent life. The young women of about 20 and others a little older left the world behind them, burning the beauty of their lives under the black mantle.

Those were times of perpetual war due to the ambitions of men, and of shipwrecks caused by the early stages of navigation and also because men did not control their desire to enrich themselves rapidly, filling to the brim the ships of the *Carreira da India* and later those of country trade.

Thus those dramatic reasons made very young widows who in some cases were already orphans, their remaining relatives, in case they had any, being in places, coasts very diverse, as in Goa, Portugal or in the cities of the Indian and Pacific Oceans like Hormuz, Jafanapatnam, Malacca, Bassein, Cochin, etc. These young women found convent life a solution, going in search of the safe port of the house of God[1] where

* Translated from the Portuguese by Charles J. Borges

their existence lay between solitude and isolation. One admits, however, that the reasons for entering the convent may have been in some cases their vocation. One lived in an age of religiosity. Other motives could be, without doubt, economic. However, their entrance in monastic life was through a dowry of 2,000 *xerafins*, a sum which was raised later to 4,000 by Archbishop Santa Catherina.[2]

It may be mentioned that the daily life of the inmates was however filled with prayers, asceticism, discipline, and manual works like handicrafts, laces, embroideries, pastry-making, craftwork and by the cultivation of a large quantity of flowers and aromatic plants filling the altars with their perfume and by the enthusiasm with which they took part in the fireworks and bonfire on the night of Saint John's feast in the valley of Lilies, a large garden of the convent around the fount of the Saviour, a circular well with abundant fresh water. Their existence was also filled by an intellectual formation of elements of general culture, Latin, Spanish, music, and as a consequence of this activity they performed sacred scores, sang in choir and produced texts in prose, in poetry and wrote theatrical pieces. The level attained seems, to me, relatively high for that time, they being women on the most distant periphery of the Portuguese world. However, in spite of being a distant periphery, it was part of the great Indian civilisation with systems of thought and the reflection of milleniums.

I give a greater emphasis to their intellectual work of the 18th century because I have some copies of some of their manuscripts[3] which belong in hypothesis to the first decades of that century. This hypothesis is based on the facts of dating and is corroborated by their own textual value regarding their form contents. These are a resonance of the literary current of the Baroque which was in vogue in Europe, in Portugal through the influence of the Spanish Baroque through the models of its conceptualists, Luis de Gongora, Quevedo, et al.

The first text "*Este Cartapácio é da Música do Terceiro Ano da Madre Francisca do Sacramento Prioresa do Ano 16...*" (This register contains the music of the third year of Mother Francisca do Sacramento, prioress of the year 16...) and the second text "*Entrada de Bonifrate para a Festa dos Reis*" (the entrance of Bonifrate for the feast of the Three Kings) are not dated. The first of these two texts has merely two figures: 1 and 6 therefore I do not have the exact date and the second text does not make any reference when it was written.

The first and the second texts by their own statements were written under the supervision of Prioress Francisca do Sacramento and Prioress Emeraciana, respectively and these two do not appear in the list of prioresses. I refer to a list written in 1699 which mentions only 33 prioresses from the foundress till the 33rd, this one governing the convent in the same year. [4]

From these facts, I can conclude that the terms of Prioress Francisca do Sacramento and Prioress Emeraciana could not have been before 1699 coming to be necessarily in the 18th century. This hypothesis is strengthened by the characteristics of the contents and the form of the texts.

The themes of the text

The first text is made up of 23 poems and some of these have common themes. We can condense the common contents to themes that constitute the daily preoccupation of the sisters. Thus we have themes like celebrating the feast of St. João, the heavenly bodies honouring the saint, offering praises to the prioress in office, Mother Prioress Francisca do Sacramento, praising the sisters in their duties in the convent, praising the fathers, recounting the follies of Cupid, the suffering of a loving and passionate heart due to ingratitude, and offering a dinner to the prioress begging her for clemency for Janona and Clarinha.

The theme of the second text begins with one of the characters giving an address to eminent persons of the audience after which the audience announces the play of Bonifrate (puppet) and in the name of the prioress, invites the convent community to attend that performance and the whole night to enter the revelry with great joy.

The structure of the texts

At the end of the first text one comes across a list in the form of an index with the titles of the songs followed by musical formulae, in a descending format probably indicating the beginning of the melody of each song.

Thirteen songs of this text are made up of a varied number of four-line stanzas, two other compositions show a hybrid structure with four-line stanzas and strophes of a varied number of verses, and eight stand out for being formally better. Its motto has four verses which express an idea developed along the rondels and the last of these verses is the refrain announced at the beginning of the motto. Of these songs some have rondels with five and others with seven verses.

The second text is a succession of scenes, not connected among themselves and featured by four actors: the Master, the Juggler, the

Canarim and the *Kafir*. The Master could be a kind of prompter and the last three probably represented the ethnic groups of the area. These scenes are separated by eight references at the entrance of the characters. They are accompanied by singing, at times in competition for example "*Cantiga do Caferinho*" (the song of the little *kafir*); by dancing as in the case of "*Baile de Milhano*" (Dance of the kite) and by the beating of drums and trumpets. Vocal sounds and whistling are also used. The text refers also to the use of harp and viola. We may notice that in the theatre of the puppet, the main scenes were sung and for this reason were designated as operas. The whole speech is written predominantly in four-line stanzas but also, though rarely seen, five-line stanzas and couplets. In both the texts a predominant number of strophes have few syllables probably to make it easier to adapt it to singing. Besides the desire to include the music in the theatre is one of the characteristics of the Baroque.

In both texts one does not come across a uniformity concerning orthography, the use of the same language along the compositions, etc.

Stylistic resources

In the first text in the group of eight songs referred to earlier, formally better, three are written in Spanish which was the current practice of the Portuguese conceptualist poets, one of the features of the Baroque style. This practice is present mainly in the songs of rondel mottos as is the case of the example presented in acetate.

The cultism, another of the features of the Baroque, prescribes the use of figures of speech, like metaphors, used with different contents of objects and materials of jewelry, heavenly bodies, flowers, fruits and socially eminent people. These elements are seen at times developed as in metaphors, therefore multiform, and when it is the case of extolling socially eminent personalities, there are the exalting metaphors. The other figures of style prescribed by the Baroque style. are hyperboles, antithesis, paradoxes and the exaggerated and repetitive eulogies.

These stylistic resources were used in the two texts "*Cartapácio*" and "*Entrada de Bonifrate*" and I will give one example of each figure of style of one or the other text.

In the first text we have an example of a metaphor which is constructed with precious stones of the East, flowers which are characteristic elements of conceptual poetry. Therefore it is a protean metaphor in which the author changes the subject.

Margarita y esmeralda	Daisy and emerald
zafiro rubín flamant	Shining sapphire or ruby
jacinto e diamante	Hyacinth and diamond
y la pérla extremada	Also pure and perfect pearl
tudo eres sublimada oriental	You are the sublime oriental
pedrería de Francisca.	Precious stone of Francisca.

From the second text I select a metaphor referring to a heavenly body.

Desmaiada a Lua	The vanishing moon
perde a valia	Has no value
competir não ousa	And dares no competition
com tal bizarria.	With such a gallantry of yours.

Again from the second text I select a metaphor using a fruit and a flower, also multiform.

Vós minha anona	You my sweetsop
de São Joaquim	of Saint Joachim.
sois uma bonina	You are the most lovely daisy
do nosso jardim.	From our garden.

Finally, from the second text, I choose a metaphor that highly exalts and which has as its object a very important social entity.

Por belo planeta	For the beautiful planet
vos dou este Sol	I give you this Sun
sendo que vós sois	For you are
o melhor farol	The best light house.

I have not taken from the first text, an example of hyperbole which makes an exaggerated comparison between the brilliance of the stars and the light of the one, to which the verses are dedicated.

As estrelas perdem	Stars lose
o seu valimento	Their shining light
vendo o brilhante	Just as they watch
do teu luzimento.	Your golden aura.

I have selected again from the second text an antithesis in which two states of the soul oppose each other, the first one of joy, expressed in the first two verses, and the second one, a moment of disillusion due to the rigour of the austerity of the cloister.

Veio-nos leda e contente	She came happy and content
sem sombrosos nem tèmores	Without gloom or fears
ignorando os rigores	Ignoring the rigours
que em si traz estas correntes.	Which these currents bring.

I choose from the second text an example of a paradox which praises the elements of water and fire.

A água e o fogo	Water and fire
que contrários são	Opposite they are
ambos se unirão	Both will unite themselves
nesta ocasião.	On this occasion.

I have selected from the second text another stylistic resource which consists of a repetitive and exaggerated elegy.

De Santa Rosa sois Joan	Joan of St. Rose you are
vós de graça superior	Your beauty is beyond words
rosa deste jardim	The rose of this garden you are
é digna de todo louvor.	Most praiseworthy.

In "*Fenix Renascida*", a collection of the best poetry of the Baroque period, the rose is adopted as the symbol of matured beauty which was inherited from the previous aesthetic currents. In the two mentioned texts of the sisters of Santa Monica, this image is also present, referring to not so young sisters of the convent. Thus, I will quote a four-line stanza from the first text dedicated to the prioress, who according to the rule in force ought to have been over forty.

A rosa como rainha	The rose like a Queen
mostra sua beleza	Irradiating her beauty
nossa amada Prioresa	Our beloved Prioress
toda formosa caminha.	Walks very beautiful.

To conclude, we come across in the second text the obsession with an improbable zoology, like the research of the marvelous, very frequent in

Baroque compositions: a phoenix reborn from its own ashes, a salamander with a great resistance to the fire, thus the Juggler in the second text says:

Certo minhas madres
estou espantado
não morrer o pássaro
no fogo abrasado.

Surely, dear Beloved Mothers
I'm really astonished
For the bird doesn't perish
Burnt in the fire.

Oh Senhoras minhas
estou espantado
este pássaro é
sem dúvida encantado.

Oh, dear Ladies
Astonished I am
This bird no doubt
Is under a charm.

In Baroque theatre it is common for many art forms to run together. The second text also includes in its plot, singing, dancing and the circus. Thus we come across a description of jugglery. A bark (ball covered with skin), remained in the fire and suspended.

Vêde bem senhoras
que vos quero mostrar
bolas de fogo
no ar passear.

Look well dear Ladies
What I want to show you
Balls of fire
In the air moving.

In both the texts appear small comic sketches interspersed, taking the theme of Cupid, and in the form of a play. The sisters start to involve themselves in his plot, which is forbidden due to their state as sisters. Thus, they infringe the rules of austerity of the convent, afterwards they sentence him to death so that they might redeem their sin. However, they end up accepting Cupid, which allows them to reaccept the breaking of the convent rule. Besides, life in society demands the breaking of rules and their acceptance.

Thus we have the involvement:

Loucuras que amante fazei
ele já toma paixão
com raiva e com aflição
todo juízo já perdi.

Foolishness you lovers do
He is passionate already,
Full of rage and afflicted
I have lost all my common sense.

After that they condemn Cupid to death

O pregão tereis ouvido	You have heard the notice
e a sentença está dada	The sentence is given
e a forca aparelhada	The gallows are ready
para morrer Cupido.	For Cupid to die.

But at last they save him.

Um embargo já sai	The stay is given
de tudo seu vassalo	For such a vassal
que por Rei conhecido	Known by the king
não pode ser enforcado.	Hanged cannot be.
Da morte já escapa	From death he escapes
este rei de patarata	This fancy king,
sobre ele justiça venha	Let justice be done
tenha vida mal lograda.	Let his life be a burden.

The entry of the daughters of aristocratic families into the convents gave rise to and spread throughout the whole country the art of convent pastry-making, which in the convent of the sisters of Santa Monica of Goa, as it would be hoped, wrapped itself in local tastes and aromas.

Thus, in the second text the recipe for a cake of wheat, *rawa*, jaggery and coconut, which are local products, is described.

Sem ser padeiro	Without being a baker
quero fazer bolo	I want to make a cake
bolo jagra e coco	Of jaggery and coconut
que não tem miolo.	Which is not fluffy.

In the second text another interesting interspersed drama is, "The dance of the Eagle" (*Baile de Milhano*) in which the attentive kites hover hiding their treacherous intentions to capture the little chicken under the beauty of their flight.

Criei cinco pintos	Five little chicken
com grande cuidado	Very carefully I bred
todos levou milhano	The kite lifted them all
por (...)	by (...)

Com graça *milhano dançai* *vossa habilidade* *a todos mostrai.*	Gracefully You kites dance Your skill To everybody you show.

In the second text, "*Entrada de Bonifarte*", is also present the charming, loving poems by the sisters as in the European Baroque, which allowed through a loving verse, to disguise the austerity of the cloister. The shining examples of this verse, at times bordering on the erotic, are the conceptualist poetesses, Sister Violante do Céu and Sister Maria do Céu. The latter wrote verse in Portuguese and Spanish. However, the anonymous Goan poetesses also practised this form of catharsis. I mention some four-line stanzas as examples of this form of liberation.

Penoso chorais *sem alívio a dor* *(...) que cruelmente* *nos maltrata amor.*	You cry in pain Pain without relief, which cruelly Love ill-treats us.
Em este cofrinho formoso *Cupido vos há guardado* *encerrado vossos cuidados* *estes suspiros penosos.*	In this little charming box Cupid has locked you, Shut off your sorrows these painful sighs.
Se ausência tanto mata *como pode um bem viver* *um amor que desbarata* *esperança mal sofrer.*	If absence kills so much How can the good live, A love that wastes Hope suffering.
Anda esta mulher *por vós perdida* *promete-vos servir* *por toda a sua vida*	This woman Mad about you, Promises to serve you For her whole life long.

I will refer yet again to the eighty four-line stanzas in the second text, which are composed about objects that speak of the environment marked by religious experience, such as the chapel, angel, cherub, rosary, etc.; of nature, such as tower, fortress, trumpet, sword, spear, quiver, etc.; of the maritime world suggested by ship, anchor, chain, fishing hook, etc.; finally of everyday life as spectacles, silver pitcher, annuity, key, umbrella, mirror, bottle, fan, etc.

As we can notice in their poetry, the life of the sisters of Santa Monica at Goa was made up of mists of fiction of that reality that existed, because they were capable of, in spite of all the adversities they faced, spending their day dreaming with dancing stars, appreciating the precious stones of the East, knowing a Greek Apelles of the court of Alexander the Great, who had painted the beauty of the "valiant Miguel", the saint, dealing intimately with Homer and Cicero, walking happily towards the vegetable garden "to dance and frolic" and not forgetting the "magnificent Christmas sweets". And, how astonishing to be addressing bold wooing to the handsome Graciano priests, "repositories of perfections", and meanwhile spinning jokes, in verse, with arrows, wounded hearts, bows and amorous tricks of Cupid.

And one of the most healthy things and of evident intellectual superiority was undoubtedly that the sisters were able to live together in an atmosphere of women coming from the four corners of the Portuguese world, at that time carrying with them the colours of their own culture for refraction from a common kaleidoscope, and in this coloured and beautiful diversity, they knew to value each one of the colours because they completed each other.

This kind of life is evident in their poetry and the letters reflect always the experience of the language and the culture in all its manifestations in their personal and collective longings that emerge from the community life of a people and of an age.

NOTES AND REFERENCES

1. Frei Agostinho de Santa Maria, *História da Fundação do Real Convento de Santa Monica de Goa,* Lisbon, 1699, p. 660.
2. M. J. Gabriel de Saldanha, *História de Goa* (*política e arqueologia*), vol. II, Delhi: Asian Educational Services, 1990. p. 136.
3. The copies of the manuscripts which are in my possession have been kindly given to me by Prof. Artur Teodoro de Matos, who in the course of his researches in the East found these documents in the archives of the Curia Patriarchal of Goa. These documents were organised in groups according to their organic affinity, designated as texts and numbered.
4. This list is in *História da Fundação do Real Convento de Santa Monica de Goa,* pp. 475-84.

19

Contrasting Images

Religious Orders in Goa before their Suppressions and after their Reinstatement in the 18th-20th Centuries

CHARLES J. BORGES

This paper is about contrasting images and about how the needs of the hour forced Religious Orders operating in Goa to take on a different stance of work after their reinstatements in the 19th and 20th centuries. All along the 16th to the 18th centuries members of the main Religious Orders adopted a style of working that combined enthusiasm, understanding for local problems with a strange aggressiveness resulting in local tensions in many fields. With the law often on their side, they could move along without any appreciable attempts to change the manner of their operations. The shocks of their being suppressed (though at different times in the 18th and 19th centuries – the Portuguese government suppressed all Religious Orders by a decree on May 30, 1834) led them to a re-evaluation of their workings on their return to their former areas of activities.

I

Many studies have highlighted the work of the Religious Orders (Jesuits, Franciscans, Dominicans, Augustinians and others) in Africa and the East since the 16th century dwelling more on the creditable work undertaken and the far-reaching consequences of these.[1] The Society of Jesus had since 1542 houses and missions in Goa, in the North Province, in the Mughal kingdom, in parts of south India, and in its overseas provinces of Japan and China. The Society had four provinces in all in

Asia: Goa, Malabar, Japan and China and had various houses in them. Among the many secular activities that they attended to were the maintenance of fortifications at Daman and Chaul and the management of rice granaries in the North Province.[2] The overseas Portuguese Dominican Province included Goa and extended from Mozambique to Malacca with houses at Macau and in Indonesia.[3]

Some recent studies, based on archival documentation, while noting the creditable charitable and evangelical work done, have also been critical of some of the methodologies adopted by the Religious Orders during their periods of operation in the East.[4] We do know that the activities of all Religious Orders in Goa were backed since the start by the financial and political power of the Portuguese government. Initially, the Crown advanced subsidies to them but these in the course of time were intermittent and turned insufficient for the vast missions that came to take off in Goa, and in other parts of India. The Jesuits, at least, soon developed a system of economic networking among their own four Provinces which assured them of funds for the various works that needed more money than the Jesuit headquarters or the Crown could provide during the time prior to their suppression in 1759. Their financial dealings involved lay people as well and in many cases Hindus.[5] Other Religious Orders operating in India also had their own systems of getting funds in addition to Crown subsidies but did not attract so much antagonism due to the smaller scale of their financial operations.[6]

A look at the workings of the Jesuits in Goa shows that early in their stay they incurred the anger of a good enough segment of the local population and the various memoranda to the Crown against them bear this out. There were complaints of their immediate gains in land acquisition particularly in the villages of Salcete in south Goa with the result that land was slowly slipping out of the hands of the local *ganvkars* or settlers. Together with financial power grew a disdain for the villagers and their problems. True it was not an approach by the entire group, but those connected with financial matters in the Provinces had much to answer for. If the picture on their arrival in Goa was one of understanding and tolerance, the Jesuit attitude soon changed due in large measure to their strong economic base which helped them wield power aided by their vast tracts of land and money. Reactions against them on many fronts were evident, and seen for instance, in a memorandum that the local Goan Brahmin clergy sent the Crown accusing the foreign-born Jesuits of persecuting them, and of being ignorant of the local language. They accused them of lacking the fear of God, and of preventing the general assemblies of Salcete villages from meeting. The latter refuted them convincingly listing their many achievements in education, in providing jobs for the poor, in composing liturgical and spiritual books, and in arresting converts in the act of worshipping their former idols. The local clergy, they added, were dark-skinned and unworthy of any respect.[7]

For a realistic picture of the state of the church in Goa in 1656 one can read Fr. Pedro Borges' memorial on the church in Goa. He had been secretary of the tribunal of the Inquistion of Goa. He mentioned that in Goa (Salcete, Jua, Divar, Chorao and Bardez) there were 85 parishes. The number of religious was 900 (Franciscans, Augustinians, Discalced Carmelites, Jesuits and Theatines). The religious had the care of 53 parishes in all, 5 in the islands around Goa, 23 in Bardez (under the Franciscans), and 25 in Salcete (under the Jesuits). In the islands around Goa the local secular priests cared for 21 parishes, while the 11 parishes of the city of Goa itself were in the hands of Portuguese secular priests. All of them had Indian assistants. His conclusions were that foreign priests did not know the local language sufficiently. There were not enough sermons preached in the vernacular. The catechumens were baptised without sufficient instruction. That was one reason why those instructed in the faith by the religious fell away often and easily from the faith while that was not the case of those prepared for baptism by the Indian priests.[8]

What was strange and harmful to the faithful was the refusal of the Religious to allow the local priests to preach in the vernacular in the churches in their care and to hear the confessions of those who did not know Portuguese. The parishes of Bardez and Salcete were all entrusted to the Religious while the local priests were not admitted even as their co-adjutors. In Bardez the Franciscans would not allow the people to call a local priest for sermons and confessions during Lent, even when they undertook to support him at their own expense. In 1628 the archbishop of Lisbon informed the viceroy of Goa that news had reached him that the parishes of Bardez were governed badly because the parish priests were not familiar with the local language. The Provincial of the Franciscans however defended his men by stating that in Bardez there were three professors of Konkani and three preached in the same language. Overall, as a matter of policy Religious Orders in India were not opposed to the admission of Indians to their ranks. The Franciscans at first admitted Indians liberally as did the Dominicans who opened their doors to Indian candidates with the necessary qualities. The Augustinians received local vocations from 1619. The Discalced Carmelites had been directed by their Fr. General in Rome not to admit locals. The Theatines believed that the locals were looked down upon and to accept them would discredit the entire congregation before the Portuguese and hinder its apostolic activity. After 1759, however, they did accept Indians and became an exclusively indigenous congregation.[9]

A shot in the arm for the Franciscans came from the archbishop who had the following to comment on their good work:. "I, Dom Augustinho da Annunciação, metropolitan Archbishop of Goa, certify that visiting in 1698 all the churches which the Franciscans of St. Thomas province administer in the peninsula of Bardez, I found them all cleanly kept, and in proper order for divine service. Some of them are magnificent buildings, according to the income of the villages in which they are situated. In all the villages there are numerous Catholics, well instructed according to their individual capacities." He went on to say that these religious because of their vow of poverty did not receive legacies. "In no village do I find any complaint against these religious, neither any fault pertaining to their person nor as to the parochial ministry which they exercise. They preach in the mother tongue of the people and pagans see their errors refuted in their own tongue". [10] Seen in the light of the facts stated above, this might seem a strange comment.

Overall, the Portuguese right of ecclesiastical patronage gave widespread powers to the Religious Orders to preach the faith. It empowered them to coerce the unbelievers to give up their idol-worship, their diabolic rites and customs adding "so that in this manner all might be united and joined together in charity of law, and love, since we are created by one (common) Creator and redeemed by one Redeemer. But if the people are stubborn as to reject the true faith they should be put to fire and steel". And Pope Leo X had asked King Manoel of Portugal in 1515 to "receive this warlike sword in your always victorious and warlike hands. With this you will wage wars under the most happy auspices; you will subject the enemies of the Faith, as you have done up to now....may you use your force, strength, and power against the fury of the infidels; may you consecrate, not only your most religious spirit, but also the kingdom itself, and the forces of the kingdom, to the giver of them, to God the best and the greatest, so that having received through this gift the help of heaven in battles, you may bring back abundant spoils and most famous triumphs." [11]

II

Thankfully, not all took these words in the same spirit that they were intended. Many missionaries in India went about their tasks in the churches and in the schools with dedication and took up innovations in many fields as time went on. Jesuit innovations there were during the 16th to 18th centuries in the fields of State diplomacy, literature and printing, inter-faith dialogue, the crossing of frontier territories, etc.[12]

For purposes of religious instruction, a local literature easily intelligible was created in which the catechism, booklets on confession, and the lives of saints were given pride of place. Fr. Alessandro Valignano, the important Jesuit Visitor had himself composed two short catechisms which he sent to the fathers in all the mission stations and before his departure for Japan he gave instructions to have them translated into the local languages. He also took care that other missionaries should write similar booklets. St. Francis Xavier had led the way with *Catechismo da Doctrina Christiana*, Fr. Henrique Henriques composed a grammar and dictionary in Tamil, two catechisms, lives of Christ, of the Blessed Virgin and other saints, and many other apologetic and devotional works. Fr. Joseph Constant Beschi wrote a masterful poem, *Tembavni*, in honour of St. Joseph. Fr. Thomas Stephens wrote the *Krista Puran*, a work setting forth the mysteries of the Catholic faith in poetic form. The Franciscan Fr. Manuel Banha wrote a dictionary in Konkani and Fr. Amador de Santa Anna translated the *Flos Sanctorum* in Konkani and the Carmelite Fr. Francis Xavier de Santa Anna wrote a scholarly Konkani grammar.[13]

In the field of popularizing devotions,[14] the Jesuits showed much skill and their reports for the 16th century at least, show the varied forms these took. These speak of the variety of religious expressions of the people. Being converts from Hinduism they needed these to feel at home in their new-found faith and events like processions, baptisms and feasts helped in this process. These expressions of their religiosity did not differ very much from the European religiosity of the time or for that matter from the Hindu practices. The Church in Goa allowed them to unfold lest the new converts felt the absence of their former practices and reverted to them. These Christian religious devotions, the processions in particular, marked an important time in their lives. They had very little else to look forward to in normal days and longed for the special days when the processions to mark the Corpus Christi (Body of Christ), the rosary, and the passion of Jesus, came around. The many accounts of the miraculous show the desire on the part of many to prove the efficacy of the new faith, and rival Religious Orders outdid each other in proving they had been more successful.

For a Europe eager to know more of India, the European Catholic missionaries stationed in 16th century India, were ready to oblige. These were the Jesuits, the Franciscans and the Dominicans, mainly. Their studies in humanities and other disciplines had given to most of them a keen sense of observation and analysis. Many of them picked up local languages. They wrote regular reports to those who managed their affairs in Europe. These reports are a mine of information for the times during which they were written. They describe the various kingdoms, wars, local traditions, the growth of Christianity, the money received, and the reactions positive or negative to the work of evangelization.[15]

If the picture of the Jesuits as successful and forceful does appear from the above portrayal, they appeared rather different in other parts of India where they worked. The fact that the Portuguese State had no territorial acquisitions in parts outside of Goa and the North Province, made them and all Religious Orders operating in those parts tread cautiously.[16] They were financially dependent on Goa and the properties they had acquired there for their ongoing work in parts outside Goa. But the manner of their operations there was very different, marked by more understanding and tolerance. They knew that they could not afford to antagonize the people too much lest they turn against them and their rulers withdraw whatever privileges had been extended to them.

Records do speak, however, of tensions in various parts, and there were disagreements between the Jesuits and the bishop of Cochin and also with the Portuguese captain at Tuticorin whose duty it was to protect the Christians against Muslim traders and soldiers.[17] There was a long-standing dispute among the Jesuits of the Goa and Malabar provinces regarding the ownership of three villages (Velim, Ambelim and Assolna in south Goa); differences about land held in north Goa on behalf of the Malabar and China Jesuit missions; lands in Goa and at Bassein for the Jesuits in South India; confirmation of the grant of temple revenues to the College of St. Paul's; ownership of the *casabe* (seat of province) of Karanja by the Cochin College; decree granting the Province of Japan the right to acquire a certain property in 1686; the Betim palm-grove for the Malabar mission, properties in Bandra for the China Province, and claims of the Goa Province concerning some diamonds.[18] The Jesuits in the Zambezi Mission of Africa had been without the promised royal stipends. Fr. Rodrigo da Estrada and three other Jesuits had been involved in a land dispute over inheritance there and were asked to return to Goa. The mission had bought land in Kumbarjua (Goa) to pay off some of their debts.[19]

The Religious Orders had such a strong presence in Portuguese India that their affairs affected many in the government. The Count of Linhares, for instance, had a personal preference for the Discalced Carmelites, over the Augustinians whom he termed "a nest of thieves and malefactors", and believed the Jesuits did what they wanted.[20] A royal letter had mentioned that the Religious parish priests of Bardez and Salcete in Goa were in the habit of punishing the laity, not paying them for services rendered by them. Another letter to the Fr. Provincial stated that the Rector of the college of St. Roque, Fr. Thomas de Barros and a Fr. André Ferreira had used the pulpit to attack the government ministers. The Provincial was asked to place the priests under house arrest.[21]

The Dominicans first arrived in Goa in 1548, and soon set up houses at Bassein, Mahim, Tarapur, Chaul, Daman, Diu, Cochin, Nagapatanam and Mylapore. They were supervised by a vicar general resident at Goa where the Order had its three convents (St. Dominic, St. Thomas and St. Barbara), and he was .assisted by a procurator to take care of business and recruitment at Lisbon.[22]

About the Franciscans and the Jesuits at the royal courts in south India we are informed: "In the time of Vijayanagar kingdom, a considerable number of Jesuit Fathers resided in the city, and appear to have obtained great privileges from the ruling king. How far they influenced State matters we have little data to bring forward, but on the great House of Victory, a cross has been super-imposed on the Hindu carving on the walls. It has been suggested that this is an evidence of their influence in the kingdom" And about the Franciscan Frei Luis it is said that he carried in one hand the Bible and in the other the orders of King Dom Manuel, his efforts having borne immense diplomatic fruits for Portugal. The King had been impressed by his narratives hoping that he would convert the kings of Vijayanagara to Christianity.[23]

The Franciscan Fr. Paulo Trindade in his volumes describes the Mughals as "a very warlike race, good archers and dexterous with horses (hardworking, proud and cruel). They were big eaters, big-built and broad-shouldered". He speaks about Cambay, and its peoples, made up of Gujaratis and Banias, a very weak race that do not engage in arms but in commerce selling very fine and precious cotton and other goods. He mentions the great devotion of the people of Daman to the memory of St. Francis.[24] And in a report Baltasar de S. António, writing from Goa on November 20, 1755 to the Viceroy Dom Luiz Mascarenhas, Count of

Alva, speaks about Goa saying that mission work was not possible outside Goan territories since the people resented the presence of the Portuguese.[25]

The Augustinians as a group of religious arrived in Goa on September 3, 1572 and built their Nossa Senhora da Graça between 1597 and 1602. Here they taught sciences and letters. Though the Jesuits (in the persons of Francisco Fernandes and Domingo de Souza). and other secular priests were the earliest to have come as missionaries to Bengal, the place remained the grand mission ground of the Augustinians. The Augustinians came to Bengal around 1599 and built their house dedicated to San Nicholau of Tolentino.[26]

In 1605 the Portuguese Augustinian Province sent one of their men, Fr. Felix of Jesus to India with the brief of writing a history of the newly-founded missionary congregation in India. He was a native of Lisbon and spent the last thirty five years of his life in the Augustinian monastery of Our Lady of Grace at Goa, where he dedicated himself with great zeal to his task as chronicler. He wrote two distinct chronicles. His history does not only give a detailed description of the various Augustinian foundations and the work accomplished by the missionaries of the Order but the account gives one some colourful sketches of local scenes and customs. The descriptions help one to understand the spirit of the time.[27] Another Augustinian to be sent to Bengal in 1628 for 13 years, Fr. S. Manrique, wrote much about Bengal and about the rites and ceremonies, dress and fruits of the region. Born in Porto at the end of the 16th century, he left for India in the beginning of the 17th and took his final profession at the convent of St. Augustine in Old Goa in 1604. He was missionary in Asia from 1628 to 1642. He wrote also about the Mughal empire and about the richness of its emperor. He stated that his congregation was the first to spread the word of God in Bengal with its blood.[28]

Mention can also be made of an important work by a Portuguese Jesuit, Fr. Diogo Gonçalves, entitled *História do Malavar.*[29] Born in 1561 in Portugal he reached India in 1591 and from 1597 for about 40 years he was at various places in South India. Up to the last days of his life, he strongly attacked the Muslims in all his sermons. In his *História* (based on his experiences from the latter years of the 16th century), he gives us a reliable and complete knowledge of the people of the South India coast and offers an instruction on how Hinduism with its corrupt morals and its polytheism can be overcome by Christianity. His book was supposed to be a kind of manual for the young missionaries of

Travancore in order to make it easier for them to get accustomed to the living conditions of an unfamiliar people whom they wanted to win over for the kingdom of God. The book with scholastic argumentation describes the mythology in Hinduism and represents (Catholic) Christianity as the only true religion.

Chronicles like the above, by their very purpose, were meant to instruct but more importantly to change ideas about a particular people. In a recent paper (which I mention here by way of example), I have described the destabilising methods employed by some Religious Orders in Sri Lanka as a distinct missionary enterprise. The process aimed at de-structuring Sinhalese political and religious systems. The Religious Orders (Franciscans, Jesuits, Augustinians) and the Oratorians used their powers well, and even the Dutch presence on the island did not prevent them from working at a de-structuring of Sinhalese life to bring about a society patterned on and beneficial to Portuguese interests and culture.[30] F. Houtarat in his book[31] has analysed well the role of colonization in the destruction of a local society. Christianity, he states, could only exist by destroying the meaning and the organization of the existing religious systems in Sri Lanka. Many of the kings there who converted to Christianity realised that if they wished to retain their power they had to adopt the conqueror's system of meaning.

Compared to the above attempts, how different was the approach of the Italian Jesuit Fr. Roberto de Nobili (1577-1656) who worked in south India under the Padroado Portuguese system. With a similar breadth of vision like his countryman Fr. Matteo Ricci, he was able to make progress only after he had discarded European for Oriental dress and adopted Indian ways. Fr. A. Saulière (a great de Nobili scholar) comments on his innovative methods: "The method he (de Nobili) followed and the means he used may be discussed and found impracticable for us.... Nor did he attach to them a permanent value: he modified them as he went along, now wearing the thread, now disregarding it, now living as a recluse and now as an itinerant preacher. These were means, tools, which he used or set aside, according as they did or did not serve his purpose". But what really did de Nobili use and discard? He had decided to understand Hinduism from within and went through a most difficult part of his life in India learning Hindu scriptures, changing into a Hindu attire and lifestyle while his own Jesuits and others were ideologically pitted against him. The aim of de Nobili's apostolate, however, was not just to convert the brahmins but through them to bring India to Christ. Largely due to him, comments one author: "Christianity was no longer considered a foreign religion. Like Buddhism, Jainism, Saivism, Vaishnavism, etc.

it became a national religion, rooted in the soil, enriching the ancient culture of India with a new life and a new message".[32]

Though not gifted with the same intellectual gifts, yet equally zealous in the cause of knowing sympathetically Hinduism was the Portuguese Jesuit St. João de Brito (1647-1693). He had worked in many places in south India. He would dress in the garb of a Hindu mendicant, align himself with the socially lowest castes, and for his forthrightness was tortured to death. And we have a beautiful pen picture of the saint from A. Saulière. "He was a man of the rank and file. He may not have had the zeal and enthusiasm of a St. Francis Xavier but he was never called upon to exercise them on the whole East, his labour being practically confined to Tamilnad. Nor was it his lot to inaugurate new missionary methods like Robert de Nobili. He came to a field ripe for the harvest and without casting about for new tools or new methods he seized the old sickle and joined the reapers".[33] Though there were other missionaries too like Fr. Joannes Ernestus Hanxleden (1681-1732), the German poet and Orientalist or the Italian Tamil scholar, Fr. Joseph Constant Beschi who did much for dialoguing with and understanding Indian literary culture, yet the work of Roberto de Nobili and to some extent of St. João de Brito were pioneering attempts to adapt the Catholic faith and practice to Indian culture.[34]

III

After spending over an eventful two hundred years in Goa, the events concerning their suppression overtook the Jesuits in 1759, though the other Religious Orders in Goa were suppressed only in 1834. Jesuit opponents had believed that their exit would help towards the much-needed reform in education and morals. They had been accused of keeping distinctions between foreigners and locals, and between brahmins and chardos and of having changed the original aims of the College of St. Paul's.[35] The eventual restoration of the Society of Jesus worldwide took place with the issue of the decree *Solicitudo Omnium Ecclesiarum* on August 7, 1814 by Pope Pius VII restoring the Society of Jesus to its former status. Jesuits returned to India by October 8, 1834, with eight Jesuits coming to Calcutta. On October 24, 1837, four French Jesuits arrived at Pondicherry on their way to Madura and in 1848 two Irish Jesuits were in Bombay. Fr. José Manuel Gonçalves was the first Jesuit superior of the new Goa Jesuit Mission started in 1890. In 1886 as a result of the Concordat between the Holy See and Portugal,

Belgaum which had belonged to the Bombay-Poona diocese was incorporated into the archdiocese of Goa and in 1889 the Archbishop of Goa, Dom António Sebastião Valente had wanted Portuguese Jesuits to replace the German Jesuits in Belgaum. Portuguese Jesuits were also invited to give retreats in Goa for seminarians of the Rachol Seminary and for priests. The Instituto de S. Francisco Xavier was started in Panjim in 1935. "It served", wrote a Jesuit, "as a link with the Society's glorious past .... with all that it means now, ruins and desolation in the old city of Goa and the flourishing Christianity that is today a giant centuries-old oak with its grandiose monuments of religious cult and active faith in the islands of Goa and in the province of Salsette." The Constitution of 1933 in Portugal allowed Jesuits to return to Goa. "Goa too was feeling the long absence of Jesuit ministry. Great was the yearning of the people to have them in Panjim to take care of their youth," said one writer while another mentioned that "this relative stagnation in conversion work has been, we believe, one of the saddest consequences that has resulted from the suppression of the Religious Orders in the Portuguese dominions. The secular priest for obvious reasons does not possess the efficiency of the religious whom his vows, detachment from country and family and the special training he receives, render better fitted for successful missionary work among pagans. Moreover the secular cannot receive the financial aid that members of religious societies obtain from their order and that goes to help their apostolic activities to a considerable extent".[36] G. Moraes remarked that "in the educational field the damage caused by the retrograde policy of the Republic was repaired by the invitation to the Jesuits to open their institutions in Goa. They opened two first-rate schools in Margao and Mapusa".[37]

The Portuguese Jesuits established a centre for the Apostleship of Prayer at Panjim and Goan Jesuits like Fr. Fortunato Coutinho and Fr. Sylvester de Souza who had joined the Goa Mission would come from Belgaum to Goa to preach novenas in preparation for the feasts in Konkani. This Apostleship of Prayer was well established in Goa when the revolution came in 1910. Open retreats were common. Fr. Adrian le Tellier (the first Jesuit of the restored Society in India to die in Goa on July 12, 1961) set up a popular retreat mission at Baga. In 1935 families asked for a Lyseum to give a Christian education to boys. But it was closed down soon after its inception. In 1954 when the freedom struggle in Goa was on, the Goa mission was terminated by the Jesuit Superior-General on July 14, 1954 and from July 31 of the same year,

Goa became a section of the Portuguese Province and Belgaum part of the mission. In 1963 Goa was joined to the Goa Poona Jesuit province. Laudable though the work of the Portuguese Jesuits was, they had nothing to show with regard to conversions, believes Claude Saldanha, a veteran Jesuit missionary himself. "If any conversion work was undertaken, that was exclusively the initiative of the Indian Jesuits who joined the Mission in Belgaum". And "the Portuguese Jesuits were much more anti-Indian in their attitude to Congress politics than the English missionaries were."[38]

A Jesuit whose litany of misunderstandings at the hands of his superiors makes painful reading, was Fr. Albert Mendonça, an erudite and nationalist Jesuit of the Goa Mission who taught philosophy for many years at St. Xavier's College in Bombay. His disagreements with the Jesuits began in 1942 when for his liberal ideas with regard to Goa's struggle for freedom, he was transferred to the Jesuit mission of Mangalore in an unjust manner. When the liberation movement began, he took every opportunity to refer to it in his lectures and writings. He was soon forbidden to do so by his superiors. In 1940 his ordination to the priesthood had been kept in suspension because he had visited Mahatma Gandhi in 1932 and had taken an interest in the freedom struggle.[39]

Other Religious Orders that had served in Goa prior to their suppressions in 1834, returned to Goa in the course of the 20th century. The Franciscans did so in 1957 and have two friaries at Ponda. As an Order only in 1925 could they return to India, to set up missions at Hyderabad and Bellary with the help of the Franciscans of the English Province and later of the Dutch Province in 1934. The Dominicans are in Goa only since 1990. The Society of St. Francis Xavier was started for the first time in 1887 and grew out of the Associação dos Missionários (1873-1883). A diocesan congregation, it was meant for the evangelization of peoples in the New Conquests of Goa. One of its most important and well-known figures was the saintly Fr. Agnelo de Souza who died in 1927 at Rachol Seminary where he was the spiritual father.[40]

IV

Though not deliberately intended, some of the Religious Orders that once operated in Goa in the 16th - mid 19th centuries, and which have returned here, portray an image quite different from the times they once operated in. Gone is the strong political backing and sturdy financial support they once enjoyed. The tensions and misunderstandings with the government and the people then from a position of occasional intolerance and aggressiveness, are things of the past, while today the Orders alongside other congregations and the secular clergy engage in works mirroring the needs of the people and of the Church at large.[41]

NOTES AND REFERENCES

1. Charles R. Boxer, *The Portuguese Seaborne Empire 1451-1825,* Middlesex: Pelican Books, 1973; John Correia-Afonso, *Jesuit Letters and Indian History 1542-1773,* Bombay: Oxford Univ. Press, 1969, *Jesuits in India*, Anand: Gujarat Sahitya Prakash, 1997; William V. Bangert, *The History of the Society of Jesus*, St. Louis: Institute of Jesuit Sources, 1972; James Brodrick, *The Origin of the Jesuits*, Chicago: Loyola Press, 1940; Frei Paulo da Trindade, *Conquista Espiritual do Oriente*, F. Felix Lopes (ed.), vols. I-III, Lisbon: Centro de Estudos Históricos Ultramarinos, 1962-67; Achilles Meersman, *The Ancient Franciscan Provinces in India 1500-1835*, Bangalore: Christian Literature Society Press, 1971.
2. Fernão Guerreiro, *Relação Anual das coisas que fizeram os Padres da Companhia de Jesus nas suas missões, I (1600-03)*, Artur Viegas (ed.), Coimbra: Imprensa da Universidade, 1930, pp. 3-4; António F. Cardim, *Bathalhas da Companhia de Jesus na sua gloriosa Província do Japão*, Lisbon: Imprensa Nacional, 1894, p. 290; *Historical Archives of Goa (HAG)*: Cartas e Ordens, codex 2595, fl. 7v; *HAG*: Cartas e Ordens, codex 58, fl. 342; Ludovicus Carez, *Atlas Geographicus Societatis Iesu*, Paris: Georgium Colombier T., 1900, p. 42.
3. Hugh Fenning in "Records of the Dominicans of Goa 1700-1835", *Archivum Fratrum Praedicatorum,* 60 [1980], pp. 387-410. He tells us that there are complete volumes for the most part of account-books at the *HAG*, while even the miscellaneous papers have as much to do with finance as with the salvation of souls. There is in them information on the Dominicans of Goa along the coast of Mozambique and for hundreds of miles up the Zambezi river, with source-material equally rich on their activities in the East Indies.
4. William F. Rea, *The Economics of the Zambezi Mission: 1580-1759,* Rome: IHSA, 1976; Charles J. Borges, *The Economics of the Goa Jesuits 1542-1759: An explanation of their rise and fall,* New Delhi: Concept, 1994; Dauril Aldin, *The Making of an Entreprise: The Society of Jesus in Portugal, its empire and beyond 1540-1750*, California: Standford Univ. Press, 1996.
5. C. Borges, "The Portuguese Jesuits in Asia: Their economic and political net-working within Asia and with Europe", in *A Companhia de Jesus e a missionação no Oriente*, Braga, 2000. The Jesuits traded with an important family in Goa, the Camotins and they lost when the Society of Jesus was suppressed in 1759 since the Province of China had owed it 2,03,370 *xs.*

(Teotónio R. de Souza, *Goa to me*, New Delhi: Concept Publishing Co., 1994, pp. 117 ff.); yet other reports suggest that this same family network helped themselves to loans from the Jesuits (Charles Borges, "Native Goan Participation in the Estado da India and the inter-Asiatic trade", *A Carreira da India e as Rotas dos Estreitos: Actas*, Artur T. de Matos & Luis Felipe F. Reiz Thomaz (eds.), Angra do Heroismo, 1998, pp. 667-86).

6. C. Borges, "The history of the Society of Jesus during the presence of the Portuguese in India 1542-1759: Archival Sources" (unpublished paper).
7. *Archivum Romanum Societatis Iesu* (Rome), *Fondo Gesuitico*, 1443/9, file 23; *Goa* 22, I, fls. 59-65; C. Borges, "Foreign Jesuits and Native Resistance in Goa 1542-1759," *Essays in Goan History*, T. R. de Souza (ed.), New Delhi: Concept, 1989, pp. 69-80; Carlos de Melo, *The Recruitment and Formation of the Native Clergy in India (16th-19th century): An Historico-Canonical Study*, (Henceforth *Recruitment)*, Lisbon: Agencia Geral do Ultramar, 1955.
8. *Recruitment*, p. 157.
9. *Recruitment*, pp. 158, 164, 167, 169, 175; J. M. do Carmo Nazareth, "Occidentes e orientaes nos conventos religiosos de Goa", *O Oriente Português*, vol. IV, 1907, pp. 72-76. The Theatines were also known as Clerics Regular of Divine Providence of St. Caetano and were part of a group founded by Italian clerics in 1650 and since 1751 admitted local boys in Goa into their ranks due to the lack of European priests. See also Vicente Xavier Isidóre Lobo, *Esboceto–Histórico da Casa da Divina Providência dos Tiatinos de Goa*, Panjim: Tip. Bragança & Co., 1929.
10. Given on December 2, 1698 (A. Meersman, *The Friars Minor or Franciscans in India 1291- 1942*, Karachi: Rotti Press, 1943, pp. 42-3); Meersman, *The Franciscans in Tamilnadu*, Schoneck-Berkenried: Nouvelle Reuve de Science Missionaire (NRSM), 1962, p. 121. The Franciscans were the first religious group to work in India. By 1629 they had two provinces and by 1635 they had 423 friars in the St. Thome Province and 177 in the Mother of God Province (Meersman, "The institution of commissaries general for the Portuguese Franciscans in the East", *Archivum Franciscanum Historicum*, (Rome), An. 59, 1966; Ricardo C. Teles, *Os Franciscanos no Oriente e seus conventos,* Nova Goa: T. Rau & Irmãos, 1922; Meersman, *The Franciscans in Bombay*, Bangalore: Everybody's St. Anthony, 1957).
11. *Recruitment*, pp. 17-18.
12. *Economics of the Goa Jesuits.*
13. Capuchin Mission Unit (Maryland), *India and its Missions*, New York: MacMillan Co. 1923, p. 57; L. Besse, *Fr. Beschi of the Society of Jesus: His times & His writings*, Trichinopoly: St. Joseph Industrial School, 1918; F. X. Schutte, *Valignano's Mission Principles for Japan*, Anand: Gujarat Sahitya Prakash, vol.I, pt. 1, 1980, pp. 175-76.
14. Borges, "Christian Life in Goa during Colonial Times", *Jnanadeepa* (Pune), vol. 1, no. 2, July 1998, pp. 34-41; See also Borges, "Catholic missionaries in the Estado da India and their insights into Indian culture, science, medicine,

life and manners" (unpublished paper); Borges, "Popular Expressions of Religiosity in 16th century Catholic Goa", *Souvenir of the Holy Family Chapel*, Goa, 1992.

15. Borges, "How True?: the "Discovered India" as reflected through the eyes of Catholic missionaries into Europe in the 16th century" (unpublished paper).
16. See D. Ferroli, *Jesuits in Malabar*, vols. I-II, Bangalore: King & Co., 1951/ Kozhikode: Xavier Press, 1955.
17. A. da Silva Rego, "The Monsoon Codices at the National Archives of the Torre do Tombo", in John Correia-Afonso (ed.), *Indo-Portuguese History: Sources and Problems*, Bombay: Oxford Univ. Press, 1981, pp. 51-71.
18. John Correia-Afonso, "Indian History in the Cartorio dos Jesuitas," in *Indo-Portuguese History*, pp. 72-85. About the three villages (Velim, Ambelim and Assolna), Teotónio R. de Souza states that the Jesuits had more than doubled the output of their lands through their more rational approach to cultivation. These villages were valued in 1578 at 2,010 *xerafins*. They were given as a grant to the Jesuits and by 1635 their yield was assessed at 5,500 *xs*. ("Voiceless in Goan Historiography: A case for the source-value of Church records", *Indo-Portuguese History*); *Archivo Historico Ultramarino* (*AHU*), no. 61, fl. 1, dated April 17, 1743 lists the petition of the "os gancares de tres aldeas Assolna, Vellim e Ambellim ..." against the Jesuits.
19. Rea lists the following numbers in his *The Economics of the Zambezi Missions 1580-1759: ARSI* [Rome], Goa 25, fl. 192v; nos. 9853, 9854, 9855 (*British Library*, London) about the Jesuit Missions 1601-1693; *AHU, codice* 449, fls. 133v-136v, maço 90 (India), codice no. 441, fl. 240.
20. Anthony Disney, "The Viceroy Count of Linhares at Goa, 1629-1635", *II Seminário Internacional de História Indo-Portuguesa: Actas,* Luis de Albuquerque & Inácio Guerreiro (eds.), Lisbon, 1985, pp. 303-315.
21. *AHU, codice* no. 208 (1643-1678), fls. 110v, 116 is a letter of the King of Portugal to the Viceroy dated March 2, 1645. Fl. 116 is the royal letter to Fr. Provincial dated January 23, 1649.
22. Hugh Fenning, "Records of the Dominicans of Goa 1700-1835", *Archivum Fratrum Praedicatorum*, 1 (1980), Rome, p. 187. Fenning, a Dominican historian had attempted to reconstruct the Dominican archives of Goa as they were in 1835 and to list whatever government records of the post-suppression period bore directly on the convents of the Order.
23. Bernard Anderson & John Correia-Afonso (eds.), *Indological Studies*, "The Jesuit influence in the court of Vijayanagar", New Delhi: Promilla & Co.·1990, p. 109; Jorge Manuel dos Santos Alves, "A Cruz, os Diamentes e os cavalos: Frei Luis do Salvador, Primeiro missionário e embaixador portugues em Vijayanagar (1500-1510)", *Mare Liberum*, no. 5, July 1993, pp. 14-15.
24. Paulo da Trindade, *Conquista Espiritual...*, vol. II, pp. 40, 52, 66-68, 87. About Trindade's frequent recourse to miracles, Meersman writes: "It is written in the spirit of the times. It is simply loaded with miracles, visions,

apparitions and what not. He was not one to allow a miracle or what he considered a miracle, to pass unheeded and unheralded" (*The Franciscans in Tamilnad*, p. 73).

25. Meersman (ed.), *Annual reports of the Portuguese Franciscans in India 1713-1833*, Lisbon: CEHU, 1972, p. 136.
26. N. Figueiredo, "Os religiosos eremitas de Santo Agostinho no Oriente", *Boletim Eclesiastico da Arquidiocese de Goa (BEAG)*, no. 2, August 1942, pp. 54-63; J. A. Campos, *History of the Bandel Convent and Church*, Calcutta: Catholic Orphan Press, 1922, pp. 26-42.
27. Arnaulf Hartmann (ed.), "The Augustinians in Golden Goa: A manuscript by Felix of Jesus, O.S.A", *Analecta Augustiniana*, no. 30, Rome, 1967, pp. 5-12.
28. Luis Silveira (ed.), *Itinerário de Sebastião Manrique*, vols. I-II, Lisbon: Agencia Geral das Colonias, 1946; Maria Ana Marques Guedes (ed.), *Breve Relação dos Reinos de Pegu, Arrãcáo, Brama, e dos Impérios Càlaminhã, Siammon e Grão Mogol de Sebastião Manrique*, Cotovia, 1997, pp. 9, 59-62.
29. Diogo Gonçalves S.J., *História do Malavar*, Josef Wicki (ed.), Munster: Aschendorffsche Verlagsbuchhandlung, 1955, pp. ix–x, xv. The English translation has been edited by Charles Borges.
30. Borges, "Goa's role in the destabilising of Sri Lanka: A Missionary Enterprise" (unpublished paper); V. Perniola, *The Catholic Church in Sri Lanka* (The Portuguese, Dutch and English Periods 1505-1844), Dehiwala (Sri Lanka): Tisara Prakasakayo, 1989-1992. *passim.*
31. *Religion and Ideology in Sri Lanka,* Bangalore: TPI, 1974.
32. V. Cronin, *A Pearl to India: the life of Roberto de Nobili*, London: Rupert Hart-Davis, 1959, p. v; A. Saulière, *His Star in the East*, S. Rajamanickam (ed.), Anand: Gujarat Sahitya Prakash, 1995, pp. xvi, 457; A. Amaladass, "Jesuits and Sanskrit Studies", in *Jesuits in India: In historical perspective*, T. R. de Souza & C. J. Borges (eds.), Macau: ICM, 1992, p. 213; See Ines G. Zupanov, *Disputed Mission: Jesuit experiments and brahmanical knowledge in seventeenth century India*, New Delhi: Oxford Univ. Press, 1999.
33. A. Saulère, *Red Sand: a life of St. John de Brito, S.J. Martyr of the Madura Mission*, Mathura: De Nobili Press, 1947; Borges, "St. John de Britto: a bibliographical survey", *St. John de Britto: his spirit and mission*, V.M. Gnanapragasam (ed.), Dindigul: CIS Publications, 1995, pp. 3-26; Josef Wicki (ed.), *Documenta Indica*, Rome: IHSI, 1988, vol. XVII, doc. 21, p. 82.
34. J. J. Pallath (ed.), *Arnos Padiri - the first Malayalam poet scholar Orientalist*, Kozhikode: Arnos Padiri Publications, undated.
35. *AHU*: *India*, maço 93, April 2, 1761; António Sergio, *Breve Interpretação da História de Portugal*, Lisbon: Livraria Sa da Costa, 1979, pp. 123, 268; J.S. Cummins, "The Suppression of the Jesuits 1773," *History Today*, 1973, pp. 839-848.

36. Walter Mathias (ed.), *Jesuits: The Golden Jubilee of the Goa Mission 1890-1940*, Belgaum: St. Paul's, 1941, pp. 15-16, 24; Claude Saldanha, "The restored Society of Jesus in Goa", *Indian Missiological Review* (Shillong), vol. 9, no. 4, December 1987. p. 311.
37. H.C. Perumalil & E.R. Hambye (eds.), *Christianity in India: A history in ecumenical perspective*, Alleppey: Prakasham Publications, 1972, p. 137.
38. Saldanha, "The restored Society of Jesus in Goa", *op. cit.*, pp. 312-14. Today the Jesuits run nine institutions in Goa, among them schools, retreat homes and research centers.
39. Zotico Praxedes de Souza, *The case of Fr. Mendonca, the Jesuits and Goa*, Bombay: Azad Gomantak Dal, 2nd ed., 1959, pp. 60-61.
40. F. X. Gomes-Catão, "Associação dos missionários na arquidiocese de Goa 1873-1883", *BEAG*, no. 2, February 1958, pp. 51-7; S. P., "Sociedade Missionária de S. Francisco Xavier, Pilar, Goa, para a conversão da India", *BEAG*, no. 1, July 1947, pp. 36-42; Conceição M. Rodrigues, "Sociedade Missionária de S. Francisco Xavier e o Seminário das missões do Pilar", *BEAG*, no. 3, September 1953, pp. 78-82; *Missionary Society of St. F. Xavier – Pilar*. Silver Jubilee, 1939-1964, lists the group's achievements since its reorganization in 1939. Today it runs a number of popular schools, technical institutes and parishes, and has a major and minor seminary in Goa.
41. Borges, "The changing faces of Christianity in Goa: From being Portuguese to being India?" (unpublished paper)

20

Goan Oratorians

CARMO DA SILVA

The Oratory of the Holy Cross of Miracles of Goa is the first religious congregation of clerics, of indigenous origin, ever founded not only in India but in Asia too. It flourished for about a hundred and fifty years till its extinction by the Portuguese government. Its showpiece is the flourishing church in Sri Lanka. The Goan Oratorians saved it from extinction by the sweat of their brows and by their missionary methods that stood the test of time and contributed in large measure to its revival and expansion, in spite of persecution.

Its origin is linked to the greatest missionary that Goa, and India, for that matter, has ever produced, Blessed Joseph Vaz. The church in Sri Lanka owes to the Oratory of Goa not only its first two Vicars Apostolic, Bishops Vicente do Rosario and Caetano António but also its most distinguished Catholic writer, Fr. Jacome Gonsalves of Divar, Goa.

But the congregation of the Holy Cross of Miracles began, as all things divine, in a small way. In those days, the doors of the existing Religious Orders were not open, for this or that trifling reason, to Indian aspirants though there was no dearth of vocations either to the priesthood or religious life.[1]

Fr. Pascoal da Costa Jeremias, an elderly diocesan priest of Margao, Goa, with four others willing to live in community had to blaze a new trail. So on October 28, feast of Sts. Simon and Jude, in 1682, Fr. Jeremias realising the aspiration of his life, along with his four companions, began the experiment of a life in common with a brief and elementary rule, approved by the Archbishop of Goa, Dom Manuel de Souza e Menezes. They took residence in the chapel of St. John of the Desert at Batim, Ilhas taluka, not very far from Panaji.

But the building was in a very bad state of conservation and situated on a lonely and not so healthy hilltop to boot. It was not suitable for a decent community life. Disheartened, the other four deserted Fr. Jeremias, who, this way, had to fend for himself in the solitary place. Later on, however, a priest, Fr. Custódio Leitão from Azossim, and a layman, Bernardo Coutinho, from Margao, joined him, sharing in his deprivations and hopes. Unfortunately, in the monsoon of 1683, the already dilapidated building collapsed. As there was no hope of rebuilding it due to the forays of the Marathas, under Sambhaji, our well-meant spiritual adventurers had to shift elsewhere. So they settled in Old Goa in the abandoned church of the Holy Cross of Miracles. It was so called because there was a cross on which Christ is said to have been seen in bodily form in 1619.

The Confraternity of Our Lady of Good Success that was holding the charge of the church was good enough to approach the Cathedral Chapter and obtain the necessary permission. The request was granted by the Chapter, by its capitular decree on March 14 1684. According to the chronology compiled by Sebastião do Rego, it was granted on March 4, 1684 as stated in the *Documentação* published by Manuel da Costa Nunes.[2] The question being of just the digit "1", it may due to oversight. Hence the members of the congregation were later on called by the Portuguese *Milagristas*.

But the small community without prospective candidates seems to have been doomed to fade away in the course of time when God's hand on September 25, 1685 brought by his unfathomable designs, a young and zealous priest, Fr. Joseph Vaz who would give a new orientation to the community. He was back in Goa after a stint as a missionary in Kanara but with the intention of going to Ceylon badly in need of priests.

At first sight, apparently, it looked like that joining the fledgling and unnamed community, Fr. Vaz would have to put aside his cherished dreams of going to Ceylon to look after the stranded folks there. But instead of spelling ruin, to his plans, it only strengthened them.

Heartily welcomed, Fr. Vaz was immediately elected superior of the community at the suggestion of Fr. Jeremias. After consulting his companions and on the advice of the Theatine, Fr. António Ventimiglia, it was decided by the new Superior not to found a new congregation but to constitute an Oratory of St. Philip Neri. The Oratories of St. Philip Neri are congregations of diocesan priests living under obedience but without vows. Their aim is to pray, preach and administer the sacraments.

In this connection they wrote to Fr. Bartolomeu de Quental, founder of the Oratory of Lisbon, on January 9, 1686. Fr. Ventimiglia recommended the application.

The first task of Fr. Vaz as Superior was to put his own house in order. He repaired the old building, in spite of the scarcity of financial means and no sympathy of the ecclesiastical authorities, boarding off the corridor into rooms or cubicles to suit the needs of a religious community. Then he introduced spiritual and charitable activities and trained his brethren to give missions, taking them along with him, one by one, to the parishes. And after about six months of this type of apostolate in the city of Goa and around, in March 1606 he set out for Ceylon in secrecy as needed by circumstances. He took along with him the latest members of the community, Fr. Paulo de Souza and Bro. Estevão de Siqueira and also a faithful servant, João, a family servant from Sancoale.

To avoid all suspicions that he wanted to go to Ceylon, he ministered along with his companions to the spiritual needs of the faithful in Kanara for about nine months and finally at Tellicherry he let it be known to his companions his real intentions of continuing the journey further southwards to Ceylon. Unwilling to enter unknown land lying under the jurisdiction of the heretical Dutch, his two companions returned home to Goa without going to their community at Santa Cruz dos Milagres to which they belonged. This is how Fr. S.G. Perera, S.J., outstanding historian of the Oratory of Goa, puts it.[3] However in the article, "The Oratory of Goa,"[4] he simply writes that they "shrank from peril and left him at Tellicherry and, sad to say, did not return to the community".

But the "Report of the Mission of Ceylon" (1697) written by the Superior of the Oratory in Goa and submitted to the Viceroy to be forwarded to the King of Portugal states: "Not to be discovered, they decided to reduce their number as they were four. Fr. Paulo de Souza and Bro. Estevão de Siqueira returned to the mission of Kanara while Fr. Joseph Vaz and his servant, João, continued their journey to Ceylon to find out what obstacles the heretics would place in their way".

On the departure of Fr. Joseph Vaz to Ceylon, Fr. Jeremias was made superior. But unfortunately he died in 1687, the very year the Lisbon Oratory replied favourably and he was succeeded by Fr. Custódio Leitão.

The new Archbishop of Goa, Dom Alberto da Silva, to whom the Lisbon Oratory had recommended the Goan initiative was the carrier of the statutes. However, he died soon after his arrival and Dom Pedro da Silva, bishop of Cochin, became the administrator of the archdiocese. He was not favourable to the idea of an Oratory in Goa because it would be exempt from the episcopal control. For the Oratories enjoyed exemption from the jurisdiction of the bishop and his vicar general was also openly against the *Milagristas*. The reason, according to the latter, was the instability or lack of perseverance shown by the four companions of Fr. Jeremias and also the fact that Fr. Vaz was deserted (?) by his two companions. Another objection, and a more serious one, though not mentioned in the official documents but found in an anonymous manuscript,[5] was that the Oratory was intended only for brahmins and that the other castes rightly looked upon it as a piece of arrogance.[6]

To take the last objection first, for it is more serious, the least one can say is that it flies in the face of evidence available. The ms. mentioned by Fr. Perera seems to be the "*Notícia*" written about the Goa archdiocese by Fr. Bravo de Moraes and sent by Archbishop Teresa on December 27, 1722 to the Royal Portuguese Academy. In this ms. it is stated unequivocally that it was open to all irrespective of the so-called castes. We quote it literally:

"É como estes Pes erão Bramnes de Nasção, e os povos de muitas castas, os q. o não erão, objectavão q isso só era em utilidade daquelles e não mais; ao q lhes respondeu q hu dos pontos de seus estatutos era em q pudessem entrar na dita Congregação homens de todas as castas, sem excepção de algua; e para isso fez q logo se recebessem alguns charodos; que são de outra casta mto oposta a dos Bramnes, o q visto p todos se resolverão a dar-lhe trinta mil xes".[7]

(And as these priests were brahmins by nation, and the peoples of many castes, those who were not, used to object that it was only for their benefit and not of others; to this it was answered that one of the points of its statutes was that men of all castes without exception could join that Congregation, and it was decided that some chardos who are of the other caste very much opposed to that of the brahmins, be received and all decided then that 30,000 *xs.* be given).

Otherwise the same Fr. Perera[8] notes that the *Milagristas* replied that it (Congregation) was open to all, and actually received some members of the other castes. But in spite of all this, it is written that the Congregation was an exclusive preserve of one caste only.[9]

One could mention also that Fr. Vaz, founder member of the Congregation taught Sinhalese, Tamil, and even Latin to his *fidus Achates*, João, faithful to his master through thick and thin and sent him to Goa in 1697 to be ordained a priest. He was a kunnbi of Sancoale. But after having been in Goa, says Fr. Perniola, "we do not hear of him any longer" and adds, "the Oratory was open only to brahmins",[10] which is not true as has been shown above. As the deadlock, regarding the institution of the Oratory continued, it is said that some members of the community even thought of joining the Society of Jesus *en masse* and asking that the convent of the Holy Cross of Miracles be constituted into an Indian college of the Society with one of its present members as Rector. But the Provincial and General of the Society rejected the proposal forthright. It is said, however, that Fr. Francisco Souza, author of the famous *Oriente Conquistado*, was very much in favour of the idea.

What finally came to the rescue of the community of the Holy Cross of Miracles, in spite of the opposition, also of the new archbishop Dom Frei Augostinho da Anunciação, is the work of Fr. Vaz and companions, Fr. Menezes and Fr. Carvalho, who had followed his uncle in Ceylon under very trying circumstances. On the other side, the Oratorians of Lisbon stood faithfully by their Goan brethren and appealed to the king who placed the matter before the *Junta das Missões*. This board, however, advised the king to obtain more information from the archbishop. Notwithstanding the favourable recommendations from prominent people like the bishop of Mylapore and the Indian bishop of Hierapolis, the archbishop was not ready to act.

The *Milagristas* then turned to the Viceroy of India who requested the archbishop to relent. On his part the Viceroy paid surprise visits to see things for himself. He appreciated the good work being done and specially their gift of preaching the word of God and requested them to raise their patrimony. Meanwhile the municipalities of Ilhas, Salcete and Bardez again came to the aid of the community and contributed 30,000 *xerafins*.

In this way the archbishop was finally forced to act, but he introduced modifications in the Constitutions of the Oratory and to keep it under his thumb he even presided over the elections.

The Oratory of Lisbon, once more, approached the king of Portugal who approved the Oratory in Goa on the advice of the *Junta* but with modifications imposed by the archbishop.

Meanwhile Rome came to know about the happenings in Ceylon and how the *Milagristas* had succeeded in gaining the goodwill of the Sinhalese king and were tending the stranded flock till then without a shepherd, even in Dutch territory, often risking their own lives. So when the Oratorians of Lisbon and Rome placed the matter regarding the Goan Oratory before the Pope, the Roman authorities did not hesitate at all to grant the permission of an Oratory in Goa and to the surprise of all concerned did it putting aside the changes introduced by the archbishop in the Constitutions. Naturally, Rome wanted an Oratory as founded by St. Philip Neri. And so the bull of approval, establishing an Oratory in Goa was issued by Clement XI in 1706.

Though the *Milagristas* were happy to hear the good news, the archbishop wanted to suspend the execution of the papal bull as it was against the royal decree that had subjected the Oratory to the jurisdiction of the archbishop but refrained from doing so at the request of the Viceroy on condition that the members accepted his direction.

Again the Lisbon Oratorians came to the rescue of their Goan brethren and the king accepted the papal bull. And finally on March 30, 1709, the Oratory of the Holy Cross of Miracles was duly constituted in Goa with papal and royal approval. This is the saga of the foundation of the Oratory in Goa, so far the only Oratory not only in Goa and India but also in the whole of Asia.

After the canonical erection of the Oratory, novices started coming in and the convent of the Holy Cross of Miracles could not accommodate all of them. So the *Milagristas* set their hopes on the Carmelite convent that was practically vacant and obtained it. For the Italian Carmelites had been expelled from the Portuguese territories.

The island of Ceylon and the mission of Kandy became exclusive fields of the missionary activity of the Goan Oratorians. So much so that Fr. Pedro Ferrão who went to Ceylon after having heard of the good work of Fr. Vaz with due permission of the ecclesial authorities in Goa, joined the Oratory in 1700 and wanted to continue to work in the mission. Another priest, Fr. Francisco Jesus, who was sent to Ceylon in 1702 by the bishop of Cochin, at the request of Fr. Vaz, died there after having worked for almost twenty years. But we hardly know anything about him. For he did not join the Oratory.

Recognising the work of the Oratorians, the Holy See granted them ample spiritual faculties and the king of Portugal, a monthly subsidy of 25 *xerafins* to each missionary working in Ceylon. The amount was increased later on. At the request of the king of Portugal, the Goan Oratory also sent missionaries to Malabar, Madagascar, Solor and Timor. And on the suppression of the Society of Jesus, when the colleges of Chorão and Rachol were instituted into diocesan seminaries, the Oratorians were entrusted with their direction. The latter at one time under the Vicentians was again reverted to the direction of the Oratorians.

We lack precise statistics of the number of the Oratorians. According to a ms. in the Torre do Tombo, Lisbon, there were, about the middle of the 18th century, 66 of them, 47 in India, 14 in Ceylon and 5 in other missions. In 1775 they were 72 of whom 16 were in Ceylon. In 1784 there were only 61 members but in 1800, there were 45 of whom 16 were in Ceylon. In 1804 they were only 42 and in the year of extinction, that is, in 1834, there were only 36. But the number of those working in Ceylon was almost the same. The extinction of the Oratory took place when the king of Portugal suppressed all religious orders in Portugal and the overseas territories.

The Emerald Island and, specially, the mission of Kandy, for almost 150 years were the fields of extraordinary and heroic activity of Goa's Oratory. That is why, the flourishing Church of Sri Lanka, as Ceylon is now known is *aere perennius*, perennial monument to their glorious memory. Many left their bones there, unwept, unsung and unhonoured.

NOTES AND REFERENCES

1. Carlos de Melo, *The Recruitment and Formation of the Native Clergy in India*, Lisbon, 1955, p. 245.
2. Mariano J. Dias, "The Congregation of the Oratory of Goa", *Blessed Joseph Vaz Bulletin*, no. 2, 1999, pp. 9ff; no. 3, pp. 12ff; See especially M. da Costa Nunes, *Documentação para a História de Congregação do Oratório de Santa Cruz dos Milagres do Clero Natural de Goa (Documentação)*, Lisbon, 1966, p. 14.
3. S. G. Perera, *Life of the Venerable Father Joseph Vaz*, Ranchi, 1943, pp. 43ff.
4. *Biblioteca da Ajuda de Lisboa (BAL), MU* 51-VII-57, fls. 1-4; *Documentação, op. cit*, pp. 127ff. A yearly report on the mission of Ceylon was usually drawn up by the Fr. Superior of the Oratory of Goa and submitted to the Viceroy to be forwarded to the king of Portugal. In 1697, the Fr. Superior of the Oratory seems to have been Pedro Paulo and the Viceroy Dom Pedro António de Noronha, Count of Vila Verde. The English translation is by V. Perniola, *The Catholic Church in Sri Lanka*, p. 143.
5. *Notícias da India, Fundo Geral,* Lisbon: Biblioteca Nacional de Lisboa, pp. 149ff, 176ff.
6. S. G. Perera, "The Oratory of Goa", in *Historical Sketches*, Colombo, 1963, p. 188.
7. M. Dias, "Goa Congregation of the Oratory", *Bulletin of Instituto Menezes Braganza*, no. 176, 1996, pp. 88ff; Carmo da Silva, "Goan Oratorians", *Blessed Joseph Vaz Bulletin*, no. 2, 1999, pp. 12ff.
8. S. G. Perera, "The Oratory of Goa", in *Historical Sketches*, pp. 184-96; *The Oratorians in Ceylon*, Colombo, 1936.
9. K. Cottineau, *History of Goa*, p. 95; A. B. Bragança Pereira, *Etnografia da India Portuguesa*, vol. II, Bastora, 1940, p. 287.
10. V. Perniola, *The Catholic Church in Sri Lanka*, vol. I, 1985, p. xxi; Sebastião do Rego, *Vida do Venerável Padre José Vaz*, 1962.

21

Religious Rituals and their Positive and Negative Impact on Hindu Society

ARCHANA KAKODKAR

This essay is an attempt to reflect on some of the religious rituals prevalent during the 19th and 20th centuries in Goa, some of which are prevalent even today. The major part of this paper is directed to the rituals that are performed in the temple of Shri Mahalasa of Mardol in Ponda taluka, in particular, to some general family rituals.

India's recorded civilization is one of the longest in the course of world history and its mythology and religions span the whole of that time and beyond. For some periods (as Hindu scholarship traditionally had little interest in history as such), religious mythology and sacred lore constitute the sole record and the changes that may be noted in such traditional material are thus vital clues to our knowledge of the socio-political changes over the years.[1]

For historical reasons, Hindus in Portuguese India were a very self-conscious community. The impact of the Portuguese rule, destruction of Hindu temples, and the subsequent policy of conversion further enhanced this awareness.[2] One must remember that the Hindus in Goa were not very different from the Hindus in the rest of the country. But the destruction of the beautiful Hindu temples created panic amongst the followers of these gods and goddesses. The Portuguese colonizers did not stop at that. They burnt the holy books of the Hindus, books like the *Vedas, Puranas, Ramayana, Mahabharata* and even the sacred scriptures (*pothis*), with the intention of wiping out Hinduism and Hindus from Goa. The colonizers believed that these scriptures contained precepts of idolatory.[3] But this was a futile attempt.

Hinduism is based on oral traditions passed on from father to son and so on. The chain continues. Besides, Hindu religion and mythology recognize nearly 330,00,000 gods and goddesses. But how many could be destroyed by a few Portuguese masters? This was a task more difficult than discovering Goa. They soon realized that their policy of intolerance was not going to bring results. But by this time most of the prominent Hindu temples of Shri Mahalasa, Shri Manguesh, Shri Shantadurga, Shri Ramnath, Shri Mahalakshmi and many others had shifted their deities to the safer places in Antruj Mahal of the Adilshahi kingdom which was under the raja of Saundia or of the Saundekars. Most of the major temples came to the Ponda taluka. The temple mahajans took *prasad* and *kaul* of the gods and shifted them to safer places. It was really a great risk. By this time the tempo of harassment of the Hindus had tapered down. The reasons being that the Marathas on one side and the Muslims on the other were building pressure on the colonizers to adopt a "live and let live policy". By then most of the Hindu temples had built their own new edifices for their *gramadevatas* (village deities), *kuladevatas* (clan deities) and *istadevatas* (favourite or personal deities).[4]

History and rituals at Shri Mahalasa Temple

The detailed description of the beautiful precincts of the temple of Shri Mahalasa at Old Mardol or Vernem, is found in the contemporary correspondence of the missionaries. Fr. Gomes Vaz in his letter dated December 12, 1567, states that he has not seen such beautiful premises in the whole of Europe.[5] Fr. Luis Goes who took the initiative to destroy these premises liked the temple and the building so much, that he made efforts to preserve the building for converting it into the church of Our Lady of Conception or Queen of Angels.[6] But this request was turned down. The detailed account of the destruction of this architecturally and aesthetically the best temple in Goa is described by P.S.S. Pissurlencar who comments that surprisingly this is the unique example where the foundation of the temple survives till this day. The Portuguese did not construct any church or chapel on the demolished temple.[7]

Devi Shri Mahalasa

According to Hindu mythology, Vishnu incarnated himself in the visage of Devi Mahalasa in order to infatuate the demons (Titan in Hindu mythology). Seeing the recklessness of the demons, Shri Devi took away the jar of nectar (*amrit*) in order to give rebirth to the deceased gods. She is seen standing on one demon, holding in one hand the head of another and the severed head of a third. The blood which drips from them is lapped up by a lion. Of her four hands, she holds the trishool in one, and in the left, the jar of nectar. There are lot of ornaments on the person of Shri Devi and a beautiful crown on her head.[8] Apart from the main temple of Shri Mahalasa, there is a separate temple of Shri Santeri, in the same premises at the right hand side of the main temple. Shri Santeri always occupies the right hand place in all major functions which are celebrated with a combined procession of both the deities. It is believed that Shri Santeri had offered Shri Mahalasa a place in her village who in turn promised her the honour of *agrapaja* in all the major celebrations.

In the temple premises, there are two panchishtas of Shri Santeri and of Shri Mahalasa. The panchishtas of Shri Santeri in the temple are Shri Lakshmi Narayan and Shri Ganapati. Behind the temple are Shri Grampurush, Shri Bhagawati and Shri Samhar Bhairav. The panchishtas of Shri Mahalasa in the temple are Shri Ganapati, Shri Sahastrapal, Shri Sankashti, and Shri Mhal Purush at the feet of Shri Mahalasa. Besides Shri Chatuh Shasti, Shri Kalbhairav, Shri Dadha, Shri Malhar, Shri Sinh Purush, at the *tali* (lake) there is another idol of Shri Mahalasa and Shri Naga. All these deities are related to each other. During the ritual of Hari Jagar (awakening the gods) which falls from Ashwin Pornima to Kartik Pornima, all the deities are offered *kakad aarti* and *naivedya* at early hours of the morning. In front of this temple there is a large *deepstumbh* and another *stumbh* of *pancha dhatu* (five metals). Besides this, there is a very big *nyandeep* made of brass weighing 25,552 kgs. The total number of wicks required are 567 and oil from seven large tins.

Shri Mahalasa is adorned as Bala after the *nirnalaya visarjan* in the morning. After the *abhisheka*, the deity is fully adorned with select ornaments. Though the same ornaments are retained for the rest of the day, it is widely believed that the deity is a *yuvati* (young lady) at noon and *proudha* (old woman) in the afternoon. This astonishing fact is experienced by the devotees through all the seasons.

Oath under the bell of Shri Mahalasa Temple

The paramount importance of Shri Mahalsa is that nobody dares to tell a lie in the temple. Even during the Portuguese rule, the government had to officially take cognizance of this fact and the decisive oath under the bell on the chawk of Shri Mahalasa temple was recognized by various decrees and orders.

The *Carta Regia* of the municipality of Ilhas dated March 26, 1532, shortly after the establishment of the rule, provided for official recognition of the oath under the bell. The *Codigos dos Usos e Costumes* (Code of usages and customs) of 1853 and later of 1880 had also granted official recognition for the said process of taking oath under the bell of Shri Mahalasa temple. "In the court, Hindu brahmins shall always take the oath on the book of Shri Bhagvad Gita and other castes on the coconut, betel, areca and rice. In cases where the decision is based solely on an oath, the parties may demand that the same be taken before the deity Mahalasa, the expenses of the transport, the emoluments of the judges, the honorarium of the advocates and fees of the employees of the court being paid by the applicant."[9]

As per this order any accused person prosecuted in the court of law, could opt to deny the charges, on oath under the said famous bell of this temple.

The ritual of taking the oath

The court used to assemble in the temple premises along with the pleaders and court officials. The accused had to take a bath in the temple tank and was then garlanded with red flowers of a plant locally known as *pitkuli*. He would then arrive in the temple accompanied by a drummer and stand below the bell facing the deity. He would next declare on oath his involvement in the litigation, in the presence of the judge, advocates and all concerned.

Socio-legal-psychological acculturation of the colonisers

It is really very surprising that Shri Mahalasa temple is the only Hindu temple in Goa, which was recognized by the Portuguese rulers, even though it was a Hindu temple. It is worth researching as to why this special favour was bestowed on this temple. Perhaps it was the first Hindu temple which impressed them or it was the result of the psychological effect or guilt of having destroyed this beautiful edifice. Or since the first demolition was so successful leading to the consolidation of their power in Goa, they recognized this deity in order to return the favour. It was indeed a sociological and psychological acculturation of the colonizers.

Some Rituals

Women and Rituals : During ancient times the status of women was very high in Hindu society. But with time women lost their higher status, and were placed in a secondary position to men. In Hinduism except for fasting and the *vatasavitri* ritual which a woman can do on her own, she cannot perform any other ritual. If she is married, she has to sit next to her husband for the performance of any domestic or temple ritual and touch his right hand reciting '*mama*' which means 'I also'. She had no choice to choose a mate, since her elders would fix her alliance and decide the dowry (*streedhan*). Her marriageable age could be between 6 and 16. Ceremonies lasted from eight to ten days. One must be grateful to the Portuguese for increasing the marriageable age. Women from the Kalavant Samaj who practised the matriarchal system of marriage were more respected and free than women of the other communities. They were the bread-earners for the family. One of the girls from such families would usually be 'devoted' to God and would undergo a ritual called '*shens*', which was a proxy wedding ceremony. The Portuguese banned this practice.[10]

Birth and Death: According to Hinduism, birth as well as death is a religious taboo. Whenever a child is born in a family, '*suer/suver*' is observed for three days and whenever someone dies, his or her family observes '*sutak*' for a period of twelve days. They abstain from doing any religious *pooja* during the period. Women are not allowed to attend the funeral procession and a male whose father is alive, cannot attend the funeral of another person. Brahmins performing the rituals for the dead cannot perform any other religious poojas.

Death Rituals and the Portuguese

Hindus in Goa during the Portuguese rule were forced to cover the entire body except the head of the deceased person and had to place it in a coffin and carry it to the crematorium. This helped to avoid disease and pollution. The rituals for the dead person could not be performed on the banks of the Mandovi or Zuari or of other rivers or at ocean sites. At Aravelem in Sankhali which has a waterfall, is a temple for the performance of the rituals and for immersing the ashes in the water. Some immerse the ashes of their deceased at Dona Paula where the Mandovi and the Zuari meet in the Arabian Sea, termed by Hindus 'a holy *triveni* or *sangam*'. Thanks to the Portuguese, Goa, the Konkan Kashi was saved from greater pollution as has not been the case of the Ganga, the Varanasi (Benaras/Kashi) situated on its banks, or Trimbakeshwar in Nasik, Maharashtra, another holy place where one can perform the last rites of the dead. Though today many claim that Goa is environmentally clean, the credit for keeping Goa clean and pollution-free must go to the colonizers for their far-reaching legislation in this regard.

Negative and Positive impact on Society

There are more positive than negative impacts of religious rituals on society. Irrespective of caste or creed, people perform rituals and take part in zatras whole-heartedly. The village economy is boosted as a result of the presence of temples. Flower-sellers, grocery-sellers, hoteliers, and cloth merchants make a lot of business due to the visitors at the temples for the festivals. Artisans find jobs throughout the year. Rituals also help devotees strengthen their faith in the deities of their forefathers. Children are taught about their faith. Rituals also have their place. But religion can turn into mere superstition if rituals are performed mechanically.[11]

The negative impact of rituals on society is that the age-old tradition of *sevas* performed by the *devdasis* (who no longer exist) are curiously sought out by visiting devotees and tourists, who look for women prostitutes in the temple vicinity. Such acts demoralise present-day society. A small village may also find it difficult to accommodate the hundreds and thousands of devotees who visit it and civic amenities get disturbed. Yet the temples of Goa are more peaceful and clean and the rituals carried out in them for hundreds of years keep Hinduism alive.

NOTES AND REFERENCES

1. Veronica Ions, *Indian Mythology*, New Delhi: Standard Literature Co., 1983, p. 6.
2. See Archana Kakodkar, in *Vasco da Gama and India,* coord. João Pedro Garcia, vol. II, Lisbon: Fundação Calouste Gulbenkian, 1999, p. 204.
3. V.N.S. Dhume, *Devasthanache Itihas*, Margao: Sahitya Prakashan, 1978, pp. 22-23.
4. Varsha Kamat, "Socio-Political and Religious life in Goa, 1900-1946", (unpublished Ph.D dissertation, 1996).
5. *Shri Mahalasa Saunsthan Jeernoddhar Samiti*, Mardol: Temple Information Book, 1993, pp. 21-24.
6. Madhav Narayan Vaidya, *Mhaddolchi Yatra*, Nova Goa, 1913, pp. 5-8.
7. Vyankatesh Vishnu Vaidya, *Shri Mahalasha Devasthanacha Itihas Va Varnan*,

Khanepur: D.C. Sadekar, 1931, pp. 30-33. See also *Documentação para a história das missões do Padroado Português do Oriente*, vol. X.

8. Narayan Vishnu Naik, "Devi Mahalasa - the destroyer of all evils", *Navhind Times* (Goa), March 20, 2000.
9. *Family Laws of Goa, Daman and Diu*, vol. 1, Advocates Association of Goa, Daman and Diu, 1979, p. 161.
10. Kakodkar, "Kalawants and temple lords" (unpublished seminar paper, 1991).
11. Kakodkar, "Urban temple towns in Goa: A case study of Ponda" (unpublished seminar paper, 1998).

Note: Shri Mahalasa Narayani, the kuladevata has now found a new abode: http://www.geocities.com/shrikantshenoy

All can now have a daily '*darshan*' of the goddess - the Mohini Roopa of Lord Vishnu, and visit her Mardol temple from their homes. The web site contains her story, temple information on *sevas* (services), her '*alankaraas*' (appearances), interesting facets of this deity, pictures, etc. This site has been created by a devotee in Dubai, U.A.E. ("Shri Mahalasa goes on the Net", *Navhind Times*, February 3, 2000).

22

The Construction of Goan Interculturality

A Historical Analysis of the Inquisitorial edict of 1736 as Prohibiting (and Permitting) Syncretic Practices

ROWENA ROBINSON

Introduction

Some scholars have tried to show that Goan politics is often characterized by communal colour. Issues are given 'Hindu' or 'Christian' overtones and used to garner community votes. Even politics in Goa, however, is marked by moderation and Hindu and Christian politicians are found across parties. Moreover, Goa has not seen communal disturbances or conflicts as other areas of the country.

Outside of politics and aside of it, in the realm of popular culture, vast majorities of Goans speak proudly of the cultural unity that binds the Hindus and Christians. There is sharing of cultural codes and modes of mediating difference. While the symbols and rituals of Hinduism and Christianity clearly differ in religious content, at operational and compositional levels there are many parallels between them. Fieldwork uncovers these areas. In the areas of collective and individual ritual, one perceives the persistence and vitality of Hindu-Christian cultural interface.

Catholics in Goa are the descendants of 16th century converts to the faith. Though the Inquisition and other decrees were used by the converting regime to prevent recourse by the Christians to rituals and rites considered 'Hindu' in nature – not just religious rituals but also socio-cultural ones – the lives of even present-day Catholics show a wide variety of syncretic interculturalism in many areas. This paper will seek to try and explore how these aspects of interculturality in Goa came to persist, given the fact that the Inquisition, in particular the Inquisitorial edict of 1736, which is the principal focus of this paper, sought hard to put an end to all manifestations of similarity in practices between Hindus and Christians.

This paper begins with an examination of the Goan Inquisitorial practices through an analysis of the edict of the Inquisition issued in 1736. The paper will probe the logic of the prohibitions imposed by the edict and will then examine the ways in which, it would appear, a number of prohibited practices – particularly those related with the celebration of certain life-cycle rituals, especially marriage – were actually tolerated within the Portuguese Goan domain. The paper will try and understand the reasons for this leniency, given the stance of intolerance associated with the Portuguese and the missionaries who functioned as a part of their oceanic empire. In other words, the paper will argue that, in some ways, the regime actually tolerated interculturality rather than stamping it out altogether.

The records of the Inquisition, the most important source of information on the workings of this infamous institution, are, for most of the period of its functioning, not available either in Goa or in Portugal, and they are believed to have been destroyed[1]. The accounts we have, therefore, depend mainly on documents in the official archives in Goa and on published contemporary correspondence of the Inquisitors or Jesuit missionaries. The Inquisition was instituted in Goa in the 16th century and was primarily to prevent recourse to non-Christian practices among converts from Judaism and Hinduism. It could also be used against Hindus if it was proved that they had tried to prevent persons from converting .[2]

The Inquisition was established in 1560 in Goa and completely withdrawn in 1812. The Goan Inquisition was styled on that which then existed in Spain and Portugal to control apostasy among converts to Christianity from Judaism. The establishment of the Inquisition in Portugal took place in 1531 and it was thirty years later that it came to Goa. The Inquisition would have been quite effective,[3] for novices of various religious orders kept an eye on the people and state forces and prisons could be used to detain those who disobeyed the laws. They could be fined or face jail sentences.[4] While death at the stake was the most severe punishment possible, it appears to have been rarely enforced. It is possible, though, that a number of people died imprisoned without ever having had their cases come up for trial.

Over the next two and a half centuries, after the phase of mass conversions initiated in the 1540s in Goa, the Portuguese made concerted efforts to firmly establish the faith among the new converts. Recourse to Hindu sacred rites and modes of worship was sought to be prohibited. A multitude of indigenous cultural practices came to viewed with suspicion and the Inquisition was used to eradicate them. The edict of the Inquisition published in 1736 gives us an indication of the practices that the missionaries wished to forbid the converts.

These included ceremonies in honour of ancestral shades, the maintenance sacred rites, festivals, fasts and holy days, the use of the *tullshi* plant or of rice-flour, oil, flowers or leaves for ceremonial or ornamental purposes. The use of betel leaves and areca nuts in ritual exchanges, such as on the occasion of marriages, or as marks of social precedence was also prohibited. The singing of celebratory verses at marriages and other festive occasions and the employment of traditional musical instruments were prohibited. The use of garments such as the *dhoti* and the *choli* was frowned upon. The maintenance of particular pollution beliefs and practices considered inimical to Christian principles was prohibited.[5]

It is going to be one of the tasks of this paper to analyse the logic of these prohibitions and proscriptions and to enquire into why these particular kinds of elements and practices were set apart and tabooed. Most writers who speak about the Inquisition address it primarily as violent and arbitrary. It signifies and epitomises the coercive nature of the conversions that took place in Goa, the intolerance of the missionaries towards all and everything that smacked of 'Hindu' or indigenous influences, and their desire to stamp these out in a sweeping and indiscriminate manner. It will be argued here, however, that certain patterns manifest themselves in the sorts of customs banned that speak of a particular intent and coherent design on the part of the Portuguese. Therefore, the items listed for prohibition in the edict of the Inquisition of 1736 should not be viewed as bundles of rituals and practices arbitrarily thrown together and lacking in sense or rationale.

Secondly, if an edict of the fourth decade of the 18th century was required to list and eliminate such a wide variety of practices among Goan Christians, then clearly such practices had been existing for a very long time – since the 16th century – regardless of the violence and coercive character of conversion. This, it seems to me, indicates the struggle required to weed out indigenous customs and, perhaps, also the inherent and ultimate failure, or at best limited success, of any such exercise.

What you adored, burn ...

It has been argued by various writers[6] that conversion to Christianity in 16th century Goa took place mainly due to 'bribery, threat and torture', which were freely used as 'instruments of proselytism'. The lure of material rewards and the threat of violence and force, rather than choice or genuine commitment to the new faith, were responsible for conversions and it is, therefore, not surprising that these were only nominal conversions, the converts maintaining their old customs and rituals clandestinely. It is against this background, therefore, that one must understand the institution of the Inquisition: the missionaries used it to eliminate all such heretical practices that had not disappeared among the converts.[7]

I have not here the space to enter into a systematic discussion regarding the nature of conversions in 16th and 17th century Goa. However, a few remarks are clearly in order here. I would strongly dispute any view of conversions that attributed them mainly or primarily to the use or the threat of the use of force and violence. Such a view is difficult to maintain for two reasons. Firstly, it assumes a fundamental distinction between the temporal and the spiritual motivations for conversion. Conversion has to be motivated by true faith. However, such a distinction is hard to defend. As various writers[8] have shown, for the converts the two were inseparable: they saw the missionaries' offerings as an undifferentiated 'package deal'. The same is true of the missionaries, who set out with a clutch of motives wherein the religious was not strictly separable from the economic or the political.

Secondly, this view assumes that the converts were passive victims of the faith thrust upon them from above. This denudes them of all agency and misses the component of, what I would like to refer to as, strategic election in the adoption of the new faith by various groups. My argument, which I have elaborated with substantial evidence elsewhere[9] is that while the element of force was not absent, the local population itself accepted conversion out of a variety of motives.[10] In other words, an exclusive emphasis on either constraint and coercion or election and intent gives an incomplete picture of the conversions. Force and the use of a system of disprivilege played a significant role, but we cannot deny the agency and motivation of the converts themselves. When the Portuguese closed in upon the Hindu world, choice was exercised by those who were tracked down, if only within the limits of the given situation.

Sustained Evangelization

Affiliation with Christianity through conversion, thus, had its dramatic phase in the 16th and early 17th centuries. Over the next two and a half centuries, the Portuguese made concerted efforts to firmly establish the faith among the new converts. Recourse to Hindu sacred rites and modes of worship were sought to be prohibited. A multitude of indigenous cultural practices came to be viewed with suspicion and the Inquisition, as we shall see, was used to eradicate them.

Among the converts, therefore, Hindu religious rites and symbols came to be replaced by Catholic liturgical celebrations, feasts of Christian saints, church-centred solemnization of life-cycle rites and Christian symbols and prayers. Hence, the church and its missionaries clearly also influenced people through the slow process of teaching them about such religious practices. Those who learnt about Catholicism became familiar with it through the liturgy of the mass and practices associated with various stages in the life-cycle of the individual and elaborated in the annual calendar of the church.

In time, perhaps, the converts may have also come to realize that the new religion could be adapted to their own social and religious needs. For instance, the annual ritual cycle of the church came to be slowly adapted to suit the Christians' own needs. This process must have been helped along (or at least not hindered) by the missionaries. The latter were apparently prepared to allow church rituals to be adapted to local custom, as long as the object and means of worship were Christian in content. The *Documenta Indica*[11] for instance gives us an example of how the harvest festival might have come to be incorporated into the Catholic calendar of the church in Goa.

The people of the village of Divar in north Goa requested the priest to come and bless their harvest as in the past the Hindu priest had done. They went to the field carrying a banner with the name of Jesus and St. Paul on it. The priest came carrying his stole and surplice. When they reached the field, the priest blessed them with holy water and blessed the sheaves. These were carried back to the church, where the priest laid his sheaves on the altar-steps first, followed by all the others. The people of other villages such as Navelim, Malar and Goltim did the same. One can argue that it is from beginnings such as this that the Catholic calendar was adapted to indigenous social and religious needs.

At first the missionaries attempted to stifle the local language and impose Portuguese on all classes of people. They soon realized, however, that learning and teaching in the local language, Konkani, was essential to propagating and sustaining the faith. Catechism lessons were instituted for both adults and children in each village to spread knowledge of Catholicism. Villages had their priests and church in which the community worshipped. Various kinds of religious literature had come out by the early 17th century in Konkani and Marathi, including stories about Christ and the lives of saints. These might have been read out to the faithful in the churches regularly on Sundays and days of devotion.

Thus, the examples given above show us that the missionaries clearly recognized the limits to coercive measures of evangelization. The faith had to be sustained by appropriate processes of adaptation and, even, perhaps compromise. This point needs to be kept in mind when looking at the proscriptions of the Inquisition edict of 1736, to which I now turn attention.

The Inquisitorial Edict of 1736

The large body of proscriptions,[12] altogether fifty-two in number, may be divided into three areas based on what I discern as their central concern. There are some eight prohibitions, which have to do with pollution practices. Some of these relate to food practices: bathing before cooking, for instance. Some twenty-two proscriptions are directly related to the use of Hindu objects and modes of worship. Hindu ritual symbols and attributes including such things as dress and names and songs or instruments of music that might have particular religious associations or might be employed in temple devotion. They also prohibit the maintenance of Hindu fasts, feasts and holy days.

The rest of the proscriptions are largely related to life-cycle celebrations and annual rituals. Their main concern appears to be with the limitation of the authority or prestige of certain categories of persons, traditionally owed respect, such as lineage and family elders. Among these are also certain prohibitions relating directly to the control and discipline of space, time and movement and modes of assembly. There are, of course, cross-linkages and certainly some practices would have been prohibited for a complex of reasons: for instance, pollution rites, which also employed the use of proscribed Hindu ritual substances. The general validity of the categorization, though, might be manifested through the use of some illustrations.

"The natives of India resident in the island of Goa are hereby ordered that on the days of the confinement of their wives, neither before nor after such confinement, should they coat with cow-dung the place in the house where the confinement has taken or is to take place.

The natives of India resident in the island of Goa are hereby ordered that in their houses cooking of food should not be done by the principal woman or women wearing wet cloth nor should they bathe in their clothes before entering the kitchen for cooking food, in the manner which is customary among the Hindus.

The said natives of India are hereby ordered that on the day on which a married woman commences her first menstrual period, they should not arrange a banquet or any other festive demonstrations or send gifts of bananas, flowers or any other things on account of the said occurrence.

... are hereby ordered that when some person dies, they should not coat with cow-dung the place or the house where he dies, as a condition for such place or house being habitable; if it becomes necessary to clean the said place, this should be done in a manner other than that of coating it with cow-dung.

... are hereby ordered that they should not throw the clothes used by the deceased person or his bed into the sea or river; and when it is necessary to avoid contagion, these things should be burnt"

It is interesting to see how these prohibitions relate in a detailed way to intimate transactions and events within the household, not merely to public ritual or worship, inter-group relations or collective activities. The question one might try to address, therefore, is: why did the edict try to control such minor and, apparently, insignificant everyday practices? This is a complex issue and I shall address it in greater detail later. It involves an understanding of the constitution of religion as 'habitus', in Bourdieu's[13] sense of the term or as discipline, including bodily discipline.[14]

Here I would like to make the point that once one uncovers the detail in these prohibitions one observes that the central concern they express has to do with the continued maintenance of purity-pollution practices among the converted Catholics. Once seen in this light, one could argue that such practices might have been found as objectionable as the more visible and harmful pollution practices associated with inter-caste relations.

All the proscriptions relate to rituals performed to discharge pollution or attain a state of purity: for instance, at death or before commencing the task of cooking. The Portuguese were certainly aware of the pollution taboos of the Hindus, particularly those related to food exchange and caste divisions.[15] And caste taboos were the object of much missionary indignation and condemnation. They were seen as inimical to Christian principles, based on common worship and, in particular, the communal sharing of the Eucharist.

The causes of pollution, which require specific ritual cleansing, are many. They include certain life-crisis events, contact with polluting materials such as bodily discharges, the skin and carcasses of dead animals or dead bodies and contact with polluting persons or caste groups, which deal with such materials. Involvement in bodily activities, such as the intake of food increases vulnerability to pollution. However, the prescribed practices to do with such forms of pollution also vary with position in the caste hierarchy: for instance, the length of death pollution is higher for the higher castes.

Here, in the edict; the kinds of practices that I have shown proscribed, all have to do with purity maintenance and pollution elimination in connection with household or life-cycle events. It is possible that the Portuguese understood the ideas about pollution associated with caste to be related in some way to notions of bodily and other pollution centred around particular life-cycle events. Probably they saw the taboos as cognate, without necessarily having a clear conception of their association. If this is true, then it is apparent why pollution practices concerned with birth, menstruation and death, and ritual taboos related to the preparation and serving of food are given their marching orders wholesale. Everything associated directly or indirectly with Hindu notions of caste pollution had to be stamped out.

I turn now to proscriptions dealing with Hindu days, objects and modes of worship, ritual substances and the like.

"All the natives of India, resident in the island of Goa and other adjacent islands and in the sub-districts of Salcete and Bardez, are hereby ordered that during the celebration of their marriages, before or after it or on occasions connected therewith, they should not use *gaitas*, or any other Hindu musical instruments, as they have been accustomed to do till now".

I would like to make a connection between this and another prohibition, which deals actually with public processions held during church feasts and festivals. The connection I see is in the rationale given for the taboo placed on the use of Hindu musical instruments.

"The said natives of India and all the residents of the said districts, even the Portuguese, are hereby ordered that in the processions, *camisades* or any other festivals which they may hold in praise of God or His saints, no Christian individual should go clothed in Hindu apparel, nor should

Hindus be admitted in the said functions for dancing or participating in any entertainment *nor should in these be used robanas, gaitas or any other Hindu musical instruments which the Hindus are accustomed to use in the solemnities of their temples ...*"

It appears to me that the ban on the use of musical instruments is placed because these are seen to have particular religious associations or are used in temple worship. In other words, I am arguing that it is the religious associations or connotations of these particular substances and objects, the fact that their use is identified with temple devotion or deity worship, that is the basis of their being culled out from the cultural repertoire and labelled as taboo. The same is true of items such as the *tullshi* plant, particular flowers, rice, coconut, turmeric or betel leaves and areca nuts, all of which have an important place in Hindu modes of devotion. It is, then, not so much the rituals that are being opposed, but, more significantly, the substances used therein. Not surprisingly, therefore, as I shall try to show, once such substances were replaced by others acceptable within the Christian religious framework, the rituals themselves could be allowed to persist.

Some other examples

"The said natives of India are hereby ordered that when on the occasion of their marriages it becomes necessary to make new *choolas* [stoves] for cooking food, they should not place under the said *choolas* betel-leaves, areca nuts or any other things which are not necessary for making the said *choolas*.

... are hereby ordered that in the functions of their marriages or any other functions ... in connection therewith, they should not anoint the bridegroom or bride either together or separately, with a mixture of ground turmeric, milk, coconut oil, rice powder, crushed leaves of '*abolim*' ...

... are hereby ordered that when dowry is taken to the house of the bridegroom, wedding presents are handed, or betrothals are celebrated and in any other functions pertaining to weddings whether held on, before or after the wedding day, they should not send from the house of the bridegroom to that of the bride, or vice-versa, flowers of any kind, betel-leave, areca nuts ...

... are hereby ordered that they should not have in their home gardens or *anganas* (house-yards), coconut gardens or other properties, the plant known as *tulosi*, and if it exists in any place, it should be uprooted immediately".

Again, Konkani verses or *vovios*, sung particularly at marriage rituals were also prohibited, possibly because they began with an invocation to particular Hindu deities and the refrain also contained petitions to divine beings.

"... are hereby ordered that on the occasions of their marriages and all other functions which they might order or direct to take place for solemnizing marriages, either in the house of their bridegroom or of the bride, songs, which it is customary to sing in the language of the land and are commonly known as '*vovios*', should not be sung, either publicly or in private; and when they desire to hold celebrations in demonstration of their joy ...

... are hereby ordered that in their houses should not be sung on any occasion and under any pretext, songs called *vovios*, either in public or in private so that the use of these songs among the faithful Christians would thereby effectively cease".

Some proscriptions are clearly meant to devalue and destroy the practice and modes of maintaining Hindu feasts, fasts and holy days. Also prohibited is the vigil kept on the sixth night of the birth of a child, when the goddess of destiny is believed to come and write the future of the child on its forehead. Interestingly, there is a prohibition regarding the celebration of the harvest with the holding of feasts. This contradicts the practice, referred to above, of allowing the ritual observance of the harvest feast (*Novidade*). Law and practice clearly diverge here, and this must have occurred in other areas as well, as we shall try to point out later. Alternatively, one might argue that while the church appropriated certain indigenous practices (such as the harvest festival) into her own annual calendar, this was combined with a wish to stem any observances that were held separately in the domain of the household, where no priest or cleric led the proceedings.

"... are hereby ordered that they should not observe fasts on the eleventh day of the new moon or full moon, nor on any other days on which the Hindus are accustomed to fast in observance of their sect, and when it happens that on such days they have the duty to fast according to the teachings of the Church, they should do so in conformity with the said teachings, but the fast should be observed in the manner of the Christians and not in the manner in which the Hindus are accustomed to fast, not eating or drinking anything except at night and using only dry food and fruit.

... are hereby ordered that they should not observe as feast days Wednesdays, days of the new moon or full moon, or the twelfth day following the new moon or full moon, nor any other days which according to the Hindu custom are so observed; and when on any such day falls one which is to be so observed according to the teachings of the Church, it should be observed merely in conformity with such teaching.

... that on the sixth day of the birth of their sons and daughters they should not celebrate the function of keeping vigil with banquets, public or private, or gathering of many persons at their houses. When they believe that special care of children is necessary against the risk which children run on that day, they should not perform any act or ceremony which would exceed the requirements of such care.

... that during the season of appearance of new crops (*Novidade*) they should not arrange feasts in their houses".

The use of Hindu modes of naming and dress are prohibited: a device manifestly aimed at the defining and maintaining of community boundaries, at separating out and keeping control over the body of believers/converts.

"... are hereby ordered that they should not refer to or address any Christian person by the name or surname of a Hindu.

... that men should not either in public or at home wear *purvem* (dhoti) as it is the custom of Hindu men to do, and that women should not wear *cholis*, as it is the custom of Hindu women to do.

... in the processions, *camisades* or any other festivals which they may hold in praise of God or His saints, no Christian individual should go clothed in Hindu apparel ..."

The third set of prohibitions deals mainly with life-cycle celebrations, particularly marriage. Again, rites are described in some detail and the use of certain ritual items is prohibited. Further, it appears that sometimes the prohibitions aim not merely at banning the use of particular ceremonial substances but, more centrally, at trying to abolish their employment in ritual presentation as markers of social precedence in the kinship, caste or lineage group. The particular category of elders in the kinship and lineage group who were customarily honoured on such occasions as marriage are called, in the proscriptions, *daijis* or *gotris*. Also prohibited is the honour due to traditional leaders such as the headman of the caste or village (referred to as *mully*).

"... are hereby ordered that at the functions of their marriage or other related occasions they should not send from the house of the bride or bridegroom any gift of flowers, betel leaves, areca nuts or fried cakes ... to the houses of the *daijis*, *gotris* ...

... are hereby ordered that they should not invite, at the time of fixing their weddings, making payment of dowry, or giving wedding presents, relatives of the bridegroom and bride, whether male or female, who commonly are known as *daijis* or *gotris*, to attend such functions; and should any of them happen to be present uninvited, he should not be the one who receives in the name of the bridegroom dowry or wedding presents from the bride, but this work should be done by the parents or guardians of the bridegroom or, if desired, by any other respectable person, whether ecclesiastic or secular, who may be authorized for the purpose by the bridegroom or bride.

... are hereby ordered that neither before or after the marriage nor in connection therewith, they should offer anything to the person who has served in the office of *mully* (headman) of a village, ward or district".

There are also some proscriptions of which the explicit intention seems to be to establish and maintain control over the ritual marking of space and time, the movement of groups of people or their assembly. Non-Christian ways of symbolically marking space or designating time were banned. Perhaps some of these prohibitions were designed to prevent the possibility of rebellion or upheaval of any kind that would threaten the authorities. For instance, there is a proscription on marriage processions, which accompany the couple home, taking place at night when, perhaps, such gatherings of people – should they turn hostile or violent – might be difficult to control. [16]

"... are hereby ordered that their weddings should be celebrated at such hours that the married couple can reach home before sunset; and *under no pretext should they be delayed on the way so that they may reach home after sunset.*

... are hereby ordered that on the occasion of their marriages, whether in the house of the bridegroom or bride or at any other place, they *should not commence on fixed days* preceding the marriages, to crush rice, grind condiments or flour, fry cakes and prepare other things necessary for wedding feasts; nor should these services be carried out in the first instance by any particular relative or *daiji* of the bridegroom or bride.

... are hereby ordered that they should not erect *pandals* with festoons of leaves at the gates of the houses of the bridegroom and bride.

... are hereby ordered that on the day of the wedding when the bride and the bridegroom return from the church to the house of the bride, and on the following day when they go from the house of the bride to that of the bridegroom they should not be received at the said houses by the relatives of the bride or bridegroom nor be seated under a canopy built for the purpose, but should be conducted immediately to such apartment as may be convenient ...

... that during the functions of their marriages, whether in the house of the bridegroom or that of the bride, they should not place in any basket, *supa* (a basket for sifting corn), earthen pot or any other place, rice, beans, coconuts, betel leaves, areca nuts ... for being preserved at an *assigned spot* for being cooked and eaten on a *fixed day*"

Unmaking the Hindu 'Habitus'

My argument is that the Inquisitorial edict of 1736 is not to be perceived as intending to bring together arbitrarily an assortment of rituals and practices for their prohibition. It is certainly important to notice the care with which minute and, sometimes, apparently insignificant details of everyday life and ritual events are recited and occasionally repeated across the range of prohibitions. Overall, here, we are dealing with the attempt to construct a 'micropower' of control[17] which starts from the body and its 'habitus' as the key objects to be manipulated and re-constituted after severing them from their location in the 'pagan' universe.

Most scholars have read the Inquisitorial edict as an expression of an excess of power, a sovereign coercive control imposed from above; a veritable theatre of violence and compulsion.[18] They see it as setting out a whole range of prohibited ritual activities and catching hold of anyone who breaks the law for exemplary, public punishment. However, if one looks carefully, it becomes manifest that the slant of the Inquisitorial prohibitions is towards a different kind of control and exercise of power: a power that seeks invisibility rather than visibility and display. The coercion might at first require public or visible punishment to make itself felt. Hence, the infamous *auto-de-fé*. However, the incline is ultimately towards a coercion that becomes self-discipline by getting inscribed in the taken-for-granted shape of the world – in definitions of the body and its movements, of space or of time. By such means, discipline is to be interred in habit.[19]

Bourdieu[20] has argued that inhabited space – and the actions, directions and rites contained or carried out in it – is a locus for the objectification of classifying and taxonomic principles that underlie the socio-cultural system as a whole. These loci and the social and cultural processes they produce and sustain hence become the principal agencies of socialization, invisibly tuning minds and bodies to their inner logic. Thus, a practical mastery of the fundamental schemes of the socio-cultural world is achieved, through bodily experience within an environment that has been structured according to the principles of that world.

The 'habitus' is created: the individual is appropriated by the structures of the world and internalizes them. Lasting dispositions are produced in the individual, habits and perceptions, ways of thinking, feeling and acting, that successfully maintain, re-create and reproduce those structures. The structures themselves, thus, become part of taken-for-granted experience and are seldom explicitly articulated. To make clear the connection between the notions of the 'habitus' and internalized disciplines and dispositions and the intended logic of the edict, it is worth quoting at some length, once again from Bourdieu.[21]

"If all societies and, significantly, all the "totalitarian institutions", in Goffman's phrase, that seek to produce a new man through a process of "deculturation" and "reculturation" set such store on the seemingly most insignificant details of *dress*, *bearing*, physical and verbal *manners*, the reason is that, treating the body as memory, they entrust to it in abbreviated and practical, i.e. mnemonic form the fundamental principles of the arbitrary content of the culture. The principles em-bodied in this way are placed beyond the grasp of consciousness and hence … cannot even be made explicit... The whole trick of pedagogic reason lies precisely in the way it extorts the essential while seeming to demand the insignificant ..."

One can see in the range of prohibitions dealing with the minutiae of everyday existence and ritual processes, the attempt to extend the tentacles of control deep into the functioning of households and the lives of individuals, to disengage the body from practices that link it with a Hindu world-view. Practices of bathing the body before cooking, of clothing it in a particular way, of destroying bodily garments at death, of naming, of fasting (denying the body food) or feasting (allowing the body an abundance of food), of marking the body with particular ritual substances, all become taboo.

These are all practices that link up with certain Hindu notions – of purity and pollution, for example. Certain banned substances, such as areca nuts or betel leaves, or objects, such as musical instruments or the *tullshi* plant, have religious associations and a particular significance in Hindu devotional arrangements. Fasts and feasts are also to be held only 'according to the teachings of the Church' or 'in the manner of the Christians'. The body should be subject to Christian, not 'pagan' law.

The convert is also required to go through a process of deculturation with regard to modes of denoting or marking space and time that are significant from the Hindu point of view. Hindu sacred/holy days should not be marked – the sixth day after the birth of a child, new moon or full moon days or the twelfth day after these, for example. Space should not register any meanings that could be consonant with a Hindu ethos – 'assigned spots' must not be ritually marked on formal occasions, property and *anganas* should not be marked by the sacred *tullshi*, canopies and *pandals* of mango leaves marking space ceremonially must be avoided.

Finally, modes of honour and precedence that mark out certain categories of relatives or elders for respect are to be discontinued. Kin, caste, lineage-based and such traditional authority structures are devalorized and denied esteem. In their place, other 'ecclesiastic or secular' persons, authorized by the bride or groom are to preside over ritual functions. In establishing its hegemony, the church needs to devalue and, in fact, eliminate any possible counter-structures to its own authority.

In assigning the right of selection of the presiding figures to the bride and groom, the church is acting in accordance with its own view of marriage, enshrined in canonical law. In contrast to the Hindu view, for the church, marriage is perceived as bringing together by mutual consent two adult individuals, rather than two families or lineage-groups. Parental and familial consent is not superfluous, but the husband-wife relationship is held to be central. Their consent to the marriage is a must, and this idea has been extended here to other arrangements connected with the ceremony.

Striking a balance: Resistance and the recognition of the need for negotiation

The previous section attempted to analyse the intent of the provisions of the 1736 edict of the Inquisition. But, if available historical and ethnographic evidence is to be believed, these prohibitions detailed and ponderous though they were, did not succeed in full measure. The story of their miscarriage has two components. It recounts the resistance that must clearly be read into the history of convert strategies. And it takes into consideration the compromises that the regime must necessarily and inevitably have made along the way.

The thrust of the prohibitions was to break contact between Christians and Hindus and Christian and Hindu ways. The particular pattern of conversion must itself have been of some aid: it ensured that Catholics and Hindus did not intermingle to any great extent in their everyday lives. Conversion in Goa was largely limited to the four coastal districts of Tiswadi, Salcete, Mormugao and Bardez. Here, whole villages were converted to the new religion. In the inner districts, away from the coast, conversion was very minimal and these areas were predominantly Hindu. Thus, the Hindu society of the interior districts surrounded the Christian areas, but were also in many ways distinct from it.

Despite the absence of everyday, mundane interaction, there were areas where Catholics and Hindus came into contact during the colonial period. The markets in the towns constituted one such area. There are also references in Jesuit documents to visits made by Catholics to Hindu religious specialists.[22] Folk songs from the Portuguese period record the memories of Hindu society that the convert community carried as part of their cultural baggage. Such songs imaginatively recreate for us the converts' concern with and consciousness of Hindu ways.

Pereira and Martins[23] render some verses:

Aj somaratso diso	Today is Monday
Deva y at-panyem pot-tttai-i	They fall on their hands and feet to their god
Faro murdongi vaztai faro	thumps resound on the earthenware drum

Fam xettingé lognankga	It is the signal of the goldsmith's wedding
Fam xettingé lognako	A Sign of the goldsmiths wedding

Fulo mallunum
Kely'm y anvem satem
Tantum falto
Y eko tsampem.

Wearing flowers in my hair
I made a pretty cluster
In it is lacking
A champak is all it needs now.

Soronam rati
Ravonom zagem
Nomoskar kot-tam deva
Tolloxi bountem.

The night does not end
I will stay awake
I worship, my god,
Going round the sacred *tullshi.*

These stand as one type of evidence of the continued receptivity to Hindu ways among the converted Catholics. The seeds of other forms of evidence are also available. And the struggle over the maintenance of the purity of the faith is already visible right from the 16th century, where we find orders forbidding the use of Hindu names among converts and prohibiting participation in Hindu processions or fasting in conformity with Hindu norms. The 17th century also saw the promulgation of various regulations, including one that prohibited Christians from holding childbirth celebrations in accordance with Hindu custom.[24]

The edict of the 18th century, which I am analysing, is much more explicit, detailed and elaborate than any of the legislation passed earlier. Perhaps it became clear to the missionaries that even after more than a century in the faith, after all the teaching and familiarization with Christianity, the continued presence of practices associated with a Hindu worldview was unacceptable. The 18th century was, all in all, a period when conversion itself had slowed down considerably;[25] the focus would then be more towards consolidating the faith among those already converted.

Earlier, the laws appear to have been more rigid than their implementation, if the edict of the 18th century is still attempting to proscribe particular customs and practices, some of which were decreed prohibited a century or more earlier. However, a much stronger and more sustained intervention is initiated now, with the 1736 edict.[26] Even so, based on this earlier record, one may discern already the presence of the element of compromise: the implicit, unstated acceptance of the gap between principle and practice on the part of the authorities concerned. This element of compromise with indigenous custom is perceived more explicitly in certain other contexts. We have already spoken about the incorporation of the harvest festival in the Catholic ritual calendar.

Again, when it came to caste, the missionaries were explicit about their abhorrence of the norms of purity and pollution. However, they themselves encouraged the persistence of hierarchical distinctions through, for example, the formation of caste confraternities within each parish. Each confraternity was host to a different feast within the church's annual calendar. Again, the Portuguese were also very conscious of the notion of the purity of blood, on which their own social hierarchy was based. A somewhat similar idea of purity of descent also pervaded Hindu caste notions. In course of time, Catholics appear to have lost any strain of other Hindu ideas regarding pollution, but they retained the idea of blood purity, maintained by caste endogamy. This becomes clear from evidence related to the turn of the 20th century. [27]

One may also draw on contemporary ethnographic evidence to demonstrate the point, apart from considering evidence that is available from the late 19th and early 20th centuries.[28] The use of such varied evidence, from different periods, may be questioned. What does it tell us? What can it tell us? It suggests, certainly, that the process of eliminating Hindu customs did not take place without struggle. And that it was not an even process. Moreover, it suggests that compromise on the part of the missionaries must be postulated as also the selective adaptation and adoption by the converts.

Finally, I would argue that the use of the kind of evidence I draw on suggests that the processes of adaptation and adjustment must have established themselves before the withdrawal of the Inquisition, which took place in 1812. Today, some of the life-cycle practices, for instance, that I refer to below are part of the taken-for-granted socio-cultural world of the Christians: they are hardly reflected on and their syncretic character raises no query. Evidence shows that such practices were also part of the life-world of Goan Catholics already in the late 19th and early 20th centuries.[29]

If such practices had been suppressed completely during the Inquisition and then resurfaced after it was withdrawn, the form in which we would find them would be different. They would/should have re-emerged with their pre-Inquisition character intact, given that there would have been no requirement for any cover-up or transformation. However, as I shall try and demonstrate below, the form in which we find these practices, shows that they bear clearly the impress of the Inquisition.[30] And speak of the kinds of selective adjustment and negotiation made by the converts in the face of the prohibitions placed on them.

In other words, the practices have changed and been transformed by the Inquisitorial proscriptions, in certain specific respects. The way in which Christian images, prayers and symbols have been mapped onto Hindu practices, as in the examples I give below, suggests that these latter have been reconfigured against something, in the face of something. And given the nature of the reconfiguration that has taken place, that something can only be the prohibitions of the Inquisitorial edict. I would, therefore, hazard a guess that though the evidence available to me relates mainly to the late 19th and early 20th century in some cases and to contemporary practice in others, the basic contours of rituals such as these must have been established before the close of the Inquisitorial regime, i.e. prior to 1812.

One could take for instance marriage practices. Ethnographic evidence from contemporary Goa shows that many of the practices suppressed by the Inquisition have continued to persist, but in modified form. Let us look at the marriage practice of bathing the bride and groom. The Inquisition prohibited Catholics from maintaining the Hindu practice of ritually bathing the bride or groom with a mixture of substances such as milk, turmeric, coconut oil, rice powder or the crushed leaves of the *abolim* plant. The practice is still maintained among Catholics today and such rituals are referred to even for the 19th century.[31] However, the use of the particular substances mentioned has been dropped and they have been replaced by coconut milk or *ros*.

Again, the ritual of setting up the stoves or *choolhas* for cooking may be mentioned, which takes place a few days before the wedding. Stoves of mud are made and new cooking pots placed on them. All the major cooking for the wedding is done here. Behind the stoves a cross of palm leaves is placed 'because it is a happy occasion and everything should go well' and the 'Our Father' is said. We noted that the Inquisition prohibited Catholics from placing betel leaves or areca nuts under *choolhas* constructed for cooking at marriages. These are used by Hindus to symbolize the auspiciousness of the occasion.

They appear to have been replaced by another symbol here, one admissible within the Christian tradition – the symbol of the cross, made of palm leaves. A Christian prayer is said for God's blessings that everything may 'go well'. Christian symbols dominate but the web of signification reveals (or conceals?) other associations which are the complement of the Hindu ritual. Both are identified with notions of the auspicious, 'happy' or celebratory aspect of the event.

Yet again, at the celebration of the betrothal or when the dowry is taken to the house of the bridegroom, in place of the prohibited flowers, betel leaves and areca nuts, fruits and sweets, usually known as *ojem*, form part of the gift-giving pattern. Moreover, though several prohibitions could be related to the attempt to displace traditional caste, kinship and lineage-based authority structures among the Catholics, we find that such authority may not have been easily relinquished.

Despite the fact, mentioned earlier, that the church centres the 'husband-wife' relationship and requires their consent to the marriage, from the point of view of the Catholics, marriage remains principally a relationship between families and lineage groups, rather than just between individuals and their parents. It is the parents and other elders who generally decide on marriage partners. Though the couple concerned may be consulted, this is more a formality. They usually have to give in to the choice of their parents and elders. Further, while the priest solemnizes the Christian marriage in the church, the bride and groom are still required to receive blessings from their family and lineage elders at the *ros*, before they go to church and also on their return from the nuptials.

Again, a few days before the wedding, a ceremony is held in honour of the dead ancestors (*purvoz*) of the bride and groom. This takes place separately for the bride and groom at their native homes. Food is served to a certain number of poor people, who are said to represent the dead ancestors of the house. We noted that the Inquisition had prohibited the holding of feasts in honour of ancestors. However, they remain a part of Catholic practice, as seen here. Perhaps they were tolerated as a folk version, inevitably found among peasants or the more superstitious Catholic masses, of the Christian notion of the remembrance of the deceased of one's family and the poor souls in Purgatory.

Perhaps the ritual itself was 'christianized' by the converts. Among Hindus, the invitees to these feasts are certain categories of relatives, usually affinal. At the annual *shraddha* ceremonies of the higher castes, brahmins are invitees. Among Catholics, it is poor persons who are invited for the feasts. Is it possible that the shift came about with the Inquisition? Was it a means of preserving the meal for ancestors by merging it with notions acceptable within the Christian tradition? Was it in fact induced by the missionaries as a way of bringing an existing practice into harmony with Christian beliefs? We can only speculate. It is significant, though, that folk theology blends the two traditions without disharmony: Catholics experience no conflict in explaining the ritual as being held in honour of their forebears while simultaneously constituting it as an act of Christian charity.

The use of songs called *vovios* was prohibited, as we noted. However, they continue to be sung on occasions such as weddings, except that the invocations to Hindu deities, with which such songs commenced, have been replaced by supplications to Catholic divinities such as 'Sucor Saibinni' or 'Sant Khuris', for example. In the refrain, the names of Hindu deities have been replaced by the simple and innocuous 'viva re', the Portuguese victory chant. A process of negotiation seems to have taken place. The preservation of these songs suggests that by dropping references to Hindu deities and substituting Christian divinities and prayers for them, indigenous ritual modes may have been retained.

In sum, therefore, it may be seen from the analysis above that the wedding in the church, which is central from the point of view of doctrinal Catholicism, is clearly framed within a sequence of rituals involving the *ros*, the exchange of gifts, the blessing by elders, the feast for ancestors and the like. The meaning of these practices is not strictly to be found within Catholic doctrine. Rather, such practices are located within a different socio-cultural universe, fed more by Hindu notions and ideas.

Other cases may be cited. The ritual of marking the sixth night of the child's birth, for instance, carried well into the 20th century and is found even today, particularly among the lower castes.[32] However, these occasions are privately marked and banquets and 'the gathering of many persons' at the house do not take place. These groups also continue to visit Hindu religious specialists on critical occasions such as illness or the death of a kinsperson. Such beliefs, perhaps, continued to be tolerated because they did not pose a serious threat to the church itself. Or because the converters were aware that such folk beliefs and practices existed particularly among the lower social groups everywhere, even in their own society.[33]

Again, the use of European dress, for instance, and the use of Portuguese language also show up caste differences. The upper castes were privileged in the hierarchical social order of the colonial period. They were allowed to enter the priesthood and they were given certain rights and honours in the celebration of church feasts in the annual ritual cycle of different village churches. It is quite possible that, in their case, the dropping of prohibited rituals and the adopting of those prescribed had more to do with keeping on the good side of the rulers than the fear of the consequences of disobedience.

Also, for these groups, adopting these new ways, taken over from the Europeans, of expressing the differential social status between castes could well have become a substitute for the maintenance of pollution taboos, which had come to be prohibited. It may be possible to argue, therefore, that the combination of the prohibition *and* converts' desire –

particularly the higher castes – to align themselves with the Portuguese and stay within the limits of the new rules established by them, were together responsible for them giving up pollution taboos and practices.

In the absence of notions of ritual pollution, other diacritical marks are used to demarcate caste status. Let us look at some examples. When low-caste persons come to the house of an upper-caste, 'decent' family, they usually enter from the back of the house and leave their slippers outside. They sit at a lower level than the *oontz lok* (high people). The high castes are *borem munis* (good persons) or *sobit munis* (fine people) while the lower castes are *sokol* (low) *munis*. The implication is clearly of higher and lower status, and ranking along a certain scale of moral value or 'goodness' and the patterns and idiom of deference give expression to it.

Certain other ideas to do with status distinctions seem to have come directly from the converters. It is the wealthy, upper-caste Catholics who stress the eating of beef and pork and the 'cutting of a pig' as a mark of status. As already noted, the upper castes also distinguish themselves from the other social groups in part on the basis of their association with the cultural attributes and language of their (former) rulers. It may, therefore, be possible to argue that the adoption of these attributes could become diacritical marks by means of which status distinctions between different caste groups could be expressed.

From all this it appears that the Catholics reworked their caste practices in keeping with Portuguese notions. Indigenous Hindu notions such as those about purity of descent that were similar to particular ideas held by the converters were retained. Practices condemned by the new regime, such as pollution taboos, were suppressed and, finally, new cultural elements made available by the Europeans may have been seized upon as signifiers of status within the 'traditional' order. This would have benefited the upper castes, in particular.

For all groups, moreover, adoption of the new faith and familiarization with it might have led, in time, to the realization that it could be re-configured to fit their own social and religious needs. Christian symbols, prayers and divinities could bear meanings other than those prescribed by strict doctrinal Catholicism and could be mapped easily onto rituals carried over from the Hindu habitus. In other words, apart from force imposed by the prohibitions, we have to also stress the agency of the converts and the creative and selective way in which they absorbed the impact of the proscriptions placed on them. Sometimes, the logic of their response may have had more to do with questions of status and privilege, as I have tried to show, that solely with the dread of the repercussions of defiance.

In any case, it seems to me, overall, likely that the regime must itself have had to come to terms with the limits of control. In the case of Konkani, for instance, that realization becomes clear. Further, it becomes manifest that once the rituals, such as those described above, were changed to the extent of eliminating the offending 'pagan' symbols or substances, the regime must have permitted them to persist. Hence, I speak both of the resistance of the converts, who held onto their traditions while adjusting them in accordance with the new faith adopted and the limits placed by the Inquisitorial regime, and the compromise effected by the missionaries, who clearly yielded in many cases to the retention of indigenous custom.

The reasons for their thus yielding might be many. Perhaps it arose out of a desire to establish a link at some level with the converts, the wish to smooth the process of adherence to the new faith, the realization that there were certain parallels between prevalent European practices and native customs or the need to establish alliances with local elites. Whatever the reasons, the compromise was clear. The church permitted caste honours and privileges to outlive conversion and allowed the impress of indigenous custom to mark its annual ritual and festive cycle. It also manifestly gave in with regard to the persistence of rituals, as those related to particular life-cycle events, in which Hindu symbols and prayers were replaced by others admissible within the parameters of the new tradition.

Brief comparative analysis demonstrates that the Inquisition was by no means unique in its prohibitory character. Visvanathan[34] speaking of Protestant missionaries effecting conversions in south India says that they 'were earnest that there must be outward symbols of this change of beliefs. The missionaries wanted their Tamil converts to shave the *kudumi*, that tuft of hair which signified high status, and separated them from Muslims, Christians and low castes. The missionaries believed that this was a symbol of idolatry'. According to her:

"There were other customs which the missionaries abhorred, some examples being, the celebration of puberty among Tamil Christian girls, the use of cowdung and rice flour for decorative purposes, oil baths on Saturdays and Wednesdays, chewing betel, expressing relationships of honour through the use of sandalwood, flowers and betel".

It is interesting that these prohibitions bear a startling resemblance to those we found instituted in the case of Goa. And there is no Inquisition to which one could attribute them. On the other hand, among colonial territories, the Inquisition was not unique to Goa. It functioned in many areas under Portuguese and Spanish rule. It was used in Africa and South America to eradicate a number of so-called 'pagan' customs including menstruation rituals and ancestral rites. It was applied to Portuguese pockets in south India. With the Synod of Diamper, Portuguese missionaries in Kerala tried not only to bring about changes in the liturgy of the Syrian Christians but also to eliminate all traces of Hindu belief and socio-ritual practice found among them.

Across regional, temporal and denominational boundaries, missionaries seem consistently to seek visible signs of religious change from their converts.[35] The various historical examples reveal to us that conversion as a sociological phenomenon is rarely limited only to a transformation in religious beliefs. Social and cultural changes always accompany it. There is accommodation and negotiation, though, rather than an elimination of indigenous ways. There are therefore 'limits' as Mills[36] puts it, to coercive evangelical methods.

The similarity in Hindu and Catholic social patterns and ritual practices revealed by my data suggests that the missionaries do forge links with local practice and people themselves must adjust to the limitations placed on them without giving up completely their own cultural modes.

NOTES AND REFERENCES

1. A. K. Priolkar, *The Goa Inquisition*, Bombay: A.K. Priolkar, 1961, p. x.
2. Stephen Neill, *A History of Christianity in India: The Beginnings to AD 1707*, Cambridge: Cambridge Univ. Press, 1984.
3. Sanjay Subrahmanyam, *The Portuguese Empire in Asia 1500-1700: A Political and Economic History*, London: Longman, 1993, p. 119.
4. Neill, *op. cit.*, p. 31.
5. Priolkar, *op. cit.*, pp. 97-107; B. G. D'Souza, *Goan Society in Transition: A Study in Social Change*, Bombay: Popular Prakashan, 1975, pp. 125-33.
6. Priolkar, *op. cit.*, p. 50.
7. Priolkar, *op. cit.*; R. P. Rao, *Portuguese Rule in Goa 1510-1961*, London: Asia Publishing House, 1963; Rui Gomes Pereira, *Goa (1): Hindu Temples and Deities*, António Victor Couto (trans.), Goa: Rui Gomes Pereira, 1978.
8. J. Guiart, "The Millenarian Aspect of Conversion to Christianity in the South Pacific", in S. L. Thrupp (ed.), *Millennial Dreams in Action: Essays in Comparative Study*, The Hague: Mouton & Co., 1962, pp. 122-138; L. Caplan, *Class and Culture in Urban India: Fundamentalism in a Christian Community*, Oxford: Clarendon Press, 1987.
9. R. Robinson, *Conversion, Continuity and Change: Lived Christianity in Southern Goa*, Delhi: Sage Publications, 1998.
10. The force was of many kinds. For instance, in the 1540s, a number of laws were enacted against the Hindus. These laws included the banishment of the Hindus from the Portuguese territory if they did not convert, so that they lost

their property, the banning of the performance of Hindu religious rites, festivals and ceremonies and the prohibition of the religious activities of Hindu priests.

11. J. Wicki (ed.), *Documenta Indica*, vol. IV, Rome: Institutum Historicum Societatis Iesu, 1956.
12. Translations of the prohibitions reproduced below have been taken from Priolkar, *op. cit.*
13. P. Bourdieu, *Outline of a Theory of Practice*, Richard Nice (trans.), Cambridge: Cambridge Univ. Press, 1977.
14. Michel Foucault, *Discipline and Punish: The Birth of the Prison*, Alan Sheridan (trans.), New York: Vintage/Random House, 1979.
15. Robinson, *op. cit.*, p. 55.
16. This is not an altogether implausible argument. The Portuguese had to face rebellion several times: missionaries had even been killed in 1583 in the attempt to establish the faith. Cuncolim and certain other villages in the Salcete district of Goa were for a long period restive under the colonial regime. The strength of the Portuguese – ecclesiastical, military and political – was also not that high. According to B.W. Diffie and G.D. Winius (*Foundations of the Portuguese Empire 1415-1580*, vol. I, Minneapolis: Univ. of Minnesota Press, 1977), there were never more than 6000-7000 Portuguese in or subject to military service in the Orient at any one time … and if one adds to this a figure of about as many clerics, European dependents, servants and half-bloods who came under European law, the figure comes to 14,000 at the most. And these were scattered from Mozambique to Macau. If the regime was clamping down on custom in such a minute way, there is no reason why it could not expect a backlash at any time.
17. See M. Foucault, *op. cit*,
18. See Priolkar, *op. cit.*
19. P. Bourdieu, *op. cit.*; Foucault, *op. cit.*
20. Bourdieu, pp. 89-91.
21. *Ibid.*, pp. 94-5.
22. Wicki , *op. cit.*, vol. IV.
23. José Pereira & Micael Martins, *A Sheaf of Deknnis*, Bombay: The Konkan Cultural Association, 1967, pp. 23, 36-37. A *champak* [*pulmeria acutifolia*]; basil [*tullshi*]
24. P. P. Shirodkar, "Socio-Cultural Life in Goa during 16th Century", in Charles J. Borges and Helmut Feldmann (eds.), *Goa and Portugal: Their Cultural Links*, New Delhi: Concept Publishing Co., 1997, p. 36; Fátima da Silva Gracias, "The Impact of Portuguese Culture on Goa: A Myth or A Reality?", in *Goa and Portugal: Their Cultural Links*, p. 47.
25. Subrahmanyam, *op. cit.*
26. There may be reason for this. Maria de Jesus dos Mártires Lopes (personal communication) argues that the Inquisition, in actual practice, began with focusing more on the Jews in Goa than on the local Christians. Records of the Inquisition available from 1660 onwards show the gradual decrease in the number of accused Jews and corresponding increase in the number of local

Christians accused. Thus, though the law decreed many practices prohibited for the local Christians, perhaps the regime looked upon them with a more tolerant eye until the faith was more firmly established, the regime itself more stable, the period of consolidation initiated.

27. A. N. de Bragança Pereira, *Etnografia da India Portuguesa*, vols. I-II, Delhi: Asian Educational Services, 1991[1923], pp. 266-306.
28. The evidence that I draw on was gathered during anthropological fieldwork done in south Goa between 1992-1993 for my doctorate on popular Catholicism.
29. Bragança Pereira, *op. cit.*, pp. 275-306.
30. It is interesting and instructive, in this light, to view the rituals and practices of Mangalorean Catholics. These Catholics of South Kanara fled from Goa (mainly from its northern districts) in successive waves. A large number fled to escape the scrutiny of the Inquisition. Among them, the ritual substances banned by the Inquisition such as betel leaves, areca nuts, rice and flowers continue to be employed in domestic celebrations and the pattern of ritual practices appears much more to resemble forms described in the Inquisitorial edict. See A. B. D'Souza, "Popular Christianity: A Case Study among the Catholics of Mangalore", Ph.D. thesis, University of Delhi, 1993.
31. Bragança Pereira, *op. cit.*, p. 295.
32. *Ibid.*, p. 275.
33. A. H. de Oliveira Marques. *Daily Life in Portugal in the Late Middle Ages*, S. S. Wyatt (trans.), Madison: Univ. of Wisconsin Press, 1971.
34. Susan Visvanathan, *Missionary Styles and the Problem of Dialogue*, (occasional Paper 6), Shimla: Indian Institute of Advanced Study, 1993, pp. 12-13.
35. Nonetheless, the missionary acceptance of particular indigenous modes, despite the stance of intolerance articulated most dramatically through the Inquisition, may not raise surprise. Here are reverberations of an ancient Catholic attitude. For instance, during the early period of Christianity, while the church was attempting to establish itself firmly against existing Jewish and other pre-Christian cults, it took over many aspects of pre-Christian religion that constituted a threat to it. Hence, the birth of Christ was seen not only as the herald of a new world order but also as the culmination of all that had gone before him (Marina Warner, *Alone of All Her Sex: The Myth and the Cult of the Virgin Mary*, London: Weidenfeld & Nicolson, 1976). In keeping with this idea, Christianity at this stage of its development did not visualize itself as a destroyer of all previous religious traditions. It consciously sought to take account of the best and most important of these and make them its own. Hence it incorporated much of pre-Christian symbolism. Just to give one example, the most potent threat to Christianity during this period was the worship of the sun god, Helios, which during the first four centuries of this era was the most important cult in the Roman empire. To overcome the power of this cult, Roman Christianity fixed the birth of the Lord on the very feast of *Sol Invictus*, the Unconquered Sun, and invoked Christ by that name (Warner, *op. cit.*; A. W. Watts, *Myth and Ritual in Christianity*, London: Thames

& Hudson, 1953). Incidentally, in practice, Protestants often proved less accommodating of indigenous modes (Jean Comaroff, *Body of Power, Spirit of Resistance: The Culture and History of a South African People*, Chicago: Univ. of Chicago Press, 1985; Saurabh Dube, "Issues of Christianity in Colonial Chhattisgarh", *Sociological Bulletin*, 41 (1 and 2), 1992, pp. 97-117).

36. K. Mills, "The Limits of Religious Coercion in Mid-Colonial Peru", *Past and Present*, 145, 1994, p. 84.

PART IV

LITERATURE

23

Saudades and the Goan Poetic Temper

Globalising Goan Cultural History

VICTOR ANAND COELHO

Among the many educational, literary and cultural projects relating to Goan history initiated by George Victor Coelho, it was his work on Goan literature that had particularly far-reaching and multi-disciplinary implications. He believed that a comprehensive study of Goan poetry – preceded, of course, by making this material widely accessible in modern scholarly editions – could provide a methodology for guiding the many branches towards the central trunk of what makes up Goan history. Such an endeavour is particularly relevant today, given the way the discipline of history in all countries is struggling to accommodate new paradigms of subjectivity, gender, myth, and sub-alternity, none of which are particularly compassionate bed-fellows, with the more traditional aims of military history, economic history and archival research. Combining the subjective experience of an insider who "experienced" British colonialism, Portuguese post-colonialism, Indian nationalism, Catholic conversions, English emigration, U.S. immigration, and finally poetic exile, George Coelho understood the strategic and favourable position that late 19th-20th century Goan poets occupied at the crossroads of European and Indian cultures, village customs and urban modernism, Latin and Sanskrit, Catholicism and Hindu and Shiva and Saint.

To many western historians and those Indian scholars who have turned their interest towards colonialism, post-colonialism, and Orientalism, in recent years, this seemingly conflicting allegiances towards Europe and India have often been simplified as a binary relationship of oppressor and oppressed, resulting in apologetic empathy for the latter. As Dipesh Chakrabarty has argued recently in an important article about the problem of an "Indian" history, as long as the history remains a discourse "produced at the institutional side of the university .... Europe remains the sovereign".[1] In other words, Indian history when filtered through the typical western genre of history is but a variation on a master narrative. This observation is true of much colonialist literature in this area.[2]

However, Goan scholars and writers – and I consider George Coelho's sympathies to lie mainly with these groups – have been attempting to narrate a rather different history – one that is based not so much upon documentary sources and the notion of conflict, but rather on exploring certain psychological and cultural tensions that are the long term result of being Goan. This troubled *mentalité* can be understood in three main ways:

1. The uneasiness towards the *a priori* acknowledgement of Indo-Portuguese assimilation that has long been part of the Goan history.
2. The problem of how and by whom Goan history has been written.
3. The problem of how the cohesion within diasporic Goan communities – whether in Toronto, Calgary, London, Boston, or elsewhere – has been loosened through the way they choose to "remember" (or *historicize*) Goa. Some have mythologized it through community manifestations like their "Night in Goa", cultural programmes; other sectors of the diaspora maintain a rigidly Catholic view of history; and a final group which includes many Jesuits, openly question what it means to be Goan, and wonder where they fit into this history.

It is through its ability to express its complexity of themes that Goan poetry represents the intersection of two roads: one, the scenic, nostalgic, and mythical, *Goa bela* lined with palm trees, and the other, a Main Street that is but an historical façade constructed by Portuguese and ecclesiastical history that leaves its inhabitants searching for their real identity, yet trapped at the same time by their insatiable longing for its myth. George regarded these poetic conceits as a vital source of Indo-Portuguese history – as he himself experienced within the Indo-Portuguese culture in which he was born. Saturated with ancient troupes, reflections of uprooted Hindu philosophy, stories of epic voyages, a yearning for Europe and a parallel nostalgia for Goa, and echoes of the Classical tradition, this poetry reflects the torn and confusing cultural allegiances that overwrite the Goan identity to the present day.

Stimulated by, but working independently of my father's work, I explored similar topics in the context of my own archival work concerning

Portuguese music brought to and institutionalized within Goa during the 16th and 17th centuries.[3] I have argued that ingredients of an early Goan music are a unique blend of archival "facts" as well as a subjective component that is arbitrated by experience and assimilation. Relying initially on written archival documents, I soon began to see first-hand the numerous issues that impinged upon how a Goan history might be written, and I am now convinced that a documentary study to the exclusion of human voices cannot hope to capture a picture of Renaissance Goa (whatever that is). As Teotónio de Souza has written in his "memoir" *Goa to Me*: "historical *objectivity* is the sum total of the *subjective* reconstructions of individual historians" (my emphasis).[4]

In this paper, I rely on drafts of George Coelho's proposed paper on the theme of *saudades* in Goan poetry and "complete" them with thoughts from my own on Goan musical historiography to form a dialogue that will pose – and try and answer – the following questions: How does one validate the subjective experience in the service of history? How is Goan cultural history tied up with its poetic and musical traditions? How does the Goan cultural experience offer models for interdisciplinary and cross-cultural work in a more global fashion? What is the relevance and potential impact of this material on Goan culture and education? And finally, how does the history of music in Goa affect the future educational and economic initiatives of the new millennium?

The foundation of George Coelho's work on Goan poetry was his projected anthology of Goan-Portuguese writings entitled the LILA Project (Luso-Indian Literature Anthology). This project is organized around the central theme of Goan people's affiliation and attachment that he – a social psychologist interested mainly in assimilation and uprooting – perceived as defining salient features of the Goan character, and hence, history. The contents of the anthology explore various contexts of attachment to the land and *comunidade*, liberty, family and friends, faith and providence, classical and romantic muses and myths, ideas of the European Enlightenment and ancient Indian civilization and the female.[5] As an example, in a recent article George examined the literary stances adopted by such poets as Floriano Barreto (1877-1904), and Mariano Gracias, among others, in profiling the temple dancer. The tension here between seductress and mother serves to locate the evolving image of the feminine through different Christian and Hindu voices. George hypothesized that "the aura or at least the penumbra of the Dancer in the sacred artform haunted the Goan Christian poet seeking to reclaim Goa's ancient heritage of the ritual... of the dance ... as the principle of universal harmony".[6] Arriving at such perspectives convinced my father who believed that Goan creativity in literature and in the fine arts should be understood as taking shape out of the crucible of cross-cultural interactions with the Portuguese during four centuries of Luso-Indian history of educational, linguistic and socio-economic relations. Furthermore, the perennial Goan traditions of sea-faring adventurers and emigration to various continents may be perceived as illustrating another theme, namely, the awareness of separation and loss, the sense of alienation and exile, and proactive transformations in nostalgia and *saudades*.

In addition to the temple dancer, George probed other things within this rich corpus of poetry such as nostalgia which manifests in Christian Goan poets like Armando Menezes (1902-83), Manoel C. Rodrigues (1908-91) and Joseph Furtado (1872-1947) and the theme of exile which carries with it the themes of longing for homeland and voyage, but also takes on a political function.[7] The exilic and nostalgic conditions are the result of displacement and uprootedness as well as the affirmation of change –as I read it. But it is also a statement of hopelessness, deprivation and alienation among the colonized Konkani and Portuguese, whose ancient Indian traditions were deracinated.

In a related fashion, *saudades* is a feeling of love and loss that is variously expressed in Portuguese life and literature and evokes a universal sentiment and complex moods of close attachment and separation. Specifically, it refers to the nostalgia or homesickness felt by persons when separated by time and distance from persons and places they have loved and it resonates in Goan lyric poetry in Portuguese.

As a philosophical and metaphoric paradigm of a people's legendary history, *saudosismo* has been elaborated by Teixeira de Pascoaes (1877-1952). *Saudosismo* is envisioned as a collective memory of the Lusitanian soul and a legendary projection of a Golden Age in Portugal's past. In this context, *saudades* is conceptually extended from its function in the traditional Portuguese lyric to an ethnic intuition. In George's view *saudades* is a nuanced Lusitanian retrospection – an autumnal mood. In Goa *saudades* intones the sad and tender reverie of darkening and lengthening shadows of church spires and palm trees in the final embrace of sunset. More subjectively (as if *saudades* is anything but subjective), it evokes a mood of painful dislocation from primary bonds. These bonds may involve one's childhood habitat, and friendship recalled in a particular place. In interpersonal relations *saudades* defines a sad sense of loss resulting from one's separation by time and distance from close attachments that are felt to be irreplaceable. Within the Goan expatriate experience *saudades* may evoke a people's mythic visions of a Golden Age. We can thus extend the scope of *saudades* from the traditional Portuguese lyric to both a cultural symbol of the Portuguese ethos and an ethnic intuition.

Let me now return to the questions I posed at the beginning of this paper and answer them in the general recommendations that George Coelho was prepared to make at the conference on "Goa and Portugal: History and Development". As a University professor in the west, working at a major institution with over 20 million dollars of Research grant money awarded to its faculty every year as well as a member of the Research Council of Canada Grants Committee (SSHRC), I am only too well aware that the main initiative in all faculties, as well as the destination of virtually every research envelope, is internationalization and globalisation. I teach at a young university built in the mid 1960s and as a result we react quickly to the changing economic, technological and sociological factors that affect all society. Cross-cultural collaboration, work study abroad programmes, technology transfers, arts and humanities links, degree programmes and institutes devoted to the study of popular culture, sports, medicine, rock and jazz music, cultural studies and the creating of cross-disciplinary research areas are all areas that have been identified as constituting the new curricula of the year 2000. Institutionalizing these fields which all hinge around the wheel of interdisciplinarity, requires a major change in what and how we deliver information and this in turn demands a major rethinking of how we do things. We see this as the biggest challenge to the survival of universities of the year 2000.

I have talked at some length about integrating aspects of what some call "metahistory" or subjectivity, as *a modus operandi* within our programmes. This theory embraces the more post-modern view that the past must continue to change for history to be relevant, and this, in turn, requires history to allow the various participants to create it from our perspective. George Coelho's call for Goan University programmes in the fine arts to emphasize interdisciplinary issues in comparative literature within the framework of Goan cultural development is based on the idea of allowing Goans to write their own history – to allow their own literature to become an historical genre that is different from the normative varieties that have dominated Western thought. This could show that Indian history does not have to be sublimated to the role of a mistress of Western history as Chakrabarty has said. Moreover, the genres of memoirs, mixed-genre histories, as that jumble of postcolonial *cum* autobiography that fills the pages of Rushdie, Seth, Roy and Naipaul are increasingly looked upon in the West as a valid source of history, just as the field of post colonialism has gone from a splinter group to an imposing arboreal presence in all sectors of academe. These stories are retellings of oral histories and experiences frozen in time through memory, and for this reason George's LILA project holds great promise for the future of Goan history.

One cannot speak of Goan literature without, of course, evoking music, since there are so many analogous issues between the two fields. The Lusofone Goan poets traveled easily in a language that was not foreign, but familiar to them, indeed even parochial. In the pre World War II colonial years, these Goan poets including Joseph Furtado (1872-1947), *Primeiros Versos*, Nascimento Mendonça (1884-1926), Paulino Dias (1874-1910), Adeodato Barreto (1905-1937), Floriano Barreto (1877-1905), and Floriano Pinto (1887-?), experienced their Catholic formation and higher education in Latin and Portuguese at the Liceu Nacional in Goa. Brought up in the well-to-do Catholic families of those colonial days, these writers were quite at home in the Goan art song and social dance, the mando. The mando, while influenced by the courtly Portuguese minuet of a century ago, is uniquely Goan in origin and composition. These Goan poets were also exposed to great works in Portuguese literature, European classical and religious music and popular Portuguese songs. In this context, they assimilated the passionate mood of *saudades* that is evoked by the Portuguese fado. Thus, *saudades* in an important thing of the expatriate Goan intellectual: it evokes a mood of melancholic reverie and pathos when he recalls his grandmother's stories that told of her young days about a hundred years ago when an autonomous Goan personality evolved and the Goan mandos were composed as a cross-cultural expression of the Goan soil and soul.

The other half of George's main case that he was intending to plea concerned the role of musicological studies within Goan/Portuguese cultural developments. The history of Goan music is a naturally cross-disciplinary and cross-cultural area of work, combining classical and Church traditions, Portuguese and Indian styles, but more importantly allowing for both hard archival source study as well as more anthropologically-oriented ethno-musicological field work. This is precisely the kind of syncretic topic, cross-disciplinary in both methodology and musical styles, that represents the most promising area in musicology today, and it would allow for Goan scholars to begin writing a music history based on their own perspective, as Mario Cabral e Sa has attempted to do recently.

In conclusion, the two areas I have highlighted here: 1) the study of literature in a cross-disciplinary, historical and comparative fashion, and 2) the expanding of offerings in musicology with an emphasis on Goan musical sources and traditions, are not only topics that occupy centre stage on a global level, but are precisely the kinds of perspectives that have emerged as the main research areas among young scholars in the West. Consequently, these topics can be used to trigger and promote cross-cultural partnership, exchanges and collaboration with international institutes. They tap into the enormous interest in comparative literature, world histories, and ethnomusicology in the West today, and on a broad geographic scale these topics can fulfill the aim of strengthening the global Lusofone triangle that exists between Portugal, Brazil and Goa, themselves representative of the Old, the New and the Ancient but rapidly developing worlds.

NOTES AND REFERENCES

1. Dipesh Chakrabarty, "Postcoloniality and the Artifice of History: Who speaks for 'Indian' pasts?", *Representations*, no. 37, 1992, p. 1.
2. I am thinking of such books as Walter D. Mignolo, *The Darker Side of the Renaissance: Literacy, Territoriality and Colonization*, Ann Arbor: University of Michigan Press, 1998.
3. See, for example, V. Coelho, "Connecting Histories: Portuguese Music in Renaissance Goa," in *Goa and Portugal: Their Cultural Links*, C. Borges & H. Feldmann (eds.), New Delhi: Concept Publishing Company, 1997, pp. 131-47; also V. Coelho, "Kapsberger's *Apotheosis*... of Francis Xavier (1622) and the Conquering of India", in *The Work of Opera: Genre, Nationhood and Sexual Differences*, eds. R. Dellamora & D. Fischlin, New York: Columbia University Press, 1997, pp. 27-47 and "Music in Portuguese India and Renaissance Music Histories", in *Vasco da Gama and India*, eds. Teotónio de Souza & João Manuel Garcia, vol. III, Lisbon: Gulbenkian, pp. 185-94.
4. Teotónio de Souza, *Goa to Me*, New Delhi: Concept Publishing Co., 1994, p. 31.
5. George V. Coelho, "Images of Women in Goan Portuguese Poetry: The *Bailadeira* theme and Variations," in *O rosto feminino da expansão Portuguesa*, Lisbon, 1996, pp. 365-79.
6. *Ibid.*, p. 368.
7. See George V. Coelho, "Voices of Nostalgia in Seven Goan Poets", *Boletim do Instituto Menezes Braganza*, no. 171, 1994, pp. 79-112.

24

José Custódio de Faria, The School of Nancy and Sigmund Freud

An unknown Goan source for psychoanalysis

HANNES STUBBE

I. Introduction: On the importance of Faria

In the history of modern sciences of the western nations and of the economic-cultural centres, the scientific sources which do not have their origin in Europe or in the United States of America have been till now ignored. Here, the ethno-centricism and Euro-centricism in sciences become apparent, which in the age of so-called globalisation, seems to me, even less acceptable. A remarkable example of this type of vision is the significance of Abade Faria (May 31, 1756 – September 20, 1819) for the development of psychoanalysis. He was born exactly 100 years before Sigmund Freud.

In compendia and manuals of the history of psychoanalysis, normally only European sources and origins are mentioned. Those quoted are Greece and ancient Rome (the Oedipus Complex), the German Romanticism (dreams and the role of the unconscious), Judaism (psychology of religion in the writings of Freud, Stroeken and Peters),[1] European philosophy and psychology (Fechner, Brentano, Schopenhauer, Nietzsche, Carus, Wundt), the research on sexuality, European poetry (Goethe, Heine, Shakespeare et al), among some others. On the other hand, the non-European sources and influences are not generally mentioned, outside Portuguese literature. Among the diverse basis of psychoanalysis and the study of the unconscious, the research of the hypnotic phenomena also forms part,

* Translated from the Portuguese by Charles J. Borges

about which Robert Heiss wrote the following in the 1950s: "The knowledge of the hypnotic processes and especially of the auto-suggestive and auto-hypnotic processes, extends over a large area outside of our cultural milieu. A large part of these phenomena which are known as techniques of yoga and which originate from the Indian cultural milieu, are some of these".[2]

Hippolyte Bernheim (1837-1919), an important researcher of hypnosis wrote in 1892: "Thus already the fakirs and yogis do in India for more than 2,400 years; they concentrate for 45 minutes on the tip of their noses, control or stop their respiration and concentrate their attention to the point that someone tells them a blue flame arises at the point of their noses. There, then, they take the extraordinary position of a kataleptic".[3] Especially in relation to the research of hypnotic phenomena we have to call attention to the significant role, until now, of the Goan Abbé Faria as a mediator between the Indian and European thought at the beginning of the 19th century.

While the father of Faria is seen as one of the many intellectual parents of the first political movements for the liberation of the colonial areas during Illuminism and the French Revolution (1789), Abade Faria can be characterised as a precursor of psychology, as a modern science, of psychoanalysis, psychotherapy and dynamic psychiatry, and this by the fact of his having turned famous as the first psychological experimenter, hypnotherapist and theoretician of psychology. It is exactly here, in my opinion, that his importance lies. For this I am going to concentrate in the following exposition on these scientific points.

In the modern German, French, Anglo-American and Portuguese literature, on the history of hypnosis, Faria occupies frequently a distinct place. The Portuguese psychoanalyst, Pedro Luzes[4] dedicates to him in his collection a complete chapter and calls him "an important precursor of psychoanalysis". Already the Portuguese doctor, winner of the Nobel prize in 1949, Egas Moniz (1874-1955) dedicated to Faria in 1925 an essay of deep significance. He classifies the work of Faria in the following manner: "His book, omitting the philosophical part is even today a compendium of important information on hypnotism... It is the moment of we giving justice to the great majority of contemporary French authors who give today to Faria the place that he deserves as the creator of the doctrine of suggestion in hypnotism that today we all profess."[5] Also in the work on the history of medicine entitled *Histoire de l'hypnose en France* of Barrucand, Faria is treated minutely as the initiator of the psychological currents between 1819–1884 in the French movements of hypnosis. Barrucand certifies that "Abbé Faria is the first to propose a psychological system to explain lucid sleep".[6]

I tried to visualise in the following **Table I**, the relations within the scope of the history of sciences between Indian ethno-psychology and Faria following the school of Nancy and Sigmund Freud in order to finally return to psychoanalysis in India which is the theme of my presentation.

Table I

Abbé Faria and psychoanalysis

Psychoanalysis in India

- Freud: References on psychoanalysis in India[7]
- Bose: First tentative psychoanalysis in India and his correspondence with Freud;
  Indian Psychoanalytic Society in 1922[8]
- Sinha : Psychoanalysis in India[9]
- Petzold: History of psychoanalysis in India[10]
- Karkar: Psychoanalysis in India[11]

↑↑

Sigmund Freud (1856-1939) and Hypnosis

- From October 13, 1885 to February 23, 1886, Freud was at Salpêtrière in Paris with Jean-Martin Charcot (1825-1893), whose hypnotic experiments with hysterics he could observe.
- 1887 (December): First application of hypnotic suggestion.
- 1888: Freud presents without critical annotations the fundamentals of the technique of hypnosis of Bernheim.[12]
- 1889: Freud visits Bernheim in Nancy; translates two of his books. [13]
- 1891: Freud writes "Hypnosis"[14]
- 1892: Freud writes "Ueber ..."[15]
- 1892/93: Freud writes "Ein Fall ..."[16]
- 1918: He calls attention in his letter to Simmel of the utility of the use of hypnosis in the treatment for neurotics of war.[17]

↑↑

The School of Nancy (Liébault, Bernheim et al)

- Ambroise A. Liébault (1823-1904) takes up again the simple method of suggestion of Faria.[18]
- H. Bernheim: "The School of Nancy."[19]

- 1886: *De la suggestion et ses applications à la thérapeutique.*
- 1891: *Hypnotisme, suggestion, psychothérapie, études nouvelles.*

↑↑

Abade Faria (1756-1819)	*European Psychology*
– Hypnosis through suggestion	– Mesmerism (Anton Mesmer, 1734-1815)
– Meaning of concentration	
– Post-hypnotic suggestion	
– Refutation of the hypothesis of fluid	– Somnambulism (M. de Puysègur, 1751-1825)
– Hypnotic anaesthesia	
– Somnambulism lucid sleep	
– Brahman	– Christian Wolff (1679-1754)
– Goan Influence	Psychology of Illuminism

↑↑

Indian Ethno-psychology

- Techniques of meditation
- Auto-hypnotic techniques
- System of Yoga: Position of relaxation (*asanas*), withdrawal of senses (*pratyahara*) of all external reactions; concentration (*dharana*) on a specific object; consequent stopping of meditation (*dhyana*), total immersion in fire, in God or in a specific object, till the point of individual consciousness to insert itself totally in it and to stop understanding.[20]
- *Vedas*, for example *Atharvaveda* (ethno-psychology)

Sources[21]

Faria, the School of Nancy and Sigmund Freud

When Freud opened his consultancy in Vienna, on Easter Sunday, April 25, 1886, he understood immediately that with neurology, as he had learnt it at university, it would almost be impossible to help his patients.

Most of his patients did not suffer from organic neurological disorders, but yes, of nerves, or as we would diagnose today, were neurotics. "My therapeutic arsenal has only two solutions, electric therapy and hypnosis", writes Freud much later in his self-introduction.[22] He applies always more frequently hypnosis (first application of the hypnotic suggestion in

December 1887). During his stay in Paris (October 13, 1885 – February 28, 1886), he could see how Charcot led hysterical patients to provoke their symptoms and take them again to their removal with the help of hypnosis. "Freud utilizes hypnosis from the beginning like Charcot. He places the patient into a trance and suggests to him the disappearance of the symptoms when turning to the normal conscious state. He would pass soon to utilize other methods which would have great importance in the growth of his work. The patient was asked to remember when his symptoms arose for the first time and to relate with the maximum details the conditions in which the symptoms had appeared".[23]

At the end of the 19th century there arose in Vienna a great interest in hypnosis caused among other things, by the writings of Obersteiner in 1885, 1893, as also by the publications of Freud in the years 1888, 1891 and 1892/93. Freud was seen for this reason during much time as a specialist of hypnosis.

Freud then took note of the school of Nancy which used hypnotic suggestion with or without hypnosis as a therapeutic means. As he was not able to attain with his patients the desired hypnotic depth, he decided in the summer of 1889 to go to Nancy for some weeks to improve his hypnotic techniques.

"I saw the old and moving Liébault practicing his work with women and children of the poor working class. I was witness of the admirable experiments of Bernheim with the patients of his hospital and I had the most strong impressions of the possibility of the powerful psychic process which lies hidden to the human consciousness".[24]

The results of his diverse lively conversations with Bernheim is the decision to translating the two works of Bernheim from French into German.[25] In these two works of Bernheim, Freud comes across Abade Faria probably for the first time since they treat in detail the thought of Faria.

The translation of Freud deals with Faria as follows: "In reality it was Abade Faria who around 1811 provides us the first correct and true description of the hypnotic phenomenon, which he called the lucid sleep. According to him, the cause of this sleep is the will of the person. There exists neither the magnetic fluid, nor any other influence of this type which the magnetizing agent can exercise over the magnetized. The cause of the changes which occur in the organism, has its unique cause in the brain of the person, in his imagination ... The notable report of Husson, which was read in the Academy of Medicine in 1831, confirms the real existence of almost all the phenomena that Abade Faria describes uniquely to the conviction of the person".[26]

He goes on in his translation: "However the correct way of hypnosis had already been discovered by Abade Faria since 1814 ... He asked the persons to sit comfortably; he would order them that they should think in sleep and look to him (Abade); he would look at them from far with large eyes, and would show them the back part of his hand which was raised; he would take some steps in their direction, and then, would lower suddenly his arm in front of the person and would ask him to sleep. On some rare occasions, he went very close to the person and placed his finger on the forehead of the magnetised and repeated the order Sleep! ... "About 3 to 5 times", says General Noizet, "I saw him reach his objective in less than a minute"... Without doubt, it belongs to Faria the merit of being the first known proponent of the theory and method of hypnosis through suggestion and to free the same of strange and superfluous processes that it possessed and concealed the truth".[27]

In the translation of Freud,[28] one also comes across, in similar form, in the seventh chapter, references to Abade Faria and hypnosis through suggestion.

Thus, we can confirm a direct line in the history of sciences that link Abade Faria to the school of Nancy and from there to Freud.

The Canadian historian of sciences, Henry Ellenberger puts down definitely, in his basic work on the history of dynamic psychiatry, Faria as one of the founders of modern dynamic psychiatry, and writes: "Pierre Janet (1859-1947) showed much later that Faria through the path of Noizet and Liébault, was the true father in the geneaology of the school of Nancy."[29] Even in his rejection of the hypothesis of fluid of Anton Mesmer, Faria was a precursor of Bernheim with whom Freud in the summer of 1889 studied the technique of hypnosis. I want to add also that the school of Nancy had a very important role in the development of psychoanalysis.[30]

Psychoanalysis in India

On the path of the expansion of psychoanalysis from Vienna to the world, there was started later on *Zur Geschichte der psychoanalytischen Bewegung* (*History of the Psychoanalytic Movement*, Supplement 1923) in British India (Calcutta), a branch of special protection of analysis [31] for which Havelock called attention already in 1911. Fundamental in such a process was Dr. Girindrashekar Bose (1887-1953) who also got interested in hypnosis and started in Calcutta in 1912 with tentative attempts at psychoanalytical treatment. He presented his thesis of medicine, *The*

Concept of Repression (1921), a study in the psychoanalytical line, which he sent to Freud, a new moment in the history of psychology in India. It was also Bose who called attention in his article "The psychological outlook in Hindu philosophy" for the parallels and similarities existing between psychoanalysis and the Indian philosophical concepts. Bose kept up also a correspondence with Freud[32] and he was president of the Indian Psychoanalytic Society which was started in 1922.

Thus, closes the circle between Indian ethno-psychology and Faria through the school of Nancy and Freud back to India.

NOTES AND REFERENCES

The present paper has its origin in the context of an ongoing research project on culture and psychology in the Portuguese-speaking countries (Hannes Stubbe, 1987, 1992, 1997, 1998, 1999) and is directed this time to the cultural relations between India and Europe.

1. Harry P. J. Stroeken, "Der Einfluß von Freuds Judentum auf sein Leben und die Psychoanalyse", *Forum Psychoanalyse*, 7, 1991, pp. 323-335; Peter Kuttter (ed.), *A guide to psychoanalysis throughout the world*; S. Karkar, *India*, vol. II, Stuttgart: Frommann-Holzboog, 1992, pp. 105-116.
2. Robert Heiss; *Allgemeine Tiefenpsychologie*, Berne: Huber, 1964, 2nd ed., p. 53.
3. H. Bernheim, *Neue Studien ueber Hypnotismus. Suggestion und Psychotherapie,* Uebersetzt von Dr. Sigm. Freud, Leipzig: Franz Deuticke, 1892, p. 43.
4. *Cem Anos de Psicanálise*, Lisbon: ISPA, 1997, pp. 4ff, 35-50.
5. Egas Moniz, *O Padre Faria na história do hipnotismo*, Lisbon: Faculdade de Medicina de Lisboa, 1925, pp. 86, 88.
6. Paris: Presses Universitaires de France, 1967, p. 69.
7. Sigmund Freud, "Zur Geschichte der psychoanalytischen Bewegung", (1914), in S. Freud, *Selbstdarstellung*, Frankfurt/M.Fishcher, 1971, pp. 165, 169.
8. G. Bose, "The psychological outlook in Hindu philosophy", *Indian Journal of Psychology*, 5, 1930, pp. 119-46.
9. T. C. Sinha, "Development of psychoanalysis in India", *International Journal of Psychoanalysis*, 47, 1966, pp. 427-39.
10. M. Petzold, *Indische Psychologie, Eine Einführung in traditionelle Ansätze und moderne Forschung*, Munich: Psychologie Verlags Union, 1986, pp. 155ff.
11. Sudhir Karkar, *Die Gewalt der Formmen. Zur Psychologie religiöser und ethnischer Konflikte*, Munich: Beck, 1997.

12. Freud, "Hypnose durch Suggestion", *Wiener Medizinische Wochenzeitschrift*, 38, 1888, pp. 898-900.
13. *De la suggestion et ses applications à la thérapeutique* (1886) and *Hypnotisme, suggestion, psychothérapie, études nouvelles* (1891).
14. Freud, "Hypnosis", in A. Bum (ed.), *Therapeutisches Lexikon*, Vienna: Urban & Schwarzenberg, 1891, pp. 724-34. A basic medical work of that age; new editions 1893 and 1900; not included in the historical work.
15. Freud, "Ueber Hypnose und Suggestion", *Aerzte Centr. Anz.*
16. Freud, "Ein Fall von hypnotischer Heilung: nebst Bemerkungen über die Entstehung hysterischer Symptome durch den Gegenwillen", *Zeitschrift für Hypnotismus*, 1, 1892/93, pp. 102-107, 123-129, 258-272.
17. Ronald W. Clark, *Sigmund Freud*, Frankfurt/M : Fischer, 1985, p. 139.
18. Bernheim, *Neue Studien ueber Hypnotismus, Suggestion und Psychotherapie*, S. Freud (trans.), Leipzig: Franz Deuticke, 1892, p. 59.
19. Bernheim, *Die Suggestion und ihre Heilwirkung.* Autorisirte deutsche Ausgaabe von Dr. S. Freud, Leipzig: Franz Deuticke, 1896, vols. I-II, p. 117.
20. Margaret Stutley, *Was ist Hinduismus? Eine Einführung in die große Weltreligion*, Munich: O. W. Barth Verlag, 1994, pp. 70ff.
21. *Sources*: Freud, 1914; Bernheim, *op. cit.*, 1888, 1892, 1896; Stutley, *op. cit.*; Petzold, *op. cit.*; Edward Conza, *Eine kurze Geschichte des Buddhismus*, Frankfurt/M: Suhrkamp, 1986; Hannes Stubbe, 1998, 1999; Christiane Hartnack, "Indische Psychologie", in Siegfried Grubitsch & Gunter Rexilius (eds.), *Psychologische Grundbegriffe*, Reinbek, 1990, pp. 478-84.
22. S. Freud, *Selbstdarstellung*, (Complete Works, G. W.), vol. XIV, pp. 39-40.
23. Clark, *op. cit.*, p. 119.
24. S. Freud, *Selbstdarstellung, op. cit.*, p. 41.
25. *Neue Studien ueber Hypnotismus, Suggestion und Psychotherapie.* Uebersetzt von Dr. S. Freud, Leipzig: Franz Deuticke, 1892; *Die Suggestion und ihre Heilwirkung.* Autorisierten deutsche Ausgabe von Dr. S. Freud, Leipzig: Franz Deuticke, 1888 (1896), vols. I-II.
26. Bernheim, *Vierte Verlesung. Entdeckung der Suggestion durch Faria* (Fourth Class. Discovery of Suggestion by Faria), 1892, p. 45.
27. Bernheim, *Fünfte Verlesung. Das Suggestiveverfahren des Abbé Faria* (Fifth Class. The Suggestive Method of Abbé Faria), 1892, p. 56.
28. *Die Suggestion und ihre Heilwirkung* (the suggestion and its therapeutic effect), 1988, pp. 101ff.
29. Henry F. Ellenberger, *Die Entdeckung des Unbewußten*, Bern: Huber, 1973, vols. I-II, p. 122.
30. Heinz Schott, "Fluidum – Suggestion – Übertragung. Zum Verhältnis von Mesmerismus, Hypnose und Psychoanalyse", in *Wunderblock, Eine Geschichte der modernen Seele.* Vienna: Löcker Verlag, 1989, pp. 83-95.
31. S. Freud, *Selbstdarstellung: Schriften zur Geschichte der Psychoanalyse*, Frankfurt/M: Fischer, 1971, pp. 165, 169.
32. Sinha, *op. cit.*; Petzold, *op. cit.*, pp. 155ff; Psychoanalysis International, 1922.

BIBLIOGRAPHY

Ackerknecht, Erwin H., *Kurze Geschichte der Psychiatrie*, Stuttgart: Enke, 1967, vols. I-II. 2nd ed.

---------, *Geschichte der Medizin*, Stuttgart: Enke, 1979, vols. I-IV.

Bernheim, Hippolyte, *Die Suggestion und ihre Heilwirkung*. Autorisirte deutsche Ausgabe von Dr. Sigm. Freud, Leipzig & Vienna: Franz Deuticke, 1888.

Borges, Charles J. (ed.), *Goa and the Revolt of 1787*, New Delhi: Concept Publishing Co., 1996.

Boss, M., *Indienfahrt eines Psychiaters*, Freiburg, 1966.

Cabral e Sa, Mario & Nou, Jean Louis (eds.), *Goa*, New Delhi: Lustre Press, 1993.

Cabral e Sa, Mario & Rodrigues, Lourdes, Bravo da Costa (eds.), *Great Goans*, Pune: Kirloskar Press, 1985.

Eliade, Mircea, *Yoga-Unsterblichkeit und Freiheit*, Zurich: Rascher, 1960.

---------, *Die Religionen und das Heilige*, Darmstadt: Wissenschaftliche Buchgesellschaft, 1976.

Faria, L'Abbé de, (Bramine, docteur en Théologie et en Philosophie, ex-Professor de Philosophie a L'université de France, Member de la Societé Médicale de Marseille, etc. etc. etc.), *De la cause du someil lucide ou Etude de la nature de l'homme*, Paris: Horiac, 1819.

Freud, Sigmund, "Hypnose durch Suggestion", *Wiener Medizinische Wochenzeitschrift*, 38, 1888, pp. 898-900.

----------, "Hypnose", in A. Bum (ed.), *Therapeutisches Lexikon*, Vienna: Urban & Schwarzenberg, 1891, pp. 724-734.

---------, "Ueber Hypnose und Suggestion", *Aerzte Centr. Anz.*, 4, 1892.

---------, *Gesammelte Werke*, vol. XVIII, Gesamtregister, Frankfurt/M. Fischer, 1972.

Mesmer, Franz Anton, *Abhandlung über die Entdeckung des thierischen Magnetismus* (1781), Tübingen: Diskord, 1985.

Obersteiner, H., *Der Hypnotismus*, Vienna, 1885.

------------, *Die Lehre von Hypnotismus: Eine kurzgefaßte Darstellung*, Vienna: Breitenstein, 1893.

Pattie, Frank, *Mesmer and animal magnetism: A chapter in the history of medicine*, 1994.

Pereira, Oscar, "Goa in Vergangenheit und Gegenwart", ABP, *Zeitschrift zur portugiesischsprachigen Welt*, 1, 1994, pp. 131-147.

Santos-Stubbe, Chirly dos & Stubbe, Hannes: "Quem foi "Katharina"? História familiar e ambiente psico-social do caso de Sigmund Freud (1895)", *Psicologia Clínica* (PUC-Rio de Janeiro), 2, 1987, pp. 17-29.

Sinha, D., "Psychology in the context of Third World development", *International Journal of Psychology*, 19, 1984, pp. 17-29.

Sloterdijk, Peter, *Der Zauberbaum. Die Entstehung der Psychoanalyse im Jahr 1785. Ein Epischer Versuch zur Philosophie der Psychologie*, Frankfurt/M: Suhrkamp, 1987.

Stoll, Otto, *Suggestion und Hypnotismus in der Völkerpsychologie*, Leipzig: K. F. Koehler's Antiquarium, 1894.

Stubbe, Hannes, *Geschichte der Psychologie in Brazilien, Von den indianischen und afrobrasilianischen Kulturen bis in die Gegenwart. Beiträge zur Kulturanthropologie*, Berlin: Reimer, 1987.

-----------, "Experimental psychologie in den Tropen", *Psychologie und Geschichte*, nos. 3/4, 1993, pp. 278-99.

------------, "Sigmund Freud in den Tropen. Zur Frühgeschichte der Psychoanalyse in Brasilien", *Kölner Beiträge zur Ethnopsychologie und Transkulturellen Psychologie*, no. 3, 1997.

----------, *Der Goaner José Custódio de Faria (31.5.1756 - 20.9.1819) und die Hypnose. Ein Dialog indischer und europäischer Psychologie?* (in press).

Vaz, J. Clement, *Profiles of Eminent Goans: Past and Present*, New Delhi: Concept Publishing Co, 1997.

Wolf, M., *Psychologie ou traité sur l'âme, contenant les connoissances, que nous en donne l'expérience*, Amsterdam: Pierre Moutier, 1745. Reprint Hildesheim: Georg Olms, 1998.

Wundt, Wilhelm, "Hypnotismus und Suggestion", *Philosophische Studien*, 8, 1893, pp.1-85.

25

Abade Faria (1756-1819) in Scientific and Fine Arts Literature

CHIRLY DOS SANTOS-STUBBE

> "The publication of a scientific production supposes always in the author the intention to discover new truths or to correct the ones considered as truth. If in the process they aspire to attain glory to the author, I consider it shameful. The hope of celebrity in this area is always mixed with sorrow."[1]

The name José Custódio de Faria (May 31, 1756 – September 20, 1819) known worldwide as Abade Faria, was known as much in scientific literature as in fine arts literature through the image that one has of this Goan, as a man of deep theoretical knowledge and immense interest in intra-psychological phenomena to which he had access through the utilisation of the technique of hypnosis. Abade Faria influenced through his hypnotic experiments many generations of doctors (among them, especially psychiatrists and neurologists) as well as, psychologists, psychotherapists, et al. Among these, we can state that the renowned father of psychoanalysis, Sigmund Freud (1856-1938) also was influenced by this religious man.

The bibliography below gives us a brief but differentiated idea of the influences of Abade Faria in scientific literature on hypnotism till our times, although I here limit myself only to some authors and works of scientific literature in French, English, German and Portuguese respectively.

The first news that we have of the activity of Abade Faria as magnetiser is of the year 1802 and is given by Count Françoise René de Chateaubriand (1768-1848) in his *Memórias de além-tumulo* published in 1843. Chateaubriand refers to Abade Faria, with whom he dined in the house of the marchioness of Custine, in circumstances little pleasant for Faria.[2]

But in spite of the large diffusion of this method of psycho-therapeutical treatment in almost the entire world, we can state that the greater diffusion of the person of José Custódio de Faria was not provided by scientific literature, but, yes, by the literature of fine arts. This world-wide diffusion is linked in the first place to the name of the Romantic French writer Alexandre Dumas, father, (July 24,1802 – December 5, 1870) who gave Abade Faria[3] a privileged place in one of his better known and debated works, especially by the Catholic Church which banned it for decades, *Le Comte de Monte Cristo (The Count of Monte Cristo*, published in 1845/6 appearing in the beginning in parts like *roman-feuilletons*, in *Journal de débats)*, followed by its publication in 18 volumes in Paris. This work was translated in all European languages.

A short resumé of the work can be presented in the following manner. Edmond Dantès, a humble, hardworking and sincere young man with immense possibilities to rise professionally in the marine transport services, residing in Marselha, is implicated in 1815 to be the spy of Napolean Bonaparte by his false friends, Fernand and Danglar. Dantès is implicated by a young and ambitious judge Villeforts, is imprisoned without the right of defence and without trial in Chateau d'If, neighboring Marselha, where he remains imprisoned for 14 years. In prison, he comes to know an eccentric priest, called thus for offering all who believe, that he could take them again to freedom, to his treasure which is hidden. Dantès and the eccentric priest, alias Father Faria, develop a strong friendship, linked deeply to the theoretical and linguistic lessons which the learned priest gives Dantès. After his flight from Chateau d'If, Dantès searches the island Monte Cristo mentioned by the priest, and really finds the treasure. He returns again to his world of youth as a rich man, as the Count of Monte Cristo, to take his revenge on all those guilty of his imprisonment.

Well, after this short resumé to bring up the unfolding romance, a fundamental question arises: what makes us affirm that this eccentric priest of Dumas' novel, called Faria, is the experimenter and hypnotizer José Custódio de Faria born in Goa, precisely in Candolim, on May 31, 1756?

There are many parallel facts between the character of the novel and José Custódio de Faria which makes us state that it is the same person, although it may be clear that Alexandre Dumas did not intend to make Father Faria a historical biographical figure. In the first place, we can call one's attention to the more evident fact: both Farias are Abades. Besides this, we can affirm that Abade José Custódio de Faria lived exactly at the time of the lifetime of the figure of the novel (1811-19), a time in which he turned into a celebrity. Dumas presents him as learned, as a linguist, as philosopher and a personality with profound moral sense, the characteristics we can apply in complete form to the real Abade Faria. His religious formation allowed him the knowledge of ancient philosophies, as well as, of the various languages, a fact also related to the biography of José Custódio and to his years of living in Portugal, from there, Portuguese; in Italy, besides Italian, also Latin, and in France, where he lived and developed his hypnotic method, French, although he did not master this language so fluently. The five languages spoken by the character of Dumas (German, French, Italian, English and Spanish)[4] are not totally the ones the Goan Abade really spoke.

The Goan birthplace of Abade Faria is not generally recognized either in scientific literature or in fine arts, although I think it a little probable, that the many authors that have written on him or based themselves on his thoughts and on his works may not have known really his place of birth. What is also a little probable is that Dumas may not have known that Abade Faria was an Indo-Portuguese descendant, above all by the colour of his skin[5] to have been frequently the motive of comment, especially, on the part of the enemies of Abade, which I doubt did not reach the ears of Dumas. The character of Father Faria in the novel is a native of Rome, the Italian city in which the real Abade Faria lived for eight years, where he studied and was born morally and intellectually. It is interesting that one of the few experiences and adventures that the young Dantès has to relate to his friend of so profound knowledge in prison, is the journey which he made to India. This is the only mention of India related to Father Faria in the novel.[6]

There are also other curious facts that give us a more exact identity of Abade Faria to Father Faria of Dumas. One of these facts, is the coincidence of the dates in the novel, which mark really various phases in the life of José Custódio de Faria.

The action unfolded by Dumas in the romance takes place in 1815, the time of Faria's life. Dumas imprisons Faria in the castle, or better, the fortress of If, in the Marselha Bay, 2 kms distance from the port[7] in 1811, exactly in the year in which Abade Faria became professor of philosophy in Marselha. The so-called eccentricity of the figure in the novel takes place in the prison of the castle of If and was dated by Dumas as the year 1813. And it is in the same year that Abade Faria opens, in Paris, his conference hall of lucid sleep on the Rue de Clichy, 49.

In the novel of Alexandre Dumas, Father Faria is visited in 1816 by the General Inspector of the castle of If who asks him about the conditions of the prison, about the food, as well as about his demands. The response of the eccentric priest, in my opinion, till now, is a response as much ironic as socio-political. "The food that is normally given in prisons, is very bad. The prison is, as you can see, humid and dirty but all in all tolerable for the aim for which it is intended" (Dumas). During this meeting that has something of cynicism and irony at the same time, Father Faria offers the Inspector, as representative of the State, part of his treasure in exchange for his freedom. In the real life of Abade Faria, he is visited in this year, 1816, in Paris by the actor Potier who exposes him soon after in the comedy *Magnétismomanie* to the jeers and the face-to-face ridicule before the people of the theatre of Variétés.

Faria of the novel took four years to prepare the tools which he used to dig the tunnel in the wall of the prison and two to three years to dig the hard wall of the prison. In real life Abade Faria gave conferences during four years and took two to three years writing his scientific work. As we see, there also exist parallels in the production of the work between the real and the fictitious figure.

Just like Edmond Dantès, the companion in prison of Father Faria in the castle of If believed that his master had supernatural mental faculties, in the novel he is described as a man "of shining and deep eyes as the prophets would have."[8] Those who frequented his classes at Rue de Clichy, in Paris, also considered Abade Faria as possessing extraordinary occult powers.

One more factor is that of the age. Dumas attributes to the prisoner Faria the age of 63 years, the age which the Goan Abade was, really, when he died.

There are other factors mentioned by Dumas which tally with the real Abade Faria, such as the fact of having a command of many languages, of having a deep knowledge of history and philosophy (José Custódio was professor of philosophy), as also the fact of his having had apoplexy (*apoplexia fulminante*) as the cause of death, the same which took the Goan Abade in Rua dos Orties, no. 4 in Paris (today Avenida da Ópera, no. 9) to his final end. Besides this, Dumas shows him as a believer that Abade Faria really was always. Exactly like José Custódio de Faria, Father Faria of the novel, dies and leaves a book completed but hidden. In the case of Abade Faria, the book was published in the year of his death (1819). We cannot fail to mention that many years after his death, his knowledge was made public and respected through the publication, in Paris, of the book of his student General Noizet in 1854 by the "Prussian Academy of Sciences" of Berlin, which summarised the doctrines of Abade

Faria. In the case of Father Faria of Dumas the book remains hidden in the wall of the castle of If and was only rescued by the Count of Monte Cristo, also many years after the death of the character. [9]

All this is mere coincidence? I think not.

Dumas used the name and some knowledge that he had of the biography of the Goan Abade to construct his Father Faria. Dumas did not want to reproduce Faria as a copy of the Goan Abade. He moved José Custódio away from all the suffering that he underwent in Paris, to create a priest in another environment of suffering, completely fantastic, within the historical castle of If.

It is interesting I think, also the question not as yet clear about the knowledge of A. Dumas, about the familiar life of Abade Faria. Did Dumas know that the father of Faria, Caetano Vitorino de Faria, was involved in the freedom movements of 1787? Did Dumas know that he had been a prisoner in Portugal and was accused of conspiracy? These questions appear to me of interest, since as we know, Dumas was a keen republican fighter for the independence of Italy in 1860. Besides this, it seems to me very coherent with the history of the Faria family, the motives by which Dumas takes Father Faria to prison; he is accused of conspiracy in Italy. The history of the life of the father of Abade Faria seems to me as a good parallel to the history of the priest in the novel, but including there, autobiographical elements of Alexandre Dumas

Attempting a literary and psychological analysis of the Father Faria of Dumas, I would like to state the following points:

Dumas places the figure of Faria at the beginning of the novel, but precisely in chapter 8, of the first volume (approximately from p. 80 of his book of 1200 pages),[10] giving him thus, a central role. Strengthening this position still further, Dumas places into the hands of Father Faria, the change of personality of Edmond Dantès. It is through the priest that Dantès changes into a man, not only of money but also of knowledge, since the priest gives him lectures on many different areas of knowledge in prison. Faria enters into the history of Dantès to substitute emotionally and intellectually his father. The relationship of the two turns, really, into a relationship the one existing between a father and son. At the end of the life of the father, which means, after the death of Faria in prison, he gives as a inheritance to his son, the possibility of liberty through flight, as well as a treasure, which means a new life.

As we know, Abade Faria never more returned to his native land Goa, but the Count of Monte Cristo, returns to his ungrateful land, to the castle of If. Almost at the end of the novel, the Count returns to his prison, to recall, to turn back to consciousness, and to free himself from the psychological trauma which the years in prison were and to say goodbye and almost pray, in the best manner, for his mentor Father Faria. The Count kneels down and makes an altar of the bed of the deceased father and says: "O my second father, you who gave me the freedom, knowledge and riches! You, similar to the one being of supreme form, knower of good and evil ..., pure heart, deep soul and elevated spirit!"[11]

It is interesting to differentiate here the treasure. Dumas presents Faria in his novel as a man possessing at least two big treasures. The first refers to his deep intellectual and practical knowledge, that he shares with Dantès giving him classes in prison, and to his firm morality, as we can verify in the case in which after the plan of the flight then not being given a certainty, Dantès proposes to the Father the killing of a guard, a behaviour that is refused categorically by Faria, who says: "You do not know, my friend, what type of courage this is. I drilled a wall and destroyed a staircase but I am not going to pierce a chest nor destroy an existence ... The laws of society do not condemn the murder but the laws of the human nature condemn it."[12]

The second treasure, is the material treasure, real and buried in the so-called island of Monte Cristo, from there the name of the Count. It is interesting to remember that what provides the development of the novel as such is the discovery of the treasure, this one being linked uniquely and exclusively to the person of Father Faria.

If we refer to the figure of Father Faria of Dumas remembering the hypnotist Abade Faria, we can interpret that the treasure imagined by Dumas may have been an allusion to the doctrine of somnambulism of Abade Faria, a treasure that served for enjoyment as much as in the prison of the novel, as much as in real life of Abade, but whose existence was confirmed by scientists, in the novel by Dantès, some decades after the death of José Custódio of whom many had profit.

The success of this novel of Alexander Dumas, father, had, not only in his age widespread publicity, and this not only in its literary form. In 1848 the first theatrical play based on this novel of Dumas was performed in *Théatre Historique* of Paris,[13] in which Abade Faria maintains the same fundamental role in the course of the plot and which was a great success. This play was followed by many others, culminating in the adaptation of the novel to the film screen in France in 1942 (director R. Vernay). The last renowned film was made in 1998 and shown also on television with Gerard Depardieu in the main role as Edmond Dantès.

It is interesting to observe that as much in theatre as in cinema the prison scenes and the appearance of Father Faria cannot be hidden in any scene and in no literary reference, since it is, exactly, through this encounter and this relationship that the story of the novel can unfold, since without Father Faria there would not have been the Count.

After years of work as a experimenter and hypnotist, after years of disillusion and disgust for being badly treated and for lack of respect and admiration that he suffered, Abade Faria dies on September 20, 1819 in great poverty and almost total oblivion. Which motives could have taken the famous French romanticist, Dumas, father, to rediscover this figure seen frequently as gloomy and till the date of the release of the novel still forgotten, and bring it up more than 26 years after its death?

It is interesting to observe here from the beginning that Alexandre Dumas had an end of life similar to that of Abade Faria. He died poor after having been so rich, forgotten and ignored by the dominant realism movement.

We can affirm that Dumas did not have knowledge, at the time of working out the novel, of the scientific work of rehabilitation of the work and of the personality of Abade Faria. What we know with some certainty is that Dumas did not take part in any session nor knew Abade Faria personally. I surmise that Dumas may have heard many times about Abade Faria, the personality that developed in the writer a great admiration.

Dumas had a great preference for questions of the occult. It is quite probable that he already may have taken part at *Villers-Cotterets,* where he was born, the discussions of the time on somnambulism and hypnotists. Besides this, we know that Dumas took part in the Congress and the demonstrations of Hyppolite Bernheim at Hôtel-Dieu.[14] His conviction of the existence of supernatural forces he published in the article "Etudes sur le somnambulisme".[15]

Many facts lead us to believe that on arriving in Paris in 1823, three and half years after the death of Faria, Dumas may have heard about this master, about his life and practices.[16] We cannot say with certainty if Dumas had known, through his own readings, the work of Faria which had been released in the year of his death 1819. What we can affirm is that the French romanticist believed in animal magnetism and that he promoted sessions on somnambulism in his house.[17]

All this proximity of Dumas to magnetism and somnambulism becomes even more clear to us if we consider that this theme also appears in his other works, like , for example in novels *Der Ratschluß des Magiers*, and in the trilogy *Mémoires d'un Médecin* (*The Reminiscences of a Doctor).* In the first part of this trilogy about José Bâlsamo and written during 1846-48, soon after the death of the Count of Monte Cristo, the author makes a mix between real political history and fiction, and develops his figures basing himself on real history as in the case of Father Faria, but giving them fictitious characteristics. Bâlsamo (also called Count Cagliostro) has extraordinary hypnotic talents and knows the power that he possesses in manipulating persons through his techniques. His ambitions are high, he wishes to change society, but not in a positive manner. Through the manipulations of hypnosis he becomes an obscure "doctor of magic", making many persons his victims. In this novel linked to the history of French Masonry, Dumas demonstrates once more, his positive position before hypnotism. In an age in which magnetism moves away from scientific circles, and charlatanism encompasses a large number of hypnotists, reaching in this way public opinion, Dumas calls attention to this situation, aligning himself once more, for a serious and respected hypnotism.[18]

Naturally, not only Dumas was interested in that age by the phenomena of somnambulism. The enthusiasm was present in academic circles, in the halls of the aristocracy and in literary circles. Honoré de Balzac published in 1841 *Ursula Mirouet* which could be seen as a manifesto for Anton Mesmer (1734-1815) and for Mesmerism.[19] Victor Hugo (*Les Misérables*, 1862), E.T.A. Hoffman (*Der Magnetiseur*, 1814-15), are only some of the great names of European literature, which within the so-called "fantastic stories" concern themselves deeply with the essential questions of animal magnetism and hypnotism.[20]

A. Dumas, father, gave a real name to a fictitious figure, becoming thus unquestionably, responsible for the publicity of Abade Faria in world literature. Today one comes across news about the existence and role of Abade Faria in diverse literary forms. Tourist guides of France, India and Germany (Merian and Goa-Dumont, 1997) for example, and even on the Internet, one comes across many addresses, referring to Abade Faria. In one of them we read, "Very important personality of Goa. Founder of Hypnotism." [21]

I wish to end with a line from the novel which I think represents well Abade José Custódio de Faria and his work, as well as Alexandre Dumas: "Do you know, Faria asks Edmond Dantès, that from the collision of the clouds comes light?. No", replies Dantès. The readers of the two writers also did not know the truth about magnetism.

NOTES AND REFERENCES

1. Egas Moniz, *O padre Faria na história do hipnotismo*, Lisbon: Faculdade de Medicina de Lisboa, 1925, p. 72.

2. Faria stated that he could kill a bird by hypnotizing it. He was asked to prove it and he failed for he did not succeed in killing the bird. Chateaubriand concluded: "Chretien, ma seule presence avait rendu le trépied impuissant" (Moniz, p. 61).
3. To distinguish more clearly the real Faria from the fictitious, I will refer in the course of the text of Abade Faria to the real José Custódio de Faria and to Father Faria, the fictitious figure of the novel of Alexandre Dumas.
4. Alexandre Dumas, *Der Graf von Monte Christo*, Frankfurt/M: Insel Verlag, 1978, vol. I, p. 142.
5. In the play of Jules Vernet, "Magnétismomanie" which was presented in the theatre of Varietés, on September 5, 1916 in which Abade Faria was ridiculed, we can see, among other negative moments, an open racism against Abade. An example could be the following passage in which the figure of Soporito (which represents Faria), says: "*Vê bem, tudo está em nos entendermos. E agora não diga que sou tão mau como sou negro* (See well, it is all about we understanding ourselves. And now I do not say that I am so bad as I am dark" (Moniz, p. 152).
6. Dumas, *op. cit.,* p. 146.
7. This was constructed by the decree of king Francis I, who decided to construct a fort there. The castle was completed in 1528 and from 1580 it became a prison of the state. Imprisoned there, were important figures of French literature created by Alexandre Dumas, father, like Edmund Dantès and Father Faria and "O Homem da máscara de ferro" (The man of iron mask). But in the castle of If there were not only fictitious figures. The Count of Mirabeau (Honoré Gabriel Riqueti, 1749-1791) was one of his real prisoners of renown. In 1515 the castle of If kept the first rhinoceros which came to Europe. It was painted in the same year by Albrecht Dürer (1421-1528).
8. Dumas, *op. cit.*, p. 136.
9. Dumas, *op. cit.*, vol. II, p. 1156.
10. I use the 1978 edition, Editora Insel, German translation.
11. Dumas, *op. cit.*, vol. II, p. 1155.
12. Dumas, *op. cit.*, vol. II, p. 139ff.
13. In 1862 the play was staged once more in *Ambigu* and in 1880 in *Gaité*. The presentations of October 1,1883 - also in *Gaité* - served to increase financially the collection for the statue of Alexandre Dumas, which was inaugurated three days after the first show in the Malesherbes Square.
14. Dominique Barrucand, *Histoire de l'Hypnose en France*, Paris: Presses Universitaires de France, 1967, p. 173.
15. Ingrid Kollak, *Literatur und Hypnose. Der Mesmerismus und sein Einfluß auf die Literatur des 19 Jahrhunderts*, Frankfurt/M: Campus Verlag, 1997, p. 158.
16. Basing myself on the biographical notes that I have of Dumas, this seems most probable that he may have attended the classes of Bertrand on somnambulism, which were of his time. In these lectures, the name of Abade Faria was frequently cited.

17. G. A.. Gentil, *Initiation aux mystères-secrets de la theórie et de la pratique du magnétisme, residue simple et facile quant a la pratique, simple et explicative quant aux principaux phènomènes derivant du somnambulisme, etc., suivi d'experiences inèdites faites à Monte-Christo, chez Alexandre Dumas, et de la Biographie de J. B: Marcillet*. Paris. 1848.
18. Barrucand, *op. cit.*, p. 49.
19. *Ibid.*, p. 47.
20. Kollak, *op. cit.*, pp. 154-166.
21. 207.92.103.87/goa/manyear.htm

BIBLIOGRAPHY

Ackerknecht, Erwin H., *Kurze Geschichte der Psychiatrie,* Stuttgart: Enke, 1967, 2nd ed., p. 84.

Adler, Alfred, *Dumas und die böse Mutter. Über zehn historische Romane von Alexandre Dumas,* d. A. Berlin: Erich Schmidt Verlag, 1979.

Barrucand, Dominique, *Histoire de l'hypnose en France,* Paris: Presses Universitaires de France, 1967, pp. 69ff.

Bernheim, Hippolyte, *Neue Studien ueber Hypnotismus, Suggestion und Psychotherapie (Hypnotisme, suggestions, psychothérapie, études nouvelles,* 1891*).* Uebersetzt von Dr. Sigmund Freud, Leipzig: Franz Deuticke, 1892, pp. 45, 561.

--------, *Die Suggestion und ihre Heilwirkung (De la suggestion et ses applications à la thèrapeutique*, 1896), Leipzig: Franz Deuticke, 1896, p. 105.

Bertrand, *Traité du sonambulisme*, Paris, 1823.

Bonin, Werner, *Lexikon der Para-Psychologie und ihrer Grenzgebiete*, Munich: Orbis Verlag, 1988, p. 174.

Burkhard, Peter, "Hypnotherapie", in Raymond J. Corsini (ed.), *Handbuch dèr Psychotherapie,* Weinheim: Psychologie Verlagsunion, 1987, vol. 1, p. 338.

Chateaubriand, Françoise R., *Mémoires d'outre-tombre*, Paris, 1843.

Crocq, *L'hypnotisme scientifique,* Paris: Societé d'Editions Scientifiques, 1895, (1st ed.), 1900 (2nd ed.), p. 9.

Dalgado, D. G., *Mémoire sur la vie de l'abbé de Faria. Explication de la charmante légende du chateau d'if dans le roman Monte-Cristo,* Paris, 1906.

--------, *Préface et introduction à la deuxième édition du livre de l'abbé Faria.*

Doucet, Friedrich, *Geschichte der Psychologie. Von den vorchristlichen Philosophen bis zu den Seelenärzten des 20, Jahrhunderts*, Bindlach: Gondrom, 1971, pp. 91ff.

Ellenberger, Henry F., *Die Entdeckung des Unbewußten,* Bern: Huber, 1973, vols. I-II.

--------, *The discovery of the unconscious,* 1973, p. 121.

Faria, L'Ábbe de, *De la cause du Someil Lucide, ou Etude de la Nature de L'Homme*, Paris, 1819, tome I.

Fröbes, Joseph S. J., *Lehrbuch der experimentellen Psychologie*, Freiburg/Brsg.: Herder, 1920, Bk. II, p. 589.

Goa, Dumont Reisetaschenbücher , Cologne: Dumont, 1997, 2nd ed.

Hehlmann, Wilhelm, *Geschichte der Psychologie*, Stuttgart: Kröner, 1963, p. 219f.

Kindler Neues Literaturlexikon, Munich: Kindler Verlag, 1988.

Langen, D., *Kompendium der medizinischen Hypnose,* 1972, p. 109.

Pitres, A., *Leçons clinique sur l'hysterie et l'hypnotisme faites à l'hôpital Saint André de Bordeaux,* Paris, 1891, vol. II, p. 114.

Schmidbauer, Wolfgang, *Psychotherapie. Ihr Weg von der Magie zur Wissenschaft,* Munich: DTV, 1975, p. 169.

Siwek, Paulo, *Psicologia experimental,* São Paulo: Editora Anchieta, 1949, p. 399.

Trömner, E., *Hypnotismus und Suggestion. Aus Natur und Geisteswelt,* Leipzig: Teubner, 1922, Bd. 199, 4th ed, pp.15f.

Völgyesi, Franz, *Die Seele ist alles. Von der Dämonologie bis zur Heilhypnose*, Zurich: Orell Füssli, 1948, p. 313.

Wilpert, Gero von, *Kröner Lexikon der Weltliteratur,* Stuttgart: Kröner Verlag, 1988, 3rd ed.

26

Morphosyntactic Realignment in Dravido-Portuguese Creoles Under a Diachronic Perspecitve

SEBASTIÃO IKEN

With the arrival of the fleet of Vasco da Gama in India in 1498, the first language contact between speakers of Dravidian languages and speakers of European Portuguese or Portuguese-creole took place. Within five hundred years of continued contact between these language communities there are influences and interferences on both involved languages. This language contact has some very peculiar characteristics that are very interesting for the linguistic analysis and specially for the theory of the origin of Portuguese-based creoles.

In their historic evolution, the Romance languages and the Dravidian languages developed divergent syntactic structures that are typologically incompatible. Dravidian languages, like many other Indian languages, maintained the SOV (subject-object-verb) predominance in the syntax while Romance languages opted mainly for the SVO structure. So, with the discovery of the sea-route to India, two languages with completely antagonistic syntactical structures were brought together. In this conflicting situation, the contact languages like Indo-Portuguese creoles had to decide whether to follow the Romance or the Dravidian syntax pattern. The crucial question formulated by Schwarz and others before, is, "If SVO is set in conflict with SOV, what will emerge?" (cf. Theban 1985, 271).

While the European Portuguese preserved the SVO structure, former studies on Indo-Portuguese proved that in the Indo-Portuguese creoles the syntax converged mainly to the Indian language substrat (cf. Theban 1975, 1977; Smith 1979a, 1979b; Goonatilleka 1985 et al) that relegates the verb to the final position. These synchronic studies finally showed that the Indo-Portuguese creoles were formed mainly by a lexicon of Portuguese origin and a syntactic structure based on Indian languages:

Eu vou a/para casa	(modern European Portuguese, SVO)
Eu ca:sa pa tanda (está andar)	(Batticaloa Creole, SOV)
Mama ged r yan va	(Sinhala, SOV)
Na : n viTT po : ran	(Tamil, SOV)
Eu como arroz	(modern European Portuguese, SVO)
Eu aro:s ta cume (está comer)	(Batticaloa Creole, SOV)
Mam bath kan va	(Sinhala, SOV)
Na : n so : ru sa : ppiTuran	(Tamil, SOV) (Goonatilleka 1985, 162)

When and how did the change from SVO to SOV happen? Was this process spontaneously given since the first moment of the language-contact or is it a younger process that developed slowly during the last hundred years as is supposed by Smith and others (cf. Smith 1979a, 1979b, 1984; Bartens 1995; Clements 1996). The other question is, what role does this process of syntactic reorganisation play in the formation of Indo-Portuguese creole? Two hypotheses will be analysed in diachronic perspective:

1. the syntactic reorganisation in Indo-Portuguese based on the Indian morphosyntactic patterns is older than supposed and
2. it is not necessarily bound to the "pidginisation and creolisation" process.

The theory of creole studies developed various explanations for their historical evolution (cf. Couto 1996). We will not discuss these models here but limit ourselves to the fact that they are undoubtedly the result of language contact. In the basic model it is supposed that during the first contact between two different languages an artificial and elementary language (pidgin) is automatically created for essential communication in trade and cultural exchange. This simple structured contact-language of a bilingual or multilingual community could establish itself as first and exclusive language or natural mother tongue of the first generation resulting from the given contact of the two speaker communities. This new natural language, denominated creole, has its own structures and gets more and more complex in its structure during further evolution. Apart from its own evolution and while the creole language is kept in contact with one or the other language that participates in the original language contact, it can converge successively to the structure of one or the other language pattern (cf. scheme 1). In this process the creole language can also disappear when the specific traits of the creole language are eliminated in case of perfect acquisition of one or the two languages brought into contact.

<u>**Scheme 1**</u>

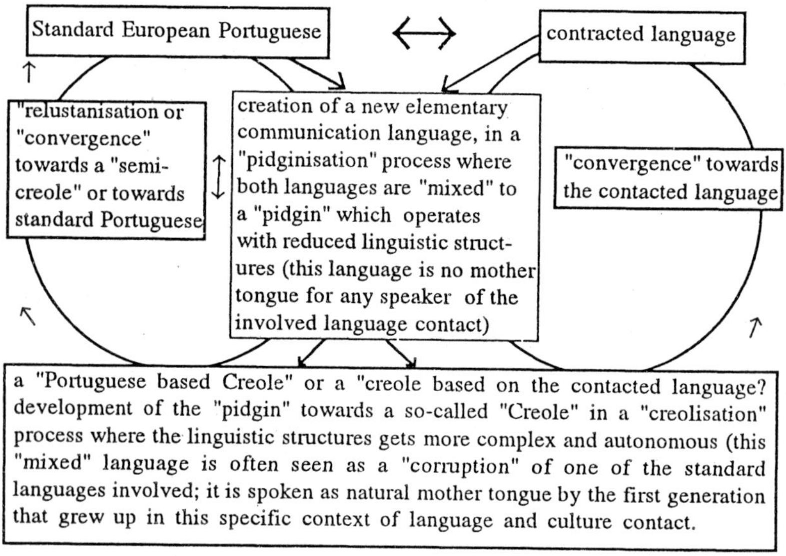

Creole language theory discusses also the base of a given creole supposing that there has been a language that has taken the role of substrat and another that has taken the role of superstrat on the formation of a specific creole-language. In view of the world-wide similarities in structure of the Portuguese-based creoles the hypothesis of a monogenesis for all these creoles as opposed to the pure language-contact model or others (e.g. "baby-talk" theory, cf. Couto 1996) is discussed. So we have many evolution models in the creole theory that could not been proved because there is no historical evidence for them (cf. Smith 1984, 298). In this context we want to present some historical documents that may show the diachronic evolution of a morphosyntactic structure, the conflict of preposition or postposition of the verb-auxiliary in analytic tenses in combination with the SVO-SOV conflict. Thus we expect to give an answer to the chronology of the syntactic reorganisation in the formation of the syntax structure found in creoles today. The further discussion can be schematised as follows: (See next page)

The oldest Portuguese documents produced in Asia were generally written by the Portuguese themselves and reflect, of course, metropolitan standard Portuguese. In these documents, which generally reveal a high language level, the SVO-order is maintained. Some Portuguese texts partly written by non-native speakers for instance, present "corruptions" that allow us to reconstruct the diachronic evolution from SVO to SOV. As shown before there are SOV-sentences found in the Portuguese Bible translated by João Ferreira de Almeida, a Portuguese Protestant missionary in Batavia, and later on corrected by German Protestant missionaries at Tranquebar in the 17th and 18th centuries respectively, that possibly could be calqued on the SOV-pattern of Indian languages (cf. Iken 2000).

E fallando elles d'estas cousas, o mesmo Jesus no meyo delles se pós e lhes disse: (Batavia 1693)
E fallando elles destas cousas, o mesmo Jesus se poz no meyo delles e lhes disse: (Tranquebar 1760)

E entrou pera com eles se ficar (Batavia 1693)
E entrou para ficar com eles (Tranquebar 1760)

O que elle tomou, e diante de seus olhos [o] comeu (Batavia 1693)
O que elle tomou, e comeo (sic) diante delles (Tranquebar 1760)

Ainda que também alguas mulheres d'entre nosoutros nos tem espantado,
as quais de madrugada a o sepulcro forão: (Batavia 1693)
Ainda que também alguas mulheres dentre nosoutros nos espantaram,
as quais de madrugada forão ao sepulcro: (Tranquebar 1760)

Porque a o vivente entre os mortos buscais? (Batavia 1693)
Porque entre os mortos buscais a o vivente? (Tranquebar 1760)

Another even older document, a trilingual Portuguese, Latin and Tamil prayer book (*Cartilha em Tamul e Português*) published 1554 in Lisbon (Almeida 1970) deals obviously with the syntactic conflict between SOV and SVO. By giving a interlinear Portuguese translation of the Tamil version, it reorganises the Portuguese syntax following the Tamil pattern.

Scheme 2

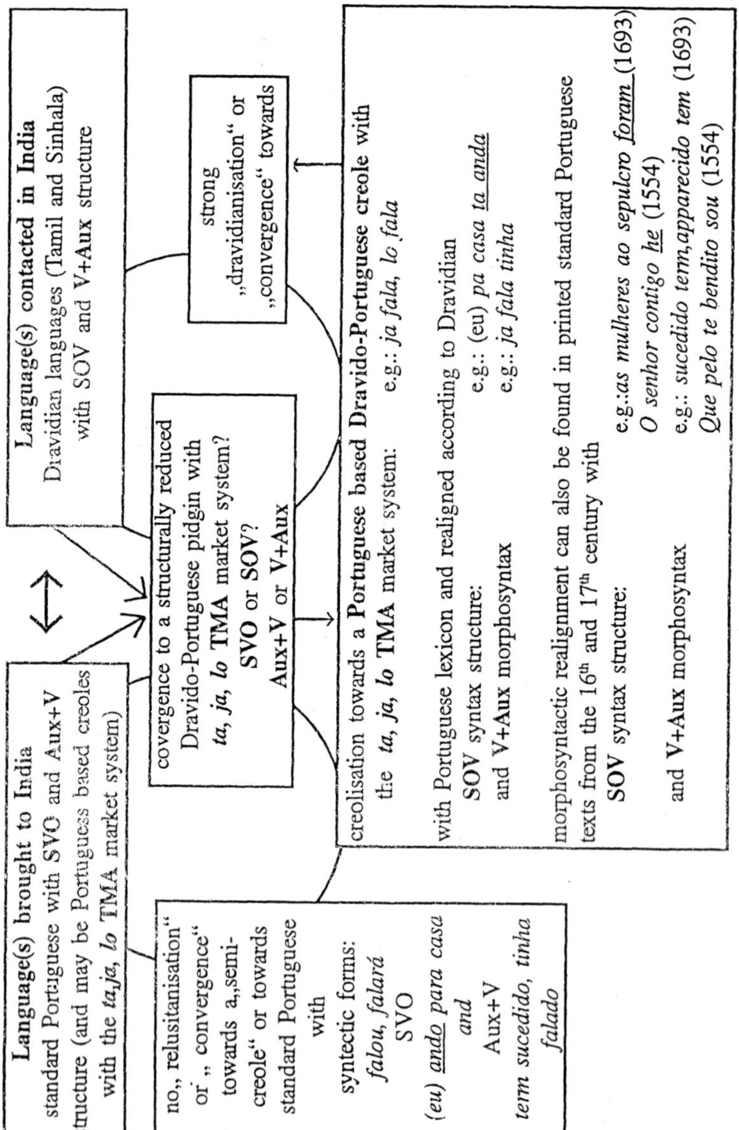
Language(s) brought to India
standard Portuguese with SVO and Aux+V structure (and may be Portuguess based creoles with the ta,ja, lo TMA market system)
Language(s) contacted in India
Dravidian languages (Tamil and Sinhala) with SOV and V+Aux structure
covergence to a structurally reduced Dravido-Portuguese pidgin with ta, ja, lo TMA market system?
SVO or SOV?
Aux+V or V+Aux
no„ relusitanisation“ or „ convergence“ towards a„semi-creole“ or towards standard Portuguese with syntectic forms:
falou, falará
SVO
(eu) ando para casa
and
Aux+V
tem sucedido, tinha falado
strong „dravidianisation“ or „convergence“ towards
creolisation towards a Portuguese based Dravido-Portuguese creole with the ta, ja, lo TMA market system: e.g.: ja fala, lo fala
with Portuguese lexicon and realigned according to Dravidian
SOV syntax structure: e.g.: (eu) pa casa ta anda
and V+Aux morphosyntax e.g.: ja fala tinha
morphosyntactic realignment can also be found in printed standard Portuguese texts from the 16th and 17th century with
SOV syntax structure: e.g.:as mulheres ao sepulcro foram (1693)
O senhor contigo he (1554)
and V+Aux morphosyntax e.g.: sucedido tem,apparecido tem (1693)
Que pelo te bendito sou (1554)

interlinear translation from Tamil	original version in standard Portuguese
de graça chea es maria acc. deos salve	*Deus te salve maria cheia de graça*
O senhor contigo he	*O senhor he contigo*
Antre as molheres tu es benta	*Benta es tu entre as molheres* (Almeida 1970)

In opposition to the evolution model given above, this example shows that the syntactic reorganisation of the sentence with Portuguese lexicon does not necessarily have to have undergone a reduction of the linguistic system in the sense of a pidginisation and then extended in the sense of a creolisation as supposed by Smith in another context.

"The paradox here is that in this very type of situation there is usually little evidence of prior pidginization (defined [...] as "reduction in inner form, with convergence, in the context of restriction in use") or creolization ("expansion in inner form, with convergence, in the context of extension in use" [...]). The process involved seems not to be one of reduction and expansion, but rather of realignment of aspects of the grammar of one (or more) of the contact languages until congruence is attained. I shall thus refer to convergence involving neither reduction nor expansion as *realignment.*" (Smith 1979a, 194).

Following Smith we define morphosyntactic realignment as reorganisation of the grammar of the sentence or the verbal syntagma in consequence of the interference of the pattern of another language in contact without necessarily having passed through a reducing and expanding pidginisation and creolisation process. We even go further admitting that the morphosyntactic realignment is a special Indo-Portuguese trait that is not necessarily linked to the evolution of the creole-universals that possibly are the prior results of these pidginisation and creolisation processes. Therefore we will analyse the morphosyntactic realignment in combination with the *ta, ja, lo* tempus-modus-aspect-system (TMA-system known in many Portuguese-based creoles world-wide) on the basis of examples from the Dravido-Portuguese creoles.

Today in Tricomalee and Batticaloa in Sri Lanka there are still small communities speaking Dravido-Portuguese creoles. It has been supposed that these creoles emerged during Portuguese colonial period (1517-1658). With the invasion of the Dutch in this area the creole communities lost their direct contact with the Portuguese undergoing other linguistic influences. They become bilinguals preserving creole as mother-tongue and acquiring Tamil or Sinhala as second language. Because of the strong and multisecular influence of the Dravidian languages in these Portuguese-based creoles, the SOV word order predominates nowadays (cf. Theban 1975, 1985; Smith 1979a, 1979b, 1984; Goonatilleka 1985). According to Smith, one of the most distinguishing characteristics of Sri Lankan creoles is the high morphosyntactic correspondence between them and the two local native Dravidian languages (Tamil and Sinhala). Some of the morphosyntactic structures of Sri Lankan Portuguese converged to the Dravidian pattern while others did not (cf. Smith 1984, 198).

Smith gives us a description of the verbal system of the Indo-Portuguese dialect spoken in Sri Lanka. Basically the time aspect is expressed with the following markers *ta* (< ptg. *está*, PRES), *ja* (< pt. *já* PASS), *lo* (< pt. *logo*, POT, FUT) and *ja:-ka:* (< ptg. *já acabar*, PERF) as known in other creoles (cf. Smith 1979a, 200):

	Creole	Tamil	English	Portuguese
pres.	*ta-prenda*	*paTi-kk-r-an*	"he is learning" "he learns"	"ele está a aprender/está aprendendo/ aprende"
adj. verb. pres.	*ta-prenda*	*paTi-kk-r-a*	"learning/who learns	"aprendendo/ que aprende"
pass.	*ja: -prenda*	*paTi-cc-an*	"he (already) learned"	"(já) aprendeu"
pass. perfectivo	*ja:-ka:-prenda*	*PaTi-cc-ir-ran*	"he has (already learned) (and finished)"	"(já) tem aprendido (e acabado)"
Potential	*lo-prenda*	*paTi-pp –an*	"he will learn"	"studaria/ estudarei, estudo, posso estudar"
perfectivò pot./fut.	*lo- ka:-prenda*	*paTi-cc-iru-v-a*	"he will learn"	"ele irá aprender, aprenderá"

A similar description of this verbal system is already given in *A Grammatical Arrangement On the Method of Learning the Corrupted Portuguese as Spoken in India* published by Berrenger in Colombo, Sri Lanka in 1811. Here the future tense and the present tense have the same forms of today's creoles, but the analytic forms of the past tense seem to follow the morphosyntax of standard European Portuguese using the auxiliar *ter* (cf. Berrenger 1811, 24 ff.):

	Corrupted Portuguese	English	High Portuguese
Present tense	eu te ama or eu tem amor	I love	eu amo
Future	eu lo ama	I will love	amarei
Preterperfect	eu já ama or já tinhe amor	I have loved	eu tenho amado
Preterimperfect	eu tinhe amor	I did love	amava
Preterimperfect Definite	eu tinhe ama(do) /tinhe amor	I loved	amei
Preterpluperfect	eu ja tinhe amor	I had loved	eu tinhe amado

Apart from the *ta, ja* and *lo* TMA-markers, Smith distinguishes two groups of auxiliaries in the Sri Lanka creole that have similar morphosyntactic functions. These auxiliaries can be colocated in two different positions in relation to the main verb. There are auxiliaries that were colocated left of the main verb, as in European standard Portuguese and others on their right, as in the Dravidian languages. The auxiliaries imported from Dravidian languages generally have a postverbal position while the auxiliaries originating from Portuguese are mostly located in a preverbal position. Only the Portuguese auxiliary *tem* can also assume preverbal and postvèrbal position in Sri Lanka creole. Thus Smith concludes, that there must be auxiliaries that are more or less bound than others in their morphosyntactic position.

> There are a number of preverbal elements which may be treated as prefixes: e.g. *ta-* (PRES), *ka:-* (PERFECTIVE), *pa-* (INFINITIVE), *se:m-* (ABẸSSIVE PARTICIPLE: 'without V-ing'). These are tightly bound in that they are not free forms and nothing may intervene (except other prefix) between them and the verb root. These forms have resisted being transferred to post-verbal position in analogy with the corresponding markers in Tamil and Sinhala. There is another set of forms which can be classed as auxiliaries – these are more loosely bound than the prefixes as they are free forms. One of these auxiliaries, *te:m* (ANTERIOR), is preverbal in Ptg. but post-verbal in SLP [Sri Lanka Portuguese]. The auxiliary *po:y* 'can' is still used preverbally, but may also be used postverbally in an infinitival construction calqued on Tamil/Sinhala. (Two other auxiliaries, *kera* 'want' and *nikara* (NEGATIVE HABITUAL) are found only in preverbal position. All 'new' auxiliaries (i.e. not tracable to Ptg. auxiliaries) are postverbal). (cf. Smith 1984, 297)

It seems that in Sri Lanka creoles the tempus aspect is expressed by a very complex system of markers, auxiliaries and synthetic forms. Apart from the perfect participle also used in these creoles, there were three different systems for the expression of the temporal aspect with auxiliaries and markers that partially concur in the development of the Sri Lanka creole:

1. the characteristic creole *ta, ja, lo* TMA-marker system; these markers were tightly bound to creole preverbal position;
2. the Portuguese auxiliaries system (*tem*, *haver, poder, ser*, etc.); these auxiliaries were loosely bound to the European Portuguese preverbal position and sometimes also found in postverbal position, and
3. the Dravidian auxiliaries system; these auxiliaries were bound to Dravidian postverbal position.

Although in modern European Portuguese the particle *já* does not have the same modifying value as in creoles, it also marks a perfective aspect to constructions of the type *já tem aparecido* or *já apareceu* as we can observe in the following versions of a sentence taken from various Bible translations from 1693, 1760 and 1960.

> *Que dizião: verdadeiramente o Senhor resuscitou, e ja a Simão apareceu.* (Batavia 1693)
> *Que dizião: verdadeiramente resuscitado he o Senhor, e ja a Simão tem apparecido*. (Tranquebar 1760)
> *Os quais diziam: O senhor ressuscitou e já apareceu a Simão!* (Rio de Janeiro 1960)

In the constructions of the type *já tem aparecido* or *já apareceu* the "perfective" aspect and the notion of "conclusion" or "anteriority" is obviously stronger than in the simple constructions of the type *apareceu* or *tem aparecido*. As we already showed, in Sri Lanka creole these aspects can be expressed with the particles *ja* and *ca* (cf. Smith 1979b, 192). But to express "perfectiveness" this *ca* and *ja* tempus-marker-system is also complemented in mixed type constructions formed with a creole marker and a past participle form from the European Portuguese:

> part. perfectivo ***(ja:)-prenda-tu*** *paTi-cc-ir-r-u*
> "(já) tendo aprendido (e acabado)" (Smith 1979a, 200)

With the second group of auxiliaries, with Portuguese origin and less tightly bound to their preverbal position we can observe the development of this process of system interference. The auxiliary can be colocated between the marker and the verb MAV (marker, auxiliary, verb) in analogy to the construction of the type MMV (marker, marker, verb) shown above:

osTr kumere ja-ka-kume (MMV)
"He has eaten the food up" (Smith 1979b, 192)
(ele comeu, ele já açabar comer/ "ele já acabou de comer"

Passado Anual Grandi Juntumantu sua minutas lo fica ler (MAV)
([...] "will have been read", [...]logo ficar ler/"vai ter sido lido")
Contas-discontas 30-8-70 ate lo fica thiradu (MAV)
Puliyadikudah escola de San Sebastião tu lo fica juntadu (MAV)
(Theban 1983, 278)

This is a frequent process expressing anteriority and perfectivity in the past also used in other Indo-Portuguese creoles:

	Corrupted Portuguese	English	High Portuguese
Preterpluperfect	eu ja tinhe amado *(MAV)*	I had loved	eu tinhe amado *(*Berrenger 1811, 24 f.*)*

cart ja ficá recebido (Indo-Portuguese from Cochin; cf. Theban 1975, 218)
(já ficar recebida/"já foi recebida" PERF. + ANT.)

But perfectivity and anteriority can also be expressed using another concurrent construction that operates with reduplication, a typical characteristic of many creole languages:

Inna: bo:s tâ – fala: âwârâ oy me: ***ja: -fâla: fâla: -tu***
Agora aqui você está dizendo, que ele lhe falou só hoje (cf. Couto 1996, 279)
(agora você está falar/"está falando", que ele já falar/"falou" falado "tinha falado" ANT. só hoje)

To express anteriority of an action in the past in relation to another action also located in the past we find another even more complex construction in creole that gives continuity to the mixed system with Portuguese past participle and creole markers:

e:li ja:fâla: e:w ja:-ka:-fâla: fâla:-tu
Ele disse que eu lhe falara (Couto 1996, 279)
(ele ja falar "falou", (que) eu já acabar falar falado "lhe tinha falado")

In order to express the anteriority in the past it is also possible to opt for another type of construction based on the auxiliary *ter* that converges to the European Portuguese pattern. But in this construction the auxiliary is located postverbally, a phenomenon of convergence to the Dravidian syntax pattern:

Ung gota je:ntis -pa me: (ja) fala: tiña
"Tinha falado a pouca gente somente" (Smith 1979, 202)
(uma gota de gente já falar tinha "já tinha falado" ANT.+PERF. para mim)
eli ***kume-tam tem/tiña***
"He is/was eating" (Smith 1979b, 194)
(ele comer está tem/tinha "ele tem/tinha de comer" IMP.)

Historical documents allow us to reconstruct the diachronic process proven by the following example taken from an Indo-Portuguese Bible from 1852 published in Colombo, Sri Lanka, in the middle of the 19th century.

E ele ja falla per elle, tua irmão ***ja vi tem****, e tua pai ja mata vaquinha.*
(cf. Schmitt 1994, 617)
(e ele ja falar "falou-lhe" (bras.: para ele!), teu irmão já vir tem "já tem vindo/viera" ANT.+CONT., e o teu pai já matar "matou" a vaquinha)

The question is whether this process of morphosyntactic realignment is also based on the morphosyntactic transformations found in a Bible translated by the Portuguese Protestant João Ferreira de Almeida and published 1693 in Batavia. Later the syntax of this translation was "corrected" by the German Protestant missionary, Nikolaus Dal in another edition published in 1760 at Tranquebar.

Porém respondendo o hum, que se chamava Cleophas, disselhe: Tu só es peregrino em Jerusalem; e não sabes as cousas que nella estes dias ***succedido tem****?* (Batavia 1693)

Porém respondendo o hum, que se chamava Cleophas, disse-lhe: Tu só es peregrino em Jerusalem, e não sabes as cousas que nella estes dias tem succedido? (Tranquebar 1760)

Mas nosoutros esperavamos que elle era o que avia de redimir a Israel; porem ainda sobre tudo isto hoje he o terceiro dia desde que estas cousas ***succedido tem****.* (Batavia 1693)
Mas nosoutros esperavamos que elle era o que avia de redimir a Israel; porem ainda sobre tudo isto hoje he o terceiro dia desde que estas cousas tem succedido. (Tranquebar 1760)

Although we did not find an example in creole with the same morphosyntactic oscillation for the Portuguese auxiliary *ser* the transposition of this auxiliary was found in various Indo-Portuguese printings from the 16th to the 19th century.

Por tuo filho unico
Te, Deos graças darei
Que pelo te ***bendito sou***
na Luz de dia andarei... (Vasconcellos 1987, 142)

Que dizião: verdadeiramente ***resuscitado he*** *o Senhor, e ja a Simão tem apparecido* (Tranquebar 1760)

interlinear translation from Tamịl version:	*Do sancto xto pois graça concebido foy da virgem maria naceo:*
Latin version:	*Qui conceptus est de spu sancto: natus ex maria virgine.*
Portuguese version:	*O qual foy concebido do xto sancto naceo de maria virgem:* (Almeida 1970)

In this last example an interference of the Latin version of the prayer could also be supposed. It has to be denied because the interlinear translation from the Tamil version has the explicit intention of reproducing the syntactic structure of the Tamil language (cf. Almeida 1970, Iken 2000). Neither these older documents or creole studies found yet prove the transposition of the other Portuguese-based auxiliaries like *ficar, estar* or *acabar* to postverbal position. The last two auxiliaries entered the Dravido-Portuguese creoles in a reduced form as markers *ta* and *ca* assuming a new morphosyntactic function in the language structure together with the markers *já* and *lo*. But they must be distinguished because *ta* and *ca* are deverbal while *ja* and *lo* are based on adverbs. Theoretically, and according to the presented realignment model, they could be translocated to a postverbal position like the other Portuguese based verb auxiliaries *ser* and *ter*. But no proof was found in the analysed texts. On the contrary, and as has been said before, there is a strong bonding of all the four creole-markers to the preverbal position. This, so Theban, seems to be a special – and maybe the only - structural peculiarity of the creoles that has not been found in any other language (cf. Theban 1975, 219).

"Em especial o hindi, o tamúlico e as outras línguas da Índia situam o paciente da oração à esquerda da base verbal, ordenando o os modificadores de tempo, aspecto e modo do lado direito obtendo desta forma uma estrutura equilibrada: PVv. Em contrapartida os crioulos indo-portugueses mais evoluidos e estáveis colocam surpreendentemente os modificadores (*tá, já, lo*) do mesmo lado do paciente deixando terminar assim a frase abruptamente com a base verbal: PvV" (cf. Theban 1975, 219)

Theban illustrates this with the following example taken from Indo-Portuguese spoken in Tellicherry:

fruita alvri su riba su ja cai (PS nS V, OSV) (cf. Theban 1975, 218)
(a fruta da árvore em cima dela já cair "caíu")

And in another study, published ten years later, Theban concluded:

"Já aludi à tendência de alguns crioulos indo-portugueses para mudar a estrutura sequencial, relegando, à maneira indiana, o verbo para posição final. Ora, a estrutura oracional com verbo posposto ao paciente, ou objecto directo, implica morfemas verbais centrífugos [...]. Na maioria dos crioulos do mundo, portugueses ou outros, a posição dos morfemas temporais e aspectuais fixou-se rigidamente no modelo centrípeto, processo este, que se dera antes de o verbo ter começado a aparecer em posição final: embora contradizendo uma regra universal de implicação os morfemas *ta, ja, lo* não tem possibilidades de ser deslocados para centrífugos." (Theban 1985, 277)

We observe that the auxiliaries *estar* and *acabar* in creole suffered a strong reduction in form. We cannot say the same for the auxiliary *ter*. On the contrary we observe that in the use of this auxiliary two declinated forms were conserved: *tem* and *tinha* while most of the verbs in the creoles were reduced to one infinitive or imperative form (e.g. *ficá, cume, prenda, falla, mata,* cf. e.g. above). This leads us to the supposition that there is a structural difference in the morphosyntactic function and use of the markers *ta* and *ca* in relation to the auxiliaries *ter* and *ser*. Considering this phenomenon I would like to put forward the hypothesis that the development of these two different morphosyntactic structures took place in different and possibly independant processes.

Finally we investigated, why the morphosyntax of the construction with *ter* is calqued on the Dravidian pattern (MVA, cf. e.g. above) while the morphosyntax construction with *ficar* is calqued on the Dravido-Portuguese creole pattern (MAV=MMV, cf. e.g. above). This phenomenon might be explained by a semantic change that *tem* underwent during the evolution of the Indo-Portuguese creoles, as suggested and exemplified by Theban:

> "Derived from P[ortuguese] *tem* "(he) has" I[ndo]-P[ortuguese] *tem*, an invariable form, has become an all-purpose vP. The Portuguese construction HABEO (with *ter*) developed, in Indo-Portuguese, into a MIHI HABET structure, patterned on the MIHI EST type of the Indo-Aryan and Dravidian languages. *Tem* has, moreover, permeated the structure of an Indo-Aryan language spoken in a Dravidian setting, i.e. the Konkani language of Cochin. In his analysis of this so-called dialect of Marathi, A. M. Ghatage glosses, without giving any etymological hint, the frequent formative *te* as "particle of assertion, *is, are.*" Now in Malayalam and Kanarese, the copula is generally dropped in equational sentences, and so it is in certain varieties of Konkani. Thus Konkani of Kanara has *hem ek sune* "This a dog (is)", while the Konkani spoken in Cochin expands this sentence to *hem ek sune tem*. This surface carry-over from Indo-Portuguese has brought about changes in the sequential structure of Konkani too, as evinced by sentences like *hem te miggale khana* "This is my food", where the medial position of vP is atypical both Dravidian and Indo-Aryan languages". (Theban 1975, 212)

Indo-Portuguese of Daman: *jinel tinh fechad (a janela está fechada, the window was closed)*

Indo-Portuguese of Mangalore: *porta tem fechad (a porta está fechada, the window is closed)*

Indo-Portuguese of Sri Lanka: *o libro tem examinado (o livro é examinado/the book is examined)* (cf. Theban 1975, 218)

This phenomenon can also be found in the examples given by Berrenger:

> Corrupted Portuguese (High Portuguese/English)
> *[...] v.m. pode enquere [...] e pode acha sabe, se eu tem um bebedor o hum ladraô (você pode inquirir e pode achar saber, se eu sou um bebedor ou um ladrão? / you may enquire and ask [...] and can learn if ever Ihve been a drunkard or thief)*
> *de quem casta vos tem (de que casta você é /what caste are you of?)*
> *isti non tem mal tem boni (esta não está má, é boa/ this is not bad, it is good)*
> *tinhe papiado assi mas tem mentira (falou se nisso mas é mentira/ there is such a discourse but it is not true)* (cf. Berrenger 1811, 145 ff.)

When the auxiliary *tem* acquires the sense of "existence" like the auxiliary *ser* in the third person singular there are various reasons to translocate this auxiliary to postverbal position. On one hand *tem* with the auxiliary function can be differentiated from *tem* in the "existential" sense depending on the preverbal and postverbal position and on the other hand a possible homophony in constructions of the type *porta tem fechad* vs. *porta ta fechad* can also be disambiguated. This means that in the creole the semantic delimitation between the sense of *ser* and *ter* is not clearly traceable, because of the interference of Indian languages. And it is remarkable that only these two auxiliaries could be found in postverbal position in the documents from the 16th to the 19th centuries.

Distinguishing two different explanation models ("pidginisation and creolisation" vs. "realignment") for the evolutions observed in Portuguese-based creoles in southwest Indian subcontinent we discussed the hypothesis that the evolution of some morphosyntactic structures possibly are not the result of a pidginisation and creolisation process but of a possibly independent complex realignment process of morphosyntactic structures. In this realignment process the morphosyntax of standard Portuguese and Portuguese-based creoles in southwest India converged to Dravidian patterns, This realignment process can be observed in old Indo-Portuguese publications since the 16th century that are presumed to be printed in standard Portuguese.

In view of the great stability of the preverbal position of the creole markers *ta, ja, lo*, and *ca* and the characteristic homogeneity of this system of markers in creoles worldwide, it can be supposed that the formation of creoles involving a pidginisation and creolisation process might have taken place prior to Indo-Portuguese language contact. On the other hand the morphosyntactic realignment, i.e. the transposition of the auxiliaries *ter* and *ser* from preverbal to postverbal positions is a process that possibly took place during the language contact between Indian languages and standard Portuguese or Portuguese-based creoles. This hypothesis may also explain why there are only traces of morphosyntactic realignment in early Indo-Portuguese documents while they do not produce other traces of the Indo-Portuguese creole languages. That confirms the hypothesis formulated by Smith that the realignment processes do not necessarily have to be linked to the pidginisation and creolisation process in their diachronic evolution. This has also been shown recently by Clements for the specific case of Portuguese-based Creole spoken in Korlai (cf. Clements 1996).

The fact that there were two declined forms of the auxiliary *ter* (*tem* and *tinha*) might be interpreted as the result of a process of "relusitanisation" of the Portuguese-based creoles in southeast India. At the other hand the convergence to SOV and V+Aux morphosyntactic patterns should be interpreted as "Dravidianisation" of the Portuguese-based creoles. During this ambivalent evolution process of the creoles, Portuguese auxiliaries were (re)introduced to extend their verbal tempus-system in order to express complex tempus relationships. In this mixed system, situated in a strong bilingual Dravido-Portuguese context, the later adopted elements, like the Portuguese auxiliaries, were less bound to their fixed morphosyntactic position in standard Portuguese than the creole markers and were consequently translocated to the position the Dravidian morphosyntax demands.

BIBLIOGRAPHY

Bible editions

Tranquebar (1760): *Primeira parte do Novo Testamento de Nosso Senhor, e Salvador Jesu Christo, que contem os quatro Evangelistos convem a saber: S. Matheus, S. Marcos, S. Lucas, S. João.* Traduzidos em lingua portugueza pelo Reverendo Padre João Ferreira A. de Almeida Ministro Pregador do Santo Evangelho na cidade de Batávia. Revistos, e conferidos com o Texto Original pelos padres missionários de Trangambar na officina da real missão de Dinamarca. Anno de 1760.

Batavia (1693): *O Novo Testamento, isto he, Todos os livros do novo concerto do nosso fiel Senhor e Redemptor Jesu Christo*, traduzido na lingua portuguesa por João Ferreira A. d'Almeida. Batávia, João de Vries.

Rio de Janeiro (1960): *A Bíblia Sagrada, Antigo e Novo Testamento.* Traduzida em Português por João Ferreira de Almeida. Ed. revista e atualizada no Brasil. Sociedade Bíblica do Brasil, Rio de Janeiro.

Studies

Almeida, D. Fernando de [ed.] (1970): *Cartilha em Tamul e Português.* Impressa em 1554 por ordem do Rei. Edição fac-símile do museu de Arqueologia e Etnologia com um preâmbulo de D. Fernando de Almeida, Lisboa.

Bartens, Angela (1995): *Die iberoromanisch basierten Kreolsprachen*, Frankfurt am Main.

Berrenger (1811): *A Grammatical Arrangement On the Method of Learning the Corrupted Portuguese as Spoken in India*, Second Edition, Colombo.

Clements, Clancy (1996): *The Genesis of a Language. The Formation and Development of Korlai Portuguese*, Amsterdam/Philadelphia (Creole Language Library, 16).

Couto, Hildo Honório do (1996): *Introdução ao estudo das línguas crioulas e pidgins*, Brasília.

Filliozat, Jean (1967): *Un catechisme Tamoul du XVIe siècle en lettres latines*, Pondichéry (Institut Français d'Indologie, 33).

Goonatilleka, M. H. (1985): "A Portuguese creole in Sri Lanka. A brief Socio-linguistic Survey", in: Teotónio R. de Souza [ed.]: *Indo-Portuguese History. Old Issues, New Questions*, New Dehli. 147-180.

Iken, Sebastião (2000): "O português "por uso das malabaricas e portuguesas escolas" da missão protestante alemã de Tranquebar do século XVIII – Contribuição para o estudo diacrónico da sintaxe do português na Àsia", to be published in: *Akten der V. Deutsch-Portugiesischen Arbeitsgespräche: Portugal, Indien und Deutschland.*

Schmitt, Christian (1994): "Portugiesisch in Südostasien", in: LRL, VI, 2, Tübingen. 597-618.

Smith, Ian Russel (1979a): "Convergence in South Asia: A Creole Example", in: *Lingua* 48. 193-222.

------, (1984): "The Development of Morphosyntax in Sri Lanka Portuguese" in: *York Papers in Linguistics* 11. 291-301.

-------, (1979b): "Substrata vs. Universals in the Formation of Sri Lanka Portuguese", in: *Papers in Pidgin and Creole Linguistics* 2. 183-200.

Theban, Laurentiu (1985): "Situação e perspectivas do português e dos crioulos de origem portuguesa na India e no Sri-Lanka" in: *Actas. Congresso sobre a situação actual da língua portuguesa no Mundo, Lisboa 1983,* volume I, Lisbon. 269-286.

------, (1975): "From Creole Syntax to Universal Semantics", in: *Revue Roumaine de Linguistique* XX, 3. 207-224.

-------, (1977): "Indo-Románica: estruturas sintácticas em contacto", in: *Revue Roumaine de Linguistique* XXII, 2. 245-248.

Thiele, Petra (1991): "Situation und Perspektiven der asiatischen Lusokreolsprachen", in: Perl, Matthias/Schönberger, Axel [eds.]: *Studien zum Portugiesischen in Afrika und Asien,* Akten des 1. gemeinsamen Kolloquiums der deutschsprachigen Lusitanistik und Katalanistik Beihefte (Berlin, 20-23. September 1990), Frankfurt am Main. 49-71. (Beihefte zu Lusorama, 3ª. Série, tomo III)

Vasconcellos, J. Leite de (1987): *Esquisse d'une dialectologie portugaise,* Lisbon.

27

Angelo De Gubernatis and Goa

Correspondence between Angelo De Gubernatis and José Gerson da Cunha (1878-1899)

MARIA LUISA CUSATI

The aim of this work is to examine the letters of José Gerson da Cunha, a doctor and orientalist, born into an old family in Goa, who wrote to the Italian Prof. Angelo De Gubernatis, a scholar of oriental culture, a man of many interests. He was a comparative scholar, studying the relationships between literature and myths, a biographer, a dramatist, a poet and a novelist. We can easily say that he had a frenetic activity. He was a great organizer, he traveled a lot and he had the chance to meet many important personalities from all over the world. He kept a correspondence with many people and he left behind a large number of letters, today kept in the Biblioteca Nazionale in Florence. They represent an important documentation for the analysis of the interests of the society of his time.

At present, an ever increasing group of scholars, lead by Prof. Maurizio Taddei at the Istituto Universitario Orientale in Naples is carrying out a research aimed at reconstructing Prof. De Gubernatis' activity[1] and studying in particular the rich international relationships he created during his lifetime.

Angelo De Gubernatis was an important personality in the historical panorama of the international relationships between Italy and India. He was born on April 7, 1840; he lived in a period in which there was an extraordinary interest, especially at the political and institutional level, for Indian culture and for oriental cultures in general. As we shall see, his initiatives got official support from ministers and even from the King of Italy. In 1863, he was given the post of professor of Sanskrit at Regio Istituto di Studi Superiori Pratici e di Perfezionamento founded in Florence[2] on December 22, 1859. This Institute, a post-graduate school, opened

* Translated from the Portuguese by Charles J. Borges

many chairs in oriental disciplines in the philosophical and philological areas.

The young De Gubernatis enjoyed the exceptional privilege of studying in Berlin for a year, thanks to a grant, where he met such personalities as Albert Weber, one of the most important Indianists of that period, and Bopp, an old man by that time.[3] He says that he was used to studying fourteen hours a day, which is why he was able to achieve such a high level of competence after just a year abroad. In the meantime, the minister Michele Amari, knowing of his great dedication to his studies, offered him the chair of Aryan languages in the Regio Istituto in Florence when Prof. Giuseppe Bardelli left Florence to teach at the University of Pisa. After a few years, in 1872, in Florence the Società per gli Studi Orientali, was founded to further the studies "... delle lingue, delle letterature, degli usi e costumi dei popoli orientale" (of the language, literature, of the uses and customs of the eastern peoples).[4] Due to economic problems, the Società became an Academy linked to the Regio Istituto and as an Academy they published the *Bollettino degli Studi Orientali*. The director was Prof. Angelo De Gubernatis.

Florence was already the centre of major development in oriental studies when Prof. De Gubernatis, who officially took part in the 3rd conference of Orientalists'[5] in Petersburg, organized by Prof. Grigorieff of the same University, elected Florence for the 4th conference. Prof. Amari obtained the title of president and Prof. Angelo De Gubernatis was appointed general secretary of the new conference, arranged for September 1878. Before that date, De Gubernatis, besides the work *Memoria sui viaggiatori italiani nell'India*, wrote four plays with an Indian setting: *Nala, La morte di Dasaratha, Maya o L'illusione*, and *Savitri*. This latter, his favourite, was read out for the first time in 1877 before the Princess Margherita of Savoia and it was considered very interesting.

The correspondence between José Gerson da Cunha[6] and Angelo De Gubernatis began with the organization of the 4th conference. They were bound together by a close-friendship, a friendship that lasted until the end of their lives. The letters owned by the Biblioteca Nazionale in Florence, are forty eight, all written between 1878 and 1899. The other earlier letters must have been written to reach the agreements, which are at the basis of the first letters, which I have examined. These are addressed to the conference office (Bombay June 12, 1878), and confirm the delivery of five boxes of Indian idols and other objects ready to be exhibited during the conference. He also mentioned the delivery of a collection of coins and some ancient manuscripts to be received by the end of August.

In a second letter, he accepted the invitation and thanked De Gubernatis for a dinner (Florence September 10, 1872). It is with the third letter that the real correspondence between the two friends began. The first two letters are written in English, in the third one da Cunha declared: "Meu prezadissimo De Gubernatis, escrevo-te em portuguez, porque não estou ainda habilitado para escrever em italiano e tu me entendes o portuguez tão bem como a tua bella lingua materna. (My most esteemed De Gubernatis, I write to you in Portuguese because I am not yet qualified to write in Italian, and you understand my Portuguese as well as you do your lovely mother-tongue)." The correspondence between the two then continued in Portuguese and, we may say, on the basis of the first group of letters, that da Cunha was received very warmly in Rome. He treats several subjects. He thanks De Gubernatis a lot "...pelos favores que me tens feito e me continuas a fazer (for the favours you did for me and continue to do)." He reports on the most important acquaintances of his social life in Rome and he comments on political events, always worried about the future of his poor India where he hoped the Russians would shortly replace the British.[7] He was present at an audience of the Pope on October 7. Afterwards he received a letter from Cardinal Meria, who invited him to visit him[8] "...qual não foi o meu espanto quando o Cardeal depois d'um largo discurso elogístico por ser eu um bom cathólico e distincto litterato disse que o Papa lhe tinha encarregado de condecorar-me com o hábito de S. Gregorio Magno. Imagine meu caro De Gubernatis a minha confusão por um acto tão inesperado. Eu apenas pude balbuciar-lhe algumas palavras de agradecimento, beijar-lhe o sagrado anel e sahir com o *Breve Pontifical* que falla nos meus trabalhos concernentes à história *veterum indianum*. Assim estou um perfeito cavaliere (what was not my astonishment when the Cardinal after a long eulogistic discourse for me on being a good Catholic and a distinct literateur said that the Pope had entrusted him to confer on me the habit of St. Gregory the Great. Imagine, my dear De Gubernatis, my confusion by this so unexpected an act. I could only babble to him some words of thanks, kiss his sacred ring and leave with the Ponfitical Brief that speaks of my work concerning the history of a veteran Indian. Thus I have become a perfect chevalier)".

He received a lot of honours, so he was unable to leave on December 27, as he previously planned. "Tive audiências privadas do Papa, do Rei e da Rainha, que me foram muito benévolos. (I had private audiences of the Pope, of the King and of the Queen, who were very benevolent to me). He was received in many important houses and by the duke of Sermoneta "...disse-me que estava contente por eu ter visitado tanto o Papa como o

Rei, que era como um mago vindo do Oriente para reconciliar os dois inimigos, que era um ângulo d'um triangulo, um elemento de concordia vossa,... (he told me that he was happy that I had visited the Pope as well as the King, that I was like a magus come from the East to reconcile the two enemies, that I was one angle of a triangle, an element of your agreement)" and he comments: "...palavras benevolas (benevolent words)."

On December 31, he stated: "Ando muito occupado. A sociedade absorve-me todo o tempo. Visitas, seratas, almoços e jantares eis o meu modo de viver em Roma. Mas não me desagrada fazer a vida de vadio por poucos meses depois de longos anos de vida médica e de devoção aos estudos orientais que são cheios de seriedade. E depois esta vadiagem não deixa de ter mais vantagens. Estuda-se a sociedade em diversas formas e phases (I am very busy. The society engages all my time. Visits, serenades, lunches and dinners, these are my way of living in Rome. But it does not displease me to make a life of idling for a few months after many years of a medical life and of devotion to Eastern studies which are full of seriousness. And then this idleness has more advantages. One studies the society in its diverse forms and phases)".

In the meanwhile, he continued his scientific activity, he studied hard and cooperated with De Gubernatis on the *Dizionario Biografico degli Scrittori Contemporanei*. He completed and sent the paper which he presented at the conference in Florence and, for this paper, he received a prize of 500 liras. This prize gave da Cunha the opportunity to create a new prize: he offered as a prize more than 500 liras to the Accademia dei Lincei for the best research concerning the relationship between Italy and India. He told De Gubernatis about this in a letter dated October 20: "...recebi effectivamente um officio do Ministerio da Instrucção Pública para lá ir cobrar a soma de 500 francos. Ocorreu-me logo a ideia de dar a essa soma uma applicação mais duradoura da que teria na minha bolsa. Tu que me conheces bem, havias de ter adivinhado que a minha intenção quando escrevi a memória não era a de adquirir um prémio pecuniário como uma glória literaria, se tivesse a fortuna para tanto. Pensei pois que seria conveniente que entregasse essa soma e mais 500 francos meus, perfazendo a quantia de 1000 francos, à Accademia dei Lincei para dar em concurso para a melhor memória que lhe fosse apresentada sobre o seguinte thema: "As relações antigas e modernas entre a India e Italia - começando com o tempo dos Romanos e passando em detalhe pelos periodos durante os quaes as Republicas de Veneza, Genoa, Pisa e Florença entretinham relaçoes comerciais com a India estudando minuciosamente os escriptores italianos especialmente os viajantes e missionários como Marco Pollo,

Ludovico de Varthema, Pietro della Valle, Marco della Tomba... " (I received effectively an order of the Ministry of Public Instruction to go there to collect a sum of 500 francs. It occurred to me immediately the idea to give this amount a more durable application than the one I would have in my pocket. You who know me well, you may have guessed my intention when I wrote the memoir was not to get a financial reward as a literary glory, had I had the fortune for so much. I thought then that it would be convenient that I may entrust this amount and another 500 francs of mine, making up the sum of 1,000 francs, to the Academy of Lincei to give it in competition for the best memoir that might be presented to it on the following theme: the old and modern relations between India and Italy – starting from the time of the Romans and going in detail through the periods during which the republics of Venice, Genoa, Pisa, and Florence maintained commercial relations with India, studying very minutely the Italian writers especially the travelers and missionaries like Marco Polo, Ludovico de Varthema, Pietro della Valle, Marco della Tomba). This proposal, discussed at the Ministry needed the approval of the *Accademia.* Afterwards he continues: "Tinha só duas condições a impor, 1ª que a memória fosse escripta em italiano, pelo amor que consagro a esta grande nação, e que no jury para adjudicar o prémio entrasses tu, sendo tuas obras um fio d'Aryadne para os concorrentes e Amari (I had only two conditions to impose, first that the memoir may be written in Italian, by the love that I dedicate to this great nation, and that you may take part in the jury to decide the prize, your works being, *A String of Aryadne* for the competitors and Amari).

He kept working on the English translation of the play *Savitri*, which he had promised in order to carry out a translation in Gujarati later on. On October 27, he confirms "...o teu bello drama *Savitri* que eu estou traduzindo paulatinamente pela difficuldade que acho em converter o verso italiano em prosa ingleza para apenas que volte para a India verter nas linguas vernáculas e levar em scena nos theatros nativos (your beautiful drama *Savitri* which I am translating very slowly because of the difficulty that I find to convert the Italian verse into English prose, in order to, as soon as I return to India to turn it into the vernacular languages and take it to the stage in the local theatres)."[9] On February 2, 1883 he is again able to write to his friend announcing: "... o dia 27 de Janeiro foi célebre nos annaes deste paiz, porque vio pela primeira vez representada a tua peça "Savitri" no Theatro da India. Grande concurso e entusiasmo do povo. Vai ser repetido o drama no dia 9 deste (January 27 was famous in the annals of this country, because it saw for the first time your work *Savitri* represented on the Indian theatre. A great audience and the enthuiasm of the people. The play is going to be repeated on the 9th of this month)." It was his birthday and he thought that this was a great coincidence. He continued to receive more acknowledgements, and on December 9, 1878, in one of his letters, he informs his friend that the *Arcadia* gave him the title of "Filasto Filoetico"; in another letter dated December 25, he gives thanks for the diploma he received from the *Accademia Orientale* and De Gubernatis, but he was not really happy, he felt homesick: "...estou resoluto a sahir de Roma até 26 de Janeiro e embarcar-me em Nápoles no vapor da Companhia Rubaltino que sahe nesse dia e vai até Bombay. Dali vou immediatamente para a minha casa em Goa onde a minha família me espera anciosa, como me dizem as cartas que tenho à mão ... (I am determined to leave Rome by January 26, and take the boat of the Rubaltino Company in Naples that leaves on that day and goes to Bombay. From there I will go immediately to my home in Goa where my family awaits me anxiously, as say the letters that I have in hand)," and, on January 24, in the last letter written in Italy, he says: "Não esquecerei nunca as numerosas provas que me tens dado do teu tão desejado affecto, nem a estima que tenho merecido à tua amabilissima Senhora, de quem levo para a minha casa o lindo quadro de Raffael, que será conservado entre nós como uma preciosa reliquia. Lembrarei sempre dos teus estimaveis Pequenos, de quem tenho muitas saudades, e fallarei delles sempre à minha mulher e às minhas pequenas. Adeus meu caro. Da India hei de escrever-te frequentes vezes e lá estarei sempre à tua disposição (I will never forget the many proofs that you have given me of your so welcome affection, neither the esteem that I have merited of your most amiable lady, of whom I take home the lovely picture of Raphael, which will be preserved among us like a precious relic. I will remember always your small dear sons, of whom I have my memories, and I will speak of them always to my wife and to my young daughters. Goodbye my dear. From India I will write to you frequently and there I will always be at your service)". The conclusion is quite personal: "Resistindo a mil encantos e fascinações da sociedade Romana levo o coração inteiro para a minha família (Resisting the thousand attractions and fascinations of Roman society I take the whole heart for my family)".

On finally reaching Goa, José Gerson da Cunha could not help writing to his friend on March 4: "Meu queridinho. Eis-me aqui em fim no meu solo natal a lembrar-me sempre de ti, a fallar de ti e da tua caríssima Família à minha... Cheguei a Bombaim aos 18 de Fevereiro. Ahi esperava-me muita gente, especialmente os doentes alguns dos quaes visitei mesmo no dia do meu desembarque. Mas estava tão ancioso por ver a minha familia que no dia 19 tornei a embarcar n'outro vapor e vim para Goa, onde me esperava a minha família e amigos e patrícios que me receberam entre abraços, lágrimas e ovações... Envio-te algumas flores do meu jardim e do jardim do meu sogro. O primeiro fica na nossa casa de campo que é uma aldeia que se chama Arporá,[10] e o segundo na cidade de Nova-Goa. De Bombaim hei de escrever-te regularmente e mais em extenso... (My dear, here I am at last in my birthplace, remembering you always, speaking of you and of your dearest family to mine. I reached Bombay on February 18. There, many people were waiting for me, especially the patients, some of whom I visited the very day of my disembarkation. But I am so anxious to see my family that on the 19th. I again took another ship and came to Goa, where my family and friends and people of the same place were waiting for me and who received me with hugs, tears and exclamations. I send you some flowers of my garden and of the garden of my father-in-law. The first is in our house in the coumtryside which is a village called Arpora, and the second is in the capital city of Nova Goa. From Bombay, I will write to you regularly and more in detail). "

From 1879 to 1884 they regularly[11] sent many letters to each other, even on scientific subjects, and da Cunha, showing great esteem and ever available, supported each initiative of his Italian friend. In the meanwhile, his exhibition of Indians artefacts, at the 4th conference of the Orientalists was considered so interesting that many people hoped that his work would not be lost and that it would form the basis for more important and lasting initiatives. Besides offering the exhibits for the conference, da Cunha gave a lot of help to Prof. Paolo Mantegazza on his journey to India in 1882, and to De Gubernatis[12] on his own journey, between 1885 and 1886. All these artefacts, fabrics and manuscripts were exhibited in the Museo Indiano, that same museum which De Gubernatis opened on November 1886, in the presence of the King , the Queen and the Prince of Italy.

Through these letters, we can observe that the life of Dr. José Gerson da Cunha was complicated and very busy. The doctor's work was always so absorbing that it left him little time to catalogue the coins he promised De Gubernatis. Meanwhile, he started building a new house which was another cause of anxiety. On the subject of his house on June 8, 1886, he asked his friend to talk with Ximenes, the sculptor. He wrote: "Quanto me agradaria se o Sigr. Ettore Ximenes me mandasse o busto que prometteo, para a minha nova caza seria um óptimo ornamento. Eu escrevi-lhe uma vez, mas elle não responde. É o modo de proceder de tratantes. Ao menos me restituisse as 800 liras, que eu empregaria melhor. O meu dinheiro é bem ganho com fadigas pessoaes sem salario nem pensões governamentaes, e não é justo que o Ximenes fique com elle. Rogo-te o favor de lh'o mandar restituir-me (How much it would please me if Mr. Ettore Ximenes sends me the bust that he promised me, for it would be an excellent decoration for my new house. I wrote to him once, but he did not reply. This is the way of behaving of rogues. At least he should have returned to me the 800 liras that I would use better. My money is well earned with personal fatigue without government salary or pensions and it is not correct that Mr. Ximenes remains with it. I request you the favour to order him to return it to me)." In the following letter of July 13, he goes on: "O Ximenes prometteu fazer o busto e não fez. Aqui eu notara a *falta de honra* porque faltara à palavra. Tu foste o primeiro a pedir-me que o encarregasse a elle desta desgraçada obra, como consta das tuas cartas que eu conservo, e quando esperava ouvir que o busto estava completo, dizes que nada está feito. Foi com espanto que o ouvi (Mr. Ximenes promised to make the bust and has not done so. Here I had noticed the lack of honour because he had broken his word. You were the first to ask me that I might entrust to him this infamous work, according to your letters that I have, and when I expected to hear that the bust was complete, you tell me that nothing is done. I heard it with astonishment)". This statement of Gerson da Cunha's seems odd when compared to the one we read in the letter of December 1, 1879: "..... teres a bondade de pedir ao escultor Sr. Ximenes para mandar-me a copia em gesso do meu busto, quando elle o não queira para si. Rogo-te pois que saibas delle se está disposto a ceder-me essa copia e quanto será a despesa..... (may you have the goodness to ask the sculptor, Mr. Ximenes to send me the plaster copy of my bust, when he may not want it for himself. I ask you then to find out from him whether he is disposed to give me that copy and what will be the expenses)" and again in the one of January 1, 1880: "Chegou-me emfim o busto, que me mandou o Sr. Ximenes, ontem de tarde. E qual não foi o meu espanto quando abri a caixa? Estava toda a caixa cheia de agua salina e o busto reduzido a pedaços. Pobre busto! Vou vêr se algum escultor Indiano pode reunir esses bocados, e reconstruir a *figura*, que esta completamente *desfigurada* (Finally the bust that Mr. Ximenes sent me arrived yesterday afternoon. And what was not my astonishment when I opened the box? The whole box was full of salt water and the bust reduced to pieces. Poor bust! I am going to see if some Indian sculptor can put together these pieces, and redo the figure, which is totally disfigured)."

Is it possible that he forgot that he had received the bust? This is what we may deduce from the last letter in which the issue is mentioned, on June 19, 1889. This is one of the last letters he wrote to De Gubernatis.

He is in Paris, to discuss a sad matter: he is considering the sale of his collection of coins in order to have the funds to pay the debts incurred for the construction of his house, and "a propósito da casa, poderás dizer-me se o Ximenes quererá dar-me o busto para a minha casa nova! Há 11 anos que elle promette.... (regarding the house, you will be able to tell me if Mr. Ximenes would want to give me the bust for my new house! It is eleven years that he promises)".

The last letters that da Cunha wrote to his Italian friend are very harsh. His attitude towards everything seems different, more strict and severe. It is possible that he was very tired, due to the difficulties he faced and to his hard work, full of responsibilities. He could no longer accept and answer all De Gubernatis' requests, the latter, in spite of not having a strong body, went on, full of enthusiasm, traveling and working hard, sometimes above the possibilities of his physical capacities. He could not, then, easily understand other peoples' difficulties. I believe that what da Cunha wrote on February 23 regarding a performance of the drama *Savitri* while De Gubernatis was in Bombay is quite significant: "The truth is the *Savitri* was performed only once, as you know, after the one private rehearsal and was never repeated anywhere in India for the last two years. It is because the drama is unpopular as it is, and even the first performance was undertaken with considerable sacrifice of money both mine and of my Ráninà. I do not think you would like me to make any such sacrifice again amidst my other duties and expenses. I am always frank, especially with friends, because there is no greater source of unhappiness than deceit and equivocation. I am going next week to Goa and hope to be back to bid you farewell.

I hope you will be able to read these lines, as I write in great haste, and I am so busy. I am sincerely J. Gerson da Cunha."

The letter of July 13 sheds some light on the deteriorating relationship between the two friends, when Gerson da Cunha says: "Está claro pois que as tuas palavras duras, durissimas, não fazem mal a mim que tenho minha consciência pura, motivos sempre elevados, e sentimentos nobres, se a maneira às vezes brusca, o estilo rispido por causa da fadiga diaria e noturna do corpo e da mente num clima quente, que sabes que faz cançar. Mas tu, meu caro De Gubernatis, não compreendes nem, parece-me agora, nunca comprehendeste a minha amizade por ti. Eu te era, desde que o conheci, tão dedicado, que ainda hoje me chama a minha família a mim teu entusiasta. Mas vejo que a tua amizade não passa de uma burla.........Tenho recebido mais aggravos teus do que tu de mim. Eu é que sou a parte aggravada e tu o aggravante...... A tua sobranceira, o ar de superioridade com que me dedicaste os teus *drami indiani* são bem conhecidos. E eu não te aceito mais dedicatórias. Obrigado. Não quero mais. Se quizeres corresponder ainda com amizade, eu também o farei, senão, não (It is clear then that your hard, very hard words, do not matter to me, for I have a pure conscience, always high motives, and noble feelings, if the manner at times brusque, the harsh style, due to the day and night fatigue of body and mind in a hot climate, that you know makes one tired. But you, my dear De Gubernatis, do not understand or, I think now, never understood my friendship for you. I was to you, since I knew you, so dedicated, that even today my family calls me your enthusiast. But I see that your friendship is but a deceit. I have received more of your affronts than you of mine. I am the aggrieved party and you the aggriever. Your arrogance, air of superiority with which you have dedicated to me your Indian plays are well known. And I do not accept more of your dedications. Thank you. I do not want more. If you would wish to correspond again with friendship, I too will make it, otherwise not)".

Probably the two friends had a friendly talk about their misunderstandings, because da Cunha wrote on February 4, 1887: "Meu caríssimo De Gubernatis. Um tempo recebi a tua estimadissima carta com os prospectos do Museo Indiano e da Sociedade Asiática, monumentos da tua incançavel e gloriosa actividade, e o livro das tuas viagens na India. Agradeço-te do coração por todos estes favores, pela minha nomeação para a Sociedade Asiática Italiana e pela tua dedicatória, provas incontestáveis da tua amizade mais do que dos meus merecimentos (My dearest De Gubernatis. Once I received your most esteemed letter with the prospectus of the Indian Museum and of the Asiatic Society, monuments of your indefatigable and glorious activity, and the book of your journeys in India. I thank you from my heart for all these favours, for my nomination for the Italian Asiatic Society and for your dedication, incontestable proofs of your firiendship more than my merits)"

The last letter comes from Viareggio on August 3, 1899: "Meu carissimo amigo. Eis-me aqui mais uma vez na tua bella e abençoada Itália. Cheguei cá depois de uma longa viagem de 25 dias por causa da monção.... estou muito fatigado com a viagem e trabalhos durante a epidemia em Bombay. Daqui a 15 dias voltaremos para Florença onde o meu endereço será .... Com saudosos abraços (My dearest friend, here I am once more in your beautiful and blessed Italy. I arrived here after a long journey of 25 days due to the monsoon. I am very tired with the journey and works during the epidemic in Bombay. After 15 days we will come back to Florence where my address will be ... With nostalgic hugs)"

It was not easy to determine exactly when da Cunha died. We have not found anything in the Academia da Ciência in Lisbon nor in the letters of his wife and brother, António Maria da Cunha, both dated November and December 1902, and probably written after his death.[13]

The letters collected in Florence give us a vision of the relationship between the two friends as one that changes over time, changes that seem to reflect the altered equilibrium in all men's lives. These are two important personalities of great interest and I hope that my contribution will represent a first step to a closer study of their letters, since they are two scholars who devoted so much time and energy to reach a better knowledge of the rich Indian culture.

Conclusion

After presenting my paper at the conference on "Goa and Portugal: History and Development", I had the opportunity, while in Goa, to consult *J. Gerson da Cunha - In memoriam.* It is thanks to some faithful friends of José Gerson da Cunha that this helpful publication was put together, in which I came across the last events of his life. He died on June 3, 1900, alone while with his mother, in Bombay, while his wife and his two daughters lived in Florence, where Emmeline and Olivia were finishing their studies, and Gilberto, his son, was studying medicine at Manchester, England.

NOTES AND REFERENCES

1. Prof. Maurizio Taddei teaches archaeology and Indian art history. He was Rector of the Istituto Universitario Orientale. Thanks to his influence I have been studying the letters of José Gerson da Cunha, that have so far not been examined. Until now, just three volumes of studies have been published: *Angelo De Gubernatis, Europa e Oriente nell'Italia umbertina,* Istituto Universitario Orientale (Collection Matteo Ripa, X), Napoli (I, 1995; II, 1997; III, 1998).
2. On the history of this Istituto, see: Eugenio Garin, "L'Istituto di Studi Superiori di Firenze cento anni dopo" in *La cultura italiana fra '800 e '900,* Bari: Laterza, 1976.
3. Angelo De Gubernatis, *Fibra, Pagine di ricordi,* Roma, 1900, pp. 175-192.
4. Besides the above mentioned work by E. Garin, *cfr.* Susanna Rosi, "Gli studi di orientalistica a Firenze nella seconda metà dell' 800" in *La conoscenza dell'Asia e dell' Africa in Italia nei secoli XVIII e XIX,* (ed.) Ugo Marazzi , Napoli: IUO, 1984, pp. 103-120.
5. The 3rd conference was very important because for the first time countries like France, Italy, Holland, Austria, and Turkey officially took part. The

first one was held in Paris and the second in London. For De Gubernatis, the 3rd conference represented an opportunity to meet many personalities, mainly Russians, and among them, to start a friendship with Dom Pedro de Alcantara, emperor of Brazil.

6. José Gerson da Cunha was born on February 2, 1844 at Panjim, Goa, into a Catholic (Brahmin) family, established there since the first years of the Portuguese domination and which later converted to Catholicism. He studied in Goa and Bombay and got a degree in medicine from the University of Edinburgh. He lived both in Bombay and Goa. He was married and had three children, Emmeline, Olivia and Gilberto. He worked as a physician but tried, at the same time, to advance his scientific knowledge. He learned different languages, studied literature and numismatics. He wrote about this and made an effort to create a collection of valuable coins. That is the reason why he was able to send not only some typical Indian artefacts but also some coins to be exhibited at an Indian exhibition during the 4th Conference of Orientalists.

7. "A dominação russa, que deve tarde ou cedo seguir a inglesa será uma phase importante na nossa evolução política ou para servir-se d'uma phrase italiana, no nosso ressurgimento (The Russian domination which, late or early, ought to follow the English, will be an important phase in our political evolution or to use an Italian phrase, in our resurgence)." *Letter of October 20, 1878.*

8. The letter is of November 29, and there he says that he was received on the 26th.

9. The play was translated and published in English (*Savitri: An Indian Dramatic Idyl* in Two Acts by Count Angelo De Gubernatis, Bombay, 1822) and translated into Gujarati by a Parsi Nánábhái Rutanigi Rániná and performed on January 27, 1883 at the Victoria Theatre in Bombay.

10. *A Gazeta de Bardez* of March 8, 1879 examined the letters and informs us that he had dinner with his family at Arpora in the house of Dr. da Cunha. His father-in-law, Mr. António José da Gama, who was present, was surgeon of the first reformed class, and knight of Nossa Senhora da Conceição de Villa Viçosa and former teacher of the medical school at Panjim. Many other personalities were invited on that occasion. This is the final comment: "We could think that it was really a great party".

11. da Cunha's letters are 48 in all. From 1878 to 1884 he wrote 34 letters and from 1885 to 1899, just 14. The relationship between the two changed a lot, when De Gubernatis went to India because, probably, he thought that his friend did not give him too much help.

12. From this journey that had official support, Angelo de Gubernatis brought back 600 manuscripts and a great number of artefacts. But, in the *Catalogo del Museo Indiano* attention is given to the role of da Cunha in the creation of the Museum: "Un primo nucleo di collezioni indiane era stato offerto nel 1878, al Segretario Generale del IV Congresso degli Orientalisti dall egregio dottor Gerson da Cunha, perché iniziasse in Firenze um Museo Indiano; erano oltre due centinaia di figurine in cartapesta, modelli di frutta e legumi, alcuni oggetti di culto dei Parsi ed una decina di idoli di cartapesta; per questi

doni, che fanno ora parte del Museo Indiano e che hanno un valore complessivo di circa mille lire, il dottor Gerson da Cunha è fra i patroni del Museo", *Fibra, pagine di ricordi*, p. 460.

13. We have two letters of his wife, M. R. da Cunha, kept at the Biblioteca Nazionale in Florence. In the letter of November 7 1902, she wrote: "My dear Count. Before the terrible shock of my poor husband's death, I have not been able to write to you nor to your dear countess and our good daughter ....". The brother, who left us two letters, on December 11, 1902, ends his request to join the Sociedade Internacional Helleno-Latina, with these words: "Renovando os meus agradecimentos pela attenção de V. E.ª que sempre soube como dos melhores amigos do meu querido e lamentado irmão doutor José Gerson da Cunha..... (Renewing my thanks for the attention of Your Excellency whom I always knew as one of the best friends of my dear and lamented brother, Dr. José Gerson da Cunha...)".

Goa as a Literary Motif and as a Historical Subject in Captain Marryat's The Phantom Ship

Preliminary considerations of a Goan identity in contemporary literature

ENGELBERT JORISSEN

I

The young Frederick Marryat (1792-1848), as we are told by his biographer David Hannay, tried three times in vain to run away from home and school until his father allowed him to become a seaman in 1806.[1] From that time till the year 1830 in which he resigned as an "active naval officer"[2] he continued going to sea. Thus, as an author - which was his main occupation from 1830 until his death[3] - he could rely on his own experiences, too, which he had during those long years, and this is true as well for his novel *The Phantom Ship*.

Today, Marryat is known mainly as the author of books for children and even if it does differ from his typical and meant-for-children books, yet, *The Phantom Ship* shows traces of this genre too. However, this novel is different from most of his other novels, first, because the stage of the plot in its most important phase is placed in a part of the former colonial world which the Portuguese claimed for themselves, i.e., in Ternate, Tidore, and Goa, while in his other novels he chose places in the Americas and, as one used to say in the language of the European colonizer, in the West Indies, places which he himself used to sail as well more often. But he could, for the novel discussed here, too, make use of personal knowledge, because he had been appointed for a voyage to Batavia during which he visited Ternate and Tidore and came, probably in 1824-1825, to Goa. The second reason for *The Phantom Ship* distinguishing itself from many of his other novels is, that it belongs to Captain Marryat's three historical novels, and R. Brimley Johnson has called it, in the foreword to the 1896 edition, "the most notable of the three novels constructed by Marryat on an historic base."[4]

Still, the historical plot is mingled with legend, and historical facts are treated quite freely, in order to create a text full of tension and surprises, in addition to which the supernatural is brought in as well. The novel has several weak points, too, and one of the shortcomings is, for example, the over-typifying of some of the figures. This is especially the case when Portuguese figures are depicted as the enemies of the Dutch during the time narrated in the novel. There is a Portuguese captain who moves only between the extremes of either drinking too much, a state in which he is either cursing São António (one of the national saints in Portugal) and other saints available, or, at the slightest foreboding of a storm appearing, beginning to shake and pray cowardly to any saint he can remember. And there is the commander in Ternate, a macho-type with whiskers and a long sword, who tries in vain to make his advance to the heroine. Another weak point lies in the sometimes unfolding speed of developments in the story, which I have tried to feel somewhat in the following summary of the plot of the novel.[5]

The novel was first published in parts during 1838-39 in *The New Monthly Magazine* and in later book form in 1839. The story which is told must be placed at about 1640. An evidence for the latter is, e.g. the first dialogue between the main male figure, Philip Vanderdecken and the Portuguese Father Mathias, who, later, will become a fatal figure for the heroine Amine, Philip's wife. Philip and Father Mathias (he is called a Catholic priest - p. 136, but he is not explicitly introduced and whether he belonged to any particular Religious Order) meet after the latter had shipwrecked - one of the many shipwrecks that fill the novel - and he relates to Philip how he has come there from Japan. This passage is rather interesting because - even if historical facts are quite wrongly presented - the narrator and author criticize the Portuguese for their greed and at the same time acknowledge the fact, that they have spread the faith among the so-called "heathens".

You are not, perhaps aware that the Portuguese, although anxious to secure for themselves a country discovered by their enterprise and courage, and the possession of which, I fear, has cost them many crimes, have still never lost sight of one point dear to all good Catholics - that of spreading wide the true faith, and planting the banner of Christ in regions of idolatry (p. 137).

The priest recounts briefly the events of the Catholic missionary work in Japan, which begin with the arrival of Francisco Xavier in Japan, contain news of how one of the lords (daimyo) in Japan had favoured the Christians and how after his death Christianity began to be persecuted, a development for which the Dutch, and especially the head of the Dutch factory, as it is said in the novel, had contributed much.

"There was a Japanese lord of great wealth and influence who lived near us, and who, with two of his sons, had embraced Christianity, and had been baptised. He had two other sons, who lived at the emperor's court. This lord had made us a present of a house for a college and school instruction: on his death, however, his two sons at court, who were idolaters, insisted upon our quitting this property. We refused, and thus afforded the Dutch principal an opportunity of inflaming these young noblemen against us: by this means he persuaded the Japanese emperor that the Portuguese and Christians had formed a conspiracy against his life and throne; for, be it observed, that when a Dutchman was asked if he was a Christian, he would reply, "No, I am a Hollander." (p. 138)

The priest continues to say that the battle had come about because the emperor had believed in certain rumours, spread, as is said, by the Dutch, according to which there would soon be a Catholic conspiracy. In this battle, the two Christian sons and the other two sons who had remained pagans of the lord - he himself meanwhile had died - had stood against each other. The Christian army of 40,000 men, the reader is told, won against an army of the government containing 25,000 soldiers. Upon this the Christian army had increased to 50,000 but had finally been beaten by 150,000 soldiers, a defeat which had, at the same time, been the end of Christianity in Japan.

It is not possible to touch here upon all historical details in their correct or distorted reflection, but I wish to mention at least the story of the four sons which reflects somewhat allegorically the opposition of the Japanese daimyo, or lords or kings (usually called so by the early Europeans in Japan) who had remained Buddhists and/or Shintoists and some of whom had become persecutors of the Christians. However there had never been a balance between these two groups, the Christian daimyo being only very few. When the story refers to the battle, this again, reflects the historical events around the uprising of Shimabara in 1637-1638, and that has led me to suggest the time as about 1640 as the time for the unfolding events in the novel. This uprising, in fact, was one of the many peasant revolts against taxation and typical of the time, a kind of revolt which had been much more frequent in the 16th century but continued as well into the early Edo period, even if the Shimabara revolt must be called the most significant of that period.

The number of the people engaged in the revolt, is today given in numbers which range from 20,000 to 40,000, but the first figure seems the more probable. The historical fact is, that the central government in Edo had underestimated the power of the uprisers, and had been defeated in the first battle, and the whole affair had endured almost through two years, and finally led to the extinction of the masses involved in the uprising at the hands of the army of the government. Christians had been involved in the revolt, but it must be stressed that it had not been a Christian revolt. However, the central government in Edo (*bakufu*) made use of the Christian elements, that is as a justification for the oppression and persecution of Christianity, while the historical reasons of this must be looked for in the political and economic interests. Catholics, in Europe, on their side made use of the events to stress the 'model' heroism of the persecuted Christians. The fact, yet again, is that there appeared even a Japanese Messiah, known as Amakusa Shiro, who played a not unimportant role. The function of this figure with all its Christian implications, however, has to be seen and interpreted, as Ivan Morris has demonstrated, together with and compared to typical Japanese figures like Minamoto no Yoshitsune and Kusonoki Masashige.[6] The historical truth, finally, is that the Dutch helped the Japanese government in bombarding the fort of Shimabara from one of their ships.[7]

The explanations by Father Mathias and their lengthy description by the narrator of the novel merit attention, because of the way they are handled, and which later should be reconsidered when interpreting the events in the second part of the novel. It may be stated here already, that the episodes told from Japan (that is from an exclusively European point of view) are also a reconfirmation that the novel, critical as it might be of the Portuguese, remains an example of the literature of Christian European colonial imperialism in the 19th century.

From where did Marryat take his information about the Shimabara revolt, I cannot as yet concretely say. Yet, to put it in a negative way, they are 'superficial enough', and could have been taken from missionary reports of the 17th century, known and accessible to the general public. I shall return to the question of the historical sources used by Marryat, but want to suggest here already that *Histoire des deux Indes* by Guillaume Raynal and Denis Diderot[8] might have been among the texts used for his critical representation of the Portuguese, a critique which despite being distorted in some details, is still quite welcome and refreshing.

II

On her deathbed, the mother of the about twenty year old Philip Vanderdecken tells him of the fate of his father. He had been a captain at sea and, once on his way to India when he had tried hard and stubbornly to make his ship round the Cape of Good Hope, had caused the death of one of his pilots who had opposed him, and cursing God for the storm had cried defiantly that in spite of the tempest he would round the Cape. As a punishment for his *hybris*, the ship sank and the captain was condemned to sail and to try forever in vain to round the Cape, a punishment which reminds us, by the way, of the *contrapasso* system in Dante's Hell of his *Divine Comedy*.

The only possibility which could absolve him from this perpetuating situation would be, it was decided, for a person dear to him to bring him a relic, a "fragment of the Holy Cross", which his wife wore around her neck, and upon which he had sworn" ..... that he would gain his point in defiance of storm" (p. 12). That dear person had to give him the relic on what had become by then a ghost ship, or phantom ship, and if he then begged God for forgiveness, his judgment would come to an end. This is of course one of the several legends or myths which tell us about the fate of the figure which became most famous as the Flying Dutchman, and several versions of which came up at the beginning of the 17th century in the Netherlands.

Philip understands that the "dear person" can only mean he himself and that his mother had always kept this story hidden from him because she was afraid to loose him. When Philip, then, goes to call Dr. Poots to come to his dying mother, he meets his beautiful daughter Amine and falls in love with her on the spot. Immediately after his mother's death he marries her (the form of the ceremony not being presented in detail). One has to notice that Philip is a Dutch Catholic, a point which is of interest for the proper evaluation of the later attacks made in the novel against the Catholic society in Goa, and especially because Philip appears in a very positive shape. He tells Amine about his destiny which predestines him to save his father's soul. Amine is inclined to understand this and thus Philip starts twice from Amsterdam in order to cross the way of the phantom ship and to bring his father the saving relic. The many episodes which make the novel a book of sea adventure must be cut short here. It should be mentioned that Philip and the crew of the ships he is voyaging with on several occasions meet with the phantom ship and that after each of such encounters something fateful and bad happens. And time and again he meets also a certain Schriften, a one-eyed pilot who repeatedly becomes engaged as well on Philip's ship as such.

On his third voyage he takes - as he had promised her- his wife Amine with him. This voyage develops in the most colourful of the three voyages described. It brings Philip and Amine near to the Cape of Good Hope, where they meet with Father Mathias, that is the encounter which has been mentioned before. Father Mathias has become one of the victims of a shipwreck obviously after the ship which had carried him had met with the phantom ship, too. For certain reasons which seem to be of no further importance their ship now turns to the West and passes the Strait of Magellan. However, these reasons, because they mean a retardation of the development of the voyage before the catastrophe, and because they lead the ship into the Pacific region of Ternate and Tidore which the Portuguese claimed for themselves as their colonies, are considered as necessary by the narrative logic. Near the Moluccan archipelago they experience one more shipwreck, then follows a rebellion among the shipwrecked seamen after which Philip and Amine become separated.

Amine first and then Philip arrive at the Portuguese fort of Ternate. From there, Amine first again followed by Philip, starts for Goa in the hope of meeting again and return to Europe together. However, Amine very soon becomes arrested in Goa, and becomes accused for having committed sorcery. Her process begins and is quickly completed, where after she is waiting to be burnt at the next *auto-da-fé* to be conducted, as it was expressed in the contemporary Catholic language of oppression. On the very day of the *auto-da-fé*, Philip, who had heard about Amine's departure for Goa, arrives in Goa, but - this is one of the novel's climaxes - instead of taking Amine in his arms and bringing the novel to its happy end, he becomes a witness of her public final condemnation in the Cathedral. With, once again, narrative logic, in vain he tries to intercede and save her, and faints. Meanwhile Amine who for her part, too, had recognized Philip in the crowd is killed by being burnt alive at the stake.

Some years later Philip has recovered from the worst effects of his shock. And one more time he starts from Amsterdam; and this time he can indeed meet his father on the phantom ship, can give him the relic, and, with the phantom ship vanishing into the sea, father and son, they too, disappear into the sea. The salvation had become possible because Philip, in one of the last scenes of the book, forgives the pilot Schriften, who once more had been a member of his crew, that is to say, he forgives a person who had been his enemy. And exactly that was the condition which Schriften - who, what at this stage of the events already is not a surprise at all, had indeed been the very pilot who had been killed by Philip's father, and who must have moved through the novel as a kind of *Wiederganger*, or ghost - had demanded as one more condition for his murder's salvation to become possible.

"..... when your Father, defying the Almighty's will, in his rage took my life, he was vouchsafed a chance of his doom being cancelled, through the merits of his son. I had also my appeal, which was for vengeance: it was granted that I should remain on earth, and thwart your will. That as long as we were enemies, you should not succeed: but that when you had conformed to the highest attribute of Christianity, proved on the holy cross, that of forgiving your enemy, your task should be fulfilled. Philip Vanderdecken, you have *forgiven your enemy,* and both our destinies are now accomplished." (p. 402; emphasis as in the original)

III

Now it becomes necessary to return to the events in Goa, and before that something should be said about Amine's life and her character. Her father, Dr. Poots must have lived an adventurous career in the Arab world and there he had married, too, his wife from an Arab family (p. 53). While the mother must have died somewhere, Dr. Poots finally returned with his daughter to Middleburg in Zeeland, at that time a prosperous port town of the Netherlands. But it is her mother, whose fortune remains almost totally in darkness in the novel, to whom Amine always tries to communicate through a kind of incantation by which she is eager to call back the spirit of the dead, an art which she is said to have learnt from her mother. Some details of that art are explained in the novel:

They resembled exactly the phylacteries that were once worn by the Jewish nation, and were similarly applied. (p. 157)

From these words originates a certain uncertainty because of the Jewish origin of the art indicated here, because her mother is said to have been "from an Arab family" and after her father had become a "follower of Mahomet" (p. 53). This does not exclude the possibility that her mother did have Jewish roots, but it is not clear whether Marryat was conscious of the problems involved or whether it is a mere slip of continuing; the question however, is not without interest, as will be seen when discussing the end of the novel.

When Amine arrives at Goa she gets a first glimpse of the city from the deck of the ship. The captain points out to her the various buildings of importance, and after having mentioned the Viceroy's Palace, he asks her:

"The building you see now, on the water-side, is the Viceroy's palace; that to the right, again, is the convent of the Discalced Carmelites: yon lofty spire is the cathedral of St. Catherine, and that beautiful and light piece of architecture is the church of Our Lady of Pity. You observe there a building, with a dome, rising behind the Viceroy's palace?"

"I do," replied Amine.

"That is the Holy Inquisition."

Although Amine had heard Philip speak of the Inquisition, she knew little about its properties; but a sudden tremor passed through her frame as the name was mentioned, which she could not herself account for. (p. 327)

Soon after disembarking, Amine meets one more time with Father Mathias, who after having returned to Lisbon, could not settle down and had left again for missionary work among what he, as the Europeans would have called 'heathens'. It is he who provides for Amine a place in the "Ursuline convent" (p. 327). However, secure as the place might be, Amine soon learns that the manners in the convent were not such as she had expected them to be.

Its inmates being wholly composed of the best families, the rules of this convent were not so strict as others; licenses were given - greater licences were taken - and Amine, to her surprise, found that in this society, devoted to Heaven, there were exhibited more of the bad passions of human nature than she had before met (p. 330).

There has never been an Ursuline convent in Goa, and one may here at once think instead of the historical convent of Santa Monica, the only convent for women in Goa, and this comes to mind all the more when thinking as well of some brief observations published together with some documents by Alberto Osorio de Castro in 1923 under the title "Um documento da vida conventional em Goa" (A document about the convent life in Goa),[9] the contents of which might be of interest to be compared with the passage in the novel indicated here. How exactly Marryat received his information in this case is not sure, but as will be seen there had been rumours about the infamous moral life in Goa from the 16th century onwards and Marryat must have transferred what he had heard about the convent of Santa Monica to his "Ursula convent".

The convent of Santa Monica was founded in 1606 as an institution according to the rules of the Augustinian order by Archbishop D. Fr. Aleixo de Menezes. During the 17th century it developed into becoming one of the largest Portuguese monasteries.[10] According to Osorio de Castro its establishment originated from the necessity of a refuge for women, after fifty two women had been killed by their husbands in the span of about two years. The complicated relations between men and women, not seldom the cause for death, much before the foundation of the convent have been described e.g. by the Dutch author, John Huygen van Linschoten, who expresses a certain maliciousness but not without being interested.[11] It may be said already here, that Marryat uses the circumstances in the monastery as presented by him in order to add one more aspect to his critique of the hypocritical society in Goa. A Puritan attitude of his mind cannot be ignored here.

As opposed to this, Osorio de Castro cannot help show some sympathy for the sisters who are secluded from the outside world and from unhindered love when describing the life in the convent. He cites some verses, composed secretly by a sister in the 18th century, verses which mention longingly the Augustinians who live in the neighbouring monastery, and ask if love would not be the cause for inconsiderate acts:

O amor he criança	Love is child
Q. faz enlouquecer,	who makes loose one's mind
Não sei se he bangue	I do not know if is hashish
Q. faz doidicins fazer."	which seduces to commit
	inconsiderate acts.[12]

Because of the bad experience in the convent, Amine decides to live in the household of a widow and her little son situated directly in front of the palace of the Inquisition.

Taking leave of the nuns, Amine quitted the convent with Father Mathias, and was soon installed in her new apartments, in a house which formed part of a spacious square called the Terra di Sabaio (p. 331).

One day when visiting the "bazaar" Amine finds the utensils which are necessary to enter into contact with her mother whom she wants to call for help in order to learn about Philip's fate. Because she needs the help of someone during the procedure, she asks Pedro, the little boy of the household to assist her, but at the same time she begs him not to tell anybody of what will happen. However, as the development of the novel forces this, the child informs his mother that something strange has happened, and on the second occasion of Amine's trying to get into contact with her mother not only Pedro's mother but Father Mathias, too, are informed. The latter, on the occasion of his arrival in Goa, is described in an anticipatory manner in the following way:

"He is a good man, thought Amine, as she descended - and Amine was right. Father Mathias was a good man, but, like all men, he was not perfect. A zealot in the cause of his religion, he would have cheerfully sacrificed his life as a martyr, but if opposed or thwarted in his views, he could then be cruel and unjust" (p. 328).

Amine is arrested at once and brought to the "Santa Casa, or Inquisition of Goa" (p. 335). There follows then a quite detailed description of the Inquisition and its proceedings:

There are two Inquisitors at Goa: one, the Grand Inquisitor, and the other his second, who are invariably chosen from the order of St. Dominic; these two are assisted in their judgement and examinations by a large number selected from the religious orders, who are termed deputies of the Holy Office, but who only attend when summoned. (p. 336)

And about the beginning of a process it is said: The first question put to a person arrested by the Inquisition, is a demand, "What is his property?" (p. 337)

Most of the descriptions given by Marryat rely on the famous description of the Goa Inquisition made by the French doctor of medicine, Charles Dellon, who was imprisoned in Goa between 1673 and 1679. His description soon became well known and famous throughout Europe with four editions in French appearing until 1700 - after it had been put on the Index of forbidden books in 1690 - and with translations into German, Dutch, and English. The suggestion that Dellon's description delivered the model for Marryat's novel is not difficult to be made and was offered already e.g. by Richard Burton, the author of *Goa and the Blue Mountains*, who came to Goa in 1846 and who made an interesting description of the contemporary state of the Palace of the Inquisition. According to him the only monastery with residents at that time was the convent of Santa Monica.[13] However it is still worth looking for further sources for Marryat because this would shed more light on the state of information about the Goa Inquisition in then contemporary Europe, and this is again of interest because Amine is not accused for being of Islamic or Jewish creed or having belonged to these religions in the past but because of sorcery. Marryat and/or his narrator himself comments on this occasion:

At Goa the accusations of sorcery and magic were much more frequent than at the Inquisitions at other places, arising from the customs and ceremonies of the Hindoos being very much mixed up with absurd superstitions (p. 340).

It is probably that Marryat had known texts of the 18th century about the handling of cases before the tribunal. The nature of such texts can now be learnt about e.g. in a recent publication of some old documents "Ultimo Regimento e Regimentos da Economia da Inquisição de Goa" (Last Rule and Economic Rules of the Goa Inquisition). In one of the two texts, that is in this case from 1778, one finds a chapter about "Dos feiticeiros, sortílegos, adivinhadores, astrólogos, judiciários e maléficos". As already mentioned Marryat, if being somewhat prejudicial against Catholics, does share certain Christian European-centered views with them. Thus it is not only regrettable that he could not make any critical remarks about the practices against the original population as mentioned here, but that he evokes further the impression that he cannot help accepting these oppressions because for him too, the "customs and ceremonies of the Hindoos" were full of "absurd superstitions".

While her process is on, Amine, as was done in historical cases too, firstly is not told why and for what kind of crime she has been arrested, and finally she is condemned to death.

Another fortnight passed, when Amine was again summoned to the Hall of Judgement, and again asked if she confessed her crimes. Upon her refusal, the accusations against her were read. She was accused by Father Mathias with practising forbidding arts. (p. 346)

On the day on which she would be burnt to death in a public *auto-da-fé*, she had to walk together with the other victims in a procession through the city of Goa, and e.g. here as well, Marryat must have taken his description of the victims dressed in *sambenitos* and *samarios* from Dellon's book. But when he describes the climax of the *auto-da-fé* and the heroic death of Amine who until her death refuses to admit a crime and the wish to die as a Christian, and who refuses therewith to the officials of the Inquisition the satisfaction of admitting her to be strangled in an act of mercy before being burnt, Marryat should have read more about such proceedings. A description including this last stage of the process can be read in a description of the very first Inquisitional process in Goa, long before it was established officially, that is in 1543, shortly after the arrival of Francisco Xavier in Goa in 1542, in a process against Jerónimo Dias who was arrested and killed for what was called "judaizing". He was asked too whether he wanted to die as a Christian, upon which he in his desperation chose to be strangled in an act of mercy as the church called it cynically. The case of the bachelor Jerónimo Dias, a New Christian who became accused of "judaizing", that is of having secretly continued certain practices of his old faith, is given with many details, many of which resemble directly the case of Amine, in *Lendas da India* by Gaspar Correia. Correia's description of the inquiring members of the Dominican Order and secular priests sitting at the desk of the Inquisition with the victim standing before it, illustrates that already in 1543, that is seventeen years before its official institution, the Inquisition in Goa was already able to display its horror with institutional rigour. In addition, Correia mentions that the bishop on the Sunday after Dias had been killed appeals to the Goan population to expose anyone practicing what was called "heresies against the Catholic faith". His report hints, what might have not been the very intention by Correia, at a society of spies, as it appears in Marryat's novel.[14]

Going back here one time more to Marryat's text, one is attempted to more considerations; after having mentioned the "absurd superstitions" as the reason for the many cases of "sorcery and magic" handled by the Inquisition in Goa. Marryat continues:

"These people, and the slaves from other parts, very often embraced Christianity to please their masters; but since, if they had been baptised and were afterwards convicted of any crime, they were sentenced to the punishment by fire; whereas, if they had not been baptised, they were only punished by whipping, imprisonment, or the galleys: upon this ground alone many refused to embrace Christianity." (p. 340)

First, again is the striking injustice in the description of the Indians' conversion, and no mention is made by Marryat to the violence with which the Hindu and Islam population often was driven to conversion. To the violence with which they were punished after their conversion is added, by Marryat, too, the insult of their 'calculation' to convert or not. Then, of interest is, secondly but on another level, the description of the greater strictness with which the converted are punished than those who had not converted. This demonstrates that the practice which was used, especially in the 16th and 17th centuries, against Jews and New Christians, that is Jews who had, because of being forced to, converted to Christianity, was repeated against the Indian population. The New Christians in Goa, too, had been observed and, if 'convicted', more cruelly and harshly punished than those Jews who had not converted; the latter, however, not being free from oppressions either.

In other words, the Christians who came from the Hindu and Islam sections of the population and who continued some of their original customs or who, after being baptised, returned to or retook some of them were treated in the same way as those New Christians who became known as "*relapsos*", who 'relapsed' wholly or partly or just by some superficial customs, as by eating certain foods that they had been accustomed to, in their former faith. It should not be necessary to mention that what is here called "absurd superstitions" were, in fact, customs and practices in the daily life of the nourishment and clothing of the Indians, etc.[15] It is not clear how far Marryat was conscious of these implications here and when he collected his material for the description of Amine's case, if only once, is as well brought into a relation with 'Jewish customs (phylacteries)'. Before Philip and Amine were married by a priest named Father Seysen, Amine was instructed to a certain degree by the same priest; however it remains unclear whether she was baptized (pp. 59-64). Later, when Amine is tortured before the Inquisition one finds the following dialogue between the Secretary of the Inquisition and Amine:

"You [i.e. Amine] say you are from the East: are you a Christian?"
"I reject your [i.e. the Secretary] creed."
"Did you enter into the bosom of the church? Did he venture to marry you without your being baptised?"
"Some ceremony did take place which I consented to."
"It was baptism, was is not?"
"I believe it was so termed."
"And now you say that you reject the creed?" (pp. 341-342)

Even if there remains a certain ambiguity about Amine's baptism it seems, at least, that Marryat wanted to make appear her process as one directed with all its cruelty as against a *relapso*, somebody who relapsed from her faith once accepted.

IV

In Marryat's novel the Portuguese society in Goa is described as collaborating almost too willingly with the Inquisition. However, there are historical texts which document, that beside some dramatization there was no need for Marryat to exaggerate. The Portuguese Catholics in his novel are hypocritically serving a God and preach falsely compassion and justice, *misericordia* and *justitia* as they appear in the very peculiar emblems of the Goan Inquisition, two concepts which are continuously denied by the Inquisition's officials and which, in the novel, are exactly what is demanded from Philip to do at the end of the novel, that is when he forgives his enemy.

The Inquisition, and Marryat as well, never could forgive. Even those victims who were condemned but had died in the prison of the Inquisition before they could be killed in an *auto-da-fé* were still burnt, as was done e.g. in the case of the famous philosopher and doctor of medicine, Garcia da Orta. In his lifetime he had gained great fame in India and Europe with his *Coloquios das Drogas e Simples da India* (Dialogues about the Drugs and Medicines of India, 1563) which had been translated into Latin immediately by C. Clusius (Ch. de l'Ecluse).[16] He had been acknowledged in the Goan Jesuit seminary too, as is documented e.g. by the Jesuit Luis Frois in one of his letters from India.[17] Twelve years after his death in 1568, his body was exhumed and burnt in 1580. Some aspects of the process which unfolded at the same time against da Orta's family have been documented by I. S. Revah in his *La Famille de Garcia da Orta.*[18]

V

Welcome as the critical description of the Inquisition in Goa in Marryat's novel is, regrettable it is that in no way is mentioned the victimization of the Goan and Indian population. Of course one must not forget the victims among minority and/or deviating groups who came from Europe as were the New Christians, Protestants and as well homosexuals. They became oppressed by those who felt themselves as the victorious group of what was called 'the Age of Discoveries'; and among these persecuted were as well many who had come fleeing a surveying and persecuting society in Europe only to run into the same society again. The oppression and persecution of deviations, which from the beginning had been directed against the Indians, more and more was turned against them. Impressing is a poem by Jennifer Marie Bayer in which she describes the horror originating from the table of the Inquisition and illustrates the export of intolerance from Europe. It expresses the experience of the Goan and Indian, under the oppression of Europeans who not only wanted to annex territories not belonging to them but as well to monopolize their culture, including language and religion.

The table
the inquisition table
The Table
at which they say
thousands of innocent people
were declared to die

On the other side
the table
has three structures
of the local man
Of man
powerless and subordinated

to be burned to death
for not having converted
to Christianity
now lies in the
Art Gallery

The legs of the table
are different
from the rest I know
For each of its legs
represent different emotions

On one side of the table
has two beautifully carved lions
to signify
strength, power and domination,
the eagle in the middle
represents
watchfulness.

Yet
of strength and power
of body and spirit
for having refused
to convert.

The very structure of the table
still carrries the horror
of those who faced
Inquisition
at this table.

The table
I now feel
generates in me
that horror
I would have had to face
had I lived
four centuries ago
And refused
to surrender
my religion, my language, my
culture.[19]

One task which becomes necessary is to turn to the historical facts of the colonization suppression of the Indian society in Goa. Another task, as necessary, is to look at the condition and identity of the Goan people in today's India. One possibility is to go to literary texts and analyse the comprehension and description of the Goans as well by Goans as by other Indian authors.

As was already indicated as mentioned in Marryat's novel, it were not only the officials of the Inquisition who rejoiced on the day of the *auto-da-fé* but thousands of the Portuguese people, too. Further, there are the many members of noble families who in the novel collaborate with the Inquisition not only passively but actively as well in their various honorary functions as leading one by one the condemned in the procession to the *auto-da-fé,* this too has historical models.[20]

How did the Goans who had converted to Christianity feel towards such a society? And how has the Goan identity to be seen today before such a historical background? In case of both questions it will be useful to remember that in many cases of Indian individuals in Goa, the Euro-Catholicism was no willing one. And at the same time contemporary Christianity in India has to be recognized in its own, historically conditioned, terms. That and how it cannot be correct to transform the past into a happy and rich Indo-European symbiosis and/or a Indo-Portuguese 'Golden Goa' has been shown in a recent publication by Pratima Kamat, in her *Farar Far*, at the beginning of which she places a song which must contradict such post-colonial lies.

Farar far zatai ranantun	"Shots are being fired in the forest
Pakle martai Ranneanku	The Portuguese are killing the Ranes
Ranne martai pakleanku	The Ranes are killing the Portuguese
Farar far zatai ranantun	Shots are being fired in the forest."

At the moment for me it is only possible to look at Indian literature written in English and, if there are few, in Portuguese. There appears, to begin arbitrarily with just one example, the figure of the Goan painter in Salman Rushdie's *The Moor's Last Sigh*. He bears the 'beautiful' name Vasco Miranda, a mixture of Vasco da Gama, the colonizer, and Shakespeare's Miranda who in *"The Tempest"* at one point exclaims "O wonder! ... How beauteous mankind is! O brave new world that has such people in't" (*The Tempest*, 5.1.181-184). He comes from Loutulim in Goa. When, on the occasion of the communal clashes between Hindus and Muslims due to the partition in 1947 he is asked what he intends to do, he answers: "Oh *me* ... Don't worry about me. I am *Portuguese*"[21] (emphasis as in the original). And when the Portuguese rule in Goa ends and he is encouraged "to see the event as a liberation, as many Goans did" he remains "inconsolable" and turns for forty days nostalgically to Portuguese food ("all pork") and historical anecdotes. And still it is said, that he had lost or even cut all his roots from Goa, which is seen as well as a sign of a certain "instability", and that he "was his own invention."[22] Vasco Miranda, as his name implies, is standing between two cultures, and even if he tries sometimes quite ruthlessly to make his fortune, he remains a tragic figure. Very different is the case of Jacqueline from Goa who works in a Bombay Parsi household in Rohinton Mistry's short story "The Ghost of Firozsha Baag". First it seems that she is merely depicted as a superstitious Catholic woman, but looking more keenly at the text, she appears as always indulging in memories of a Goa with a Hindu tradition as well.[23] Jacqueline's case is of interest for example because she is living in a Bombay Parsi household which makes her identity one time more inflected. The Parsi family does not even care to pronounce her name correctly, but in the end the Parsi lady and Jacqueline meet on the same level of superstition. Then, for Jacqueline Europe is only something which she knows like a phantasma from a fairy tale, her grandfather had been there a long time ago, which makes the reader ask, what her Catholicism really consists of. However the essence of this short story should not be taken only from the negative points hinted at, it can easily be read as well, as a *plaidoyer*, besides being for religious and cultural tolerance, as well for an individual religious syncretism on which level this might be.

Finally there is a poem by Eunice de Souza which contains the refreshing lines, which remind me of one of the philosophies described by Fernando Pessoa in which he shows how to be happy without an identity bound by history and religion. Positively E. de Souza describes this freedom:

> No matter that
> my name is Greek
> my surname Portuguese
> my language alien
> There are ways
> of belonging. [24]

NOTES AND REFERENCES

1. David Hannay, *Life of Frederick Marryat*, London: Walter Scott, 1889, pp.15-16.
2. *Ibid.*, p. 55.
3. *Ibid.*, pp. 58ff.
4. R. Brimley Johnson, *The Novels of Captain Marryat*, vol. X; *The Phantom Ship*, London: J. M. Dent & Co., Boston: Little Brown & Co., 1896, p. ix. All citations from the novel are taken from this edition and given as from *The Phantom Ship*.
5. Other failures of the novel have been pointed out as well; Hannay lists the book among those which "must be taken for what they are worth in place of the possible better", but still acknowledges that the "value" of *The Phantom Ship* is "considerable" because, as Hannay writes, even if the material of the sea legend is not original, Marryat "made good use" of it, *Life of Frederick Marryat, op. cit.*, p.122. Johnson attests to the novel's "general success" but sees it blurred e.g. in that "his religious discourses, coloured by prejudice against the Romanists, are conventional and unconvincing", *The Phantom Ship*, p. x. This argument, without doubt, cannot be overseen here. However,

if Johnson cannot be blamed for his judgment, the novel remains an interesting testimony for the indicated 'popular' prejudices because of the historical facts, as the terror by the Catholic Inquisition in Goa, from which they originated. Hannay and Johnson agree upon the bad taste of the novel's final scene, which "trenches on the namby pamby" (Hannay, p.123), and which "savours of the Sunday-school" for Johnson (p. x).

6. Ivan Morris, "Amakusa Shiro: The Japanese Messiah", ch. 7, in: I. M., *The Nobility of Failure. Tragic Heroes in the History of Japan* (1975), Rutland, Vermont & Tokyo: Tuttle, 1982, pp.143-179; *cf.* also ch. 5 (Victory Through Defeat) and ch. 6 (Seven Lives for the Nation) on Minamoto no Yoshitsune and Kusunoki Masashige respectively (*Ibid.*, pp. 67-105, 106-142).
7. *Cf.* e.g. Charles Ralph Boxer, *The Christian Century in Japan 1549-1650* (1951), University of California Press, 1974, p. 381.
8. *Histoire de deux Indes* by Guillaume Raynal and Denis Diderot, first published under the name of Guillaume-Thomas Raynal only, under the title *Histoire philosophique e politique des etablissements et du commerce des Europeens dans les deux Indes*, Amsterdam, 1770, Geneva, 1774, 1780, appeared in English translation by J. O. Justamond in the form of a general account as *A philosophical and political history of the settlements and trade of the Europeans in the East and West Indies*, Dublin, 1784; a German translation was published in 1782-88. The extent of the contribution by Diderot, who had written already for the first edition but much more for the third edition became evident when his literary bequest became known, *cf.* Hans-Jurgen Lusebrink in G. Raynal and D. Diderot, *Die Geschichte beider Indien, Ausgewahlt und erlautert*, Nordlingen: Greno, 1988, p. 346. It might be of interest that Raynal (1713-1796) had been a member of the Society of Jesus, which he left in 1747, and most probably would have heard about the activities of the Jesuits in the overseas colonies of the Europeans during the instruction he must have received from the Jesuits.
9. Alberto Osorio de Castro, "Um documento da vida conventual em Goa", in Azevedo Neves (ed.), *Archivo de Medicina Legal*, vol. II, nos. 1, 2 and 3, 1923.
10. *Cf.* A. Lopes Mendes, *A India Portuguesa*, vols. I-II (1885), New Delhi: Asian Educational Services (AES), Reprint 1989, vol. I, pp. 83-84.
11. Arthur Coke Burnell (ed.), *The Voyage of John Huyghen van Linschoten to the East Indies*, vols. I-II (1885), New Delhi: AES, Reprint 1988, vol. I, pp. 208-217.
12. Osorio de Castro, "Um documento da vida conventual em Goa", *op. cit.*, p. 2.
13. Richard Burton, *Goa and the Blue Mountains* (1849), New Delhi: AES, Reprint 1990. In Burton's travelogue one finds as well a description of the, at that time, already decaying Old Goa, *cf.*, especially pp. 123-143.
14. Gaspar Correia, *Lendas da India*, ed. Rodrigo José de Lima Felner, Lisbon: Academia Real das Ciências, vols. I-IV, 1858-1866, vol. IV, pt. II, chs. 26-27, pp. 292ff.

15. Seen from the point of the cultural-anthropologist, aspects of the only natural process of a certain degree of syncretism in religious daily life are shown by Rowena Robinson in her *Conversion, Continuity and Change. Lived Christianity in Southern Goa*, New Delhi: Sage Publ., 1998. Robinson's subject is contemporary Christianity. However, her study offers interesting possibilities for working up the conditions in the 16th and 17th centuries too.
16. *Cf.* also Garcia da Orta, *Coloquios das Drogas e Simples da India (*1891), Lisbon: Imprensa Nacional/Casa da Moeda, vols. I-II, 1987. For the life and career of da Orta, *cf.* C. R. Boxer, *Two Pioneers of Tropical Medicine: Garcia d'Orta and Nicolas Monardes*, Cambridge: W. Heffer & Sons Ltd.; A.J. Andrade de Gouveia, *Garcia d'Orta e Amato Lusitano na ciência do seu tempo*, Lisbon: ICALP, 1985.
17. In a letter from Goa dated November 12, 1559, Frois mentions da Orta as a member of the board of examinations at the Jesuit college in Goa and as "one of the best men of letters in this region." Josef Wicki (ed.), *Documenta Indica*, Rome: MHSJ, 1948, vol. I, vol. IV, pp. 269-300, 296-297.
18. I. S. Revah, "La Famille de Garcia da Orta", *Revista da Universidade de Coimbra*, vol. 19, Coimbra, 1960.
19. Jennifer Marie Bayer, "The Inquisition Table" in *Boletim do Instituto Menezes Bragança,* Panjim, no.172, 1994, pp. 119-121.
20. Detailed information about the institution of the Inquisition in Europe and Goa, about the observation before someone became accused, the process, the procession, and the *auto-da-fés* are given in Francisco Bethencourt, *História das Inquisições: Portugal, Espanha e Italia. Temas e Debates*, 1996.
21. Salman Rushdie, *The Moor's Last Sigh*, London: Jonathan Cape, 1995, p. 167.
22. *Ibid.*, pp. 156-157.
23. Rohinton Mistry, "The Ghost of Firozsha Baag", in his *Swimming Lessons and Other Stories from Firozsha Baag* (1987), New York: Vintage Books, 1997, pp. 41-56.
24. Here cited from Dennis Walder, *Post-colonial Literatures in English. History Language Theory*, Oxford: Blackwell, 1998, p. 93.

29

O Signo da Ira (The Sign of Anger)

Ethno-literature and neo-realism in a case of literary excellence

RUI DE AZEVEDO TEIXEIRA

With a controlled, well-distributed abundance of ethnographic indices and a "disobedient obedience" since suspicious and creative, to the guidelines of neo-realistic aesthetics, *O Signo da Ira* narrates the story of a cycle of rice, of the rabi crop till the harvest and the subsequent theft of the same harvest. The action centres on a miserable settlement of "earthen huts, blocks covered by dry coconut palms and broken tiles" in Goa, in the Portuguese state of India, and unfolds at the start of the fourth decade of this century when "to the rumours of a war far away followed its first signs in the year 42".

Side by side with the history of the novel of Orlando da Costa, runs the thread of a loving adolescent, platonic plot between the kunnbi girl Natél, the kunnbi boy Bostião and a white man (*paklo)*, a soldier of the expeditionary Portuguese corps. In his turn, the narrator is the owner of a big narrative authority - he is a narrator, absolute lord of Romanesque material; the language, being very careful, does not fall in the plot of "over-written"; the rhythm is slow, translating with exactness the slow cycle of rice, and the tone of the novel is one of supreme sobriety, making the "voice" of the book reach prudence, once it promises "to understand things not more but better." (Armindo Rodrigues)

Ethno-Literature

In what touches the anthropological cultural material of the work, its indicators are not given in a block, in the style of a dry, literally

* Translated from the Portuguese by Charles J. Borges

unproductive inventory. Much, on the contrary, Orlando da Costa sows the more expressive and more suggestive ethnographic data in the ground of the novel with discretion, in a strategic and artistic sense, giving them thus a functional relevance and a literary meaning. The low sense of the exotic or the neutral mood, characteristic of the scientific discourse, of traditional ethnographic discourse – it may be remembered by the way, that in the post-modernist anthropology of Clifford Geerts or of James Clifford, the "literary" starts to impinge on the "scientific," - never emerges to the surface of the text and much less are brought up passages, small though they may be, of the novel.

And it is thus, with the informative-ethnographic load wrapped in a literary form, that the novel presents the small and unjust world dominated by the landlord (*bhatkar*) Ligór, a brahmin landowner, physically imposing, of Aryan profile. Ligór – who has the mysticism of the Earth, of Strength, of the Family and of Tradition and who like a strong defender of the patriarchal education, makes one remember "the Baron" of Branquinho da Fonseça – he has under his medieval command, beyond a foreman (*mukkadam*, an overseer), shudras and kunnbis. The shudras offer him subordination as servants in "the big house" and the kunnbis work hard, whether as *mundkars* (rural settlers who obey the *bhatkar*) or as *begarins* (casual workers without a fixed type of work).

Apart from the clans, which give us the essential of the social original pyramid – the others, the Portuguese, place themselves on the edge of the story, more on its horizon than in its centre,- other indices of ethnographic roots are bound up for importance:

- with habitation, with the poor dwellings of "cowdung-spread threshold" that contrast with the insulating opulence of "the big house" of Ligor.
- with food, for example, "the dry skins of *kokum* and "roasted tamarind seeds" that the hungry children crack.
- with drinks, like for example with *feni*, the distilled cashew juice, the typical drink in opposition to macheira (corruption of brandy "Macieira", drunk by the Portuguese in the "big house").
- with tobacco, with the kunnbis who "smoke their beedis of jackfruit leaves."
- with the distinction of castes, as one sees during the feast in the house of Ligor or in the scene of the procession.
- with marriages arranged by the parents of the bridegrooms and brides.
- with burials, while the dead bodies are covered and melted with lime.

and with the feudal "right of leaping", the privilege of the first night, practised with brutal and scornful desire, by Ligor on the women of the lower castes than his own.

Neo-Realism

In what touches the second characteristic of *O Signo da Ira* which we propose to examine – its affiliation in neo-realistic aesthetics – diverse are the elements that fit the novel in this literary genre that is going to drink of the very Italian of the past century and of the Spanish customs. Here there are the core elements: the central opposition between plenty and penury, between a landowner and his workers (the opposition between Portuguese and Goans is secondary); a socio-economic medieval structure, of open exploitation, which is faced as the natural order and not as the cultural order of things; the alienation of the kunnbis, their lack of awareness regarding the exploitation they are subjected, until well near the end of the book; and, finally, the seed of the revolt, son of an emerging conscientization.

In short, the whole classical situation and movement of a neo-realist novel, in which a burnt-out structure, dirtied by the tradition and by the injustice begins to be shaken by a movement that points out, if not for the substitution, at least for the coexistence between a new – the socio-economic progress – and the old – the world stopped and motionless and privileged world of Ligór, this world a little different from the "medieval paradise" of the big lord of *"Barranco de Cegos"* (Ravine of the Blind), of Alves Redol.

But, if the general movement, the phasing of the novel is typically neo-realist this does not prevent Orlando da Costa from refusing the bureaucratic obedience of the school, from denying a schematization more simple in the question of economic deprivation, from diverging from a Manichaeism of a political agent infiltrated in literature. Costa opposes the blessed revolutionary optimism "of the tomorrows that sing", fights the frozen orthodoxy of a dogmatic mentality. The author of *O Signo da Ira* through a very minute attention to the reality of the settlement and through an incessant desire for Truth places frequently in the cause the theoretical nucleus of a more helpful neo-realism. And the better example of this unyielding obedience to neo-realistic dictates, of this rinsing of more crass materialism, is the importance and goodness with which in the novel are treated figures like those of Fr. Antu and of Christ himself, a Christ of "sweet and compassionate look" in front of all that "collective despair". The kunnbis themselves, who after the loss of the harvest, wander about like Lazaruses, in a scene which evokes powerfully that of the beggars who walk through the marshy land in *"Gaibéus"* of Redol, are classified as "messengers of Christ".

But it is not only through religion that Orlando da Costa displays his autonomy and literary non-orthodoxy. Opening still more to the true life and to the true literature, he creates characters in the roll of exploited who, or are of a refined wickedness like the grandfather of Natél, who denounces coldly a Portuguese soldier for a crime that he did not commit, or on the contrary, creates characters who are capable of seeing the good also on the side of those who in some way make up the camp of the exploiters, as is the case of Natél, when she says that "not all", thinking of the already referred to soldier, are bad.

Conclusion

In *O Signo da Ira* the ethnographic elements and the neo-realistic aspects submit themselves always to a literary essentialness and do not separate ever from the more profound questions of truth and being. In this novel, whether they be the cultural and anthropological traces, or the materialistic characteristic, without negating the weight and impact of necessary information, they do not abstract themselves from the creation; do not remain without an aesthetic meaning. Or maybe, to an unedited information (for a non-Goan reader) joins itself with the aesthetics, and it is precisely this fusing of information with aesthetic creation that creates better the persuasion which more easily leads the reader to believe in the more direct thesis, the neo-realism of the book.

With this strategy of writing, with this philosophy of the novel, Orlando da Costa ends in equating in his book much more than a local phenomenon with creation, information and smooth persuasion besides the constant, honest search of the Truth and of the Being. He manages to take the local reality of a human experience to the higher plane of a universal experience. By the other way, the key of his literary knowledge consists in the capacity of, beginning by presenting a local form, structuring it afterwards, lifting it later in an archetypical way.

And it ends (or begins) in biblical wisdom, with an irresistible resonance of "*Ecclesiastes*" – in the passage in which it is said that everything passes, that one generation comes and goes and another appears, but that the Earth, this remains always – when at the beginning of the novel, in the words of the author, he clarifies that, in his narrative, persons and facts are imagined and "that only the earth intends to be true and the nature in which it is integrated and expressed".

30

Reports About Goa for the Royal Academy of History (1726)

ANA ISABEL BUESCU

During the modern epoch, the academies flourished in Europe having as their inspiring example the Italian model, established mainly by the Platonic Academy of Florence (*Academia Platónica de Florença*) in the 15th century. In the 16th century and above all in the following, the academies multiplied in all of Europe, even at the regional level, forming in the ambit of ideological and cultural affirmation of the ideology of the *Luzes*, a narrow and active net in the exchange and diffusion of ideas, in the social legitimacy of men of letters and in the progressive broadening of peoples.[1]

In Portugal, too, from the middle of the 17th century, there began to appear circles of erudite classes, whose periodical meetings had as their aim the discussion of varied matters and themes, above all, of a historical and literary character.[2] Although hardly known, the academies, in relation to which there still lack for the Portuguese case monographic studies that might allow an appreciation of the whole,[3] line up as forums that intended to correspond to new patterns of sociability in the area of letters and of sciences, attaining in time, a significant renown in Portugal, too.

One may refer, among the large number of private academies that flourished among us, by the importance that they came to have, to the *Academia dos Singulares* (Academy of the Singular) started in Lisbon in 1628, with a new term of activity in 1663-65, and the *Academia dos Generosos* (Academy of the Generous), started by D. António Álvares da Cunha in 1647, also characterised by an interrupted activity, interrupted in 1696 by the tireless Count of Ericeira, D. Francisco Xavier de Menezes, under the designation of *Conferências Eruditas* (Erudite Conferences). To the Academy of the Generous, considered by Fidelino de Figueiredo as

* Translated from the Portuguese by Charles J. Borges

"the most important of the 17th century for the quality of its members and the comparative regularity of its works":[4] space of aristocratic bearing that the very name indicates (generous), belonged for example, D. Francisco Manuel de Melo, and in it participated, during various times of its functioning, intellectuals and men of culture like Rafael Bluteau, Manuel Caetano de Souza, Francisco Leitão Ferreira and José Barbosa. Many others, like *Academia dos Solitários* (Academy of the Singles) Santarém, 1664, *Academia dos Únicos* (Academy of the Unique) Lisbon, 1691?, *Academia Instantanea* (Instant Academy) Porto, end of 17th century, *Academia dos Illustrados* (Academy of the Learned) Lisbon, 1716, *Academia dos Laureados* (Academy of the Laureates) Santarém, 1721, *Academia dos Problematicos* (Academy of the Doubtfuls) Guimarães, 1721, give an account of the vigour which these type of institutions had at the end of the 17th and in the 18th century in Portugal.[5]

In the first phase, it is therefore the movement of literary academies of a private and essentially aristocratic nature, that distinguishes itself in Portugal.[6] In the second phase, the very State would be interested in the phenomenon. The foundation of the academies by royal initiative throughout Europe, in accordance with the French model started by Richelieu in the 17th century, constitutes a decisive element in the affirmation of the monarchical cultural apparatus to which Portugal of D. João V (1689-1750) also was not alien. In fact, the political project of the exaltation of the royal power in Portugal of King John passes also, and by a decisive form, through the artistic and cultural politics to which the monarch gave, as we know, privileged attention.

We have referred earlier to the outstanding figure in the ambit of the movement of the academies, of D. Francisco Xavier de Menezes (1673-1743), Count of Ericeira. Having distinguished himself especially as a man of culture, author of historical, philosophical and scientific works and owner of a very rich collection of about 15,000 books which constituted one of the main poles of the spread of the culture of the *Luzes* movement in Portugal,[7] the fourth Count of Ericeira started in 1696, the celebrated erudite conferences, whose members were in large part, the same as those of the Academy of the Generous. In 1717 the erudite conferences gave rise to the *Academia de História Portuguesa*, (Academy of Portuguese History) whose main objective was the study of national history.

D. João V was interested in the project and decided to give it royal protection. In this concrete case the form as also the academies are visible in the larger area than the institutions of knowledge of the old regime in Portugal, and allowed themselves to be protected by the power.[8]

On December 8, 1720, the decree was published which gave official birth to a new institution, the *Academia Real da História Portuguesa,* whose first director was Manuel Caetano de Sousa, a cleric of the Theatines Regular and a man of trust of the monarch[9] and whose members had belonged to the *Academia dos Anónimos* (Academy of the Unknown) and to the *Conferências Eruditas.* The decree for the creation of this new institution established as the central work of the academy "to study and write the ecclesiastical history and the history of these kingdoms and their conquests" in order to perpetuate "the actions so worthy of memory that in these kingdoms have been performed in building up the service of God, of the Catholic church, of kings, my predecessors and mine", the objective inscribed in the symbol adopted at the time, *Restituet Omnia,* or rather, to bring to light of knowledge, the information of the deeds of the Portuguese.

The members of the Academy were given certain facilities of access to documentation which was necessary for them. In this respect, it interests us, particularly to remember an order of the early 1721; by the royal letter of 11th January and notices of 16th and 18th March of this year. It was to order those responsible for archives and registries of the kingdom that they should give copies of documents under their keeping to all the members of the Academy who might have asked for them.[10]

In *Memórias para a História Ecclesiastica do Arcebispado de Goa e seus Suffraganeos* (Memoirs for the ecclesiastical history of the archbishopric and its suffragans), a codice preserved in the National Library of Lisbon[11] and of great importance for the history of Goa, we come across a direct echo of the royal decree with a view to the dynamism of the works of the Academy. In fact, the *Memórias* (Memoirs) include a set of news and information addressed to the Academy, consisting of *Progresso da Memória das Notícias que El Rey N. Snor que Deus Gde ordena se dem a Academia Real da História Portugueza dos Cartorios e Archivos desta nossa Sta. Provincia da Madre de Deus dos Reformados Filhos de Nosso Serafim Patriarcha S. Francisco* (Progress of the Memoirs of Information that the King our Lord that God may guard the Royal Academy of Portuguese History of the Registries and Archives of this our Holy Province of the Mother of God of the Reformed sons of our angelic Patriarch St. Francis), dated 1726 and collected by order of Fr. Simaõ de Jesus Maria, then Provincial Minister of the order.[12]

As the very title indicates, *Progresso da Memória,* treats of a complement and sequence of news and information previously sent to Lisbon in compliance with the royal order referred to. Besides, the monarch himself, determined, as is affirmed, that "in order that the news may be sent to the secretary of the Academy, we ought not to wait that they may be all together, but to be convenient that we may send them successively as and when they might be discovered, so that the scholars may more promptly be able to use them."[13] Thus, in the monsoon of 1724-1725, in the ship of His Majesty, named *Madre de Deus*, captained by D. José Caetano Sottomayor, there had already been sent to the secretary of the Academy, Count of Vila-Maior, "a book in folio, bound in a case, enclosed in an envelope of yellow damask", in which many reports were included relating to the ecclesiastical histoiy of Goa collected during the last three years in the registries of the Franciscan convents in Goa.[14]

The information that now was gathered gave, therefore, a sequence to the royal order partially completed within the volume already sent to the Academy, in accordance with the very concrete items, consisting of the regulations of *Memória das Notícias pertencentes às Religiões* (Memoirs of news relating to the Religions) ordered by D. João V, which we are going to refer to: "that they may send the information of the old rites, relics, miracles and more noteworthy matters of each monastery" (article 7a)[15]; "that we may send copies to the Academy of all the signs of the chapels, and graves of all the convents, and colleges, both old and new, with the coats-of-arms, which might be in whatever part of the same monasteries whether in walls, arches or graves" (art. 6a)[16]; "that we may send an inventory, that with minuteness may declare all the papers, and title-deeds that are in each registry of this Religion, declaring what each contains in particular, era or year in which it was done, and of each book, or bundle that one may make an index of the papers that they contain" (art. 2)[17]; "that we may send to the Academy the catalogues of books of the libraries, of the convents, especially of the manuscripts, etc." (art. 4)[18]

The minute contents of this inquiry, that the *Progresso da Memória das Notícias*, allows one to notice to have been responded in a very complete form in the volume sent in 1724 to the secretary of the Academy, allows us, although indirectly, to evaluate the richness and source of these informations of Goa, then sent to the *Academia Real da História* (Royal Academy of History). Trying to fill in the missing elements, with the documents obtained after 1724 in the registries and convent archives, as is the case, for example, of the catalogue of the library of the Convent of Santo António of Thane, or giving an account of the successes achieved in the meantime, as may be the transference of the bodies of Fr. Gaspar, first archbishop of Goa and of Fr. André de Santa Maria, 4th bishop of Cochin, to new graves in 1725, *O Progresso da Memória das*

Notícias is, above all, an interesting cache of information relating to the ecclesiastical history of Goa. But this information is of interest also to the history of art, for one may see the minute descriptions of the grave stones of Fr. Gaspar and Fr. André de Santa Maria, accompanied by drawings that attempt to reproduce them faithfully; to the history of mentalities - "the excesses of veneration,"[19] of the relics of the first archbishop primate of Goa, which forced the transfer; to the cultural history, in the matter pertaining to the questions of books and of the libraries, with the reproduction of the catalogue of a convent book collection. Let us concentrate on this last aspect.

The book collection of the Franciscan convent of Thane, according to the inventory reproduced in *O Progresso da Memória das Notícias*, is made up of 255 volumes, a good number, which was securely higher since it is expressly said that in this number are not included the books "already completely destroyed". In spite of the order of D. João V referring to the convenience in distinguishing the manuscripts from the printed ones, such a distinction is not done, it is thus not possible for us to evaluate the composition of the book collection in this case. In terms of the contents, naturally, the bulk is on the ecclesiastical matters in their varied contexts, although it may be possible to come across works of classical authors like Virgil, Salústio, Ovid, or Quinto Cúrsio. Here is the order made in the very inventory: "Holy Priests 88, decree givers and jurists 18, canonists 15, moralists 30, humanists 13, spiritual fathers 11, theologians and philosophers 6, preachers 74.[21]

The history of the book and the reading matter have registered, in the last years, a very appreciable dynamics in the larger area of cultural history of the ancient regime, whether it may be in the perspective of the production of the book, of its circulation and of the access of various social groups to the printed object, or of the constitution of the network of reading matter and libraries.[22] With respect to the Portuguese case, the study of the composition of the libraries is going on in large measure, in spite of the undeniable importance of this type of research for the socio-cultural history in the Modern Age that can, inclusively, reveal some surprises. It may be seen, for example, regarding Goa, the case of the 18th century writers' inventories of the libraries of the rural palace of St. Inez and that of Panjim, in which we come across the unexpected presence of *Philosophiae Naturalis Principia Mathematica* (1687) of Isaac Newton.[23] In any case, the path starts to be explored, it being possible to point to some important contributions for the history of books, of literature and of libraries, as it happens, for example with the excellent study of Rui Manuel Loureiro about the library of the chronicler Diogo do Couto.[24]

Also the *Memórias para a Histórica Ecclesiastica do Arcebispado de Goa e seus Suffraganeos*, in which is included the information for the Academy which we have been referring to, contain another inventory of a convent book collection of Goa, the collection of the Convent of Santa Cruz of Miracles. Its dimension and contents merit, without doubt, a detailed study. It is an important collection with more than 500 books, in which stand out, naturally, the ecclesiastical matters in particular, the preacher-authors, with more than 200 books, as it happens, besides, with the collection of the convent at Thane – speculative and polemical theology, moral and mystical theology and canon law, but also books of grammar, rhetoric, philosophy and history.[25] In it are included, for example, among the manuscripts and printed works, various works of classical authors – Aristotle, Ovid, Quinto Cúrsio, Virgil – two *Artes* of Fr. Manuel Álvares, and *A Ásia Portuguesa* of Manuel de Faria e Souza, *As Décadas* of João de Barros, *Os Sermões* of Vieira in 11 volumes, the life of Frei Bartolomeu dos Mártires, and *O Flos Sanctorum* in Portuguese; but also "two *Artes* of the language of the land, one printed and the other in manuscript" or one *Nobiliarchia Bracmana*.

We think that this very short probing gives an account of the suitableness of a more systematic investigation of convent book collections in the Portuguese East, of certainly stimulating results on various basis. On the other hand, and on a more general level, there exist in the records of the *Academia da História* the book of *Notícias* sent by the Franciscans in 1724 to the secretary of the Academy, of which, as we have seen, we only know indirectly, yet we can be face to face with a precious testimony of Goa of the 16th to 18th centuries, particularly of its ecclesiastical history.

NOTES AND REFERENCES

1. See an excellent synthesis of Maria Cruz, *Intellettuali, potere e circolazione delle idee nell'Italia moderna (1500-1700)*, Turin, 1982, pp. 172-87, 200-33, and the study of Alain Viala, *Naissance de l'écrivain*, Paris, 1985, esp. pp. 15-50. See also Roger Chartier, "O homem de letras", in *O Homem do Illuminismo*, ed. Michel Vovelle, Lisbon, 1997, pp. 119-153.
2. José Costa Pereira, "Movimento das Academias", in *Dicionário Ilustrado de História de Portugal*, vol. I, Lisbon, 1985, pp. 16-17.
3. See José Silvestre Ribeiro, *História dos Estabelecimentos Scientíficos, Literarios e Artisticos de Portugal*, vol. I, Lisbon, 1871, pp. 154-200, 266-72; Fidelino de Figueiredo, *História da Litteratura Classica, 2a epocha 1580-1756*, Lisbon, 1921, pp. 37-48; Óscar Lopes, "Academias", in *Dicionário de História de Portugal*, vol. I, Lisbon, 1979, pp. 14-15; Elize M.H. Vonk

Mathias, "A Academia dos Generosos. Uma Academia ou uma sequência de Academias?", *Revista da Biblioteca Nacional*, 2 (2), 1982, pp. 223-241; João Palma-Ferreira, *Academias literários dos séculos XVII e XVIII*, Lisbon, 1982.

4. Fidelino de Figueiredo, *op. cit.*, p. 39.
5. See a list by Figueiredo, *op. cit.*, pp. 39-45.
6. Óscar Lopes, "Academias", *op. cit.*
7. Ofélio Paiva Monteiro, "No alvorecer do Iluminismo em Portugal. D. Francisco Xavier de Menezes, 4° Conde da Ericeira", *Revista Portuguesa de História Literária de Portugal*, no. 1, 1962.
8. António Camões Gouveia, "Estratégias de interiorização de disciplina", in *História de Portugal*, ed. José Mattoso, vol. IV, Lisbon, 1993, pp. 444-45.
9. Ana Isabel Buescu, "O Peregrino Instruido. Viagem e poder na Europa Setecentista", in *Memória e poder. Ensaios de história cultural (séculos XV-XVIII)* (forthcoming).
10. José Costa Pereira, "Academia Real de História Portuguesa", in *Dicionário Ilustrado...*, *op. cit.*, vol. I, p. 16.
11. *BNL*, Res. codice. 176, microfilm (F. 2527).
12. *BNL*, codice 176, fls. 79-95v.
13. *Ibid.*, fl. 80.
14. *Ibid.*, fls. 80-80v.
15. *Ibid.*, fl. 80.
16. *Ibid.*, fl. 88.
17. *Ibid.*, fl. 88v.
18. *Ibid.*, fl. 91.
19. *Ibid.*, fls. 80v-81.
20. *Ibid.*, fl. 93.
21. *Ibid.*
22. For this vast area of studies see, for example, Roger Chartier, *L'ordre des livres. Lecteurs, auteurs, bibliothèques en Europe entre XIVe et XVIIIe siècle*, Paris, 1992; Fernando Souza Álvarez, *Del escribano a la biblioteca. La civilización escrita europea en la Alta Edade Moderna (siglos XV-XVII)*, Madrid, 1992. See also *infra*, fn. 24.
23. *BNL*, Res. codice 1525, fl. 410.
24. Rui Manuel Loureiro, *A Biblioteca de Diogo do Couto*, Macau, 1998. See also the point of the situation in João Luís Lisboa, "Sobre a investigação actual em história do livro e da leitura", *Leituras* (BNL), no. 1, April-October 1997, pp. 105-112.
25. *BNL*, codice 176, fls. 303v-305v.
26. *Ibid.*, fl. 303v.

31

Foreigners in India in The Time of Afonso de Albuquerque

The Anonymous

Ana Maria Pereira Ferreira

India called many. There fortunes were made, there coats-of-arms were gilt, there one plotted, there others married, there, also, life was lost.

Cosmic land, included in the sense in which there was a greater hope, was in the first years of the discovery of the maritime route, the concrete and illusory food of the powerful, who already inscribed themselves in the indices of history and of the people of "little luck", those who remain in the better of hypothesis, on a skirting board, those whom the chronicler gathers like shells. Nothing or hardly anything distinguishes them, nothing gives them form, if not the name, a nationality here and there, pieces of a game in which they were pawns, a complex chess game of varied check-mates.

It is exactly, this line of anonymity that links them. In the antipodes of the big commercial interests, not knowingly, by chance, the Stozzi or the Weiser who, since the beginning, also branded the tooth in their share,[1] are dozens of varieties of firemen and of men-of-arms who served the enterprise of D. Manuel, the multinational enterprise in the capitals. People who only had to lose their lives and which in that time, was very little, because in the western Christian world disbelief and doubt only will be served ... aristocratically – about two centuries later.

To know these anonymous people who made the route from the four corners of Europe, we used the letters of Afonso de Albuquerque.[2]

From 1509 to 1514, the Lion of the Asian Seas, as Genevieve Bouchon[3] called him, signed orders of payment and also words of praise.

If well counted, the roll includes 142 names. If there is an error it will be by defect, and not by excess, since the personalities are repeated in various scenarios of war and since at times, the same scribe or different scribes, use spelling at the mercy of the moment.[4] The crossing of the data allows almost always, the non inflating of results. The percentages are said in a few words. The anonymous are modest. About 57%, being obviously foreigners, do not indicate the origin. But, the names like Anis de Lipre[5], Anes Triquer[6], Henrique de Bramar[7], among many others, suggest that the bulk of this column came from the so-called North Europe.

From there many came to whom was attached their nationality. Nine Dutchmen and 12 from Flanders (14.8%), 15 Germans (10.6%), of diverse locations, from Bruges,[8] from Anvers[9], from Bremen[10], when to distinguish them it was not enough to say Flemish Gilis,[11] or German Clement.[12] But, also from Spain (8.4%), coming from borders or closer, like Corunha, Salamanca, Galiza, although also Navarre and Castile were represented.[13] The French were prominent with 9 persons (6.3%), less the Italians, from Corsega and Saboia who in all make up five individuals.[14]

What was the weight of these men-of-war in the whole reckoning? We admit to have proceeded merely by surveys. The numbers appear, however, revealing. In Goa, at the end of December 1509, for 24 foreign firemen appears an equal number of Portuguese.[15] Among those who went to Banastarim and are paid in November 1512, the percentage is more: to the 23 nationals are joined 42 strangers.[16]

Finally, only in Cochin in 1514, the Portuguese are in the majority.

Given the numbers, it is fit to try some approximation to the man. Betraying, in a certain way, the title of the paper, let us start with some who crossed the frame of ignorance. It is the case of Corbinelli – Francisco Corvineil of letters – Italian and merchant, who started by captaining the ship *Santo Agostinho* in 1510, and in November of the same year, he is appointed factor of Goa where he is till 1515, returning afterwards.[18] Corbinelli does not belong, properly, to the group, and meanwhile becomes the border between those who go by payment and those who go by service or by their love of adventure. Before him, the examples are many, like the case of the Baron of Longuy, serving in Africa and whom D. João II will make count of Gaza.[19]

But, at the time of Corbinelli, two other names stand out: the ones of the German friars, Henrique and João who, for obvious reasons, we cannot mention in the numbers presented. If in relation to the first, we only know that he ought to have received one *cruzado* a month,[20] the history of Frei João was better narrated. In January 1511, he is in Goa serving in the hospital.[21] On 25th October of the following year, he was preparing himself to leave and Afonso de Albuquerque writes to the king a letter of recommendation, where he relates part of his journey. In the prose of the governor, the religious appears divided between the spiritual and the temporal. Perhaps serving more the temporal, having taken part in the capture of Goa and Malacca and in "all the feats after his coming", in such a way that he requested him that he may stay with him. He ends up becoming his confessor: "I gave him always an account of my evils and sins, and I have some love and affection for him". It is, then, with pity that he sees him leaving and hopes that he may return.[22]

More difficult to understand, are the others. The documentation, in its dryness, does not help. Effectively, it is plausible that many of the firemen and some commanders who were in Goa may have taken part in the campaign of Banastarim. Some will be praised, as is the case of Gilis of Flanders, fireman and commander of *Froi de la Mar*, honoured with 30 *cruzados*, in the name of His Highness, "for serving him very well from his office in these parts and for killing many Muslims and pulling down the wall of Banastarim."[23] This Gilis already was, however, in 1510 in Cochin.[24] There are, in truth, various cases of longevity and of mobility in these parts. The German Clemente,[25] the German Cristovão[26] or João from Saboia, who serving in Cochin in 1509, is in Goa even at the end of 1512.[27] Other, examples, to which we will add an unusual case, is the one of João de França, fireman of merit and for this is recompensed,[28] who appears in April of 1514 as a cook of Afonso de Albuquerque. No, it is not a overlapping of names. Specifically the Master of War indicates: "fireman, my cook".[29] Perhaps, already at this time, some refinement of French cuisine might have touched his palate.

What would this Foreign Legion achieve to risk so long a journey to plunge into the unknown? In the 500s, Georges Buchanan, professor in the College of Arts in Coimbra, was stressing that much time was needed for the insatiable thirst of gold superimposed by the fear of cold, of heat, of the ferocious animals and of the people of the jungles.[30] Buchanan was a humanist, a man of letters. His erudite logic did not capture various other gradations that form part of a less formal mentality. In the first place, India was a known space. The old memories of her riches became palpable for the common man soon after the first voyages. It is present in the example of Gonneville.[31] It is not, then, strange to find that already in the fleet of Lopo Soares between 1504-1505, he may have been able to take about 51 foreigners.[32] In truth, it is probable that some or all may have repented during and after the six months of sea where in the words of Pero Fernandes Tinoco, "two winters and two summers", were spent.[33] However, at the time of parting, it was, we believe, the salary, it varied between the 40 and 20 *réis* per day,[34] and also, this other benefit called *quintalada.*[35] It may be added the common mobility increases for the men of this age, well mirrored in the varied origins of the very Portuguese and the surprise will have to be mitigated.

If the motives of the Indian appeal were many, including, perhaps, the excess of offer,[36] the reasons why the Crown turned to so many people of the whole of Europe, also deserve some lines.

Few, for various authors, namely Luis Filipe Reis Thomaz, have shown the specificities of the Manueline project.[37] Now, Afonso de Albuquerque, had been "sent to the East when the sovereign and his advisers thought it to be an opportune time to start the assault on the Islamic block".[38] There was need of people. Repeatedly, he says this lamenting. Some of his letters show the despair of someone who needs more and more hands: "if Your Highness had sent me the equipment, men and arms, that I may carry out what you ordered me to do, I would not put myself to the people twice in the fire at Malacca nor in Goa twice, neither the Muslims of Hormuz would have your fort, that I started in their power."[39] Accounts done, he was asking for 3,000 men and only had 1,500, half of them useless."[40]

In this context, the specialists, whatever the origin, would always be welcomed, attending to that when for the second time he reached India in 1506, Albuquerque understood at once the fragility of a strategy based only on naval power and on precarious alliances with the local powers.[41]

Concluding, what is only a necessary outline, "we cannot forget the role of individual personalities, neither that of specific circumstances, nor neglect subconscious or irrational factors, so many times relevant. In the end, in the final analysis, history is made by persons".[42]

Other circumstances, that precede and overtake the short chronological period treated, gave rise to the doctrines and politics of exclusion. We refer, obvio' sly, to the *Mare Clausum* (Closed Sea), supported by secret, source of fierce polemics. The question that we make is simple: in front of the show, complemented by so many other sources that prove the sieve that was the Indico and India in this decisive stage, how does one situate the theoretical-practical schemes of the Portuguese state?[43] The answer is also simple. The Closed Sea never was prohibitive in absolute terms. It only expressed to foreigners or to nationals that only the sovereign could allow the journey. Regarding the secret, with all that it had of ambiguity, it was not thought of thus we believe, for the professionals of the war. The danger of losing the advantage of invention was thought by the Crown as a problem from within to the outside, limited to the things of the sea. However, while the maps and pilots, inspite of the repression and the forces volatilized themselves by the main maritime centres, another torrent of knowledge was building up, fruit of the experience *in loco* (on the spot), knowledge as essential as the drawing of the route.

Ten years later, what would have been the importance of this base of anonymous experiences for the voyages programmed by the financiers of beyond the Pyrenees?

NOTES AND REFERENCES

1. See for example, Manuel Nunes Dias, "Dinâmica dos metais alemães na rota do Cabo", *Bartolomeu Dias e a sua Época, Actas*, vol. III, Porto: Economia e Comércio Marítimo, 1989. pp. 564-84.
2. *Cartas de Afonso de Albuquerque* (Henceforth *CAA*). Raymundo António de Bulhão Pato (ed.). vols. 1-VII, Lisbon, 1884-1915.
3. *Albuquerque le Lion des Mers d'Asie*, Paris, 1992.
4. There are many examples. See the case of Cornelles de Tollo, fireman in Goa on December 6, 1511 (*CAA*, vol. V, Lisbon, 1915, pp. 170-71); referred to as Corniles de Tollo, at Banastarim on November 27, 1512 (*CAA*, vol. II, Lisbon, 1898, p. 101). Also, Hermão de Lamden (*CAA*, vol. V, pp. 170-71). mentioned in another document, Herman de Lemden (*CAA*, vol. II. p. 101).
5. *CAA*, vol. II, p. 102.
6. *CAA*, vol. V, pp. 170-71.
7. *CAA*, vol. II, p. 1101.
8. Nicolau de Bruges, fireman in Goa (*CAA*, vol. V, pp. 408-10).
9. Miguel Danvers, fireman at Cochin (*CAA*, vol. IV, pp. 229-30).
10. Henrique de Breman, fireman at Banastarim (*CAA*, vol. II, pp. 102-3).
11. Flemish Giles, fireman at Banastarim (*Ibid.*, p. 104).
12. German Clemente, fireman in Goa (*CAA*, vol. V, pp. 408-10).
13. See for example, Garcia Fernandes Castelhana, man-of-arms in Calicut (*CAA*, vol. VI, pp. 119-21); Luis Ortiz of Salamanca, man of grouping at Goa (*Ibid.*, pp. 107-115); João de Corunha, fireman at Cochin (*Ibid*, p. 102); António Navarro, fireman at Goa (*CAA*, vol. V, pp. 170-71).
14. Silvestre Corço was captain of a big galley and served the king of France (*Ibid.*, pp. 302-3); João Baptista Corso was cabin boy of the ship Nazaré and was at Calicut in August 1514 (*CAA*, vol. VI, pp. 119-21).
15. December 28, 1509 (*CAA*, vol. IV, pp. 229-30).
16. *CAA*, vol. II, pp. 101-2.
17. In the ships we have 8 foreign firemen among 25 and in Castelo were 8 firemen among them three foreigners (*CAA*, vol. VI, p. 98).

18. Maria Emilia Madeira Santos, "O Feitor e a sua Carreira, Alguns casos no Estado Português da India", *Estudos Orientais*, vol. III; *O Ocidente no Oriente através dos Descobrimentos Portugueses*, Lisbon: Instituto Oriental, UNI, 1992, pp. 15-22.
19. *Cf.* Ana Maria Pereira Ferreira, *Problemas Marítimos entre Portugal e a França na Primeira Metade do século XVI*, Redondo, 1995, p. 121.
20. Letter of January 7, 1513 (*CAA*, vol. V, p. 248).
21. Letter of January 26, 1511 for which Francisco Corbinelli gives him a bale of sugar, of the small, for the sick of the hospital (*Ibid.*, p. 34).
22. *CAA*, vol. I, p. 93.
23. *CAA*, vol. II, p. 104.
24. *CAA*, vol. IV, p. 204.
25. *CAA*, vol. V, pp. 170-71, 408-10; vol. II, p. 101.
26. *CAA*, vol. V, pp. 170-71, 408-10; vol. II, p. 101.
27. *CAA*, vol. IV, pp. 129-30; vol. V, pp. 170-71; vol. II, p. 102.
28. December 3, 1502 (*CAA*, vol. V, pp. 272-73).
29. April 8, 1514 (*CAA*, vol. VI, p. 57).
30. Cited by R. Hooykaas, *Os Descobrimentos e o humanismo*, Lisbon, p. 45.
31. *Cf.* Ana Maria Pereira Ferreira, *op. cit.*
32. *Cf.* Maria do Rosário S. Themudo Barata, "A Iª Viagem de Lopo Soares à India (1504-1505): Um termo e o começo", in *Bartolomeu Dias e a Sua Época, Actas*, vol. III, Porto, 1989, pp. 253-73.
33. *CAA*, vol. II, pp. 335-37. Letter to the king. The person accompanied in 1505 the Viceroy D. Francisco de Almeida. With respect to the voyages and their problems, besides the valuable works of Artur Teodoro de Matos, see the modest article of Elaine Sanceau, "Tribulações do viajante nas naus de quinhentos", in *Boletim da Biblioteca Pública de Matosinhos*, no. 22, Matosinhos, 1978, pp. 17-25.
34. There are indeed discrepancies. One may take, however, a document of July 17, 1514, referring to Cochin: João de la Camera, who is commander, 30 *réis* a day: Fernão de Álvares, commander of Castelo, 40 *réis*; the firemen of the fortress, 20 *réis* and those of the ships, 14. (*CAA*, vol. VI, p. 102). Meanwhile, it seems to be usual the firemen received 20 *réis* a day (*CAA*, vol. V, pp. 408-410).
35. *Quintalada*, this is the free transport of a fixed quantity of merchandise on the ships of the king.
36. The appeal appears to be less at the time of the wars between France and the Empire, as the documentation published by António Dias Farinha suggests, *Os Portugueses no Golfo Pérsico (1507-1538). Contribuição Documental e Crítica para a sua História*, Lisbon, 1991. Meanwhile, it is a mere hypothesis in need of verification.
37. See especially "A Política Oriental de D. Manuel I e suas contra-correntes", in *De Ceuta a Timor*. Lisbon: Difel, 1994, pp. 189-206.
38. *Ibid.*, p. 197.

39. *CAA*. vol. I, p. 37 (Letter IX).
40. *Ibid*., p. 40.
41. The book of Fernando Gomes Pedrosa. *Afonso de Albuquerque e a Arte da Guerra, Prémio do Mar 1995*, Cascais, 1998, has interest on these subjects.
42. *Cf.* footnote 37, p. 206.
43. I remember only chapter I on the Portuguese commerce in Malabar between 1506-1508 of the book of Artur Teodoro de Matos, *Na Rota da Índia: Estudos de História da Expansão Portuguesa*, Macau: Instituto Cultural de Macau, 1994, pp. 15-58. Various foreigners appear there, including a Venetian who bought appreciable quantities of precious stones.

INDEX